THE GESTAPO

A History of Horror

JACQUES DELARUE

Translated from French by
MERVYN SAVILL

Skyhorse Publishing

Frontline Books, London

Histoire de la Gestapo by Jacques Delarue
World copyright ©Librarie Arthème Fayard, 1962

All Rights Reserved. No part of this book may be
reproduced in any manner without the express written
consent of the publisher, except in the case of brief
excerpts in critical reviews or articles. All inquiries
should be addressed to Skyhorse Publishing, 307 West
36th Street, 11th Floor, New York, NY 10018.

Skyhorse Publishing books may be purchased in bulk
at special discounts for sales promotion, corporate
gifts, fund-raising, or educational purposes. Special
editions can also be created to specifications. For
details, contact the Special Sales Department,
Skyhorse Publishing, 307 West 36th Street, 11th
Floor, New York, NY 10018 or
info@skyhorsepublishing.com.

Skyhorse® and Skyhorse Publishing® are registered
trademarks of Skyhorse Publishing, Inc.®, a Delaware
corporation.

Visit our website at www.skyhorsepublishing.com.

Library of Congress Cataloging-in-Publication Data

Delarue, Jacques, 1919-
    [Histoire de la Gestapo. English]
    The Gestapo: a history of horror/Jacques Delarue;
[translated from the French by Mervyn Savill].
    p. cm.
    Includes index.
    ISBN-13: 978-1-60239-246-5 (pbk.: alk. paper)
    ISBN-10: 1-60239-246-3 (pbk.: alk. paper)
    1. Germany. Geheime Staatspolizei—History. I.
Title.

HV8207.D4513 2008
363.28'3094309043—dc22

                                   2007042961
10 9 8

Printed in the United States of America

The Gestapo: A History of Horror

This edition published in 2008 by Frontline Books,
an imprint of Pen and Sword Books Ltd, 47 Church
Street, Barnsley, S. Yorkshire, S70 2AS
www.frontline-books.com

Histoire de la Gestapo by Jacques Delarue
World copyright © Librarie Arthème Fayard, 1962
This edition © Pen & Sword Books Ltd, 2008
New Preface © Jacques Delarue, 2008

ISBN: 978-184832-502-9

*CIP data records for this title are available from the
British Library and the Library of Congress*

For more information on our books, please visit
www.frontline-books.com, email info@frontline-
books.com
or write to us at the above address.

CONTENTS

Hitler's cabinet • The Brown Terror • Goering takes over and purges the Prussian police • Despotism and a series of decrees • The terrible month of February 1933 • The burning of the Reichstag • The "emergency measures" • Rounding up the Opposition • The apathy of the trade unions • The electoral campaign and the March 5 elections • The new Reichstag • Full powers • Gleichschaltung • The comedy of Labor Day • The dissolution of the unions • Dr. Ley's Labor Front • The dissolution of the parties • The sole Party.

Hermann Goering • Goering the S.A. man • Goering and Roehm • Rivalry • Goering wounded in Munich • Flight and exile • Morphinomania, obesity, and psychological evolution • Return to Munich in 1927 • Goering, a deputy and then President of the Reichstag • Goering and Papen • Rivalry and chicaneries • Diels the policeman • Diels against the Nazis • The wind changes • Diels buys himself back into favor • Goering seduced by the political police • The opening of the first concentration camp • Goering's directives to the police.

Amnesty for the Nazi criminals • The decree of April 26, 1933, creates the Gestapo in Prussia • The beginning of the Gestapo under Diel's direction • The S.A. cries for blood • Internal rivalries between S.A., S.S., and Gestapo • Diels is overthrown only to return in triumph • The Gestapo becomes Goering's personal property • The trial of van der Lubbe • Rail and Reineking.

The police forces of the German Laender are placed under the jurisdiction of the Reich • The Nazi administrative imbroglio • Diels quits the Gestapo for good • Himmler succeeds him • Himmler's career • His deputy, Heydrich • A biography of Himmler • The

TABLE OF ABBREVIATIONS USED

ACTION A-B, Ausserordentliche Befriedigungs Aktion, Extraordinary action of classification.

A.O., Auslands Organisation, Party organization for abroad.

A.P.A., Auslands Politische Abteilung, Office of foreign police.

C.S.A.R., Comité Secret d'Action Revolutionnaire, Extreme Right French political organization. (Cagoulards.)

D.A.P., Deutsche Arbeiter Partei, German Workers' party.

D.N.B., Deutsches Nachrichten Buro, German News Bureau (Official Press Agency).

GESTAPO, Geheime Staatspolizei, Secret State Police.

G.F.P., Geheime Feld-Polizei, Secret Police in the Field.

H.J., Hitler Jugend, Hitler Youth.

KRIPO, Kriminalpolizei, Criminal Police.

K.Z., Konzentrations-Lager, Concentration Camp.

N.S.D.A.P., Nationalsozialistitsche Deutsche Arbeiter Partei, National Socialist German Workers' party.

N.S.K.K., Nationalsozialistischeskraftfahrerkorps, Motorized section of the N.S.D.A.P.

O.K.W., Oberkommando der Wehrmacht, German High Command.

ORPO, Ardnungspolizei, Civil Police.

O.S.A.F., Oberster S.A. Fuehrer, Supreme Head of the S.A.

P.O., Politische Organisation, Political Organization.

P.Q.J., Police aux Questions Juives (French Organization).

R.S.H.A., Reichssicherheitshauptamt, Reich Security Main Office.

S.A., Sturmabteilung, Assault Section.

SCHUPO, Schutzpolizei, Urban Police.

S.D., Sicherheitsdienst des Reichsfuehrers S.S., Security Service of the Chief of the S.S. in the Reich.

S.D.P., Sudetendeutsche Partei, Sudeten German party.

SIPO, Sicherheitspolizei, Security Police.

S.S., Schutzstaffel, Protective Squads.

W.V.H.A., Wirtschaftsverwaltungshauptamt, Economic Administrative Head Office of the S.S.

PREFACE

More than sixty years ago Nazism collapsed, leaving fifty million dead in a Europe ruined and economically on its knees.

Slowly the scars healed, memories faded, two generations were born who know almost nothing about Nazism and who understand Hitler only as a metaphor. But one name lives on, a name that has come to universally symbolize oppression and terror: the Gestapo.

On January 30, 1933, Adolf Hitler, who had long been considered a political agitator, became Chancellor of the Reich. Three months later (Dachau opened on March 22), the first concentration camps opened their gates to welcome political dissidents such as the Social Democrats and all Germans suspected of not adhering to the state's racist and totalitarian ideology.

Within a few months, Hitler, Goering, and Himmler's lieutenants formed the steel framework of the regime: the Gestapo. Every totalitarian regime, whether it claims to be right or left, relies upon a powerful political police force to ruthlessly crush dissent. The existence of an opponent, however weak is incompatible with a totalitarian system. Nazism gave birth to the most inhuman, the most perverse, and the most murderous police system ever conceived by man. In order to secure its power, the German people had to be brought to heel. Coming from an old and deeply rooted civilization, highly cultured, endowed with a solid legal tradition, the people of Germany could not be easily tamed, despite their innate taste for discipline. Other nations' eyes and legal barriers from Germany's own laws stood against it. Within a few months the unions, every political party, and every independent organization, be it for the arts, sports, or youth, was disbanded or absorbed by Nazi organizations. There was still the law and the courts to which the victims of the Nazis turned, and the Nazis had enough sense not to try to suddenly assault the German legal system. On the contrary, they gradually lifted legal obstacles in order to destroy them, one after another. In 1933, Goering, the founder of the Gestapo, relieved the Home Secretary, by decree, of all authority concerning the Gestapo. It became a solely self-regulated organization. Between 1934 and 1939 the Nazis passed a series of laws making it impossible for ordinary justice to exercise the slightest control on the activities of the Gestapo and the S.S. On January 30, 1934, a law took the police forces away from the authority of the "laender," and placed them under the jurisdiction of the Reich. On April 20, Goering handed over control to Himmler, and then every German police force, uniformed and plain clothes, criminal and political, was also handed over to Himmler, who was already supreme chief of the S.S., the private army of the Party.

These transfers of legal and administrative functions, these nominations, this placement of responsibilities with one man, created a legal tangle which ensured the great power of the Party's organizations. A decree of 1935 stated that decisions taken by the Gestapo could not be challenged, thereby giving the Gestapo the right to intern citizens in the camps. On the February 10, 1936, a "fundamental" law stated that the Gestapo "has the task to search for any intention which would endanger the State." A mere suspicion was enough to justify an arrest. The decree specifying how the law should be enforced made it clear that the Gestapo were in charge of the camps' administration; the law of 1938 states that they were drawing up the Orders of Internment themselves. They were extremely powerful.

All the German people were put under surveillance. From an early age each German child became a member of one of the Party's organizations and wore a uniform. The slightest misconduct was ferociously repressed. To execute the death sentence, the traditional axe was replaced by the guillotine, which was quicker (the last person beheaded with an axe was the Communist Deputy Robert Stamm, who was beheaded in Berlin on November 5, 1937). In the end, twenty-one guillotines were in use in Germany, in addition to the gallows and firing squads. Hitler and his fanatically devoted henchmen believed that the most efficient way to govern was by terror. The heads of foreign countries were well aware of the regime the Germans were subjected to; they knew of the existence of the concentration camps, the bullying and ill-treatment of prisoners. The persecutions imposed on the Jews were immediately known through direct testimonies. The diplomats' reports, as well as reports from the most important international journalists, were very explicit. They continued to treat Hitler with all the consideration owed to an honorable head of state, and the international relationships with Germany continued up to the eve of the conflict which was to bathe the planet in blood for more than five years. However, once the Occupation arrived in their countries, they appeared surprised and deeply shocked to see the Nazis apply the same principles to them.

On September 27, 1939, while all eyes were turned towards Poland, devastated by the war, a Party decree grouped together the political police, the criminal police, and the Party's secret intelligence service, the S.D., to form the R.S.H.A. (Central Security Office of the Reich). Well before Hitler came to power, an internal intelligence service of the S.S. was in charge of the security of the Party. In 1934 it became the only intelligence service of the Party. Its size increased considerably and it became the surveillance tool of the Gestapo itself, being incorporated into the R.S.H.A. without becoming a state organization, its members remaining civil servants of the Party. This was a complicated hybrid formula typical of the Nazis' administrative structure. This strange mixture ruled over all the occupied countries and caused the most terrible devastation. Theoretically, only the Gestapo had the power to arrest as the S.D.'s role was supposedly confined to research, but, in reality, on the ground everybody did a bit of everything, using the same methods. The Kripo, (the police in charge of common law crimes) also had members in these units, but their activities were practically non-existent as the local police forces were able to deal with these ordinary problems themselves.

The military occupation of the European countries was accompanied by the introduction of detachments of this police body. Some detachments of the Gestapo accompanied the first wave of troops in the occupied countries. In France, on June 14, 1940, the first day the commandos of the Gestapo entered Paris, they used their own specific methods. In the beginning, the Gestapo had no powers as the army held them all, including the powers of police. The Gestapo took possession of them slowly, until the spring of 1942 when Himmler obtained from Hitler authority for the powers of the police to be taken away from the army and handed over to the Gestapo. They operated according to their traditions and employed their usual investigation methods, using torture and deportation almost systematically. They were also entrusted with another task, more discreet: the surveillance of soldiers' ideological orthodoxy.

Quickly the persecution of the Jews, the key tenet of the Nazi ideology, in existence in Germany from the beginning of Nazism, was extended to every occupied country. First of all administratively and economically despoiling the country, they quickly became murderous, and one could see incredible scenes of old people and young children, whose sole crime was to have been born Jewish, being sent to concentration camps and killed. The Gestapo was the principal instrument of this persecution. Wars have always been an occasion to massacre civilian populations, to commit crimes of all sorts, but most of the time these atrocities took place in a climate of spontaneous and improvised violence. What differentiates the crimes of the Nazis from the others is their methodical organization, their administrative planning, and their relentless execution. The big raids which resulted in the deaths of thousands of innocent victims were organized as if they were agricultural plans or a labor recruitment schemes, in ordinary offices unique only because governed by the rule of secrecy. On January 20, 1942, during the conference held at the R.S.H.A. in Berlin-Wannsee, radical solutions were found to the "Jewish problem": every

Jew living in the occupied territories would be rounded up, sent to concentration camps, and exterminated.

The orders of deportation, the lists of arrests, the criminal accountability of the persons to be exterminated, the statistics of the dead, the orders for the poison gas, all this was drawn up in ordinary offices by civil servants of death who, once at home, would look after their wives, their children, and their dogs as would any other family man.

The deportations started in March 1942 and lasted up to the end of the conflict, even though every sensible German understood that the war was lost, that the one-thousand-year Reich was tumbling down in a bloodbath, and that soon they would have to account for their actions.

Resistance against the occupying forces was organized in the whole of Europe; it was ferociously repressed by the Gestapo, who were responsible for all the executions and deportations. The Resistance fighters were not sent to the extermination camps to die by gas like the Jews, they were sent to concentration camps to die by work, providing free labor which soon became indispensable to the war economy of the Reich, because of the large number of German workers who wore a uniform. The people sent to the concentration camps were killed in large numbers by exhaustion from hard work, malnutrition, cold, illnesses, assaults, and ill-treatment. They, too, were sent to the camps until the end. The last convoy of Jews sent to the camps left France on August 17, 1944, and the last convoy of Resistance fighters left on the 18th, the day the Gestapo left Paris. One week later Paris was liberated. It took more than eight months and hundreds of thousands of additional victims to complete the destruction of Nazism. Incapable of taking responsibility for his diabolical creations, Hitler found in suicide the only exit door he had left.

At the center of this gigantic disaster, the Gestapo continued to act ruthlessly, enforcing everywhere and up to the end their dreadful methods: arbitrary deportation, torture, and murder.

Soon the last direct witnesses, the last victims of this fiendish organization, will have disappeared. The young generation must learn how all this was possible, and how a totalitarian system works from the inside. Nazism was the ultimate model.

Those who are unaware of the past are condemned to relive it. Let us not forget that it is only by some miracle that humanity avoided total annihilation.

—J.D.

INTRODUCTION

GESTAPO! For twelve years these three syllables made Germany, and ultimately the whole of Europe, tremble. Hundreds of thousands of men were hounded by this police force operating under the cover of "social necessity," millions of human beings suffered and died at their hands or at the hands of their brothers, the S.S.

And yet, whereas thousands of volumes published in every language have studied, dissected, and commented on, the most outstanding events of the history of National Socialism and the Second World War, no work has yet appeared, seventeen years after the collapse of the Third Reich, to retrace the complete history of the Gestapo. The Gestapo was the central pivot of the Nazi State, and the events of this period are only comprehensible in the light of our knowledge of this vast political machine.

Never has an organization attained such complexity, been vested with such power, and reached such a pitch of "perfection" in efficiency and horror. In this respect, the Gestapo will remain in the human memory as the example of a social instrument perverted by unscrupulous individuals. It shows what happens when a governmental body ceases to be in the service of the nation, and passes instead into the service of a clan. The powers and weapons entrusted to it at the outset to assure the protection of the citizens, their rights and liberties, are no more than the means of enslavement and death. Gang rule prevails.

The gigantic Nazi machine and the men behind it are still almost unknown, not only to the general public but also to most historians whose works deal with contemporary events. I have tried to "dismantle" its mechanism, to reveal its implacable machinery, to show how, thanks to this armature which supported even the smallest elements of its edifice, the Nazi regime was able to assert itself. We shall see how the innumerable ramifications of the Gestapo and the S.D. (Security Police) infiltrated all the activities of everyday life, enveloping the men subjected to it in such a tight network that no action and no thought could escape their vigilance.

The men at the controls of this machine are as little known as the machine itself. I have found it essential to show them as they were. In most respects they were ordinary men. But their destiny changed on the day Hitlerism gave them a new "moral code" by substituting for their own conscience a total submission to the Nazi dogma.

The elements which have served as a basis for this book may be divided into two orders. I have used a great number of unpublished sources and also certain works which will be found listed in the bibliography. For nearly ten years, from 1945 to 1954, I amassed a considerable volume of personal notes, during the trials of the Gestapo agents in France, from their leaders and the war criminals which the French courts brought to justice. During the same period, I had occasion to meet personally most of the people who directed the German police services in France. I realized then that they were only men, sometimes obtuse, sometimes intelligent, always lacking in character, without moral fiber, incapable of distinguishing between the ideas of good and evil, obedient only to their orders.

Most of the accused felt no remorse and seemed incapable of appreciating their situation. The proceedings taken against them for their crimes seemed to them an act of vengeance exercised by the conqueror on the conquered and, paradoxically, it was in this view that they accepted their fate, for this was an idea they could understand. They acted in this manner. The most able of them thought that they could barter their lives for certain secrets or by placing themselves in the service of the conqueror. Masuy, one of the most notorious torturers of the Gestapo's "auxiliary" teams, confined for many months in Fresnes prison, planned the opening of a doll factory in Spain after his liberation, which he imagined would not be long delayed.

It is from these direct "contacts" that I have drawn the portraits of most of the agents who operated in France. I have used their statements and their recollections to reconstruct the edifice of the general organization of the Gestapo, and the stages of its development in France, in addition to the reasons underlying certain still little known events. The proceedings in the collaboration trials before the High Court, the Courts of Justice, or the Military Tribunals, have also provided me with precious information.

The most useful printed sources were primarily the twenty-three volumes of the proceedings of the International Military Tribunal at Nuremberg and the seventeen volumes of appended documents. I have used the version published by the French Government. The documentation concerning the administrative structure of the Nazi organization and their powers originates from works published by the Nazi party or by the governmental bodies of the Third Reich. I have ransacked these works for useful biographical details.

In the course of my research over a period of ten years, I have been fortunate in receiving invaluable encouragement and help, without which it would doubtless have been impossible for me to complete this work efficiently. I proffer my very sincere thanks to those people who have given me their cooperation. In particular I wish to thank Mlle Lisbonne, librarian to the Ministry of the Interior, for her inexhaustible kindness; to M. Chalret, the Public Prosecutor, who placed his library at my disposal; to M. Durand-Barthès, archivist to the Ministry of Justice; to Mlle Adler-Bresse, archivist to the Bibliothèque de Documentation Contemporaine; to M. Joseph Billig and all the staff of the Centre de Documentation Juive Contemporaine, whose records were extremely valuable; to M. Michel and the Historical Committee of the Second World War; to Mlle Fraissignes, in charge of the German documentation of the historical archives of the Ministry of War, asking them to accept this token of my gratitude.

Before embarking upon the history of the Gestapo, it may be useful to recall the events which served as milestones on the Nazis' road to power from 1919 to 1933. In actual fact, it is impossible to separate the Gestapo from National Socialism. They are bound together in their very essence. This short survey is merely to recall certain determining elements.

National Socialism was born from the complex of defeat. When Germany had to admit that she was conquered in November 1918, her soldiers refused to accept this defeat, which they did not consider they had deserved.

The traditional cadres of the Imperial German Army, dominated by the Prussian officer caste, had always cultivated militarist habits and sentiments, which they had developed to the point of hypertrophy. Considering themselves the sole masters of Germany and of the people, whom they persisted in regarding as serfs, they could not accept the idea of their capitulation. They began by spreading the concept of an army unconquered in the field but the victim of treachery. In this way was born the legend of the *Dolchstoss*, the "stab in the back." They forgot to mention that in November 1918 the

German Army had 184 divisions in the line, but only seventeen in reserve (two being newly formed divisions), whereas the Allies had 205 divisions in the field, but 103 reserve divisions, sixty of which were new, enlarged every day by American reinforcements. The Danube front had surrendered a month before. Austria had collapsed on November 6 and Germany was on her own. On November 3 the 5th Squadron of the High Sea Fleet mutinied at Kiel; on November 7 the revolt which broke out at Munich overthrew Ludwig III, the old King of Bavaria. On the 9th the Grand Council of War held at Spa, confirming that the German General Staff had lost the initiative, decided to sue for an armistice, while the Chancellor resigned and the Kaiser fled to Holland. Three civilians, Prince Max of Baden, the new Chancellor Ebert, and the Catholic conservative Minister Erzberger, had to humiliate themselves and open *pourparlers*. The same day the Social Democrat Scheidemann proclaimed the Republic from the balcony of the Reichstag.

This young Republic, born in disaster, soon became the bête noire of the military, which chewed the bitter cud of defeat and began to talk of treason.

Germany foundered in chaos. Total discipline, the famous German discipline, so often quoted as an example to liberal nations, was responsible for this. For generations this *Kadaverische Gehorsamkeit*, this "corpselike obedience," had depersonalized the Germans, maintaining them in a kind of subjection which rendered them comfortably docile. The hierarchic pyramid had crumbled and these "corpses," deprived of the brutal orders which animated them, were delivered without defense into the hands of agitators.

Unemployment and poverty added to the chaos. In order to re-establish order it was necessary to call upon the Army, which had recruited some curious formations, known as the Freikorps or "combat groups," private armies recognizing no other leader than the officer commanding them. These groups put down all local attempts at insurrection, thus taking a mortgage on the regime when, a little later, they formed the cadres of the new Army. At the same time, the soldiers discovered politics, or what they considered to be politics, creating a kind of service of psychological action, which organized "courses of political instruction." One of the animators of this institution was Captain Ernst Roehm.

At the beginning of the summer of 1919 a new *Bildungs-offiziere* (educational officer) graduated from these courses. His name was Adolf Hitler and he had just received the rudiments of the future National Socialist doctrine. Much has been said on the determining role of the German Army in the birth of National Socialism. Allied to certain big industrialists they created or supported the tiny groups which propagated anti-democratic ideas, preaching militarism and reviving anti-Semitism, which at the time had virtually disappeared.

The Republican Government seemed unaware of this agitation, confident in the excellence of the Weimar Constitution: promulgated in August 1919, this constitution was undoubtedly good but contained certain dispositions which made the Republic liable to be overthrown.

Very soon the enemies of the new regime realized that infiltration methods were preferable to a frontal attack. They feigned Republican sentiments to insure the control of power, and Noske, the Social Democrat Minister for War, was able to say in all seriousness, "With the young Republican Army I am bringing you liberty and peace."

Under cover of these soothing words the enemies of the Republic continued their work of undermining. At the *Herrenklub* (the officers' club), they perfected their doctrines, disseminating them in *The Ring*, Baron von Gleichen's newspaper. "The officers of the Reichswehr have learned since the revolution to distinguish between the State itself and its apparent form. The officers wish to serve the State insofar as it is permanent and identical with itself."

It was quite simple; as soon as the State ceased to follow the officers' political ideas it was merely an "apparent form" which they were free in future not to serve. They were soon taught that it was even their duty to impose their own laws upon it.

Captain Roehm and his friends learned the lessons and, to facilitate a return to the old order, prepared for future action by creating an infinite number of nationalist organizations. This splitting up reassured the government who did not see that, when the time came, it would be easy to reunite these groups, under a single direction, since all these "good wills" were only dispersed to outward appearance.

In September 1919 the educational officer, Adolf Hitler, entered one of these groups, the D.A.P., Drexler's German Workers' party. He soon obtained control, and on August 8, 1921, with the help of Captain Roehm, transformed it into the N.S.D.A.P., the German National Socialist Workers' party. The new

Party which had united the members of three groups—Drexler's D.A.P., Jung's N.S.D.A.P., and Streicher's S.S.D.P., the German Socialist party—could muster only sixty-eight members on its creation, rising to three thousand by November 1921. Thanks to an intensive propaganda campaign, based on the repetition of violent slogans, reiterating *ad nauseam* the legend of the treachery of the "November criminals" invented by the Army, it increased rapidly, creating a special team of "toughs" designed to silence with fisticuffs or rubber truncheons any opponents who might contradict them. This period saw the birth of the S.A.

In November 1922 a prize recruit enrolled in the N.S.D.A.P.: Captain Hermann Goering, the war pilot and last commander of Richthofen's famous "circus." He was to become the father of the Gestapo.

The best recruiting agents of the Party were the soldiers. They also formed the cadres of the S.A., transformed by Roehm into a veritable army which very soon threatened the government and exceeded the Reichswehr itself in numbers and power.

There was, however, no question of fighting against the Army; the latter gave its help, producing weapons, secret cadres, and sometimes money. In April 1923 the S.A. acquired stocks of secret army weapons, and in September of the same year General von Lossow in Munich refused to ban the Nazi newspaper, the *Voelkischer Beobachter*, preferring to be relieved of his duties.

The Nazi doctrines struck a sympathetic note with the soldiers. They resembled those of their "courses of political instruction": suppression of parliamentarianism; the concentration of power in a strong State led by a responsible chief, who consulted the people by plebiscite; no constitution, a superfluous framework which hampered evolution. The State would not tolerate opponents, who always play the enemy's game. It would crush them. No opposition press and, therefore, no "treason"; no opposition parties to undermine the power; all that counted was the "national interest."

The whole trick consisted in identifying the party in power with the Fatherland itself, a piece of chicanery which was customary in the Army. In the defense of the Fatherland (i.e., the Party) all methods were justifiable. The individual did not count. He merely existed as a member of the community to which he had to sacrifice everything. Absolute discipline, therefore, was needed and total obedience to the "leader." This is why the intellectuals were to be kept under observation and ruthlessly eliminated if they became "a danger to the country," in other words, hostile to the regime.

To these principles must be added all the racial arguments—the value of pure blood, Nordic blood, the superiority of the Germanic race, "the Herrenvolk," the need to impose its law on submen, the degenerates of bastardized inferior races, the harmfulness of ideas of charity and pity which were not in "the natural order." "In all confidence," wrote Hitler, "we can go to the limits of inhumanity if we bring happiness back to the German people."

As the N.S.D.A.P. progressed, thanks to its propaganda, others tried to seize the power. Various abortive putsches, such as that of Major Buchrucker, encouraged Hitler to try a *coup d'état*. On November 9, 1923, in Munich, he attempted to overthrow the Bavarian Government, thinking that the movement would set an example. His principal accomplice was General von Ludendorff. But the revolt collapsed in a few hours, after ten minutes' firing which caused fourteen deaths and fifty wounded.

Hitler was arrested. Goering, who was marching at his side in the procession when it was fired upon, was seriously wounded but managed to reach Austria. Another man who had participated in the affair as standard-bearer of the Reichskriegsflagge, a movement inspired by Roehm, was called Heinrich Himmler.

The setback to the putsch and the arrest of Hitler were not exploited by the Republican Government, which let slip the chance of finally liquidating National Socialism.

After a scandalous parody of a trial, Ludendorff was acquitted, and Hitler, together with his four chief accomplices, sentenced to five years' incarceration, with a remission of four years under the First Offenders Act. The accused men left the courtroom to the cheers of their friends and the strains of the national hymn!

On December 20, 1924 at 12:15 P.M. Hitler was released from Landsberg prison, after having served thirteen months and twenty days' detention. He had realized that the power could fall into his hands provided he approached it legally, in other words by using the mailed fist in the velvet glove; by violating the law under cover of solid complicity; by pretending to play the democratic game while undermining it from within.

However tempting it may be, a reconstruction of this patient undermining work would be beyond the scope of this book. Let us merely recall that the parties of the Extreme Right and the Nazis had suffered a heavy defeat in the November 24 elections and were reduced practically to nil at the beginning of 1925. From 1924 to 1932 the Left Wing parties continued to improve their positions at the polls with an increase of 3,329,000 votes in eight years. But these victories were merely relative, since during the same period the Nazis by their propaganda managed to attract an important mass of new members among the young electorate (3,000,000 new voters registered in 1930), progressively filching the clientele of the traditional Right Wing parties, from the right center and even from the center. All these good folk, timorous and traditionalist, were snared by words they had learned to respect, without realizing that in the language of the Nazis they had quite a different meaning. These same good folk had struck the first blow at the Republic by appointing the old Field Marshal Hindenburg its President in the 1925 February election. Under cover of this former national glory, the enemies of the Republic were able to install themselves in most of the key positions.

It was by playing the democratic game with stacked cards that the Nazis and their friends made the whole edifice collapse. By provoking ministerial crises (involving constant elections) they persuaded an enormous number of citizens to turn from the government and to lend a more attentive ear to Nazi propaganda. In the face of this strategy the Left Wing parties were incapable of uniting: incapable of abandoning their internal struggles to make a common front against the enemy, incapable of seizing the numerous opportunities which presented themselves for recapturing the initiative. As for the neighboring countries, the conquerors of yesterday, in particular France and Great Britain, whose role might have been decisive, their inconsequence and blindness seemed limitless, not only during the period of the seizing of power but also during the first years of National Socialism.

On May 30, 1932, when Field Marshal Hindenburg brutally dismissed Chancellor Bruening, appointing von Papen, representative of the "barons" and the Reichswehr, as his successor, the last phase of the struggle for power began. The German lower middle classes—of whom Thomas Mann once said, "They will never agree to become submerged in the proletariat—" applauded this appointment. For them the old Marshal was the man of providence, the savior of their class, and his decisions could not be anything but wise.

On June 14, less than two weeks after coming to power, von Papen raised the ban on the S.A. and the wearing of the Hitler uniform, which had wisely been decreed by Chancellor Bruening. From now onward von Papen's role became clear. At a meeting of the National Association of ex-German officers in Berlin at the beginning of September 1932, the Nationalist deputy Everling calmly stated from the platform, "Chancellor von Papen is vigorously employed in sweeping away the final debris of the Weimar Republican edifice, in order to rebuild the Reich on new foundations."

Von Papen dismissed the republican high officials and the governors of provinces, replacing them by "nationalists." In Prussia, Braun-Severing's Social Democrat Catholic Government alone put up a resistance. A simple presidential decree of July 20, by virtue of Article 48 of the Constitution, disbanded it by pleading its "failure to restore order," in other words to prevent the continual provocations of the Nazis.

Von Papen had opened the way to power, and the Nazis took it without striking a blow. In the 1932 July elections they captured 230 seats in the Reichstag, thus becoming the most powerful party in Germany. On August 30 Goering was elected President of the Reichstag. From this moment total victory was merely a question of tactics.

This ineluctable course does not seem to have been envisaged either by the parties of the Right, or by the soldiers who played the Nazi game. All of them were thinking in terms of the traditional political usages; they did not imagine that total power could fall into the hands of the Nazis, whom they judged incapable of governing on their own. They merely wanted to use their dynamism, to swim in their wake, to cause the traditional values to flow again, and to recapture their privileges. In exchange for their help they were ready to give the Nazis a share in the government. They had, however, forgotten the warning uttered by Hitler: "Where we are there is no place for anyone else!" It needed a long period of bloody experience to force them to take this phrase seriously.

Placed in the saddle in July 1932 by von Papen, the Nazis stumbled in the new November elections. They lost two million votes and thirty-four seats in the Reichstag. The lesson was not to go unheeded. Von Papen, forced to resign five days after the elections, was replaced by von Schleicher. Under constant fire he, too, was obliged to resign on January 28.

At midday on January 30 Hitler, chaperoned by von Papen, was called upon to form the new cabinet. The "old gentleman" had been forced to surrender power to the man he had always referred to contemptuously as "the Bohemian corporal."

Although the irreparable step had taken place no one as yet believed in a Nazi victory. On learning the news Thomas Mann smiled and said, "So much the better. He won't last eight months." The French and British "experts" took the same view and unanimously judged National Socialism as lost forever.

Hindenburg had thought to obtain some guarantees by placing Hitler in tutelage, by giving him von Papen as Vice-Chancellor and Commissioner for Prussia, and von Blomberg as Minister for War. These "barriers" were soon to be swept away.

On February 1 Hitler obtained from the Field-Marshal-President the decree to dissolve the Reichstag which he had refused to von Schleicher four days earlier, forcing his resignation. The elections were fixed for March 5. From this moment the Nazis decided to retain the power by all possible means. Germany entered into one of the most bloody adventures in her history, and the Gestapo, after its modest beginnings, was to play the leading role.

PART ONE

**THE BIRTH OF THE GESTAPO
1933–34**

Chapter 1
The Nazis Become Masters of Germany

On January 30, 1933, the fate of the world for the next fifteen years was decided in Marshal Hindenburg's study. Hitler had just assumed the title of Reich Chancellor. At his side, von Papen became Vice-Chancellor and Commissioner for Prussia; the former staff officer was one of the Field Marshal's "men" and the straw man of the German Agrarian League which, under the presidency of Count von Kalckreuth, was composed of the big eastern landowners. Ordered by Hindenburg to "get in touch with the parties, to clear up the political situation, and to examine existing possibilities for forming a new cabinet," he had brought him Hitler, whom the Junkers considered the only man capable of stopping by a forceful policy the developing socialist tendencies. Von Papen was also the Army's man.

The new Minister of the Interior was Dr. Frick, formerly a Munich police official, a dyed-in-the-wool Nazi, who would retain his post until August 1940. Von Blomberg was appointed War Minister; von Neurath, Minister for Foreign Affairs; Goering was still President of the Reichstag, Minister without Portfolio, and at the same time in charge of aviation and the works of the Prussian Ministry of the Interior.

This "Minister without Portfolio," the faithful Hermann Goering, a member of the Party since 1922, seriously wounded in the abortive putsch of 1923, was to play an important role during the weeks that followed the seizing of power. A Reichstag deputy since the May 1928 elections, a member of the Prussian *Landtag*, Goering had cultivated police circles and, thanks to one of his new friends, the police officer Rudolf Diels, had acquired a profound knowledge of the techniques of the political police.

The terror immediately descended upon Germany. It assumed a double form. Brutal and bloody, it manifested itself in riots and street fighting. Secretive but widespread, it manifested itself by arbitrary arrests at dawn, often ending in a swift execution by the revolver or hangman's rope in some silent cellar.

From the evening of January 30, 1933, the Nazi troops clashed with the Communists. Veritable pitched battles ensued. On January 31 Hitler made an announcement on the radio. In a moderate speech, the new Chancellor proclaimed his attachment to traditional principles. The mission of the government, he said, was "to re-establish the unity of the spirit and will" of the German people. He wanted to maintain Christianity and to protect the family, "the constituent cell of the body of the people and the State;" thus reassuringly he made himself the defender of middle-class values.

This head of state, so respectful to traditional form, obtained on February 1 the decree for the dissolution of the Reichstag which Hindenburg had refused to von Schleicher. The elections were fixed for March 5; the Nazis now operated within the framework of legality. But since victory was by no means certain, it was necessary to aid it by every means and, first and foremost, by methodically eliminating the enemy. On February 2 Goering, Commissioner of the Interior, took over the Prussian police and purged it. Republican officials long since noted and filed were liquidated, so indeed were the lukewarm ones. They were replaced by trusted Nazis. Hundreds of superintendents, inspectors, uniformed policemen, in fact two-thirds of the squads, were purged in favor of Nazis from the S.A. or the S.S. From this Nazi corps, molded by force into the framework of a traditional administration, was formed the Gestapo.

But the Prussian *Landtag* opposed these measures. On the 4th it was in turn suppressed by a decree "for the protection of the people." The same day another decree authorized the ban on meetings "capable of disturbing public order," which was to prevent meetings of the Left Wing parties and to leave the field clear for the Nazis.

On March 5 the Stahlhelm, the Schupos, and the Brown Shirts staged an official parade and procession in Berlin. It was the premature official seal given to the S.A., reminiscent of the famous Harzburg Front of the Nationalist parties. A bloody night followed, marked by Nazi raids on the meeting places and cafés frequented by the Communists. Brawls broke out at Bochum, Breslau, Leipzig, Stassfurt, Danzig, and Düsseldorf. There were many dead and wounded. The government was in the hands of the triumvirate: Hitler, von Papen, and Hugenberg (Minister of Economy and Agriculture, press and film tycoon and head of the German Nationalists).

On the 6th an emergency decree "for the protection of the German people" muzzled the press and the information services of the opposition. From the 9th onward Goering's police machine went into action. Throughout the whole country Communist branch headquarters and the houses of the party leaders were searched. The alleged discovery of weapons, ammunition, and documents "proving" a conspiracy about to explode, consisting in the main of a plan for setting fire to public buildings, was fabricated. Arrests and kidnapings increased. The S.A. tortured and murdered the adversaries who figured on lists which had been mentioned for many years.

General Ludendorff, Hitler's former friend, renounced his 1923 accomplice and wrote to Hindenburg: "I must warn you most solemnly that this sinister individual will lead our country into the abyss and our nation to an unprecedented catastrophe. Future generations will curse you in your tomb for having allowed this." Hindenburg merely sent Ludendorff's letters to Hitler.

On the 20th Goering gave an order encouraging the police to use arms against demonstrations in the parties hostile to the government. At Kaiserslautern, Bruening, the former Chancellor, had organized a meeting of the Catholic Association, Pfalz Wacht. After the meeting the Nazis attacked the procession with rubber truncheons and revolvers. The result: one dead, three wounded, and several people slightly wounded. The Catholic newspaper *Germania* appealed to President Hindenburg, but the "old gentleman" remained silent.

On the 23rd the Württemberg Minister of Economy, the democrat Maier, protested against attempts to deprive the provinces of their rights. He invited the southern Germans to unite (since the Nazis had no majority in any of the southern parliaments) in "the defense of Republican legality, their rights and liberties."

On the following day Herr Frick gave a significant reply. "The Reich," he said, "will eventually impose its authority on the southern states and Hitler will remain in power, *even if he does not obtain a majority on March 5*." Such an eventuality was deemed to warrant the proclamation of a *Staatsnotzustand* (a state of emergency) and the suspension of part of the constitution "in view of the fact that the adverse majority can only be negative."

Despite their will to retain the power they had had so much difficulty in attaining, the Nazis were worried. The opposition still resisted them. The situation became all the more alarming as events were speeded up: on the 25th the Communist activists, including the Antifa League, were placed under a single leadership in reply to the occupation of Karl Liebknecht House, which had taken place the previous day. On the 26th this new leadership launched an appeal to "erect a broad rampart of the masses for the defense of the Communist party and the rights of the working classes," and to "launch a powerful assault of the masses and a gigantic conflict against the Fascist dictatorship."

The only means of striking the Communist party and preventing its leading an anti-Fascist crusade was to crush it legally. The country had to be persuaded of the reality of the plot, of a Communist putsch; this would permit the elimination of the leaders and discredit the Party before the elections.

The staging of a widespread plot presented no difficulties to the Nazis. Thanks to Goering's purge, the Berlin police was in their hands. Thirty-thousand armed auxiliary police, wearing the swastika armlet, were masters of the streets. The Party paid them three marks a day. A decree signed by Goering, dated February 22, had enrolled members of the S.A. and the Stahlhelm as auxiliary police. Everything was ready for, the gala performance. On the 27th the curtain rose on the main act of the tragedy.

On February 27, at about 9:15 A.M., a theology student returning home along the pavement of the Koenigplatz, on which stood the Reichstag Palace, heard the sound of a window being broken. Pieces of glass tinkled onto the pavement. In surprise he ran to alarm the parliament watchman. A tour of inspection was immediately organized. A figure was seen running through the building, setting it on fire.

A few moments later the fire brigade and the police were on the spot. The leading police car, which arrived a few minutes after the firemen, was commanded by Lieutenant Lateit. Accompanied by Inspector Scranowitz and a few men, he hurriedly searched the building for the "firebug." They were all surprised by the number and spread of the fires. In the chamber an extraordinary sight met their gaze: a huge flame rose to the ceiling. It gave off no smoke, was three feet wide and several feet high. There was no other seat of fire in the hall. It had been caused by a very powerful incendiary product. The men were so impressed that they continued their search with drawn revolvers. They reached the restaurant, which was already a blazing furnace. The curtains and the carpets were alight everywhere.

A man, stripped to the waist, pouring with sweat, with staring eyes and a bewildered air, suddenly emerged from the great Bismarck Hall, in the south wing of the building. As soon as he was challenged he raised his arms and allowed himself to be searched without resistance. He carried only a few greasy papers, a knife, and a Dutch passport. Scranowitz threw a blanket over his shoulders and took him to the Alexanderplatz police headquarters. The man revealed his identity without demur: van der Lubbe, Marinus, Dutch citizen, born at Leyden, January 13, 1909, unemployed.

On the announcement of the fire, the radio broadcast the news: "The Communists have set fire to the Reichstag." Thus even before the inquiry had started it was known that the culprits could only be the Communists. The repression started the same night. The "emergency laws of February 28" were promulgated on the spot "for the defense of the people and the State" and signed by the old Field Marshal.

The Communist party was most directly affected, but all the Social Democrat newspapers were also banned. These decrees of public safety abolished most of the constitutional liberties: the freedom of the press, the right to hold meetings, the respect for correspondence, the inviolability of the home, and habeas corpus. Their effect was to deliver the German people to the tender mercies of the Nazi police, which could act without restriction or responsibility, practice secret arrests and perpetual detention without accusation, proof, public audience, or lawyer. No jurisdiction could oppose them, order a release, or demand a re-examination of the files. The Gestapo was to retain these prerogatives until the end of the regime.

That night the arrests began in Berlin. In the middle of the night 4,500 people—members of the Communist party or Democrats of the opposition—were taken into preventive custody. The police, the S.A., and S.S. shared the task; they carried out searches, interrogations, carried off truckloads of suspects who, after a stay in some private Party jail or in a State prison, were soon to people the first concentration camps, created by Goering to house them.

By three o'clock in the morning the airdromes and ports were subjected to a very strict control, and trains were searched at the frontiers. It was no longer possible to leave Germany without permission. Many of the Opposition managed to escape in spite of this, but the blow had been struck. There were five thousand arrests in Prussia and two thousand in the Rhineland.

On March 1 a second decree punished "provocation to armed conflict against the State" and "provocation to a general strike." What the Nazis feared most was a general strike, which could be the sole effective weapon of the divided Left. The Communist party had been decapitated, the Social Democrats shivered in their shoes, but there remained the unions. By virtue of their enormous size they could have opposed Nazi progress by paralyzing the country with a general strike.

In Germany at the time there were three groups of trade unions: the General German Workers' Confederation, the powerful General Confederation of Independent Workers with an affiliation of 4½ million, and finally the Christian Unions with 1,250,000 members. The German unions had the largest memberships in the world. Eighty-five percent of the workers contributed to a union. They had not forgotten the price they had paid for the war, and were deeply opposed to militarism.

This vast mass of men, despite its hostility to the newcomers, was incapable of taking the risk which might have saved it and at the same time saved Germany. Like the Social Democrats, the unions elected to wait and bow their heads.

In the midst of these disorders, polling day came, and from January 30 onward the Nazis unleashed upon the Germans a torrent of propaganda which spread everywhere, accompanying every action and moment of their daily existence. Thousands of meetings were organized for the electoral campaign. Hitler seemed to be everywhere at once, flying from town to town, appearing just long enough to galvanize his troops with harsh, hollow phrases. A gigantic propaganda machine had been organized by Goebbels—a welter of processions, flags, banners, and heroic marches impressed the poor devils who had come to hear the new Messiah. There were now more than seven million unemployed in Germany, which meant that nearly one worker out of three had to be aided (sparsely) by the Wohlfahrtsamt, the public assistance.

On March 5 Germany went to the polls. There were only 11 percent abstentions, a very small percentage compared with previous elections. The Nazis gained 17,174,000 votes as a result of their dynamism, of the countless pressures they applied, and of the gigantic swindle of the Reichstag fire.

The Communists, who should have been crushed, proved more resilient than could have been suspected. Despite the fierce repression meted out to them, the disappearance of their leaders (who had been imprisoned or forced to flee), and the suppression of their newspapers, they collected 4,750,000 votes and retained eighty-one seats. The new Reichstag was, therefore, composed of 288 National Socialists, 118 Socialists, seventy deputies of the Center, fifty-two German National People's party, twenty-eight Bavarian People's party and Independents, and eighty-one Communists. The Socialists gained nearly seven million votes. The Nazis, having obtained only 43.9 percent of the ballot, had no majority in the Reichstag. They naturally feared that the other parties might combine against them: they accordingly "invited" the Communist deputies not to sit. Realizing that to flout this "invitation" meant death, none of them took their seats.

On March 21 the anniversary of the convocation of the Third Reichstag by Bismarck in 1871, the new parliament was summoned to a solemn inaugural session. The following day the first real session of the Reichstag took place in Berlin at the Kroll Opera House in the Tiergarten. Huge swastika flags were draped behind the rostrum and the desk; the corridors were full of S.A. and S.S. squads; the Nazi deputies wore the uniform of the Party: the new order came out into the daylight.

The elimination of the Communists enabled the Nazis to dispose of 52 percent of the votes. No deputy raised the slightest protest against this amputation, which gave the Nazis complete power. The election to office took only a few minutes by "sitting or standing." Goering was elected President by a majority, excluding the Socialists.

On the 23rd Hitler read a perfectly harmless program speech, demanding full powers for four years, recalling that "the majority now held by the government could absolve him from asking for this measure." These full powers would allow the government to legislate outside the constitution. Its decrees would need neither the signature of the President nor the ratification of the Reichstag. He would also be relieved of the necessity of seeking parliamentary ratification for treaties that he might conclude with foreign powers. Thus parliamentary democracy was erased at a single blow and Germany became legally a dictatorship.

The din of the S.A. squads massed around the building could be heard in the hall, creating a disturbing, noisy background to the setting. The house voted. The Socialists alone had the courage to vote against Hitler. The plan was adopted by 441 voices to 94. Nothing remained except to dismiss the assembly. The old Field Marshal himself was dispossessed, since his signature was no longer necessary at the foot of the decrees. The Nazis were to rule as masters, and now the real revolution began.

Although they now enjoyed full power, the Nazis knew perfectly well that they had to strike a harsh blow against an opposition whose vitality had been proved by the recent elections. The future Gestapo was soon to find itself fully employed.

The first step was the *Gleichschaltung*, the "uniformization," in other words the total Nazification of Germany, the submission of the people, and the subordination of the State to the all-powerful Party. In other words to destroy, at the outset, all political organizations, to eliminate their leaders by murdering, arresting, or forcing them to flee.

The Communists had already been eliminated. On April 1 Hitler proclaimed a boycott of Jewish products and stores. The Jews everywhere were subjected to a certain amount of violence. For a long time one of the rallying cries of the Nazis had been *"Judah Verrecke!"* (Perish Judah!). On April 1 the S.S. and S.A. rampaged through the streets of Berlin inciting the crowds against the Jews, beating up those they met, ransacking and pillaging the Jewish shops, whose owners and staff were assaulted and robbed. They invaded the big cafés and restaurants and expelled the Jewish customers. This revival of medieval pogroms aroused a wave of censure throughout the world.

These acts of violence, however, were less gratuitous than one might have thought. "We must always take into account the weakness and bestiality of human beings," remarked Hitler. This exploitation of the most primitive instincts of man, industrialized by National Socialism, would materialize primarily in anti-Semitism which would be inseparable from it. The operation of April 1 was therefore in the nature of a smoke screen: while all eyes were fixed on these spectacular operations, a first decree was published which, augmented on the 7th by a second, began the centralization of the administration of the Reich. The parliaments of all the *Laender*, with the exception of Prussia, were dissolved. In their place *Reichsstatthelter*, representatives chosen by Hitler, were invested with full powers. This capital measure denigrated the resistance which had raised its head within the parliaments of the country, for example, in Bavaria. These "lieutenants of power" had the right to dismiss officials for non-Aryanism or for political non-conformity.

This precaution taken, a decree signed by a "Committee for National Action" of the Party decided upon the dissolution, on April 21, of the twenty-eight federations of the General German Workers' Confederation. Their property was seized, their leaders as well as the executive directors of the Workers' Bank were arrested. No reaction from the other trade union organizations was forthcoming.

Hitler, having decided to make May 1 "National Labor Day," the leaders of the free unions, i.e., those that remained, with a Socialist or Catholic leadership, were "contacted" amiably but firmly. They were asked to allow their members to participate in a manifestation organized by the Party on the occasion of this first feast day of the new regime. It was a question of celebrating working-class solidarity and the union of the workers in the national fraternity. It was a social, non-political act, which was also to serve as a feast of reconciliation. The day would be paid for, like any normal working day, and all those who attended the manifestation would receive expenses for their lost time and a meal. The unions accepted. From cowardice, or naïveté? Who would dare to pass judgment?

On May 1 a million workers assembled on Tempelhofer Feld, the former military maneuver ground. Hitler made a high-sounding speech, invoking God and exhorting the masses to work. The following day at ten o'clock in the morning S.A. detachments and police occupied the union headquarters, the people's houses, their newspapers, cooperatives, the Workers' Bank and its branches.

The Gestapo, which by a decree signed by Goering on April 26 had been formed in Prussia, operated for the first time under its new name in Berlin. The trade union leaders, carefully tabbed and shadowed for some days, were arrested in their homes or in the places where they had gone into hiding. Leipart, head of the Reformist Trade Unionists, Grossmann, Wissel, and in all fifty-eight trade union leaders were taken into protective custody. The records of the unions and their bank accounts were seized, including their relief and pension funds.

The same day an action committee for the protection of German labor under Dr. Ley "took over" the direction of the united unions, which now in actual fact fell into the hands of the Party factory cells. Thus, organizations embracing more than six million members, and whose annual revenue totaled 184 million marks, were destroyed without the least resistance.

On May 4 Ley announced the creation of his "Labor Front," decreeing compulsory labor. This Front was used as a giant propaganda tool for the inculcation of Nazi ideology among its millions of enforced members. The result was a leveling of the workers' living conditions. If the great Hitlerian programs lowered the figure of unemployed, it was to the detriment of the average working wage and to the benefit of the industrialists who had been won over to National Socialism. The unions thus eliminated, it was easy to administer the *coup de grâce* to the political parties.

Hugenberg, who had shared the power with Hitler and von Papen from January 30, bringing them the precious support of the German Nationalists, was terrified by the measures taken against the parties of the Center. In numerous departments, officials who were members of his party were cavalierly dismissed by applying the new decrees. However, he still held two portfolios: Economy and Agriculture. To be rid of him mass protests were organized against his agricultural policy. On June 28 he was forced to resign.

The same day the People's party, formerly Stresemann's party, considered it prudent to disband. On July 4 the Catholic party of the Center followed suit. Alone, in the midst of these scuttlings, the Bavarian People's party continued to face the threats. Its leaders were then arrested, including Prince Wrede, a cavalry officer who had taken part in the 1923 putsch at Hitler's side, and had been confined with him in Landsberg prison. He was forced to yield and in turn to disband his party.

On July 7 a decree eliminated the Social Democrat members of the Reichstag and the governmental organizations of the *Laender*. Many of their leaders had fled abroad. The others were in prison or in a concentration camp. The Nazis announced that all those who did not grasp the beauties of National Socialism would be sent there "to be re-educated." The first of these camps had been opened on March 25 near Stuttgart. There was only room for fifteen hundred, and it would soon count three or four times this number of inmates. This type of establishment was rapidly to become the principal national institution.

The same day a "series" of nineteen laws appeared. One of them put a full stop to all discussion: "The National Socialist party of German Workers constitutes in Germany the sole political party. Any person who undertakes to maintain the structure of another political party, or tries to form a new political party, is liable to a term of forced labor up to a period of three years, or to a term of six months to three years' imprisonment, without prejudice to the heavier sanctions ordained in other documents."

Doubtless many honest Germans were surprised at the turn which events had taken. They had been wrong not to heed the warning uttered by Hitler. "Where we are there is no place for anyone else!" His former friends and allies, the German Nationalists, had had plenty of time to reflect on this. The Nazis were now absolute masters in Germany. Their "new institutions" could function without hindrance.

Chapter 2
Goering Has Recourse to the Police

By the spring of 1934 sixty-five thousand Germans had left their country. A year of Nazi dictatorship had caused this flux, urging thousands of men and women, for the most part scientists, artists, writers, and professors, to run the risk of illegally crossing the frontier to seek asylum abroad. They fled from an insidious terror which now bore a name: the Gestapo.

This word became a symbol of misery and horror. But what kind of man was able with his own hands to create this monstrous edifice of terror? What monster forged this pivot of the Nazi machine, which was to cause twenty-five million deaths and to reduce Europe to ruins and ashes?

Hermann Goering by no means looked a monster. His fat face was more engaging than that of most of his companions. He was very popular and on the whole jovial. Looking back on Goering's life history, one cannot help recalling two phrases of Malraux: "The man is not what he conceals, he is what he does," he writes in *Les Noyers de l'Altenburg*, and in *La Condition Humaine*: "A man is the sum of his actions, of what he has done and of what he can do." Goebbels, Hess, Bormann, and Himmler, not to mention Hitler, very soon aroused a certain anxiety. Goering himself was reassuring. Yet Otto Strasser said of him, "Goering is a natural-born killer. He has a feeling for terror." There was, indeed, a kind of artistic refinement in the decadent style affected by this fat Marshal, swollen with superfluous flesh and pride.

This particular "feeling" had developed in him in rather strange circumstances. It will be recalled that on October 13, 1930, the new Reichstag held its first session. The National Socialist party were runners up to the Socialists, who had captured 143 seats. The 107 new Nazi deputies wearing the brown shirt uniform entered the chamber in a column, marching in swinging step. At the head of this strange company marched one of the oldest members of the party, Hermann Goering. He had entered the Reichstag two years earlier on May 20, 1928, when the Party had only managed to obtain twelve seats. At this period few Germans remembered that the new deputy was a hero of the last war, of the "Great War," which had not yet become a legend. There was something surprising about his presence in the bosom of this young, noisy, ill-famed National Socialist party. His birth and his past should have placed him on the conservative seats with the monarchists for preference, or in the Party of the Center representing the upper middle classes, his peers.

The son of Dr. Heinrich Goering, a magistrate of the old school, Hermann Goering was born at Rosenheim in Bavaria on January 12, 1893. Through his maternal grandmother, Caroline de Nérée, he had French ancestors, Huguenots from the Low Countries. His father, a personal friend of Bismarck, became in 1885 the first High Commissioner of German South-West Africa. After taking his decree at the universities of Bonn and Heidelberg, and having served as an officer in the Prussian Army, he became a magistrate, deeply ingrained with Prussian method and order.

A widower with five children of his first marriage, Dr. Goering married a young Tyrolese girl whom he took back with him to Haiti, his second colonial post, and then sent home to Bavaria to bring little Hermann into the world. Hermann's childhood was a long sequence of battles. He was constantly being expelled from schools on account of his aggressive temper and wilful character. His father solved the problem of his education by sending him to the cadet school in Karlsruhe, from where he graduated to the military school in Berlin.

He passed with honors, and in March 1912 embarked upon his military career in the Prince Wilhelm Infantry Regiment at Mulhouse with the rank of second lieutenant. He was just nineteen. Barrack life bored this violent young man, and he went gaily off to war. In October 1914 he obtained a transfer into the German Flying Corps. Here he was to cover himself with glory. An observer at the start and a pilot from June 1915, he flew on reconnaissance and finally as a bomber; at last in the autumn of 1915 he became a fighter pilot.

Alone in his machine, Lieutenant Goering came to life and gave reign to his aggressive instincts. He shot down one of the first British heavy Handley-Page bombers and was himself shot down by fighters. Wounded in the thigh and the left leg, he returned to his squadron as soon as he was fit, becoming one of the aces of the German fighter arm, and in May 1917 was given command of No. 27 Squadron. At the beginning of 1918 he had twenty-one victories to his credit and was decorated by the Kaiser in May with the Pour le Mérite, the highest German decoration. It was at this period that Goering was transferred to the famous No. 1 Air Squadron, more commonly known under the name of its first commander, the Richthofen Squadron.

On April 21, 1918, Captain Baron Freiherr von Richthofen, who had eighty victories to his credit, was shot down in turn. His successor, Lieutenant Reinhardt, fell on July 3. Goering then took command of this famous formation. On July 14 the German troops began their retreat from the Marne.

Although performing great deeds of courage, No. 1 Squadron suffered from the German reverses. It was a painful moment for Goering. In November he had to bring his men and matériel back to Germany. With the heaviest heart Goering had to pin up the news of the armistice on the daily orders board. Since its formation No. 1 Squadron had chalked up 644 victories: sixty-two pilots fell under its colors.

Goering was demobilized with the rank of captain. On his chest he wore the Iron Cross, First Class, the Lion of Zähringen with Swords, the Karl Friedrich Order, the Hohenzollern Order Third Class with Swords, and the Pour le Mérite. He could never forget this period of his life or his comrades from the Richthofen Squadron. In 1943 a Jew named Luther was arrested in Hamburg by the Gestapo. This man had been a member of his squadron. As soon as Goering was notified, he intervened energetically, had him released, and placed him under his protection.

Demobilized at the end of 1919, Captain Goering had to look for a job. He could have resumed his service in the Reichswehr, but being opposed to the Republic he refused to serve in it. In order to live he gave exhibition flights in Denmark, and then in Sweden. On Sundays he gave members of the public who were prepared to entrust themselves to his little Fokker their air baptism. He earned a living … and a wife whom he stole from her first husband and son, and brought back to Germany. He married her in Munich.

On his return to Bavaria the unemployed hero scratched a meager living. He enrolled at Munich University to take a course in political science and history, but above all to give a cachet of respectability to his enforced idleness. He lived in a charming bungalow on the outskirts of Munich on the money which his wife, née Karin von Fock, received from her family.

In the autumn of 1922 the Allies demanded from the German Government the surrender of a certain number of war criminals. Goering was even more indignant because his name figured on the lists drawn up by the French. One Sunday in November a protest meeting was organized on the Koenigsplatz in Munich. Goering attended. While listening to the speakers, who protested against the demands of the Entente, he noticed at his side in the crowd a thin man with pinched features and a small brown mustache with whose face he was familiar. It was Adolf Hitler, who was becoming known in Bavaria and whose portrait he had already seen. A circle formed around him and he was urged to speak. He refused "for fear of breaking up this bourgeois manifestation of national unity." It was said with a sort of icy contempt which impressed Goering. He, too, thought that these academic protests were ineffectual, and that violent action alone would have any chance of success. The following week Goering attended a meeting organized by the N.S.D.A.P. Hitler made a speech on his usual subjects. The conflict against the Versailles *Diktat* was the leitmotiv. The Versailles Treaty had reduced Goering, this brilliant officer, this semi down-and-out, to living on his wife's money. At the end of the meeting he approached Hitler to offer his services.

Goering was a prize recruit for a party which was still weak but in the process of vigorous development. His prestige as a former hero could be exploited, and his taste for violence, which could be sensed in his language, was in accord with the Party line. The following week he was enrolled in the N.S.D.A.P. and resolved to devote himself "body and soul" to this man whom he had only known for a fortnight. The shock troops of the Party, the *Sturmabteilung*, or S.A., lacked a leader. They had to be organized, disciplined, and coordinated, "to form an absolutely reliable unit which would carry out Hitler's and my orders," as Goering used to say later. At the beginning of January 1923 Hermann Goering, the unemployed hero, took command of the Nazi troops.

Goering transformed this already important though still badly organized troop into an army within a few months, with the help of soldiers, in particular Roehm, who was given command of the 7th Division and the control and direction of the clandestine militia. Roehm also directed the Nationalist parties "psychologically," disseminating orders and ideas. Hitler and his Party interested him, but there was a great gulf between the two men. For Hitler, the politician, the political organization of the Party came first: for Roehm, on the other hand, this first place had to be held by the soldier. The soldier had to be transformed and made politically aware.

Roehm, while illegally arming the S.A. from the secret stocks of the Reichswehr, entertained the hope of one day taking over command. A latent hostility soon made him oppose Goering, whose arrival he had viewed with displeasure and who, for his part, very soon sensed a dangerous rival in Roehm. Nevertheless, it was thanks to their collaboration that the N.S.D.A.P., at the beginning of 1923, could dispose of a real army dressed in field gray, giving the military salute and led by ex-officers recruited as a result of an appeal published by Goering in the *Voelkischer Beobachter*. The brown shirt and the Hitler salute would only appear later.

Hitler and his friends, therefore, anticipated with confidence the ordeal of the putsch improvised for November 9, 1923, and intended to bring about a Hitler-Ludendorff dictatorship. As we know this putsch, insufficiently prepared, collapsed within a few hours. The S.A. Munich Regiment had taken up positions on the right bank of the Isar, while the police were installed on the left bank. To counter any attempts at resistance Goering arrested a few hostages. The affair ended with an exchange of shots in the narrow passage of the Feldherrnhalle. Goering received two bullets in the stomach. It was in the house of a Jewish family, the Ballins, that he found asylum for a few hours while waiting for devoted friends to take him in secret to the Austrian frontier and from there to Innsbruck, where he would finally receive hospital attention. Twenty years later the Ballin family were to owe their lives to this fact.

These wounds and the ensuing period of inactivity had serious repercussions on Goering's temperament. A warrant for his arrest prevented him from returning to Germany: he had to live for four years in Austria, Italy, and subsequently in Sweden. His wounds, left unattended too long, had left deep marks in his flesh. For two years he was a morphia addict. Completely intoxicated, his brain was affected and he became dangerous. He had to be sent to the psychiatric hospital of Langbro, then to Konradsberg, and once more to Langbro, which he left half-cured, obliged to return for periodical visits. The forensic doctor Karl A. Lundberg, who examined him at Langbro, alleged that Goering had a hysterical temperament; he was a split personality, alternately a prey to attacks of lachrymose sentimentality and of rage, during which he was capable of committing the worst excesses.

His family found nothing surprising in this. For a long time its judgment of him had been harsh. According to his cousin, Herbert Goering, the family considered that the dominant traits of his character were vanity, a fear of responsibility, and a lack of scruples which would have "made him trample over corpses."

His prolonged idleness, his periods in clinics or hospitals, had completely transformed Goering. His constant tendency toward plumpness was now given free reign. At the age of thirty-two he was obese, swollen with fat which he would never lose. Cut off from his Nationalist Socialist friends, he had escaped the influence of this brutal milieu. He now disliked direct action. The unfortunate experience of Munich, which had given him food for thought for many months, had taught him that the solution must be looked for elsewhere.

The wild beast of yesterday was transformed, the fighting animal had donned a new mask. Goering would now fight with infinitely more dangerous weapons. This evolution completely alienated him from Roehm, who still remained a coarse soldier. When he finally returned to Germany in 1927, he was convinced, like Hitler, that the seizure of power could only be achieved by "political" means (in other words, by the basest means possible).

On his return to Munich after the amnesty of autumn 1927, Goering rejoined his friends—Hitler, who had long been released, Goebbels, Streicher, and Rosenberg. There was also a newcomer—Himmler, whom Hitler thought of giving the task of reorganizing his personal bodyguard, the S.A. Roehm trained this new army in Bolivia. Goering might have tried to get his hands on the S.A. again, but he felt in some obscure way that there was something better to do. He was a candidate at the 1928 elections. The Nazis obtained only twelve seats, but Goering was elected. The rather solemn aspect of the Reichstag sessions pleased him, as did the monthly salary of six hundred marks, which transformed his material situation. His bourgeois origin and former rank allowed him entree to Berlin high society and above all to the homes of the industrialists. He became "Hitler's ambassador" while waiting to be the Fuehrer's most "faithful paladin." Frequenting the Berlin salons, he no longer came in contact with Roehm's soldiery or the S.A. His affected taste for works of art and his pretensions to being a Maecenas date from this period.

Within the Party two rival factions stealthily opposed each other—the S.A. and the P.O., Gregor Strasser's Political Organization. Goering was on the worst possible terms with him. Skilfully avoiding the shoals, he followed his master Hitler, who was adept at exploiting the rivalries of his lieutenants, whom he encouraged to fend with each other in order the better to dominate them.

After the September 1930 elections Goering entered the Reichstag at the head of 107 Nazi deputies. Among these was Gregor Strasser. Goering was the only man to have foreseen this triumph: an increase from twelve to 107 seats in less than two and a half years. In October 1931 he lost his wife Karin, who had suffered from tuberculosis for many years. He plunged himself into politics, devoting his whole life to the man of whom he had made a kind of god. At the beginning of 1932 attention began to be paid to the presidential elections, old Hindenburg's mandate expiring in April. Hitler's candidature was seriously envisaged, but there was a snag. Hitler did not possess German nationality. At this juncture Goering had a brilliant idea. Thanks to his friends in the Brunswick Government—Kuechenthal, the president, and Klagges, the Minister of the Interior, both Nazis—Hitler was appointed economic attaché of the Brunswick Legation in Berlin. This nomination automatically conferred German nationality upon him. It was a piece of chicanery. Hitler was appointed on February 24, took the oath on the 26th, forfeited his salary and resigned on March 4. He had become a German in eight days!

Hitler was defeated at the April polls and the old Field Marshal resumed his post. But the elections of the following July 31 were, as we have seen, a regular Nazi spring tide. The N.S.D.A.P. won 230 seats, thus becoming the most powerful party in Germany. Goering reaped the rewards of his efforts; elected President of the Reichstag, he installed himself in the Presidential Palace opposite the Reichstag. The Reichstag was soon dissolved, and there was a return to the hustings. This was quite normal, since between 1925 and 1932 there were more than thirty general elections in Germany.

Despite the Nazi recession in the new November elections (196 seats as opposed to 230), Goering retained the presidency. His functions gave him access to the old Marshal, who was forced to consult him in periods of crisis. These crises succeeded each other almost without interruption. (He reminded Hindenburg that as an ex-officer he had had the honor of being presented to him during the war.)

In this post Goering was twice able to hasten the march of events. The first time on September 12, 1932, by leading the opposition motion which forced Minister von Papen to resign before he could use the decree of dissolution he had already prepared (and which Goering from his presidential chair pretended not to see when von Papen brandished it before his eyes); the second time on January 22, 1933, by persuading Oscar von Hindenburg, the son of the Marshal-President, to convince his father that Hitler alone could form the new government, the fall of the Schleicher cabinet being merely a question of hours. Goering had thus rendered Hitler services of capital importance. His personal action had played a predominant role in the accession to power—this power of which now, in March 1933, he held a considerable portion.

This was the man who was to play a leading role in the destruction of German liberties and in the foundation of the Gestapo.

When the old Marshal agreed to entrust the chancellor-ship to the man whom previously he had called "the Austrian corporal," he had made four formal stipulations. Firstly, von Papen was to be Vice-Chancellor. Secondly, von Neurath was to be Minister for Foreign Affairs. Thirdly, von Papen would also be Premier of Prussia, a post traditionally occupied by the Reich Chancellor himself, and the most important one in the Reich after that of Chancellor. And finally, he had insisted that the Minister of the Reichswehr should be von Blomberg, at that time absent from Berlin, since he was representing Germany at the Geneva Conference.

By making these conditions the "old gentleman" thought to put the Nazis in tutelage by subjecting them to the control of von Papen. The Nazis had agreed, firmly determined to get around the difficulty and prepared to violate their undertakings. In this once more Goering was to play a preponderant role.

On the evening of January 31, 1933, Goering spoke on the radio. Hitler had only been Chancellor for a few hours. Addressing the German people, he announced that the shameful history of the past years had now finished forever. "A new chapter opens today," he said, "and in this chapter liberty and honor will constitute the very basis of the new State." Liberty and honor! How many Germans would soon have plenty of leisure to savor the value of these words in the concentration camps or in the Gestapo jails?

In the new cabinet Goering had to submit to the counterweight of von Papen. He was Minister of State, President of the Reichstag, Prussian Minister of the Interior, and Commissioner for Aviation. Although von Papen obviously had no intention of interfering in aeronautical questions, as Premier of Prussia he was going to control Goering's activities in police matters. Now Prussia was the most important German province and Berlin was under the jurisdiction of Goering.

One of the first measures taken by Goering was to remove the police from the authority of the Prussian Premier by taking control of it himself. Frick, however, as Reich Minister of the Interior, had the right to examine the activities of the Prussian Minister of the Interior. He could give no orders but he could ask embarrassing questions. Goering also forbade the officials of his Ministry to give the least reply to questions asked by the Reich Minister of the Interior.

For several years Goering had been especially interested in the police. In fact as soon as Goering, by his functions as deputy, was able to make permanent contacts in bureaucratic circles he had been fascinated by the power represented by a well-organized political police force, directed without scruple. The idea of the Gestapo gradually took shape. He had chanced to meet a member of the Berlin Police Presidium, Rudolf Diels. The Prussian police, like all other police forces, possessed a political section, Section I A, directed by Diels. The latter had been one of those "postgraduate students" at the University of Hamburg who were more assiduous in their evenings at the beer hall than at the faculty courses. A boisterous member of a sinister association with medieval pretensions and a great womanizer, he cultivated a reputation for being a clown and a gay blade. On joining the police to put an end to his restlessness, Diels had been able to exploit his latent talents—a very acute sense of observation and great perspicacity.

He had plenty of time in the I A Branch to become appreciated. Any kind of dubious and irregular work could be asked of him. He forced himself to do it efficiently provided it brought him some advancement. Thus he was so at home in the more scabrous circles of Berlin, where all the vices flourished, that he was able to buy some private letters written by Roehm, in which the chief of staff of the S.A. made no bones about his homosexual tastes. (These letters fell into the hands of a member of the Prussian Government who had them published, hoping in this way to deal a mortal blow to the S.A.)

During the years of the struggle for power the N.S.D.A.P. had to face 40,000 court cases. Its members at the end of 1932 could boast of 14,000 years of detention and 1,500,000 marks in fines. Section I A had played a considerable part in these prosecutions. On April 13, 1932, the police went into action against the S.A. and the S.S. throughout Germany, for they had just been banned by an emergency law. Searches were instigated everywhere in the S.A. schools, the barracks, the headquarters, and the two Nazi Combat Groups were banned until the von Papen Government lifted the ban.

Diels, as much involved as his colleagues—probably a little more since he was particularly active—had the advantage over them. He was the first to realize that the situation had changed, and that the Nazis were soon to become masters of Germany.

When Goering became President of the Reichstag in August, Diels knew that he had not been mistaken. He paid discreet court to the new President, bringing him the secret files in which slumbered information capable of ruining the enemy. Knowing his métier to perfection, he also showed Goering what power, what means of obtaining knowledge, and what penetration a police force such as he dreamed of could have. It could, in fact, be all powerful. Goering appreciated Diels's services, since he had placed at his disposal files which would damn his political adversaries and allow him to consolidate his position within the Party. He also appreciated the discretion of these underhand measures. This secret power alone could check the army of braggarts which one day or another Roehm would try to use, not for the Party and the Fuehrer, but for his own ends.

Apparently Diels had other means of making himself appreciated. Goering, displaying his finery in the Reichstag or at the Presidency and courting applause at public meetings, loved to play the *grand seigneur*. Unfortunately he was a very impecunious *grand seigneur*. Diels, however, who had a finger in every pie, had excellent relations with members of the Stock Exchange. His information allowed Goering to speculate so successfully that he could now live up to his status. He, therefore, became Goering's man of confidence, paying for his position by dubious stratagems such as bind men together by making them accomplices.

When the Nazis came to power the police measures which would keep them in the saddle were ready. Diels had long since prepared a list of the Republican policemen to be eliminated. On February 8, 1933, the purge began. When all that remained was a third of the old squads, considered inoffensive, these were stiffened by dyed-in-the-wool Nazis chosen from the inner circles of the Party, the S.A., and the S.S. Goering placed Privy Councilor Diels at the head of this new service. The shady side of this creature and the intemperate habits he had retained did not scare the President. Moreover, Dr. Schacht was to say later that at this period "drunkenness was one of the basic elements of the Nazi ideology."

Diels was fully aware of the rivalry that existed between his master, Goering, and Roehm. He himself was on friendly terms with the S.A. leaders, both with Roehm and with Ernst, chief of the Berlin-Brandenburg group, with Count Helldorf, head of the Berlin S.A. later police president in Potsdam, and with Victor Lutze, the future S.A. chief of staff. According to his normal customs, he played a double game, profiting by his relationships to glean information which one day might prove extremely useful.

The police purge having been carried out in a few hours, the repression was now turned upon political adversaries. For this task S.A., S.S., and police were in close collaboration. The Communist party and then the Social Democratic party were deprived of leaders. The S.A. opened a private concentration camp at Oranienburg, near Berlin. Hundreds of prisoners arrested for no valid reason were incarcerated here. The son of the former President of the Republic Ebert; Ernst Heilmann, the leader of the Prussian Social

Democrats, languished there in company with many other well-known figures. Goering knew of the existence of this camp as well as the forty others opened by the S.A.

In Berlin itself the Gestapo had founded its own private prison. It entirely eluded the control of the Minister of Justice, a post held by a non-Nazi minister, Dr. Guertner. This prison, the Colombiahaus, was in the Papestrasse, in a large building which the Nazis jokingly called the Colombia bar, about which the most terrifying stories were soon current.

On February 22 Goering signed a decree making the S.A. and members of the Stahlhelm auxiliary police. He now had additional staff for his "vast police operations" and in addition chalked up a point against Roehm since, now that the S.A. were in the service of the police, they automatically came under Goering's authority. The fact that this semi-official recognition of the S.A. resulted in a redoubling of violence left Goering completely unworried. On the contrary he invited the men who were under his orders to display utter ruthlessness. On the 17th, addressing the Prussian police, he ordained: "No hesitation to shoot in case of need. Every policeman must grasp the fact that inaction is a more serious crime than an error committed in the execution of orders received."

In his orders of February 10 and 17 he recommended: "Each bullet which now leaves the barrel of a policeman's revolver is my bullet. If you call that a murder, it is I who am the murderer. These are my orders and I give them my full support. I assume the responsibility and I am not afraid."

On March 3 in a public speech, referring to the enemies of the Fatherland, he explained: "I am not called upon to render justice. My sole aim is to destroy and to exterminate, nothing else. The fight to the death, in which my hands will wring your necks, I will carry out with the help of the brown shirts."

After such encouragement how can one be surprised that Scheppmann, the Dortmund prefect of police, gave his men orders to fire on sight at distributors of hostile pamphlets; that every day corpses were discovered, usually bearing the marks of appalling brutality; that the German newspapers at the end of February could write that in six weeks at least twenty-eight thousand persons had been sent to camps and prisons. Moreover, this figure was lower than the true one because of the veil of secrecy which covered most of the arrests. The burning of the Reichstag, thanks to the emergency law signed on the same night, had set the seal on these measures and permitted the imprisonment of all the leaders of the opposition parties.

On March 5 the Nazis were finally ensconced in power. Goering, who had become Prussian Premier, could complete his work and bring out into the daylight his political police force of which he was so proud. But behind the scenes another man had already decided to take this force away from him.

Chapter 3
The Gestapo Is Created

On March 23, 1933, Goering opened the first session of the new Reichstag. At this first sitting an amnesty was proclaimed condoning crimes and misdemeanors "committed with patriotic intentions," in other words by the Nazis. This amnesty was complemented on June 23 by a law annulling the sentences pronounced against National Socialists during the years of the struggle for power. The law ordered the immediate release of prisoners, the erasure of their sentences from the police files and the reimbursement of their fines. The Party paid its debts and covered its men. This was at the same time an assurance for the future, but from now onward Goering wanted things to take place with strict legality, which signified that murder would now only be committed on orders.

To supervise these more or less criminal activities it was necessary to eliminate from posts of responsibility ministers who were not Nazis. Two of the basic laws of the reorganization of the Nazi State were published on April 1 and 7. In accordance with these decrees the parliaments of all the *Laender* were dissolved, with the exception of that of Prussia. In their place Reich Governors (Reichsstatthaelter) were appointed who were to serve as direct representatives of the Chancellor, charged with watching in each province the execution of the laws of the Reich and the Fuehrer's directives. With a stroke of the pen centralization had been accomolished. Also destined to disappear was the Reichsrat (the Council of States), which had become pointless, and at the beginning of 1934 was all that survived of local government. Naturally the governors were now chosen from among the most trustworthy Nazis. The members of the Party's political organization took the lion's share of these posts, battling fiercely with these dignitaries of the S.S. who proved dangerous.

In Prussia the battle was tough, since von Papen had to be dispossessed. Hitler appointed himself Statthaelter and, as the decree allowed, delegated his powers to Goering. The Reich Commissioner, von Papen, had no part to play in future. Goering was intent upon completing his great police task, and it was for this reason that the Prussian Government was not yet dissolved: its disappearance would have brought his police under the authority of Frick, the Reich Minister of the Interior.

His preparatory work completed, Goering, on April 26, 1933, issued a decree creating a Secret State Police—*Die Geheime Staatspolizei*—placing it under the authority of the Prussian Minister of the Interior, in other words himself. The same day Diels was appointed his deputy. In German *geheime* means not only "secret" but also "private." And, in effect, if this political police was to be secret, it was also to be the private police force of a party and even of a single man. The confusion between Party and State, current in all totalitarian regimes, was affirmed here as it was to be affirmed in all domains.

The same day a decree created a State police office in each district of Prussia, subordinate to the central Service in Berlin. The Gestapo, until then limited to Berlin, now had a branch in every district, but its power did not yet exceed the boundaries of Prussia. The purge was complete, not only in the police but also in the magistrature and among the State officials. A law of April 7 allowed the dismissal of officials and anti-Fascist judges, Jews, or those who had belonged to Left Wing organizations.

On June 22 a ministerial order issued by Goering enjoined all officials to supervise the conversations of State employees and to report those who dared to make any criticism. On June 30 a similar order introduced the same form of denunciation among the workers. Thus began a reign of constant spying. A net of observation and anonymous denunciations was woven, a net so complex that it was to strangle Germany in its meshes.

The Secret Police was at the center of this spider's web. Immediately on its creation, it had become the custom to designate it by its postal abbreviation "*Gestapo*," and within a few days this name became tragically well known.

From July onward the Gestapo scored several points over the opposition and gave proof of its efficiency. The clandestine organization of the Communist party, prepared and in position for years, was dismantled. At its headquarters John Scheer and all his staff were arrested. Scheer was handed over to justice for having re-formed a banned party, but the S.A. kidnaped him from prison and murdered him.

While continuing to strike at the opposition, Diel's men, on Goering's orders, began to undermine the S.A. From this moment Roehm came directly under fire. By reason of his functions, Goering was responsible for the concentration camps. But most of these camps, opened by the S.A., eluded his control. Horrifying stories were current. Goering was by no means shocked, but he could not bear his authority to be breached. These alarming rumors allowed him to attack Roehm directly. Roehm was now more dangerous than ever, for since the seizure of power the S.A. had grown out of all proportion. The Berlin group alone now comprised more than 600,000 men. Entire sections of the "Red Front" had gone over to the S.A. The Berliners had christened them "beefsteak sections," that is to say brown outside and red inside. Roehm could not have cared less. At the end of 1933 there were 4,500,000 S.A. in Germany and Roehm was a Minister without Portfolio.

For the moment Goering, forcing himself not to jump the gun, ordered Diels to inquire into the S.A. camps and to dissolve them. The official camps alone were to remain and to be administered by the S.S. Goering had come to a private agreement to this end with the head of the S.S., Himmler. In fact the S.A. settled bloody accounts, liquidated their adversaries and the accomplices of the old days who had become dangerous. They murdered the engineer, George Bell, who had acted as intermediary in the financial transactions between Hitler and Sir Henry Deterding; they shot police superintendent Hunglinger, who ten years earlier, on November 9, 1923, had opposed Hitler at the beginning of the abortive Munich putsch.

The S.A. wanted the three hundred dead and four thousand wounded who had fallen in their ranks in the struggle for power to pay the price in blood. At the Nuremberg trials, Gisevius, a valuable witness since he himself had been a member of the Gestapo for several weeks before going over to the opposition, describes this tornado in the following manner: "The S.A. organized vast raids. The S.A. searched, houses, confiscated goods, held interrogations, and imprisoned people. To sum up, the S.A. had been promoted auxiliary police and respected none of the customs or usages of a liberal system. ... Woe to the man who fell into their clutches. From this period dates the Bunker, the appalling private prison: each storm troop had at least one. Kidnaping became the inalienable right of the S.A. The value of the Standartenfuehrer was measured by the number of arrests he had made. And the good repute of an S.A. man was based on the efficiency with which he 'instructed his prisoners.'

In certain regions, the allies of former days, the parties of the Right, were disturbed by these excesses. In Brunswick the Stahlhelm opposed the S.A.: it was dissolved. All resistance, all hesitation was swept aside. Each S.A. leader had become an arrogant and cruel satrap, a district potentate who arrogated to himself the right of life and death over his fellow citizens. Each of these tyrants organized a bodyguard of heavy-jowled rogues, armed to the teeth, and insisted upon having a special office for seeking out political adversaries to liquidate; these offices were known as "I.C. Services," and corresponded to the French Deuxième Bureau. They arrested at random, genuine or false Communists and Jews and, in default of anything better, just ordinary, inoffensive citizens.

This was disloyal competition, and Goering became annoyed. Diels stuck his nose into these private camps. They apparently existed everywhere, and in them languished between forty and fifty thousand "enemies of the Fatherland." The best known was at Oranienburg, but, although created by the S.A., it had from the start been staffed by officials of the Gestapo. Since the Gestapo sent nearly all its prisoners there, it was left untouched. On the other hand three camps at Wuppertal, Hohnstein, and Bredow functioned under local S.A. leaders. The Minister of Justice had received complaints reporting the bad treatment meted out to prisoners. Minister Guertner forwarded these complaints to Hitler with the comment. "The prisoners have not only been beaten with whips and blunt instruments to the point of unconsciousness and for no reason, as in the security internment camp at Bredow, neat Stettin, but have also been tortured in various ways."

The Bredow camp had been opened by the S.A. leader Karpfenstein, the former Gauleiter of Pomerania. Goering closed this camp as well as the one at Breslau, which was run by Heines, Roehm's intimate collaborator, also a homosexual, who took a delight in inflicting the most sadistic tortures on the prisoners. The S.A. leader Ernst, a former café waiter who had become an important figure in the S.A., also had his camp in the suburbs of Berlin. He was a man with a more than dubious past. Goering closed the establishment.

On the other hand, there was no question of interfering with the S.S. camps; for example, Dachau, which was to become notorious twelve years later, was administered by the S.S. The commandant, S.S. Fuehrer Eicke, had published the following regulation: "Tolerance signifies weakness. In consequence punishment will be ruthlessly applied each time the interest of the Fatherland is involved. The good citizen will never be affected by this regulation. But let the political agitators and the subversive intellectuals, whatever their tendencies, heed this warning: See that you do not get caught, for you will be seized by the throat and reduced to silence, according to your own methods."

Every S.S. man knew what was meant by the "interest of the Fatherland." In May the former Communist deputies, Dressel and Schleffer, were murdered at Dachau. At the same period, between May 16 and 27, four other prisoners were executed by four different S.S. guards, proving that this was the normal practice. On May 24 Dr. Alfred Strauss, a Munich lawyer, was killed by two bullets in the neck after having been tortured the previous day. The doctor who carried out the post-mortem noticed that the body bore "black and blue bruises and gaping wounds." Three other prisoners, Leonhard Hausmann, Ludwig Schloss, and Sebastian Nefzger were executed in identical circumstances,

The Munich Court, which was not sitting at the time, wanted to set up an inquiry into the murders. The S.S. leadership replied that the four prisoners had been killed in an attempt to escape. But Strauss's post-mortem indicates that he was in slippers, "a sock on one foot, the other bare, obviously as the result of a wound." And the bullets were fired into his neck at point-blank range.

It is obvious that S.A. camps were closed, not because of the atrocities committed upon the prisoners, but because they were run by the S.A. Roehm and his friends understood this only too well. They therefore counterattacked.

One morning the Berlin Gestapo brought two prisoners to Oranienburg. As usual they were in a piteous state. They had obviously undergone a grim interrogation. This time there were almost indignant recriminations.

Schaefer, the camp commandant, reported the incident to his superior, Standartenfuehrer Schutzwechsler. He, too, was "shocked" by such revolting practices. The two men went to the Prinz Albrechtstrasse, the Gestapo headquarters, to "ask for explanations." They were received politely and given the assurance that the culprits would be sought, and that they would receive a reply on the following day.

On the following day in fact the reply came by telephone. The Oranienburg camp was dissolved on account of the bad treatment meted out to prisoners. A train was already on the way to transfer the prisoners to the camp recently opened by the S.S. near Ems. Schaefer had just time to rush to Berlin to report the matter to Secretary of State Grauert. The latter, sensing a bitter conflict brewing, decided to cancel the order for dissolution. The Oranienburg camp continued to function under Schaefer's paternal rod of iron.

This was only one episode in the internecine war which, from this period onward, the different Nazi organizations waged against each other, and which ended only with the collapse of the regime. Furthermore, certain personal accounts were only settled in the courtroom of the Nuremberg International Tribunal. These rivalries often attained an extraordinary degree of hatred.

Their source lay in the race for position, honors, and profits, distributed not by reason or merit, capacity, or the moral value of the individual, but by reason of temporary favor, the momentary supremacy of a clan or a powerful friend. Each organization tried to supplant the neighboring organizations, particularly those whose activities bordered upon its own. Within each organization, each service, a struggle evolved similar to that between the coteries who shared the power. The Gestapo was no exception to this rule.

The post of Diels, Goering's irreplaceable favorite man, attracted great envy. For certain people, to murder Diels was to render his chair vacant and have a chance of stepping into his shoes. For, according to a Nazi custom, the denouncer of a man usually received as his reward the post of the man he had delivered to the executioner. Goering's enemies, therefore, aimed their shots at Diels, whose departure would be a heavy loss to the Minister-President. In the midst of these intrigues Diels skillfully avoided the shoals.

One day, however, one of his enemies found a chink in his armor. After a hypocritical campaign of protest against Gestapo practices, a file was sent to President Hindenburg by generals whom he trusted. It had been drawn up by Frick, who had not yet accepted the way in which Goering had filched the

Gestapo from his control. The maneuver failed. Goering explained that it could only be a matter of isolated excesses, committed by overzealous sub-alterns. He decreed a commission charged with reorganizing the Gestapo and imposing the necessary sanctions. Naturally this commission never met. To pacify the Field Marshal, Goering had to sacrifice Diels. At the end of September 1933 he was dismissed. By way of compensation he was appointed the same day deputy director of the Berlin police. But, brought up in the seraglio, Diels, the true inventor of the Gestapo, knew the ropes. Despising his new appointment, he judged it safer to cross the Czech frontier and to wait events in Bohemia. Austria, already infested by Nazis, had not appeared to him safe enough. Goering accepted the blow which had been dealt him. The dismissal of Diels was a victory for his enemies. He parried the coup.

To replace Diels, Goering appointed a dyed-in-the-wool Nazi, one of the "old guard" whose orthodoxy could never be questioned, Paul Hinkler, a friend of Wilhelm Kube, former president of the Nazi group in the Prussian *Landtag*, Lord Lieutenant of Brandenburg.

Hinkler took over office. What Goering knew, but kept to himself, was the fact that Paul Hinkler was an alcoholic on a scale that made Diel's drunken bouts seem like a schoolgirl's tippling. He had also at one time been brought before the courts for complicity in a murder, and been acquitted as *non compos mentis*. In fact Hinkler was a congenital idiot in addition to being an alcoholic.

From his retreat Diels eagerly watched events. The trial of the Reichstag incendiaries had started on September 21, a week before his flight. Diels, who had led the inquiry and knew the secrets, realized that a great deal of excitement was brewing. Abroad, this trial was very much in the limelight. The German refugees tried to publish the truth, and Diels let it be known discreetly that, if it was made worth his while, he would consent to return to the fold.

In Berlin, Hinkler's extravagances piled up. At the end of October, after being less than thirty days in office, he had to be hastily dismissed. Diels, recalled by telegram, agreed to resume his duties. One of his first gestures was to issue a warrant for the arrest of Hinkler, who, seeing the Gestapo *sbirri* approach at dawn, had just time to flee through the windows in pajamas across the Zoo gardens. A patrol took him to headquarters, where he was able to notify his friend Kube, who came to his rescue.

After this warning Diels resumed his work and the old methods. Goering had felt the draught of the bullet. He prepared a new attack. On November 30, 1933, in his role of Prussian Premier, he issued a revolutionary decree removing the political police, the Gestapo, from the control of the Minister of the Interior. By this decree the Gestapo came under his personal direction. This separation of a branch of the police constituted a judicial enormity, but for the Nazis contempt for all judicial forms was an article of faith.

The same day Goering issued a warrant for the arrest of certain members of the Commission for Reorganization and Control created on Diel's departure, but which had never met. These warrants were never executed but they achieved their object—to serve as a warning to anyone who tried to pry too closely into what happened in the bosom of the untouchable Gestapo.

At the beginning of 1934 the Hearst newspapers in America published an article by Goering in which he wrote: "We deprive the enemies of the people of legal defense. ... We National Socialists wittingly oppose false gentleness and false humanitarianism. ... We do not recognize the fallacious quibbles of lawyers or the monkey tricks of judicial subtleties."

Admittedly the Nazis had never set store by legal "monkey tricks," but the only time they tried to employ a full-scale, well-staged trial for their propaganda, their machinations turned against them.

On September 21, 1933, the curtain rose at the Supreme Court of the Reich, sitting in the Leipzig Palace of Justice, on the second act of the tragedy which, in February, had shaken Germany and the world. Seven months earlier, when the dome of the Reichstag had half collapsed in the flames, liberal Germany had collapsed with it into an even more destructive inferno. White-haired President Buenger, in all the dignity of his ermine, surrounded by four assessors in red robes, was, in fifty-four sessions, to make the most gallant but unsuccessful efforts to preserve a little dignity during the proceedings.

For the new masters of the Reich were determined to use the trial to justify themselves in the eyes of the world, and to perpetuate the fable that this act of arson was Communist-inspired. Once the fable was established as fact, their implacable program for the repression or annihilation of their enemies could be put into practice under a cloak of legality, and their position, still by no means secure, could be consolidated.

In the dock were five disparate individuals, whom a succession of exploited coincidences had obviously brought there. To begin with there was van der Lubbe, the semi-moronic Dutchman, who had been arrested in the burning Reichstag, and who was indisputably one of the incendiaries. Next to him stood Torgler, the former head of a Communist group, one of the best known orators of the K.P.D. (German Communist party) and the most popular after Ernst Thaelmann, the head of the German Communist party. He had been imprisoned after reporting to the police of his own free will the day after the fire to give an account of himself. He had been accused on the depositions of two dubious witnesses, the deputies Frey and Karwahne, former militant Communists, who had deserted the N.S.D.A.P. They had sworn on oath to having seen Torgler on the day of the fire entering the Reichstag in company with van der Lubbe; their testimony had sufficed to satisfy the judge.

The three other accused men were more interesting. They were three Bulgarians arrested in rather strange circumstances. A certain Helmer, a waiter in the Bayernhof Restaurant on the Potsdamerstrasse, had seen the photo of van der Lubbe in the papers. He had also noticed the posters offering twenty thousand marks' reward to anyone who would help in the arrest of his accomplices. Helmer then remembered having seen van der Lubbe in the restaurant in company with three men who came there from time to time, and who were obviously "Bolsheviks." The fact that the Bayernhof was far too smart a restaurant for the ragged van der Lubbe ever to have got past the door was ignored. The police laid a trap at the Bayernhof and arrested the three regular customers on March 9. The papers of two were apparently in order, describing them to be Dr. Hediger and Herr Paneff. The third had no papers. It needed but a few minutes to discover that the papers were forged. The three men then admitted that they were Bulgarians: Blagoj Popoff, Wassili Taneff, and Georgi Dimitroff.

Dimitroff! As soon as his capture was known at Gestapo headquarters, there was unbounded joy. Dimitroff was the head of the clandestine Komintern network for western Europe. He had already been condemned in Bulgaria to twenty years' imprisonment on one occasion, and to twelve years on a second. His two companions had also been condemned in their own country to twelve years' imprisonment each for their political activity. They had fled from Bulgaria, taken refuge in Russia where they had dwelt for a long time, and had just arrived in Germany to try and return under cover to Bulgaria. They maintained that they had never seen van der Lubbe and knew Torgler only by name. As soon as their arrest was known a host of witnesses appeared. They all insisted on having seen the three Bulgarians in the company of Torgler and van der Lubbe, at the restaurant, in the street, at the Reichstag, carrying crates, spying in the parliament hall, in the most improbable places. Dimitroff listened calmly to these accusations. He had little difficulty in proving that on the day of the fire he was in Munich. Such were the five men in the dock, and such were the charges, disastrous for van der Lubbe, the human wreck caught in the act, and flimsy enough in the case of the four others.

The trial aroused enormous public interest. A hundred and twenty journalists from all over the world, with the exception of the U.S.S.R., who had not been admitted, had gathered in the court. Hitler was impatient for the "pitiless verdict" which was to conclude the sessions, in order to relaunch his anti-Communist propaganda.

But shortly before the Leipzig trial another tribunal had already pronounced judgment on this affair. The German *émigrés* who had found asylum in France, Holland, and Great Britain, some of them even in the United States, had alerted world opinion. They had started an inquiry, collected evidence, published photographs and documents, in an attempt to establish what everyone suspected: the Reichstag had been fired by the Nazis themselves to obtain old Hindenburg's signature on the emergency laws to justify the repression.

In Paris a particularly active body was formed with the aid of André and Clara Malraux, Jean Guéhenno, and the Italian Chiaromonte. Under the direction of two German Communist writers, Willi Munzenberg and Gustav Regler, a *Brown Book* was published in several languages and widely distributed. The truth gradually came to light.

At the beginning of September an anti-Fascist committee in London set up an International Communist of Inquiry, which decided to carry out in advance the trial of the Reichstag fire. Presided over by a famous British lawyer, D. N. Pritt, the Commission included French, British,

American, Belgian, and Swedish celebrities such as Gaston Bergery, Maître Moro-Giafferi, Maître Henry Torrès, Arthur Hays, and Vermeulen. The Prosecutor's chair was taken by Sir Stafford Cripps, who exposed the facts, stating that this simulacrum of a trial could have no judicial validity, and had no other object except to serve the truth, which circumstances in Germany prevented from being revealed.

During the sittings of this Commission it was obvious that even if van der Lubbe had been one of the incendiaries, he had been only a tool. In the hands of whom? Of the Nazis, replied the Commission, and more particularly of Goering, who became the principal accused. On September 11, Maître Moro-Giafferi, who since the start of the trial had received threatening letters, proclaimed in a thunderous voice:

"There is no tribunal in the world, there is no court of justice, not even the most rigorous, the most hostile to the person of the accused, which would accept for a moment this fabrication of ridiculous so-called proofs. Yes! But there must be a saving of face: behind the accused, whom it has been resolved to destroy, a face must be saved, the face of the man whom the conscience of all honest men already accuses—Goering. . . .

"Which man on February 27 in Berlin held the keys to the Reichstag?

"Which man was in command of the police?

"Which man could order or stop surveillance?

"Which man held the key to the cellar through which entrance was made?

"This man was at the same time Prussian Minister of the Interior and President of the Reichstag. In other words it was Goering!"

To save face . . . This is what Maître Moro-Giafferi had said, and this is precisely what the Leipzig Court tried to do. For panic soon reigned among the ranks of the prosecution, which was soon reduced to a prudent defense in the face of the furious assaults delivered by a wrathful Dimitroff. The other accused were harmless. From van der Lubbe, who was constantly plunged into a state of gloomy idiocy, they had difficulty in extracting a few monosyllabic replies. As for Taneff and Popoff, they did not speak a word of German. Dimitroff had taken charge of the trial. He was now the accuser, and his accusations were so precise that on October 17, Dr. Werner, the Prosecutor, announced a decision which flabbergasted the audience. He was going to take the famous *Brown Book*, published by the *émigrés*, and to follow it page by page to prove that it was a mere tissue of lies!

The accusers had therefore become the accused, and the remainder of the trial could have no other object but to exonerate them. To the bar now came those men whose names were only whispered in Germany: the S.A. leader of Silesia, Heines, prefect of the Breslau police; Count Helldorf, S.A. leader in Berlin at the time of the fire, prefect of the Potsdam police; the S.A. man Schulz, and, finally, Goering himself!

Gisevius has given a colorful account of Hermann Goering's appearance before the court. Among the numerous characters he liked to play, the popular Hermann, the faithful paladin, the national hero, was one he affected at this period and which he chose to play that day: "the iron man."

Hermann appeared dressed in a smart light hunting coat and wearing riding boots, which rang out on the parquet. He tried to assume a calm which he soon abandoned. In his rage he sweated profusely and thundered in court. The strange turn taken by the trial disturbed him. He could not understand why the judges should bother with this *Brown Book*, this work "of provocation to hatred," which he must destroy wherever he found it.

From his chair, President Buenger followed the scene in amazement. He began to realize that this trial would deal a death blow to his career. In the box Dimitroff could not conceal his satisfaction. Goering still quivering with rage fixed him with a threatening eye and tried to recover his calm. But here was Dimitroff, the accused, questioning the Minister-President, and the Minister-President replying. An incredible dialogue ensued.

"What was the Minister of the Interior doing on February 28 and during the following days when der Lubbe's accomplices could easily have been discovered?" asked Dimitroff.

"I am not employed by the judicial police, I am the Minister," replied Goering. "My main preoccupation is to busy myself with the Party, whose ideas weigh on the world and which bears the responsibility."

He had just fallen into the trap laid by Dimitroff, by involving himself in a political discussion. Although the grand strategist of the N.S.D.A.P., he was not of the stature to cross swords with an expert in Marxist dialectics. In a flash Goering's interrogation turned into a piece of Communist propaganda. Hermann, nearly out of his mind and foaming at the mouth, abused his adversary.

"You are scum!" he cried, "only good for the gallows."

The President intervened, reminding Dimitroff that he had already forbidden him to make propaganda. "Confine yourself to asking questions relative to the affair," he added in a conciliatory tone.

"Thank you, my Lord, I am already satisfied with the Herr Minister's reply."

"Scum!" roared Goering. "Leave the court, scoundrel. I'll deal with you later!"

As he was being expelled from the courtroom in the midst of an incredible uproar, Dimitroff taunted Goering. "Are you by any chance afraid of my questions, Herr Minister-praesident? ..."

For the prosecution the collusion of van der Lubbe and the other accused rested on the fact that van der Lubbe was a Communist. During the proceedings, however, it turned out that he had ceased to be one in 1931. The inquiry carried out by the criminal police had proved this quite clearly.

On December 23 the court gave its verdict: van der Lubbe was condemned to death and the remaining four acquitted. The world press reported the event and the *émigrés* were triumphant. Despite orders, the German judges had not been able to make up their minds to condemn innocent men. On hearing the verdict Hitler was seized by one of those fits of rage which his entourage dreaded.

Goering however refused to release his prey. He had said to Dimitroff, "I'll get you!" and this is precisely what he did. Despite the acquittal, the four Communist leaders were kept in jail. They were not released until February 27 under pressure of international opinion, which manifested itself more and more vigorously. Torgler had been transferred to a camp on his release from prison. He paid for his complete freedom by entering the services of the Nazis.

On January 10 it was announced that van der Lubbe had been executed in the courtyard of the Leipzig prison. In Germany many people doubted that this execution had really taken place. It was maintained that his family had on numerous occasions, in accordance with the law, asked for the body of the hanged man from the German authorities to give it burial in Holland, but that they were never able to obtain satisfaction. It is difficult to see why the Nazis, in the event of van der Lubbe having been an *agent provocateur*, should have hesitated to get rid of such an embarrassing accomplice in the most legal manner in the world. The Gestapo did not like leaving any traces.

It is tempting to quote the Latin tag, *Is fecit cui prodest*, with reference to the smoking ruins of the Reichstag. This providential fire served the Nazis too well. It was indispensable to them in order to justify the repression, to buttress the role of the Gestapo, and to stage their electoral campaign.

An hour after the discovery of the fire Hitler and Goering watched the building blaze. Diels acted as guide, leading them through the still accessible corridors of the palace, and giving a running report on the first evidence found by his men, who were already at work.

Fascinated by the flames, Hitler cried on his arrival, "This is a sign from God. No one can now prevent us from crushing the Communists with a mailed fist."

On January 31 Goebbels had written in his diary: "The broad outlines of the conflict to be waged against the Red terror have been established in the course of a meeting with Hitler. For the moment we shall abstain from taking countermeasures. Not until the opportune moment when the Communists launch a revolution shall we strike."

It was necessary for the Communists to launch a revolution for countermeasures to be unleashed. But time slipped by. There was no explosion, and the elections were drawing near. The conflagration arrived at last as a boon from heaven, a week from the date foreseen, and Dr. Goebbels was able to make capital out of it.

On February 22, five days before the fire, Goering had issued a decree transforming the S.A. into an auxiliary police force. Without the S.A. the mass arrests could never have been carried out on the night and the day after the fire. The lists of arrests had been prepared long before, but it needed a considerable staff to carry them out.

Another detail: the fire took place in the midst of the electoral campaign. As was his custom, Hitler led an exhausting campaign. His electoral calendar, drawn up by Goebbels and distributed to the Party on February 10, was a very full one. Each day he had to speak at various meetings, often far distant from each other. He must not lose an hour of his valuable time. Now on February 10 a surprising detail comes to light: no meeting was scheduled for February 25, 26, or 27, and it was stated that the Fuehrer would be unable to attend any public meetings on the 27th.

Strange coincidence: it was precisely on that evening that the Reichstag went up in flames.

And now as to the fire. The investigators, the first police to arrive on the spot a few minutes after the discovery of the fire (at about 9:15 P.M.), were all struck by the great number of small fires—between sixty and sixty-five—dispersed throughout the building. Most of them appeared to have been caused by incendiary material, particularly the huge column of fire which rose from the floor of the chamber.

In its second March number *Der Ring*, Heinrich von Gleichen's conservative weekly—he was a member of the Herrenklub—published an article which ended with these questions: "How was all this possible? Have we really become a nation of blind sheep? Where are the authors of this crime, who were so sure of what they were doing? Were they perhaps members of German high or international society?" As a result of this article *Der Ring* was banned, but these questions haunted the minds of everyone.

Goering and Goebbels had ranted on the air that this crime could only have been perpetrated by the Communists. The day after the fire, the Gestapo and the KRIPO (Criminal Police) searched Karl Liebknechthaus, the headquarters of the Communist party. Now in this house, which had already been searched several times, emptied of its occupants for more than a month and guarded by the police, more documents were discovered (according to Dr. Goebbels "stacks of documents") of capital importance, confirming the existence of a plan designed to install a Communist regime by force throughout Germany. The unleashing of the "Red terror" was to have as its signal the burning of the Reichstag. The details of this plan, which had only failed thanks to the promptness of Nazi patriots, were broadcast. These overwhelming documents were never published despite constant demands made by the foreign press, and none of these capital exhibits were produced at the trial.

What were the actions of the police entrusted with the investigation? Armed with technical information provided by the material proofs, one of the incendiaries arrested on the spot, *in flagrante delicto* in their hands, knowing thanks to these documents the political loyalties of his accomplices, the approximate number of whom was known to them, all they caught in their nets were Torgler and three Bulgarians. Diels himself, however, "followed" the affair, assisted by Artur Nebe, an old criminal police dog, the author of an authoritative treatise on criminology. Their investigation hung fire and went astray on various unforeseen paths. Rumor bruited strange reports and surprising names, and their echoes could not fail to reach one of the many thousand ears of the Gestapo.

A certain Dr. Bell had some strange things to tell about van der Lubbe. The doctor had many friends in the N.S.D.A.P. He maintained that the Dutchman had many contacts in the S.A. and, he added knowingly, he already knew the details of what happened on the night of the fire. On March 3 or 4 in the National Club in the Freidrich-strasse, he told what he knew to one of his friends in the People's party. The latter, delighted at being so well informed, wrote to several comrades so that they might enjoy Dr. Bell's revelations. One of these letters found its way to Gestapo headquarters. Dr. Bell realized that he was being followed and kept under observation. He grew scared and fled across the Austrian frontier to the peaceful little village of Kufstein. On April 3, just as he was beginning to feel reassured, he was murdered by a group of S.A. men who had come from Munich.

There was also the strange story of Dr. Oberfohren, president of the German Nationalist Group in the Reichstag, a very well-informed man. He, too, knew the strange details of the affair. He, too, had the imprudence to put this on paper. He wrote an account of what he knew of the preparations for the fire, and sent it to several of his friends. A copy found its way abroad: it was published by the French, British, and Swiss papers. On May 3 Dr. Oberfohren was found dead in his flat. The police report concluded suicide, but his family noticed that his private papers had disappeared.

Later, after the bloody "Roehm purge" on June 30, 1934, Roehm's chauffeur Kruse, who managed to flee abroad, wrote a letter to Field Marshal Hindenburg revealing that the Reichstag fire had been carried out by a group of S.A., Roehm's trusties, with the connivance of Goering and Goebbels.

But all these rumors, despite their consistency, were less revealing than certain details. How could the incendiaries have entered the Reichstag? Two doors were used—No. 2 door in the Simpsonstrasse, open only on days of session, and No. 5 door, on the Reichstag quay. On February 27 access was only possible through No. 5 door. Through this door one entered a hall barred by ropes, at which stood the porters. Every visitor had to fill in a form giving the name of the deputy required, the name of the visitor, and the object of his visit. A page took this form to the deputy, and it was only on his acquiescence that the visitor entered the building, led by the page to the deputy he wishes to see. Finally the visitors' names were recorded in a special daily list. How could seven or ten men, carrying a large quantity of incendiary material (according to the investigation they used a ladder), manage to escape these controls?

But in the cellar of the Reichstag, which housed the boiler, was a small staircase leading into a tunnel. The latter ran under the colonnade, crossed the Freidrich Ebertstrasse, ending at the Presidency on the opposite side of the same street. A door separated this corridor from the staircase of the cellar and the boiler room. It was a wide corridor with rails on which ran a small wagon to carry coal from the Reichstag to the Presidency. This was one of the perquisites of the job. The President had his heating free, and this President was Goering. It can now be seen how easy it was to introduce the whole squad by this exit into the Reichstag.

It was whispered that the S.A. leader Ernst was one of the incendiaries, together with Heines; that Count Helldorf was also a member of the party—or that he had at least participated in planning the operation. Moreover, Ernst had boasted of this exploit in his cups. Others were equally indiscreet. A certain Rall, an old lag arrested a few weeks after the fire for a civil misdemeanor, thought he might save his skin by making certain revelations. He demanded to be heard by his examining magistrate as a witness "for another affair."

"In February," he said, "I was a member of Karl Ernst's bodyguard and I took part in the firing of the Reichstag."

The fellow continued in this vein, quoting Goebbels and Goering, giving the names of the participants and the details of the operation, while the stupefied clerk of the court took down his statement. One evening toward the end of February, Ernst summoned ten S.A. men of his guard, considered particularly capable of carrying out a delicate mission. Rall was one of them. Under the leadership of Heini Gewert, they were taught, on a model, the interior topography of the Reichstag. Heini Gewert alone reconnoitered the area in company with the deputy Ernst. They were told beforehand that the aim of the operation was to set fire to the Reichstag. On the night of the fire the ten men, led by Gewert, were driven to the Presidency in a car at about 6 P.M. They were ordered to go down into the cellar, where they remained for two or three hours waiting for Karl Ernst to come and give the signal. They were each given a tin of some incendiary product, and they had been given several rehearsals of their respective roles. During their long wait another simultaneous "operation" was taking place, of which they knew nothing.

At about 9 P.M. Ernst finally arrived and gave the signal. The ten men went into the tunnel, entered the Reichstag, surveyed the building, deserted at this hour, and distributed their incendiary material. It was all over in ten minutes, after which they returned to the Presidency by the same route.

The simultaneous operation, the completion of which was to serve as the moment for the signal, could only be the "tele-guidance" of van der Lubbe, reduced to a psychological condition by his "friends." At the moment the poor creature, possibly drugged and undoubtedly hypnotized, arrived at the Reichstag, his pockets stuffed with matches, climbed the façade, and broke a window, the S.A. men ran through the halls, strewing their tins at the prescribed places and retiring under Goering's protection. For there was no possible doubt that Goering had found this operation, hatched by his friend Goebbels, brilliant and given his consent. According to Gisevius, who related these details, which only a man in a strategic position such as he held could have gleaned at the moment of the event, Goering ordered Diels to mislead the investigation, being careful to eliminate any unforeseen elements which might come to the surface. Rall was one of these unforeseen elements.

The clerk of the court, Reineking, who took down Rall's statement, was a Nazi, an obscure member of the S.A. without rank but a confirmed Nazi. He saw here an opportunity of enhancing his esteem among the pontiffs of the regime. He was convinced that Rall had spoken the truth. Too many precise details, verifiable circumstances, and, above all, the fact which he checked that he really had belonged to Karl Ernst's bodyguard at the end of February, decided him. He was also accustomed to taking down the statements of witnesses.

Reineking notified his chief. In view of the importance of the event they decided to go to S.A. headquarters, which sent them to the Gestapo. The Gestapo had Rall released from Neuruppin prison. The judge was told that they needed his testimony. He was transferred to Berlin headquarters and interrogated for twenty-four hours on end. Messengers were dispatched in all directions. The Gestapo hurried to the Leipzig Post Office to intercept the letter sent by the Neuruppin judge to the examining magistrate of the Supreme Court, containing the copy of Rall's statement.

At Neuruppin, Reineking, promoted on the spot to the rank of inspector, was ordered to get rid of the original. The Gestapo searched Rall's home—he was living with a mistress—and all the places where he might have left a letter or some note. The result was, as Rall had expected, his immediate release. It was a defensive one. His body was discovered in a field a few days later by a laborer who unearthed it with his plow. He had only been buried a foot beneath the earth. He had been strangled.

However much truth is contained in these versions, the role of the Gestapo is evident: there is very little doubt that the Reichstag fire was lit by the S.A. on its initiative and at the instigation of Goebbels, the author of the plan, with the complicity of Goering, without whom it would have been impossible.

But what was van der Lubbe doing in this company? The unhappy creature was homosexual, a fact which came out at the trial. He had often frequented the Berlin doss houses, shelters, and sordid cafes and had met many of the strange fauna which teemed there. The S.A. was riddled with homosexuals. "Virile friendships" flourished. Roehm, the Chief of Staff, set an example. The Standarten S.A. of Berlin-Brandenburg, from which the incendiaries were recruited, was also tainted. The entourage of Ernst, if not Ernst himself—Heines, Heini Gewert, and many others—belonged to this fraternity and recruited their bodyguards, chauffeurs, and henchmen from it. It was through the secret channels of this milieu that the Dutchman had entered the orbit of the conspirators, while they were making their plans. They saw at once the profit they could draw from him. It was doubtless child's play to indoctrinate this half-demented creature, to awaken his anarchist passions, to persuade him to act against this symbol of the social order which he detested, and, a poor Erostrates, to hurl a ludicrous firebrand.

Perhaps he was drugged beforehand. In the course of the trial he murmured vaguely that there were "others." Nothing else could be extorted from him and he relapsed into that state of euphoria in which certain doctors recognized the symptoms produced by scopolamine.

The story of the tunnel had been discovered by the International Commission of Inquiry held in London. During the course of the trial, the Leipzig tribunal drove to the Reichstag and descended into the famous passage, only to conclude that the incendiaries had not taken that route, the Reichstag nightwatchmen having insisted that they would certainly have noticed them!

The pathetic van der Lubbe paid with his life for the hazard which had made his path cross that of the brown shirt incendiaries. He was not the only one. Apart from Rall most of the incendiaries fell in turn to the bullets of their accomplices. The Gestapo did not like witnesses.

The burning of the Reichstag and the Leipzig trial had brought the Nazi world, its methods and men, into the fierce glare of the spotlight. The whole world had learned their techniques, assessed their morality, realizing that they were murderers of the very worst type. It would have been easy to draw the correct conclusions. But that would have demanded action. It was easier to close one's eyes and to let the killers continue with their careers. The Gestapo already knew how to keep mouths shut.

And Roepke could write several years later: "The world catastrophe today is the colossal price that the world has to pay because it turned a deaf ear to all the alarm signals which, from 1930 to 1939, announced in ever more vehement tones the hell which the satanic powers of National Socialism had unleashed firstly on Germany itself and then on the rest of the world. The horrors of this war are precisely those which the world tolerated in Germany, by going so far as to maintain normal relations with the Nazis, and organizing with them festivals and international congresses."

PART TWO

**THE GESTAPO PERFECTS ITS METHODS
1934–36**

Chapter 4
Himmler Takes Over the Gestapo

The year 1933 had ended with a blow to Goering's pride. He had been roughly handled at the trial of the Reichstag "incendiaries." This trial was a setback for the Nazis and a blow to their prestige, in Germany itself and even more abroad.

In compensation Hermann Goering received on New Year's Day 1934 a letter of good wishes from his Fuehrer. Recalling the 1923 putsch, the reorganization of the S.A. which had been his work, his "primordial role in the preparation for January 30" (the seizure of power), Hitler ended by thanking him "with all my heart" for the outstanding services he had rendered the National Socialist Revolution and the German people.

A slightly less academic satisfaction had been accorded him a few weeks earlier. The Air Supply Corps had been transformed into the Ministry of Aviation—for civil aviation of course but camouflaging the organization engaged in secretly re-forming the Air Force, forbidden by the Allies under the Versailles Treaty. Goering thus became Minister for Air and, to mark the occasion, was appointed General of the Reichswehr. Hindenburg had been persuaded that a minister who tomorrow would be in command of a powerful air force could not remain a captain.

A "League for Air Defense" directed by the retired General Grimme was created; designers such as Messerschmitt and Heinkel started to work under the orders of Colonel Erhard Milch, whom Goering had known as an air force captain in 1918. He was to become Inspector General of the Luftwaffe and finally an Air Marshal.

Goering began to take a less active interest in police affairs, having become rather disenchanted by the van der Lubbe trial. Nevertheless, he had no intention of making a present of *his* Gestapo to a stranger. He was to write in 1934: "For weeks on end I worked personally on reorganization and managed to create, by my own efforts and on my own initiative, the Gestapo

Service. This instrument which strikes terror into the enemies of the State has contributed most powerfully to the fact that a Communist or Marxist danger in Germany and in Prussia is out of the question."

On January 30, 1934, on the anniversary of the accession to power, a decree placed the police services under the jurisdiction of the Reich, their administration alone being left to the *Laender* which, since the creation of the Reichstatthaelter, were no more than archaic structures deprived of all real substance. They would, however, continue to pay the police out of their budgets until the 1936 reorganization law.

This "placing under control" which was to affect the Gestapo was merely an administrative formality: Goering kept a firm grasp on his creation. In truth he was too proud of his work to abandon it, and he needed it to destroy Roehm, his dangerous rival, whose star was still in the ascendant. What mattered most was to place *his* Gestapo in good hands. Thanks to the measures he had taken, he was able to dispose of it quite freely. The decree of November 30, 1933, had detached the Gestapo from the Prussian Ministry of the Interior, and subjected it to his authority as Premier.

Thus, in the spring of 1934, he was able to hand over the Prussian Ministry of the Interior to Reich Minister of the Interior Frick, another of his rivals. The latter would have the somewhat vaguely defined right to give orders of a general nature to the political police, but could give no specific orders. Moreover, he was to lose even this vestige of power in 1936.

The administrative imbroglio was now total, because as Prussian Minister of the Interior Frick was Goering's subordinate, but as Reich Minister of the Interior Frick could give orders to the *Laender*, and thus to Goering himself as Prussian Premier! This jungle facilitated a complete lack of control and an adulteration of responsibilities, to the point of rendering them incomprehensible. The man in the street, incapable of finding his way about this labyrinth, was even more helpless.

The reason Goering decided to make this tardy "gift" to Frick was because he had discovered a *rara avis*, a stalwart ally against Roehm, a man who would make the Gestapo, already dangerous but still imperfect, that precision instrument which two years later would be capable of overwhelming or absorbing any opposition whatsoever. This man was Himmler.

Diels was dismissed on April 1, 1934. This time Goering sacrificed him without regret, for he felt that Himmler was much more able. Diels would continue to deal with current matters until his successor arrived on the 20th. As a parting gift Diels was appointed Regierungspraesident of Cologne (a sort of super-prefect of police), before taking up the same duties with Victor Lutze, the S.A. chief of staff, after the death of Roehm.

With Diels's departure, the "first epoch" of the Gestapo came to a close. The man who arrived to take over was to leave his personal imprint, and to give it "style" and an indelible character. When Himmler installed himself at No. 8 Prinz Albrechtstrasse, he "rounded off" an operation upon which he had been engaged for several months.

At the time when Goering was organizing his Gestapo in Prussia, Himmler, thinking on the same lines, decided to establish his power by insuring for himself the direction of the political police. Since Prussia was already in the hands of a competitor, he set up *his* pieces on the chessboard somewhat differently. In March 1933 he was appointed Munich prefect of police, and a month later head of the whole Bavarian political police. He next carried out a kind of touting business, facilitated by his position as head of the S.S. His men reported the positions available and, if necessary, gave the local authorities to understand the advantages they would gain by nominating friends in certain posts. It was a hotly fought contest because the S.A. leaders and those of the political organizations were equally covetous of these posts.

By October, Himmler controlled the police of Hamburg, the second city of the Reich. Thereafter in succession fell Mecklenburg, Lübeck, Thuringia, the Grand Duchy of Hesse, Baden, Württemberg, and Anhalt. At the beginning of 1934 Bremen and Oldenburg and finally Saxony, a province hostile to the Nazis, came under his control. By the spring he controlled the whole of Germany with the exception of Prussia. At this juncture he asked Goering to give him the Gestapo. He had Hitler's support, for the Fuehrer accepted the S.S. leader's argument—that it would be "just, opportune, and necessary to pursue the enemy in the same manner, throughout the Reich." Goering was moved by the fact that Himmler, too, was determined to ruin Roehm, one of his enemies. He also appreciated the strategic skill of this encirclement movement which had been swiftly carried out by Himmler. With an ally of this stature Roehm's days were numbered.

On April 20 Goering delegated the direction of the Gestapo to Himmler. But he took a final precaution. Himmler became the leader *de facto*, but

Goering remained leader *de jure*. He would remain this until the basic reorganization of 1936, but the title would be in fact purely academic.

Although he had been police chief of a host of towns and states, Himmler had not been able to carry out his duties efficiently. He had delegated them to "substitutes," according to the fashion of this period, which allowed the Party bosses to accumulate titles. He chose these deputies from trusted members of his S.S. In Munich, and subsequently for Bavaria, he had appointed a particularly interesting character, the chief of the S.S. Security Service, Reinhard Heydrich. When Himmler finally achieved his goal and settled in Berlin, he immediately appointed him chief of the Gestapo Central Office. On the very day of his arrival, he united all the political forces of the whole of Germany. On that day the Gestapo crossed the Prussian borders and spread its network throughout Germany.

Himmler's entrance to the Gestapo was not without clashes. When it was obvious that Goering was getting rid of Diels, another serious candidate had entered the ring: Kurt Daluege, S.S. Gruppenfuehrer East, second in rank in the S.S. to Himmler, his great rival. He had been made a general of police by Goering, and was already in charge of the ordinary police forces, i.e., the uniformed police, and the Security Police of the Reich and of Prussia. Goering had delegated his powers in this field, and Daluege thought that he now had a right to the political police as well.

A silent conflict began. Daluege was in favor with Hitler, but Himmler shared this esteem. Daluege, in addition, was Frick's favorite. This fact, combined with his lack of real enthusiasm for the political police role as Goering conceived it, decided the choice. Daluege displayed too much attachment to a certain formality, and refused to admit the practices in force in the Gestapo. Goering considered this a handicap. Furthermore, his appointment would have given Frick the possibility of being informed of matters which it would have been preferable to conceal from him. In this way Himmler became the lucky winner in this remarkable lottery.

What type of a man now came into possession of such a heritage? Like Goering, he was of middle-class origin, and only the stirring times had made him deviate from a fate which had been mapped out in advance, and which would in all probability have been uneventful. Kurt Heinrich Himmler was born on October 7, 1900, in Munich. His father had been a tutor at the Bavarian court. His mother was the daughter of Savoy market gardeners.

Himmler spent his childhood and youth in the little Bavarian town of Landshut. His father was the school governor. He was a stern, authoritarian man, tolerating no infringement of the immutable rules which defined the relationship of the members of the family—respect due to institutions, work, and the social hierarchy. The Himmler family was Catholic, and young Heinrich, like his brothers, was brought up in a strict religious observance. This austere education weighed heavily on the young man, and it marked him for life. He would preserve an outward respect for certain values, without ever realizing that he only venerated them superficially.

At the worst moments of the Nazi oppression, when his concentration camps became gigantic crushing mills, he put up posters bearing the inscription: "One path leads to liberty. Its milestones are called obedience, application, honesty, sobriety, cleanliness, a spirit of sacrifice, order, discipline, and love of country." These posters were not the fruits of cynicism, but the subconscious projection of lessons received from his father, the Bavarian schoolteacher, still valid despite the bloody tide unleashed by his son, perverted as he was by the heady ferment of the Nazi ideology.

He was called up for military service at the age of seventeen. He arrived just in time to witness the collapse of the German Army, of the generals and the officers whom he had been taught to revere. His short spell in the Army gave him no military education. Paul Hauser, the Colonel General of the Waffen S.S., maintained that in the S.S. Himmler's ignorance of military questions was notorious. "It was well known," he confessed at Nuremberg, "that Heinrich Himmler had only been a soldier for a year and knew nothing of military matters, that he underestimated the task of the soldiers and their work. He loved to play the strong man by using superlatives and hyperbole!"

Young Heinrich was equally impressed by the social upheaval which accompanied the fall of the German Empire. The professors were no longer respected; shoulder straps were ripped from the officers' tunics, and men were acclaimed for making speeches for which a little earlier they would undoubtedly have been shot.

The end of the war found him in Berlin. He eked out a paltry living as a roundsman for a brush merchant, and later as an employee in a glue factory, but managed as best he could to continue his studies in estate management. Berlin at this period was a seething cauldron, teeming with the most dangerous specimens of humanity. The "difficulties of existence," the unemployment, the political and monetary instability, favored the blossoming of an active well-armed scum in the floating population of the capital. Apparently young Himmler, doubtless bewildered by the collapse of the social values which had formed the basis of his education, was drawn to this scum and lived for several months in the Berlin underworld.

It is difficult to investigate this period in the lives of the Nazi leaders, and authors who have written the history of Germany always come to grief here. Men, for example, such as Himmler, Kaltenbrunner, and Heydrich, had all the time in the world during the fifteen years the entire police forces were in their hands to get rid of embarrassing records. It is significant that a small volume such as *Nazifuehrer sehen Dich an 33* (Nazi Leaders, See Yourselves) published in Paris in German by Willi Muenzenberg and other refugees, smuggled into Germany in 1935, was sought for by the Nazis throughout the whole of Europe. This little brochure contained short, very summary, and incomplete biographies of the chief Nazi leaders. The notices are often reduced to a few aspects of their criminal activities within the Party.

The small volume was naturally on the "Otto" list of works to be destroyed as soon as the Germans entered France. The Bibliothèque Nationale possesses two copies of the work, which were hidden during the Occupation. The copy of the second edition, however, published in 1935 with addenda, has been mutilated. The chapter dealing with Himmler is missing altogether.

The fact remains that, according to André Guerber, Himmler as a young man clashed with the police and the law in the following circumstances. At the beginning of 1919 he lived in a hotel of ill repute in the Moabit district, No. 45 Acherstrasse, with a prostitute, Frieda Wagner, his elder by seven years; she was born on September 18, 1893, in Münchenberg. A police report of April 2, 1919, dictated by Inspector Franz Stirmann of Police Station 456, the Spissengerstrasse precinct, indicates that complaints were laid by the neighbors against the couple on account of their constant brawls. Young Himmler, according to the report, lived off the earnings of his "girl friend." Furthermore, he partly admitted the fact. Suddenly, at the beginning of 1920, he disappeared at the moment Frieda Wagner's body was found murdered. A search warrant was issued, he was arrested in Munich on July 4, 1920, and brought before the Berlin-Brandenburg Criminal Police Court on September 8, 1920, accused of murder. Himmler put up a strong defense and, in absence of proof, his flight being only presumed, the court had to acquit him.

At the same period in Berlin young Himmler met a youth also from a good middle-class family, Hans Horst-Wessel, who like himself was leading a strange existence in the Berlin underworld. He lived at 45 Maximilianstrasse, and a report from Police Inspector Kurt Schisselman indicates that he, too, was a "ponce." On September 4, 1924, he was sentenced to two years' imprisonment for fraud by the Berlin Court. On his release Horst-Wessel became interested in politics and met his former friend Himmler, at a meeting of the Party. This was the period when the N.S.D.A.P. was prospecting the underworld for ruthless men to form the backbone of its shock troops.

In 1929 Horst-Wessel joined the Party and entered the S.A. With a group of killers, recruited from among his friends and from the lowest quarters of Berlin, he formed *Sturm* No. 5 of the S.A. and, as a result of bloody brawls, managed to become cock o' the walk in one of the most infamous districts of Berlin, at that time held by the Communists. This exploit won him promotion to honorary member of the Nos. 5, 6, and 7 S.A. *Sturmer* in Berlin.

Horst-Wessel amused himself by writing Nazi words to the tune of an old naval ballad. This song, the Horst-Wessel Lied, was to become the hymn of the Nazi party, after the death of the lyric writer. He was murdered on the evening of February 23, 1930, by another "ponce," a Communist, Aly Hoeler, in a dispute as to the "ownership" of a certain prostitute, which ended in a brawl in a tavern of Berlin-Weding.

After the accession to power. Horst-Wessel took his place in the pantheon of the Nazi martyrs. His mother and sister were put on display at propaganda meetings.

After this Berlin interlude, young Himmler decided to return to the fold. At the beginning of 1921 he reappeared in Landshut. His father settled him in a small farm, where he could exercise his farming talents in raising chickens. He advised him to stand aloof from all political agitation. At this time Bavaria, and above all Munich, was on the boil. Himmler had already belonged to a youth movement which preached the "renovation of the German peasantry"—the "Artamans Movement," whose device was "Blood, soil, and the sword," a slogan which was to become a basic principle of the S.S.

Ignoring his father's advice, Himmler took an interest in the patriotic movements which preached the return to traditional values, demanding the death of the Weimar Constitution and of the criminals responsible for the shameful armistice. He joined the Reichskriegsflagge (the Empire Banner), one of whose leaders was Captain Roehm. At the beginning of October 1923 a split took place in this movement. The majority, led by Captain Heiss, supported the policy of von Kahr, while the group of "ultras," N.S.D.A.P. sympathizers, left the organization. Himmler was one of the three hundred extremists who, under the leadership of Captains Roehm and Seydel, remained in the movement. This was largely composed of toughs and was born just in time to take part in the November 9 putsch. Himmler figured in the group heading the procession in the famous march which ended so lamentably in front of the Feldherrnhalle. He came through the volleys of fire without a scratch.

During the period of eclipse suffered by the N.S.D.A.P. as a result of the abortive putsch, he continued as an activist in the diverse groups which served the Nazis as camouflage; for some time he was Gregor Strasser's secretary, a post in which he was succeeded by Goebbels in 1925.

At the end of December 1924 he heard of Hitler's return to Munich on his release from Landsberg prison. On February 5, 1925, he wrote, to him saying how much the patriots relied upon him to help Germany emerge from the chaos and to recover the place which was her due. Touched by this letter, Hitler, whose troops had evaporated during his absence, replied to his young admirer and invited him to pay him a visit. On March 12 Himmler knocked on the door of old Frau Reichert, who rented a room to Hitler at 41 Tierschstrasse. Himmler was given the Party card No. 1345. Hitler had decided to start again from scratch, but to impress new members the cards began at No. 500.

Hitler was impressed by the young man's respectful and disciplined air. Himmler had rediscovered the submissive attitude inculcated by his father. He listened religiously to the words of Hitler who, as soon as he had an audience, immediately lapsed into the style of the political meeting. By his temperament Himmler was preordained to play the role of the brilliant second-in-command, the faithful, indispensable servant. He was driven by ambition, but his taste for discretion always made him prefer to play second fiddle. As opposed to many of the Nazis, particularly among the "old guard," who would often try to supplant Hitler, Himmler never tried to seize the power. According to Dr. Gebhardt, one of the Nazi doctors who had known him since childhood, "he was the typical subordinate who assumes the odious character of sternness, precisely as Mahomet smiles and the Caliph executes."

During the following month Hitler had an opportunity of appreciating the qualities of this recruit. Young Himmler was one of the most assiduous Nazis at the Party manifestations. He was intent upon becoming one of Hitler's bodyguards in the course of his journeys, for a new propaganda effort had begun to relaunch the N.S.D.A.P., although in theory the Party was outlawed. But Ebert, the President of the Republic, had died on February 28, General Ludendorff was a candidate for the presidential elections of March 25, and Hitler was ready to support his candidature.

Ludendoff obtained less than 1 percent of the votes, and Field Marshal Hindenburg was elected President, but, from this moment, the Weimar Constitution was doomed. The second half of 1925 was particularly active. Hitler had realized that he must lead the assault against the Republic by legal methods, since the regime had already been undermined from within.

On November 9, 1925, the anniversary of the "glorious patriotic Munich march," Hitler decided to form a group specially designed to protect him: the *Schutzstaffel* (protection troop), which was to become famous under the initials S.S.

This "troop" was not born spontaneously *ex nihilo*. Hitler had always had a bodyguard. The first had consisted of "bouncers" recruited for the first meetings to silence hecklers. From 1920 five men were detailed for the personal protection of Hitler: Lieutenant Berchtold, the watchmaker Emil Maurice Weber, the horse dealer Hermann Esser, and the "butcher boy" Ulrich Graf. The last-named became Hitler's personal bodyguard.

The S.S. was created to reconstitute the former Stosstrupp (Hitler's personal guard), which had been dissolved during Hitler's term of imprisonment. Command was given to Julius Schreck, but at the beginning of 1926 the group was attached to the S.A., of which it now formed a specialist unit. The S.S. therefore now came under the authority of the S.A. chief of staff, Franz Pfeffer von Salomon.

In 1929 serious tension developed between Hitler and Pfeffer von Salomon. It ended the following year with the departure of the latter. Hitler realized that as head of this bodyguard he needed a man who was devoted to him body and soul. The malcontents always maintained that Hitler played the sultan. He was, however, a sultan who needed janissaries, and here was where Himmler came into his own.

When Heinrich Himmler took over the S.S. on January 6, 1929, it comprised 280 men, but they were all reliable veterans. From the first Himmler tried to observe a policy of strict selection as the basis of the group he was now ordered to reorganize. Contrary to Roehm, who was only interested in numbers, Himmler preferred "quality," in order to make the S.S. the Party's elite troop.

This difference of conception was confirmed when Roehm, taking over the leadership of the S.A. in January 1931, theoretically became Himmler's superior in the hierarchy, the S.S. still being integrated in the S.A. There was latent antipathy between the two men. From hostility it developed into fierce rivalry, destined to play a decisive part in Himmler's determination to obtain control of the police services.

Himmler's preference for rigorous selection made recruitment slow at the start. The S.S. rose from 280 in November to 2,000 in 1930, 10,000 in 1931, 30,000 at the accession to power, and 52,000 at the moment Himmler took over the Gestapo—a ridiculous figure compared with the 4½ million S.A. under Roehm's orders at the same period.

But these precious S.S. had been placed by their master in key posts. As a start, as soon as Hitler entered the Chancellery, Himmler had selected 120 superb, tall men whose courage had been tested to form the Leibstandarte Adolf Hitler, a company which would act exclusively as the Chancellery guard. This unit was to remain in being until the end of the regime. Then too, Hitler's immediate entourage was almost solely composed of S.S. Himmler placed them everywhere, around Hitler's person. Brigadefuehrer S.S. Julius Staub managed the Fuehrer's personal affairs, another S.S. Brigadefuehrer, S.S. Streck, became his chauffeur. His immediate personal safety was insured by S.S. guards under Brigadefuehrer S.S. Rattenhuber and by a group of Gestapo police officers under Inspector Hoegl. These men never left Hitler's side and accompanied him on all his journeys. Himmler, therefore, was always informed of the least incident, of each visit, and of the smallest conversation. No one could approach the Fuehrer without his being notified. His men had also entered the Gestapo. They were firmly ensconced in numerous posts during the purges and reorganizations which had followed the accession to power.

Himmler had already started a systematic attack on the S.A. and Roehm. Working on Hitler's feelings, according to the same plan as Goering, he reported the excesses committed in the camps by the S.A. and demonstrated the inconveniences which might result. It was not the methods themselves that shocked him, but the disorderly manner in which the S.A. operated.

In March 1933 the S.S. opened its own camps, and progressively eliminated the "competitor," and at the beginning of 1934 Himmler contrived that all the camps were run and guarded by S.S. alone. To this end he created a new branch of the S.S., the *Totenkopfe*, or Death's-Head regiments, charged exclusively with guarding the camps. They perpetrated the same horrors as their predecessors, until finally they became murder organizations on an enormous scale. The cost of the camps was charged to the budgets of the *Laender* and did not figure in the general budget of the Reich until 1936.

This creation of these special troops clearly showed that the camps had become a national institution. No administrative or judicial authority, no German magistrate, not even Minister for Justice Guertner raised the slightest protest against this judicial monstrosity. The S.S. continued to arrest and detain thousands of persons who had been charged with no crimes and given no trial, and who could expect to be detained there, according to Goering's expression, "until the Fuehrer takes pity on them." It was the cowardly acceptance of the *fait accompli* that allowed the progressive extension of Nazi methods, the setting aside of all legality, and, ultimately, the founding of criminal organizations.

Himmler therefore was already powerful when he settled at No. 8 Prinz Albrechtstrasse in the Gestapo office from which he could survey the whole of Germany as though from the center of a gigantic spider's web. On January 1 he had sent an unambiguous message to the S.S.: "One of the most urgent tasks incumbent upon us," he said, "is to discover all the declared or hidden enemies of the Fuehrer and of National Socialism, to combat and annihilate them. To accomplish this task we are ready to shed not only our own blood but the blood of others."

"The body bears the imprint of the inner forces which animate it," the enlightened theosophist, Jakob Boehme, wrote at the beginning of the eighteenth century. It is consoling to think that murderers bear the stigmata of brutality. The majority of the Nazi leaders conform to this rule: Roehm had the head of a killer, Bormann's physiognomy was more than disturbing; Kaltenbrunner and Heydrich had the faces of cold-blooded murderers, as we might expect. Himmler, on the other hand, reveals to us a smooth, desperately commonplace face.

He was slightly above average height but muscular. His face was rather plump and, although he was only thirty-three at the start of his police career, he had gone slightly bald on the forehead and at the temples. He had the face of a junior clerk, a modest accountant, or small tradesman, with a tiny receding chin which did not indicate very great will power. A mustache barred this flabby face with its two large, stick-out ears. A perpetual smile gave him a final touch of the tradesman's servility.

Two signs alone sound a discreet note of alarm: the very thin, colorless lips, and the small bluish-gray eyes behind a pair of steel-rimmed glasses, which hardly concealed a look of surprising penetration and icy hardness. He probably knew that these eyes betrayed him, for he always kept his head slightly averted toward the right shoulder, so that the reflection of the glasses would hide them and not betray him to an interlocuter who might perhaps be a prey. His curious, rather unhealthy-looking neck often struck his visitors: the skin was flabby and wrinkled, making it appear the neck of an old man. His hands were abnormally small and delicate, long-fingered, almost feminine, very white and transparent with blue veins. ... When he spoke or listened he often kept them curiously inert on the table in front of him. These inexpressive hands harmonized with the face which was composed, enigmatic, and motionless.

His subordinates would say later that Himmler never meted out praise or blame. His orders were usually vague. He liked to let people discover for themselves the best methods of satisfying a chief whose plans were only revealed to them in stages. He loved secrecy; he impressed it deeply in his creations, making it an absolute rule, any violation being punished with exceptional severity and sometimes with death.

He was endowed with a rare gift for work. His day usually started at eight o'clock in the morning and did not end till late at night, often at two o'clock in the morning. He never stopped working. When traveling he was always accompanied by his secretary; he would dictate letters in the train, an airplane, or a car, keeping in close touch with the Gestapo head office, thanks to radio communication. Every report, all correspondence of any consequence, had to be communicated to him. He read them all carefully, making marginal notes with a green pencil. With his own particular meticulous care, he franked every document that passed through his hands with the letters *GEL,* short for *gelesen* (read), followed by the date and his signature, two coupled capital *H*'s with a horizontal line ending in a sharp point. This choice of grayish-green pencil reflects his personality. Goering, ostentatious and gaudy, annotated his mail with a brilliant red pencil.

When Himmler was not on one of his frequent voyages or tours of inspection, which he carried out at random to check up on the activities of his services, his long day was disturbed only by breaks for meals, nearly always taken in an S.S. or Gestapo mess. He would sometimes keep a visitor for lunch; he often invited his heads of departments, showing himself to be an agreeable and talkative host, a witty conversationalist, unpretentious even when, after coming to power with his countless terrifying duties, he was in fact the most powerful man in the regime.

He had good and faithful friends, several from his early childhood, who continued to call him affectionately "Heini," as they had done when they went with him to his father's school. In the S.S. he was often called with respectful attention, "Reichsfuehrer Heini." One of the fascinating aspects of this story is to see killers cultivating the flower of friendship and using among themselves diminutives still redolent of violet ink and chalk, breathed together in the old Bavarian school. For he had carried along with him most of his comrades. Dr. Gebhardt, his childhood friend, would become one of those responsible for the scientific experiments; Bavarian officials he had met at the Munich Police Praesidium would follow him to the Gestapo in Berlin. All of them believed in his star: he had indisputable powers of persuasion. "He believed what he was saying at the moment he said it, and everybody believed it too," said Gebhardt.

Himmler lived away from home. He seemed to have no private life. His whole existence was spent within the framework of the S.S. and the Gestapo, and he seemed to live entirely for these two monsters. His apparent serenity hid a secret wound. Himmler had an unhappy married life. He had married a nurse, seven years older than himself, Marga Couzerzova of Bromberg. She had worked in a large Berlin clinic at a period when moral corruption was at its peak. She had seen so many abortions, so much illicit traffic in drugs that she had the greatest contempt for doctors and surgeons. On the other hand she attributed the greatest virtues to herbal treatments, a belief which she passed on to her husband. It was with his wife's money that Himmler had started his chicken farm at Trudering near Munich. It failed, and on her advice he changed over to the cultivation of medicinal herbs. He studied the old medieval herbals with passionate interest, but did not manage to make a commercial success. This setback did nothing to damp his ardor, and later he was to make the prisoners in the concentration camps grow medicinal plants.

These setbacks were perhaps the cause of the couple's lack of harmony. His wife despised him. In 1928 the birth of a daughter, Gudrun, brought about no change. According to Dr. Gebhardt, Himmler suffered from partial impotence and "could never overcome this inner conflict." The disagreements became so serious that he decided to part from his wife. He always refused to divorce her on account of his daughter, he said, and doubtless also under the subconscious influence of the stern religious education he had received in his youth. Later he met another woman who shared his life. He had two children from this affair, a boy and a girl, who were brought up by foster parents at Hohenlychen, where they were born.

This double life, these two homes, often brought him into monetary difficulties and occasionally forced him to borrow. Himmler was without doubt the only top Nazi official whose duties did not make him wealthy, although he was all-powerful, and corruption reigned at the very highest levels of the Party machine. His fundamental honesty made him despise Goering who, during the war, engaged in all manner of traffic thanks to his exalted position in the administration of the State and the Party.

Himmler had no real culture. This "half-educated" man was a romantic who set a particular seal on his creations and, moreover, on the whole organization of the Third Reich. He believed in magnetism, mesmerism, homeopathy, the more dubious theories of naturist eugenics, in psychic virtues of natural diet, in the clairvoyants, healers, magnetizers, and sorcerers with whom he surrounded himself throughout his life, incapable of making a decision before having consulted them. He shared this failing with several of the early Nazi leaders who frequented the salon of the Berlin astrologer, Hanussen, enabling the latter to foretell the burning of the Reichstag.

He also had the greatest respect for military discipline. According to Gebhardt, he gave an almost hysterical interpretation to the old military

conception: "An order given *has* to be carried out." He made this an absolute dogma for his troops—an easy enough task, for the Germans had never
exchanged the state of serfdom for that of the bourgeoisie, and entered the
Third Reich as sleepwalkers. His romanticism dictated his great admiration
for one of the German emperors, Henry I, known as the Fowler or the Saxon.
He admired this sovereign's order of chivalry which had enabled him to found
new towns, to expel the Danes, conquer the Hungarians, and subject the Slavs
and the Wends. This model, and the interest he took in racial questions, were
of capital importance in the organization of the S.S. Thus the swearing in of the
young S.S. men took place at midnight, by the light of torches, in Brunswick
Cathedral before the coffin containing the bones of Henry the Fowler.

According to the analysis of Dr. François Bayle, a single trait dominated
Himmler's subconscious: a congenital incapability of grasping general ideas,
which made him anchor himself in the spirit of the system; a passion and a
negative will in the form of ferocious obstinacy, expressing itself in strenuous
work; a total absence of originality and sensitivity, resulting in an almost
mechanical functioning of the brain, so deeply deformed in its nature and
range that it must be considered pathological. To this must be added an
absence of common sense, an ineradicable pretension, and an obstinacy
bordering on the absurd, an absence of intuition without any compensating
intellectual education; his erotic instinct was abnormally developed, with an
intense need for caresses and friendly society, combined paradoxically with a
profound affective indifference.

This robot was to regard Hitler as a savior. The latter was assertive, bel-
ligerent, proposed energetic and marvelously simple solutions. Above all a
conviction, a stubbornness emanated from him, which found an echo in
the numskull head of his disciple. And when Hitler spoke with eloquent
conviction on racial questions, on purity of blood, it struck a sensitive
chord. Himmler had always taken a passionate interest in these subjects:
he believed that he had given a scientific form to his obsession, since he
had studied racial selection among animals at his agricultural college. The
chicken farmer thought that men, for their great good, could be subjected
to the rules of rational farming. He had learned that, in the barnyard or the
stable, the species which did not show a profit had to be eliminated. He
found it perfectly reasonable that Hitler should write: "We all suffer from
the infirmities of impure blood. He who is not a thoroughbred is nothing,"

or again: "A stronger generation will eliminate the weak. The *élan vital* will reak the ridiculous bonds of a pretended humanity of the individual, to give place to the humanity of Nature which exterminates the weak to the advantage of the strong," or again: "Pity can only bring us dissension and demoralization."

And when Hitler announced that the National Socialist State would put these theories into practice, Himmler applauded. As soon as he was given the opportunity, he began to practice. The words of Hitler were engraved ineradicably in his mind:

"Anyone who sees in National Socialism merely a political movement has understood nothing. It is more than a religion, it is the will of a new human creation. Without biological bases and without biological goals, politics today are completely blind."

And above all: "I free mankind from the yoke of reason which weighs upon it, from the obscene and humiliating intoxications derived from chimeras, from so-called conscience and morality, and from the exigencies of personal liberty and independence of which only a few can serve."

And finally: "After centuries of crocodile tears shed over the defense of the poor and the humiliated, the moment has come when we must decide to defend the strong against the weak.... Natural instinct orders all living beings not only to conquer their enemies but to exterminate them. In the old days the conqueror had the prerogative of exterminating whole races and peoples."

One day soon Himmler would start to follow this advice to the letter.

Chapter 5
Himmler's "Black Order"

Himmler dreamed of chivalry and of a field of biological experiments to put into practice his "principles of the blood." The S.S. allowed him to realize all this. He was also going to leave his mark on the Gestapo. He was Reichsfuehrer S.S., in other words, Supreme Head of the S.S. for the whole Reich, and the S.S. would virtually remain "his chattel," his personal property, until the final collapse.

In order to understand the functioning of the Nazi administrative scheme which the superimposition of different hierarchies renders inextricably complicated: the hierarchy of State bureaucrats and soldiers of the Regular Army, the hierarchy of the Party, and the special hierarchy of the S.S., it is necessary to explain the precise nature of the S.S., for this organization was soon to infiltrate not only the Party and State administration but public and private organizations. From approximately 1940 all the important figures of the regime, all the police officials, all the heads of the main services, were S.S. men or given honorific titles in his body.

The ideology and principles of the S.S. progressively influenced German life, while at the same time all the leading posts were in the hands of people who, by belonging to the S.S., were more or less under Himmler's control. It was he who laid down the two basic principles of the S.S.: racial selection and blind obedience.

The farce of racial selection was arrayed in pseudo-scientific theories completely in the taste of the Grand Master of the Order. In a country which, down the ages, had succumbed to so many numerous and diverse influences, to important population accretions, notably the enormous influx of Slavs which impregnated the German population as far as the Elbe, the theory of "rigorously pure Nordic blood" was a joke. But no one seemed aware of this in Germany—or at least no one had the courage to say so.

These grandiloquent mouthings greatly amused the public, who mocked them, and called that distorted dwarf, Dr. Goebbels, "a shriveled German." It is also significant that, at the period when genealogical researches became the fashion on S.S. principles, Hitler strongly forbade all researches into his own personal origins, which, according to his enemies, were very mixed.

Himmler wanted to turn his S.S. into a new chivalry. He saw this as the surest foundation of the Nazi Reich. In an order signed by him in Munich on December 31, 1931, he defined it as follows: "The S.S. are a union of Germans with Nordic traits, specially selected. ... By the present order, the S.S. are conscious of taking a notable step forward. Mockery, irony, and misunderstandings do not affect us. The future belongs to us."

The racial principles, one of the bases of Nazism, which were to justify the massacre of the "inferior races," the extermination of millions of human beings, and the transformation of millions more into slaves, led in 1935 to the promulgation of the Nuremberg Laws which regulated the status of

the citizen: in future, bound by certain ethnic characters and reserved to
Volksgenosse, in other words to those who could prove that at least three of
their four grandparents belonged to the five races defined as Germanic. Only
they were allowed to exercise their political rights.

Thus we see the importance of the upheaval introduced by Nazism into
the scale of values of the Western world. Since the triumph of Christianity
and the start of its influence in the building of societies, all forms of social
organization had admitted that men had identical rights and duties. This fraternity, this equality, originating from a divine creation common to them all,
subsisted in lay societies and resulted a priori in the declaration of the rights
of man. Marxism, which rejects the Deity, preserves the same principles.

National Socialism, on the other hand, is based on the revolutionary affir-
mation of the inequality of man. It postulates that men are deeply differenti-
ated, not by their knowledge, their strength, their acquired qualities, but by
the fact of their origin. There are superior men, that is to say the Nazis, on
the highest rung of the ladder, and submen, the degenerates of bastardized
inferior races, on the lowest rung. Between them lies a whole range of inter-
mediaries which can be assessed with the aid of pseudo-scientific procedures.
A postulate which rests purely on a policy of force, a series of brutal asser-
tions, devoid of any scientific foundation, but which was to allow an attempt
to exterminate the submen.

The S.S.—and in particular the Gestapo—were the executors of this
aggressive Nazi racial policy. Their rules, those famous rules, in which
Himmler tried to revive the traditions of chivalry, were elementary. First
and foremost there was the famous oath sworn by the young candidate in
a theatrical setting: "I swear to you, Adolf Hitler, Fuehrer and Chancellor
of the Reich, fidelity and valiance. I solemnly pledge to you and to those
you have given me as leaders, obedience until death, with the aid of God."
This oath was nothing more than a commitment to blind obedience which
would "oblige" the S.S. to commit the most monstrous crimes without the
least hesitation.

"My honor is my loyalty," was the proud device of the S.S.; it was merely a
repetition of the oath of obedience; the loyalty was solely to be understood
as an obligation toward the Fuehrer, his leaders, and S.S. comrades, but not
to any rule of traditional morality. The "honor" of the S.S. man, of which
such a fuss was to be made in the pamphlets and speeches of the movement,

would actually force him to murder women, children, and old people. It was in the name of this strange honor that children arriving at Auschwitz were torn from the arms of their mothers and sent to the gas chambers, or on days when there were too many, in order to save time, they were flung alive into trenches full of burning petrol.

Honor, loyalty—in the hermetic world of National Socialism these words were perverted and emptied of their substance. The Nazi interpretation was explained by Himmler himself in a speech on October 4, 1943, at Posen before the assembled S.S. Gruppenfuehrer. "A fundamental principle must serve as a cardinal rule for the S.S. man. We must be honest, respectable, loyal, good comrades to those of our blood and toward no one else. What happens to a Russian or a Czech is of no possible interest to me." This was the application of the theory of the "Herrenvolk" so dear to Hitler at the start of the Movement.

The S.S. who were to form the world aristocracy of tomorrow were recruited on the principle of blood. Worth was a question of race. "In consequence only the perfect blood, the blood which history has proved to be important, creative, the basis of every State and all military activity, in other words Nordic blood, has to be taken into account. I decided that if I succeeded in selecting for this organization as many individuals as possible, the majority of whom possess this blood, by teaching them military discipline and in the fullness of time the value of this blood and the whole ideology evolving from it, it would be really possible to create an elite organization capable of facing up to any eventuality."

To select the possessors of this precious blood, the candidates were severely sorted. "They are examined and checked. Out of a hundred applicants we can only use on an average ten to fifteen, no more. We ask them to produce the political dossier of their parents, brothers, and sisters, their genealogical tree back to 1750 and, naturally, we insist upon a physical examination and their record in the Hitler Youth Movement. Furthermore we ask for a dossier on their heredity, proving that their parents and their family suffered from no hereditary diseases."

Himmler himself has revealed the final object of so much care: "We want to form a superior class which will dominate Europe for centuries." He also betrayed one day that the future Reich, which would then extend over the whole of Europe, would be organized on the model of the societies of antiquity, in other words, that an elite representing 5 to 10 percent of the population would rule over the rest and would dispose of an enormous mass of helots and slaves. And in fact once three-quarters of Europe had been occupied, it can safely be said that the Nazi regime was truly based on slavery.

These future "lords," these S.S. men, had special rights. When they took the vow they received the S.S. dagger. Its purpose, they were told, was to avenge their honor by washing out the insult in blood each time they considered this "honor" had been impeached. In 1935 a decree issued by Himmler specified this right—even this duty—and a court decision added that the S.S. were "free to use their arms even if the enemy could be repulsed by other means." The right to murder with complete impunity was an S.S. prerogative.

In September 1939 a member of the Waffen S.S., guarding a group of fifty Jewish laborers, amused himself at the end of the day's work by shooting the unfortunate men one after the other. The matter was reported but the murderer was not punished. It was maintained that being an S.S. made him "particularly sensitive to the sight of Jews," and that he had therefore only acted in an unreflecting manner, attributable to a youthful spirit of adventure.

To insure greater security, various decrees were issued to release the S.S. from ordinary jurisdiction and to arrange that, exclusive to their internal justice, they could only answer for their actions to S.S. tribunals. At the start the authorities were content to apply the law of August 2, 1933, which allowed the government to stop any inquiry or case in progress before a tribunal. But this method presented some inconvenient problems. On October 17, 1933, two prisoners in the Dachau camp "committed suicide" in their cells. The camp authorities maintained that they had hanged themselves by their belts. Their families, however, having notified the Munich court, two forensic doctors carried out postmortems which revealed that the unfortunate creatures had been maltreated and then strangled. Numerous contusions on the skull and on the whole body left no doubt of this: the marks visible oh the neck had been caused by strangling and not by hanging. The belts alleged to have served for the suicides could not be produced.

These facts had become known before the superior authorities could take action to suppress them. As soon as Roehm (the theoretical head of the S.S. not as yet independent of the S.A.) was notified, he dictated a note: "Dachau camp is a camp for prisoners in preventive custody and for political internees.

The incidents in question are of a political nature, and in all circumstances the political authorities have to decide in the first instance. In my opinion they do not seem to be of a nature to be examined by the judicial authorities. This is my advice as chief of staff and as Minister of the Reich. In this capacity I am interested to see that the Reich suffers no political prejudice as a result of these proceedings. I will obtain from the Reichsfuehrer S.S. an order decreeing that no investigating authority will be allowed to visit the camp for the moment, and no prisoner will be interrogated."

The Minister of the Interior demanded the suspension of the proceedings. As his motive he remarked that "these inquiries would do a great deal of harm to the prestige of the National Socialist State, for they were directed against members of the S.A. and S.S. and as a result the S.A. and the S.S., otherwise the main pillars of the National Socialist State, would be affected."

On September 27 the public prosecutor stopped the proceedings: "For inquiries have proved that there was insufficient proof that the death of these persons was due to external causes."

Matters had been "arranged," but on December 5 the Minister of Justice ordered the pursuance of the inquiry to its end. "The facts must be cleared up with the greatest possible speed. … If attempts at camouflage have been made, it will be necessary to deal with them by the appropriate means."

An unfortunate incident. Of course after such a long delay and the few methods of investigation open to justice in the S.S. milieu, it could not be dangerous. Nevertheless, "foreigners" might, as a result of these regrettable incidents, pry too deeply into the private affairs of the S.S. and learn of certain "practices" which it was not necessary to divulge. This was one of the reasons for the special S.S. jurisdiction. In future the S.S. formed a watertight world into which no one could penetrate.

Himmler treated these S.S. untouchables as human material of the highest quality, ideal for his personal experiments. The chicken farmer reappeared to watch over the purity of his selection. The S.S. man did not have the right to marry without the authorization of his superiors. His fiancée had to prove her Aryan descent back to 1800 if she wanted to marry a simple S.S. man or non-commissioned officer, and back to 1750 if she was to marry an officer. Only the *Hauptant*, the head office, could validate the proofs provided and give the necessary authorization. Furthermore the girl had to undergo a certain number of medical examinations and physical tests. She must be capable

of insuring issue to the race of Herrenvolk. After the marriage the bride had
to attend one of the S.S. special schools, where she was indoctrinated with
the political education and "ideology which springs from the idea of racial
purity." She was given courses in domestic science and child welfare, etc. The
aim was to obtain within a few years a uniform whole continually increasing
in number but rigorously identical physically and psychologically.

Himmler's system achieved its apotheosis with the creation of the
Lebensborn—the fountain of life—a sort of human stud farm where young
girls selected for their perfect Nordic traits could, free from all conjugal
bonds, procreate with S.S. men also chosen according to the same criteria.
The children born of these unions were fruits of a planned eugenics and
belonged to the State, and their education was insured in special schools. In
theory they were destined to form the first generation of pure Nazis, fashioned in the ovum. The collapse of the regime did not allow the Nazis to
pursue this experiment any further. Nevertheless, fifty thousand children
were born in these stud farms. Their average intellectual standard is in actual
fact grossly below the average; they show a percentage of mental deficients
four or five times higher than the normal. The Nazi eugenists were unaware
of what the psychologists of the "decadent" countries and "degenerate" races
know: ideology and biology cannot replace maternal love.

Himmler's biological experiments on the S.S. took on other forms. The
chicken farmer thought that nourishment influenced anatomical and psychological characters. Thus in the S.S. barracks early morning coffee was
replaced by the old Germanic breakfast of milk and porridge. For meals the
S.S. were given mineral water, and their menus were "scientifically" worked
out by the Party eugenists. Experiments in magnetotherapy were carried out
in some of the S.S. barracks. Certain leaders were submitted to massage of
the nervous system. To sum up, the S.S. were treated like luxury guinea pigs
and, far from feeling humiliated, or that their male dignity was debased by
these methods (which reeked of the cattle shed or the laboratory victim),
they were immensely proud of the fact. They were being made into men apart,
into supermen, who looked down with contempt on the rest of humanity.

For the members of this new Praetorian Guard, one of the essential
merits was "a fine soldierly bearing," exactly as Prussian tradition defined
it. Everything was based on this model: haughty indifference, a stiff poise,
inflexibility, absence of critical faculties, a feeling of power carried to the

limits of absurdity, "pride of caste, the sadism of the parade ground and the masochism of the barracks, in all their primitive or distorted forms that two hundred years of the Prussian regime had evolved," according to Eugen Kogon. And this author remarks: "A critical thought which postulates the ability to compare and to distinguish, and in consequence demands an increasing knowledge, would have been harmful to efficiency, would have rendered them anaemic, would have appeared to them demoralising, dangerous, perfidious and Jewish. To this was added an old military precept: 'Never try to understand.' "

The rights bestowed upon them, the right of life and death over their fellow men, the tolerant treatment they enjoyed, could only confirm them in the opinion of their superiority. As to the legitimacy of their actions, it could never be questioned; they were never assailed by the least doubts.

How could it have been otherwise? The entire German "establishment" accepted the most criminal actions and acquiesced by its silence. They entered into the system and agreed to cooperate with the newcomers. On becoming head of the S.S., Himmler had tried to attract aristocrats, who still enjoyed great prestige, and certain well-known soldiers. The entry of former officers of the Freikorps, presented as national heroes, into the ranks of the S.S. had aroused a certain echo. In 1928 the heirs of many famous families had joined the N.S.D.A.P. Before 1933 aristocrats had enrolled in the Schwarze Korps, by which name the S.S. was known, men such as Prince Waldeck-Pyrmont and the hereditary Grand Duke of Mecklenburg. When the Nazis came to power many others followed suit. Prince Hohenzollern-Sigmaringen, the hereditary Duke of Brunswick, the hereditary Prince Lippe-Biesterfeld, General Count von der Schulenburg, and even a high dignitary of the Church, Archbishop Groeber of Freiburg. No service was demanded of these highborn recruits, but skillful publicity surrounded their entrance into the Party. They exercised so much influence on recruitment that Himmler subsequently created honorary S.S. ranks to be distributed to high-ranking non-members of the S.S.

The effect of this policy was not long delayed in its effect, on the middle classes in particular: the S.S. regiments were soon regarded as "chic," and the black uniform as the height of masculine elegance. If the S.S. could consider the success of their recruiting drives as approval of their methods, it must be recognized that the absence of international reactions could only confirm them in their good conscience. The refugees continued to cry in the wilderness; although the crimes committed daily in Germany could no longer be ignored, no civilized country dreamed for a moment of breaking off relations with the murderers. The ambassadors continued with the same dignity to shake hands still dripping with innocent blood and to give banquets in honor of the executioners. New trade treaties were signed. France invited Nazi Germany to the International Fair of 1937 and, worst of all, the U.S.S.R. in 1939 signed a non-aggression pact with the very men who had tortured to death thousands of Communists, and who kept many thousands still incarcerated in the camps.

The chosen "supporters" of high rank were no more than a publicity stunt. Basic recruitment on the contrary delved into the lowest strata of the population. For the tasks for which they were destined, it needed men without scruples, servile brutes or organized sadists.

Such a recruitment was potentially limited, and the Nazis realized that, in order to insure a constant stream of "suitable elements," the Praetorian Guard of tomorrow had to be fashioned from infancy. The great reservoir from which the S.S. and the Gestapo could draw was the Hitler Youth Movement. Each April 20, on the Fuehrer's birthday, children who were reaching the age of ten that year were admitted into the Deutsches Jungvolk. A ceremony combined with Hitler's birthday celebrations had as sole object the captivation of their minds. They remained in this group until the age of thirteen, spending a year in one of the four sections designed to lead them progressively to the Hitler Jugend, which would prepare them more directly for the Army, or the Party formations.

Originally a junior branch of the S.A., the Hitler Jugend became independent and, soon after the accession to power, a decree of June 22, 1933 ordered the dissolution of the National Committee of German Youth Associations. Their goods were confiscated and their members absorbed into the Hitler Jugend (H.J.). In 1936 a law made membership of the H.J. compulsory for all children. Thus from the age of ten, the young German was subjected to a continual obsessive barrage of Nazi propaganda and ideology. From this tender age when the personality is easy to mold, the *Fuehrer-prinzip* was implanted in young brains as absolute dogma. A little later began the training which would allow a human being to be reduced to a state of total subordination. This "culture," alien to man, this dehumanization, provided an excellent grounding in the Hitlerian creed. In order that a handful of professional murderers might reign over a whole nation and impose its methods upon it, man had to be perverted from infancy. Oradour, the Warsaw Ghetto, the mass executions in the East and in Auschwitz were not German crimes but Nazi crimes. It is certain that the same methods applied to any race would have produced the same results. If the German people was a malleable clay, it is because their traditional militarization had inculcated the strictest habits of discipline, a deformation often quoted officially as an example in most of the "undisciplined" countries with a shade of regret. Most of the rank and file of the S.S. who set fire to Oradour were between eight and fourteen at the time Hitler came to power. All had been subjected to Nazi education from early youth and no one had given them a chance of questioning the value of this teaching. It was in the Hitler Jugend groups between 1933 and 1940 that the Oradours of the war were prepared.

In a speech in November 1935 Hitler proclaimed his intentions with regard to German youth: "When an opponent declares, 'I don't want to be on your side, and you won't make me,' I reply calmly, 'Your child already belongs to me. A nation lives eternally. Who are you? You will pass on, but your descendants are already in the new camp. In a short time they will know nothing else but this new community.'"

On May 10, 1933, under the direction of Goebbels, an auto-da-fé was organized on the square outside Berlin University. During the preceding weeks the bookshops, public libraries, and universities had been "purged." Tons of books, whose authors were Jews and Marxists, or whose contents did not conform to Nazi principles, had been seized. On May 10 Nazi students singing ribald songs carried twenty thousand volumes, of which they made an enormous bonfire in the public square. The lowest pornographic literature had been mingled with the works of "degenerate" philosophers. The pile was sprinkled with petrol and set alight while the band played the national hymn and the Party airs. Goebbels made a speech. "Today's ceremony," he said, "is a symbolic act. It will teach the world that the basic morality of the November 1918 Republic has been destroyed forever. From this pile of ashes will rise the phoenix of a new spirit."

The selected young German had to serve a compulsory period in the *Reichsarbeitdienst* (the Labor Corps) before entering the S.S. The S.S. force was divided into three categories: the Allgemeine S.S. (General S.S.)

in which service was not permanent; the S.S. Verfuegungstruppen, or regiments quartered in barracks,[1] and the S.S. Totenkopfver-baende or Death's-Head regiments, in charge of the concentration camps.

The Allgemeine S.S. formed the mother branch to which the young "candidates," whose ambition it was to belong to this elite corps, were admitted. They were given their first instruction, a period of testing, took the oath, and received the dagger of honor. The Allgemeine S.S. had to remain as active members of the S.S. until the age of fifty. They were obliged to undergo a yearly examination to check up their physical health, their military training, and their political orthodoxy.

To obtain certain posts in the State administration or certain high posts in private industry, it was soon as indispensable to be a member of the S.S. as it was to have a qualification from the famous schools or universities. Thus this strange "Black Order" fashioned by Himmler insinuated its way into the whole machinery of German everyday life, soon giving its animator absolute power. It also allowed him to eliminate his most dangerous enemies.

Chapter 6
The Gestapo Is Everywhere

Himmler, grand master of the S.S., transposed some of the principals of his "Black Order," to organize the Gestapo. The strict hierarchy was progressively modeled on that of the S.S., even reproducing it completely as soon as the members of the Gestapo received S.S. rank on assimilation. The partitioning of powers was reinforced by the protection of secrecy. Discretion was one of the basic principles of S.S. discipline. It constituted one of the essential bases of the Gestapo which Himmler, as he had done with the S.S., turned into an enclosed world, of which no one had the right to catch the least glimpse and about which it was forbidden to utter any criticism.

[1] Until September 1939 the S.S. Verfuegungstruppen totaled only four Standarten in barracks.

On its creation by Goering, the new State Police had need of premises. A number of buildings in the Prinz Albrechtstrasse were ideally suited on account of their geographical position and their interiors. As a start the Museum of Folk Lore was evacuated and occupied; next came an industrial professional school; it was commandeered simply on the pretext that some of the pupils were Communists and that the domitories were the scene of "nocturnal orgies." As soon as these premises were freed the Gestapo took up its quarters there. Reinhard Heydrich ruled over these offices. Appointed head of the S.S. Security Service by Himmler in 1931, he had been his deputy in the Munich Police Praesidium at the beginning of 1933, joining him later in Berlin when his chief acquired control of the entire Gestapo at the beginning of 1934. Himmler had immediately put him in charge of the Gestapo head office, and from Berlin he now assumed a great part of the effective direction of the whole State Police.

Here again, according to Nazi custom, we find a duplication of functions. As head of the Gestapo, Heydrich acted as a state official but as chief of the S.D., a Party organization, he was one of the important figures in the N.S.D.A.P. and could use the private organizations of the Party. This made him doubly superior to most of the officials and members of the Party under his command. It was a convenient situation, for those who might entertain some scruples of conscience with regard to certain revolting practices, and who might have been tempted to report the matter to the law, were now more sensitive to the secrecy enforced in the name of the Party than to administrative interdictions.

The Party had begun its annexation of the State. Article No. 1 of the law of December 1, 1933, was quite clear: "The National Socialist party has become the representative of the idea of the German State and is indissolubly bound up with the State."

What all these men pursued—officials or members of the N.S.D.A.P. services—was the realization of the political plans of the Party, of the Fuehrer. It was the accomplishment of his inspired predictions: the building of the thousand-year Reich which he had announced for many years and, in the course of time, the overthrow of the foundations of human societies, the disruption of world equilibrium, the advent of a race of Herrenvolk, and the colonization of the world. The Party became the repository of these sacred principles, the instrument for propagating this ideology. To sum up, the

State was the Party. To be rejected was tantamount to a death sentence. It was said that "exclusion from the Party constituted the most serious sanction. In certain circumstances it was the equivalent to the loss of any livelihood and all personal consideration." A less terrible threat, however, than that which Himmler had hung like a sword of Damocles over the heads of the S.S.: "The man who is untrue to us, even if only in thought, will be expelled from the S.S. and we shall see that he disappears from the world of the living."

The task of the Gestapo was to prevent all discussion of Nazi dogma, to eliminate by no matter what means the opponents, even those who dared to *doubt* the excellence of the regime. In order to achieve this the Gestapo had to be omnipotent. From their lair Himmler and Heydrich had to be in a position to know everything. They would need several years to perfect the structure of their organization, but from the very outset they possessed a working basis. During their years of clandestine existence, the S.S. Security Services had amassed important records. The enemies of the Party had been carefully filed. Their dossiers were often remarkably complete: political and professional activities, family, friends, domicile and possible hideouts, close relationships, human weaknesses and passions. All these details were to be found in the dossier, ready to be used when the occasion arose.

The Gestapo began to exploit these records. Opponents were arrested, tortured, and murdered. Everyone in Germany knew it, but among those who could have sounded the alarm and possibly saved their country and the world from the growing danger, not a minister, not a general, nobody dared to raise his voice. Nevertheless, as Gisevius would write: "a mere glance from the outside at the sinister darkness of the Prinz Albrechtsstrasse could have broken the spell of Heydrich." No, no stranger's eye tried to penetrate this stifling darkness and, in the words of the American Judge Advocate, Robert H. Jackson, at Nuremberg, "Germany became a gigantic torture chamber."

The Gestapo was under the control of the Party. Consisting above all of professional policemen, who remained in the majority despite the purge carried out on the accession to power, it was impossible to carry out too violent a change for fear of upsetting this delicate mechanism. From April 1934 it was subjected to a more rigorous control of opinion, and new entrants had to belong to the Party. In the same way, before an official could be promoted, the agreement and advice of the Party had to be obtained. A special card index was kept for this purpose, the U.S.C., which gave the *Politische*

Beurteiling, the political judgment upon which the appointment depended. A circular from the Chancellory defined it as "a valuable judgment on the political and ideological attitude and the character ... it must be exact and true ... based on incontestable facts and in its estimation directed toward the goals of the Movement. In order to obtain the elements of this appreciation, the competent political leaders, the technical services, and the S.D. services of the Reichsfuehrer S.S. must be consulted." Thus the Gestapo officials were subjected to the political control of the S.D., in other words, a "twin" organization, their opposite numbers in the Party, between whom an ever closer collaboration became established.

The two services, S.D. and Gestapo, placed under the direction of Heydrich, exercised control over public opinion, but the S.D. as a Party organization confined itself to the quest for information, whereas the Gestapo carried out the arrests, interrogations, house searches, and all the material police tasks.

Although as early as 1934 the Gestapo had received intelligence from the S.D., the latter was far from being its sole source of information. The basis of the Party and State organization was the *Fuehrerprinzip,* or the principle of the leader, according to which the power resided in the hands of a single man. The commandments of the Party proclaimed: "The Fuehrer is always right. For you his program must be dogma. It demands that you devote yourself entirely to the movement. ... Right is whatever serves the Movement and in consequence Germany." For naturally the Party identified itself with the Fatherland. "The basis of the Party organization is the Fuehrerprinzip. All the political leaders are considered as having been appointed by the Fuehrer and are responsible to him. They enjoy complete authority over their subordinates."

The logical conclusion of this infallibility of Adolf Hitler was the need for absolute obedience to all the leaders appointed by him. Article No. 1 already violated the indefeasible rights of the individual. "Every leader has the right to govern, administrate, or make decisions without being subjected to any control whatsoever."

The Fuehrerprinzip was introduced from school age into the life of the Germans. Below the Fuehrer in the hierarchical pyramid came the fifteen *Reichsleiter.* Among the bigwigs of the regime the most famous were Hess, head of the Party Chancellery, later replaced by Bormann; Goebbels, head of the Propaganda Department; Himmler, Ley, head of the Labor Front, Baldur von Shirach, head of the Youth Organizations, and Rosenberg, representing the Fuehrer in the control of intellectual and ideological activities. The main task of the Reichsleitung was the choice of leaders.

From the beginning of 1933 Germany had been divided into thirty-two *Gaue,* or administrative regions. Each Gau was divided into *Kreise,* or circles, each Kreis into *Ortsgruppen,* or local groups, each Ortsgruppe into *Zellen,* or cells, and each Zelle into *Blocks.* Each of these divisions had at its head a *Gauleiter,* a *Kreisleiter,* an *Ortsgruppenleiter,* a *Zellenleiter,* a *Blockleiter.*

The Gauleiter, appointed directly by the Fuehrer, bore total responsibility for delegating the sovereignty he enjoyed. This was a *Hoheitstraeger,* a wielder of authority, just as the Kreisleiter was responsible for education, the political and ideological formation of the political leaders, the members of the Party, and the general public. The Ortsgruppenleiter was also a "wielder of authority." He was responsible for a combination of cells, grouping about fifteen hundred homes. The Zellenleiter, responsible for between four and eight blocks, was the immediate superior of the Blockleiter, to whom he transmitted the Party orders and whom he controlled.

The Blockleiter, in fact, constituted the very foundation of the Party. He was the most important man, being responsible for a block, that is to say between forty and sixty homes at the maximum. He was the only official whose position brought him in contact with every category of the population. From him was expected as perfect a knowledge as possible of each of the members of the group he controlled. He had to ferret out malcontents and explain to them the new laws which were often imperfectly understood; if this proved inadequate other courses were open to him: advice and sometimes a rougher form of correction could be used if the bad behavior of an individual reflected upon himself and in consequence upon the community.

Naturally the knowledge of his district and his neighbors demanded of the Blockleiter served another purpose. It was the duty of the Blockleiter to discover individuals who spread harmful rumors and refer them to the Ortsgruppe, so that the facts could be reported to the competent State authorities—in other words, to the Gestapo. It was here that the results of this scientifically organized police spying ended. An order signed by Bormann on June 26, 1935, states: "In order to establish a closer contact between the services of the Party and its organizations and the heads of the Gestapo, the

Fuehrer's delegate demands that in future the heads of the Gestapo shall be invited to be present at all the important official manifestations of the Party and its organizations." Thus through the cell and block leaders the Gestapo disposed of thousands of ears and attentive eyes spying upon the least movements of each individual German.

The American Judge Advocate, General Thomas J. Dodd, said at Nuremberg: "In no Nazi cell or block could a secret remain unknown to them. The switching on of a radio, the disapproval of a frown, the inviolate secrets between priest and penitent, the ancient confidence between father and son, even the sacred confidences of marriage, were their stock in trade. Their business was to know." Nothing was to escape the Gestapo.

These thousands of gratuitous agents were still not enough. The man had to be watched in his professional activities, his distractions, when away from home, particularly when he was able to elude his Blockleiter-jailer.

The officials had naturally been the first to be placed under control. On June 22, 1933, an order, signed by Goering, enjoined bureaucrats to watch the words and actions of State employees and to denounce those who criticized the regime. In this way a kind of automatic surveillance resulted, because everyone spied on his neighbors and was in turn spied upon by them. To guarantee the smooth running of this system, Goering's order stressed the fact that failing to send in a denunciation would be considered as an act of hostility toward the government!

The iron corset of constant espionage was augmented still further. For example, the Sohlberg-Kreis, an organization of specially selected youths, included among its leaders a young drawing teacher, Otto Abetz. The latter arranged meetings with the committees of French youth, in the course of which useful trails were laid by the S.D. They allowed, on the one hand, the recruiting of French sympathizers, some of whom were persuaded to play the part of secret agents and, on the other hand, to introduce S.D. agents into France.

The Germans were also kept under observation at work. Each factory, each concern formed a Party cell. Robert Ley's unique Arbeitsfront, which controlled social welfare, the cooperatives, wages, etc., replaced the unions. Workers and employees were affiliated to it and closely controlled. An order from Goering on June 30, 1933, enjoined the Gestapo services to report to the work delegates any member of the Party, any worker whose political attitude appeared suspect. The peasantry was brigaded by Walter Darré's Peasant Front. In 1935 the *Reichsnaehrstand,* the body responsible for the feeding of the country, tried to group all the professions in competition for the food supplies of the Reich.

Sport was also given a leader, Tschammer-Osten; relaxation came under the K.D.F. organization, *Kraft durch Freude,* directed by Ley; the cinema and radio were closely controlled by the Minister of Propaganda. The press was naturally not forgotten: it was guided by a firm hand, the various agencies having been replaced by a State agency, the D.N.B., *Deutsches Nachrichten Buro,* while at the same time a federation and a press council were formed under Party control. Woe to the journalist who dared to write a misplaced allusion! His article, however, had little chance of being published, for the newspaper directors and editors had to be acceptable to the Minister of Propaganda and could be dismissed at the slightest slip. These measures allowed the censorship to be abolished, since no subjects except those chosen by the Ministry were permitted.

A Chamber of Writers and a Professional Association kept a close watch on all those whose profession it was to write. Only members of this association had a right to publish their work, and the only writers to be admitted into the association were the "right thinkers." The Chamber of Writers reported to the Ministry anything that appeared noxious in old or new works. The libraries were purged. The Booksellers' Federation completed this muzzling of thought.

Lawyers, doctors, and students were regimented in associations of the same order. The German Medical Society, founded in 1873, known throughout the world, was absorbed by the National Socialist League of Doctors, which "purged" the profession by eliminating Jews and Socialists, and ultimately all political non-conformists.

The Ministry of Public Health was integrated into the Ministry of the Interior, and the Red Cross came under the control of the S.S. The few scientific bodies of international repute, such as the Chemnitz Association or the Berlin Medical Association, were placed under strict control: it became impossible to give free expression to a scientific opinion. The intellectual level sank so low that genuine scientists ceased to frequent them, ceding the place to official nonentities and to Party charlatans.

The Nazi party was suspicious of the universities, considering that the scholars had been corrupted by liberalism. Between 1933 and 1937, 40 percent of the professors were purged. A decree of June 9, 1943, created a Council for Research, whose board consisted of twenty-one members; it included not a single man of science. Instead, there were men like Bormann, Himmler, Keitel, etc.; the president was Goering. This Council controlled the research institutes and placed a member of the Gestapo in each of them. This individual could be a professor, an assistant, a bureaucrat, or even an anonymous student. His task was to report on the state of mind of the members of the institute.

Two other organizations allowed the Nazis to push their clandestine investigations beyond the frontiers of the Reich and to extend their control throughout the world. These were the A.O., *Ausland Organization* of the N.S.D.A.P., and the Volksdeutsche Mittelstelle, whose job it was to bring back into the bosom of the Fatherland all men of German blood. In reality these organizations were spy rings; sometimes alone and sometimes as auxiliaries of special Nazi services, they contributed originally to the planting of a Fifth Column in Austria and Czechoslovakia, and later to the detection and surveillance of German political opponents who had managed to find asylum abroad. These rebels were pursued for years by the hatred of the Nazis.

An order issued by Goering on January 15, 1934, directed the Gestapo and the frontier police to make a note of political *émigrés* and Jews living in the neighboring countries, and to arrest them or send them to concentration camps if they returned to Germany. In the countries where they had taken refuge, these exiles were spied upon and constantly followed. On the entry of the German troops into Austria, Czechoslovakia, Poland, and subsequently France, these unfortunate people were pursued with incredible tenacity by the Gestapo. This applied to the two leaders of the Social Democrats, Hilferding and Breitschied, who had taken refuge in France in 1933. On the demand of the Germans they were arrested in the Unoccupied Zone in 1941, and handed over to the Gestapo. Hilferding committed suicide in his cell in Paris. He had been Reich Minister of Finance and had represented his country at the Hague Convention. Breitschied died in Buchenwald.

Finally, in June 1942, a message from the O.K.W. (German High Command) to the Afrika Korps transmitted a secret order from the Fuehrer giving orders that German political refugees discovered fighting in the Free French Forces in Africa were "to be treated with extreme severity. They must be shot down without mercy. When this has not been done they must, on the orders of the nearest German officer, be immediately and summarily executed unless they can be temporarily kept alive for obtaining information."

The Ausland Organization (A.O.) and the Volksdeutsche Mittelstelle also permitted the tracking down of refugees. Head of the A.O. was Ernst Bohle, with the rank of Party Gauleiter and State Secretary to the Ministry of Foreign Affairs. This special section had been created in 1931 at Hamburg by Gregor Strasser. The choice of Hamburg for the headquarters of the organization had been dictated by the fact that eight out of ten Germans entering or leaving Germany for a remote destination passed through Hamburg, the port for the two Americas, the seat of the big shipping companies, and the city with a hundred foreign consulates. Its task was to insure liaison with the thirty-three hundred members of the N.S.D.A.P. residing outside the German frontiers. In October 1933 the A.O. was placed under the control of Hess, as the Fuehrer's representative. In a few years this organization implanted nearly 350 regional groups of the N.S.D.A.P. spread over the whole surface of the globe, apart from isolated adherents with whom contact was constantly maintained.

The second organization, the Volksdeutsche Mittelstelle, was completely under the control of the S.S. The head of this body was S.S. Gruppenfuehrer Lorenz, charged with the defense of German nationals living abroad, his field of action being confined to the borderlands; with Fifth Column technique he played a considerable part in the preparation of the Anschluss and in the Sudetenland uprisings.

During the course of the war Lorenz played a major part in the population movements in Poland and the Eastern territories. On October 7, 1939, Himmler, in his capacity of Reich Commissioner for the Assertion of the German Race, supervised the carrying out of these measures with the aid of the S.S. and the Gestapo.

And finally there was a third, less known service, the Auslands Politische Abteilung (A.P.A.) or Bureau of Foreign Policy of the N.S.D.A.P. This office, directed by Rosenberg, functioned from April 1933. Its object was to spread Nazi propaganda abroad, particularly by propagating anti-Semitism, organizing university exchanges, facilitating trade agreements, and publishing in the foreign press of propaganda articles concocted in Berlin. Thus Nazi propaganda themes were distributed in the United States by the Hearst newspapers, and in France certain extreme right newspapers received regular subsidies from the German propaganda services and echoed Hitler's proclamations.

The most important branch of the A.P.A., however, was the most discreet. The A.P.A. included a press section with a group of first-class interpreters. They had a profound knowledge of all the languages in use throughout the world. According to events they could give instant translations of any text, however remote. It produced a daily press review with extracts from three hundred foreign newspapers, dispatching to the appropriate services a précis on the trends of world politics. Incidentally, these translators performed a police work which was to swell the Gestapo files. All information relating to political *émigrés* published in the world press, including, notices of marriages, births, and deaths, announcement of meetings, conferences, commercial advertisements, etc., were translated and entered on the *émigrés'* dossiers. Furthermore, the press section of the A.P.A. kept statistics of the influence of the principal newspapers of the world on public opinion, such as the audience and slant of the journalist—information which was also communicated to the Gestapo.

By these examples one can judge the extent of the network of informers and spies with whom the Gestapo covered not only Germany but the whole world. This quest for information, this exploitation, this systematic distortion of all human activities for inquisitorial ends, give some idea of the stifling universe of National Socialism which, within a few months, transformed Germany into a formidable prison.

Intelligence also came from other sources. The local police services and *gendarmeries* had to transmit any piece of interesting political news. On the other hand, the Gestapo instigated investigations from these local services for minor affairs, acting directly only in matters of a certain importance. And finally Himmler received information direct from the S.S. leaders and the other dignitaries of the Party.

Another important source of information was the tapping of telephones. Ever since the telephone has existed wiretapping has been practiced in every country of the world and under every government. A recent scandal has revealed that even in the United States private organizations exist which use this method to obtain commercial information. The Nazi regime turned this into a regular industry. With the method and care for technical perfection characteristic of the Germans, an organization was created by Goering in

1933. This establishment was given the ambiguous name of the Hermann Goering Research Institute. Although Goering was the master, not to mention the owner, it was organized by specialist naval telegraphists, aided by policemen such as Diels. The institute controlled the telephonic and telegraphic networks and also radio communications. Calls between Germany and abroad were listened in to, and telegrams sent or coming from abroad were recorded. The institute managed at times to intercept communications between two foreign countries. It also, of course, practiced these measures internally. Soundings were taken at random. In case of necessity the institute could listen in almost instantaneously to any line. Finally a special apparatus allowed the recording at will of any communication considered to be important—a considerable technical feat for the period. The institute picked up systematically and classified in the records all the Fuehrer's telephone calls.

Every day reports and extracts were compiled and sent to Hitler. On the other hand, any piece of information of interest to a Ministry or some service was immediately transmitted. But Goering, as creator and head of the institute, could always decide not to transmit certain revelations and to keep them for his own ends.

His institute gave Goering considerable power and was very effective in his conflict with Roehm. Realizing the value of such an instrument, he was determined to keep it under his control and refused to hand it over to Himmler or to the Gestapo. The Gestapo and the S.D. could call freely on the services of the institute, but the latter remained until the end under the control of Goering.

On the other hand, the Gestapo acted on its own account by secretly installing microphones and tape recorders in the homes of suspects. In the absence of the victim, or on the pretext of making repairs or of checking the telephone or the electric installations, a few microphones were discreetly installed, allowing the individual to be spied upon even in the bosom of his family. No one was safe from this type of practice. In 1934 Dr. Schacht was unpleasantly surprised to discover that a microphone had been installed in his drawing room, that his maid had been engaged by the Gestapo, and that a tapping system had enabled her to spy on the private conversations of her master even at night in his bedroom.

Spying became so universal that nobody could feel safe. The Luftwaffe General Milch confessed at Nuremberg that people were not so much afraid of the S.S. as of the Gestapo. "We were convinced," he said, "that we were kept under permanent control, whatever our rank. Each of us had our dossier with the Secret Police, and many people were later betrayed to the tribunals because of these dossiers."

In fact each of these organizations became a private citadel belonging to its creator, its leader, and each of these potentates battled fiercely against those whom he suspected of being rivals, present or future. A merciless struggle ensued with no holds barred. Hitler considered that this rivalry kept them on their toes and thought that mutual surveillance prevented people hungry for power and money from becoming dangerous.

In the midst of these intrigues Himmler navigated with consummate skill, emerging far ahead of his rivals. ... His alliance with Goering was very profitable. The fact that the "institute" with its listening apparatus was left in Goering's hands, whereas it would have been normal to have placed it in the hands of the Central State Police, is an example of the concessions which Himmler knew how to make to preserve a benevolent neutrality from the Reichsmarschall. Besides, the Gestapo and the S.D. very soon installed their own ultra-secret means of listening to Goering himself!

In this struggle for supremacy, where the coldest cynicism and the most pitiless cruelty were obligatory weapons, Himmler found a precious helper, a devoted and trustworthy auxiliary with great inventive powers, in the person of his second-in-command, the subtle, well-dressed Heydrich.

Chapter 7
The Strange Personality of Heydrich

The man who sat in the leader's chair at Gestapo headquarters in April 1934 was fascinating. Reinhard Heydrich was a young man of good family who had received an excellent education. He was born on March 7, 1904, at Halle, near Leipzig, where his father, Bruno Heydrich, was director of the Musical Academy. He spent his early childhood and youth in his native town, in a solid secondary school, living in an atmosphere of classical culture in which music played an important part. He remained devoted to it—it was always his favorite form of relaxation from his sinister duties at Gestapo headquarters.

At Easter 1922 young Heydrich entered the Navy. The young man's career evolved quite normally. He became a midshipman in 1924, sub-lieutenant in 1926, and first lieutenant in 1928.

He had long been interested in politics. In 1918–19 he had belonged to a Pan-Germanic nationalist youth association, the *Deutsch Nationaler Jugenbund* in Halle. In 1920 he joined the *Deutschvoelkischen Schutz und Turtzbund*. The same year, burning to participate in the politico-military life seething around him, he became a volunteer liaison agent with the Lucius division of the Halle Freikorps. In 1921, with a comrade, he founded a new association, the *Deutschoelkischen Jugendschar*. In these groups he was fed with extremist and violently militarist theories.

On joining the Navy he had remained in contact with the association of which he was co-founder. Appointed midshipman, he was transferred at his request to the political section of naval intelligence at Ostee. Here he made a few acquaintances who were to be useful to him a few years later. Remarkably intelligent, hard working, capable, and well disciplined, this young officer could have had a brilliant career but for one dreadful flaw. Heydrich was a sex maniac whose case history would have delighted a psychiatrist. On several occasions, troubles with women disturbed his career, and ultimately a more serious affair put an end to it. Heydrich was engaged to the daughter of a superior officer of the Hamburg naval dockyards. According to one version, the girl became his mistress, and he had then broken off with her on the pretext that an officer could not marry a girl of such easy virtue. According to the second version, he made her drunk and raped her. According to a third, he extorted money from her. The precautions taken by the Nazi leaders to erase their pasts make research into the early periods of their lives very difficult. In any case he had to face a "jury of honor." This tribunal, presided over by the future Admiral Raeder, judged that Flag Lieutenant Heydrich's behavior was unworthy of an officer and a gentleman and asked him to hand in his resignation to avoid more serious action being taken. In 1931, at the age of twenty-seven, the young officer found himself on the Hamburg streets. Like Himmler, Heydrich then went through a rather hectic period, hanging about the North Sea ports of Hamburg, Lübeck, and Kiel, living from hand to mouth and frequenting a somewhat shady milieu. He met many characters whom the Nazis, in their struggle against the authorities and rival parties, recruited to break up meetings and to start brawls in the street.

These contacts, facilitated by his political past, induced Heydrich to enroll in the N.S.D.A.P. With his education, military training, and background the party considered they had gained a valuable recruit. Heydrich entered the S.S., which was one way of finding a job. A little later he commanded the Kiel group, numerically still of little account. Himmler spotted him in the course of his duties. He quickly perceived the exceptional talents of this subordinate, and on August 1, 1931, appointed him Sturmfuehrer. Late that autumn he made him a Sturmbannfuehrer (equivalent to a major) and took him onto his Munich staff.

In July 1932 Himmler decided to reorganize the S.S. Security Service and entrusted Heydrich with this task, promoting him to Standartenfuehrer (the equivalent of a colonel). Since the creation of the S.S. each unit included two or three men in charge of "security," in other words of intelligence. Himmler himself had explained the task of these men: "At this period, for obvious reasons, wc had an intelligence service in our regiments, battalions, and companies. We had to know what our enemies were up to—if the Communists were going to organize a meeting today or not, if our men were to be suddenly attacked, and other information of this nature."

In 1931 Himmler detached these intelligence agents from the rest of the S.S., transforming them into a watertight security service. This new organization was known as the *Sicherheitsdienst* (S.D.), the Security Service of the Reichsfuehrer S.S. It remained therefore an S.S. organization, responsible for Himmler's personal safety and the safety of the S.S. in general.

As leader of this new service, Heydrich put into practice all he had learned in the naval secret service. He organized his realm on the military model and gave his men technical training. He instituted an efficient filing system, but could not develop his service to the extent he wished, for lack of staff. On the accession to power he was to fill in these gaps. Satisfied with his work, Himmler chose him as representative to the heads of the Bavarian police in 1932, then appointed him chief of the Gestapo head office in 1934. Without having been one of the "old guard," Heydrich was sufficiently senior in the Party when he came to Berlin to direct both the Gestapo and the S.D., of which he still remained the head.

This man with the hectic past, who was soon to make the Germans tremble, looked completely harmless; tall, well educated, with a few traces of red in his smooth blond hair, which was parted down the middle. He was slim, well built, and possessed the virtue, so fashionable at that period, of a "fine military bearing." Heydrich's features were revealing. The abnormally high receding forehead above two small deep-set blue eyes partially hidden by the heavy upper lids—these slanting eyes were Mongolian and this indiscreet heritage from some remote ancestor, who may have ridden with Genghis Khan or Attila, might have sufficed to upset Himmler's racial theories had the latter bothered to notice them. His face was oval, rather too long, framed by a pair of big, boldly curling ears. The long straight nose was exaggeratedly broad at the bridge and too narrow at the tip. In this somewhat masculine face the mouth came as a shock—large, well-sculpted with thick lips. Heydrich had a voice pitched two tones too high—a woman's voice in the body of an athlete. His hands, too, were white, feminine, delicate, well tended, and as expressive as his face. While Himmler affected the face of an impassive Buddha, Heydrich had difficulty in mastering his neurotic temperament. His delivery was jerky. More often than not he left his sentences incomplete. The words telescoped because his brain worked too fast. Whereas Himmler disguised his absence of thought by limiting himself to broad orders, leaving the recipient uncertain of his intentions, Heydrich always appeared afraid of not being understood.

Heydrich was very much the man of the world. An excellent horseman, a first-class fencer—one of the best in Germany—he was also a great art collector. A talented violinist—one of the reasons which made him tend his hands so carefully—he gave chamber music evenings of the highest order, at which he liked to hear his genuine talent applauded. This man, with his discreet respectability, sometimes betrayed just those disturbing traits in his temperament which he normally sought to conceal. Sexually unbalanced, he was perpetually on the chase. He loved organizing, in the company of a few friends, nocturnal expeditions to the pleasure haunts. Even when he occupied the highest posts he could never renounce these outings which, starting with a round of the Berlin night clubs (the variety of which at this period was notorious), lasted all night and finished in brothels where he would pick up prostitutes ready to submit to any perversion.

Heydrich also displayed unmitigated cruelty. The most savage torturers of the Gestapo trembled before him. This effeminate brute could beat the worst killers at their own game. These Nazi "qualities" were served by an outstanding intelligence, a cast-iron will, and an overweening ambition. He was skillful enough to hide his appetites and to appear disciplined, a quality which Himmler appreciated first and foremost. Beneath this orderly exterior, however, he was disrespectful and impudent. Shortly after the Nazis came to power, when Hitler was not yet solidly ensconced at the head of the Party and intrigues multiplied, Heydrich undertook to amass documents on the nebulous origins of the Fuehrer, at which his enemies continually hinted. A revealing example of the genealogical fetish which obsessed these men, concerns Admiral Canaris, who, on the death of Heydrich, insisted that he held the proof of his Jewish descent.

Heydrich, whose duties demanded nerves of steel, easily lost his temper. He often flew into terrifying rages when he would roar, foam at the mouth, and threaten his subordinates. But it was only at home, or in his own domain, that he allowed himself these outbursts. In his love affairs he displayed furious jealousy. He was jealous of his wife, a cold beauty who egged her husband on to get "advancement" in the hope that he would attain the highest post and thus enable her to enjoy the luxuries which were apparently indispensable to her. He had her followed and spied on to insure her fidelity. He was jealous of the success of both his adversaries and friends; he wanted power, honors, and money; he had to have first place, and made up his mind that he would do anything to obtain it.

In order to dominate he incited his chief collaborators to plot against each other. He knew how to exploit, to get the maximum out of them, and then, having squeezed them dry, to reject them ruthlessly. He acted in the same way with those whose qualities appeared to him too outstanding or whose ambition might transform them into rivals. To neutralize them he had instituted a kind of mutual surveillance on the Nazi pattern.

Heydrich also knew how to set the pontiffs of the regime at each other's throats. His maneuvers earned him bitter enemies. He remarked one day to Gisevius, whom he detested, "I can pursue my enemies even from the tomb." It was probably said for effect, but it contained a germ of truth. In this way, he was destined to hate Canaris, Bohle, and Ribbentrop; and would finally cross swords with his own chief, Himmler himself. All these fierce conflicts were waged discreetly. Heydrich combined a taste for violence with a taste for secrecy. His very real love of disguise was probably born of an inferiority complex.

In the Party his subordinates hardly ever mentioned his name, referring to him as "C," a curious nickname known only to the initiates of the mysteries of the establishment. He was incapable of looking people in the face and also, despite his bestial instincts, incapable of striking them directly. This deep-rooted harmony between his most intimate feelings and Nazi principles made him the ideologist, the theoretician, the propagator of racial concepts and the active principles of the S.S. For him, the man who commands and who justifies everything was providential. Thus the S.D. was ordered to pay attention to doctrinal conformity rather than to their "smart appearance." The murderer wore the mask of the moralist.

From his office at No. 8 Prinz Albrechtstrasse, Heydrich patiently wove the gigantic spider's web that was to cover the whole of Germany. Five years would suffice. Five years which would lead Germany to the brink of a war which clear thinkers already saw approaching, even in 1934.

From the start Hitler had determined the extent of the Gestapo's preroga-tives. "I forbid all the services of the Party, its branches and affiliated asso-ciations, to undertake inquiries or interrogations on matters which are the concern of the Gestapo. All incidents of a political police nature, irrespective of reports made through the Party channels, have to be brought immediately to the knowledge of the competent services of the Gestapo, now as before. ... I particularly stress the fact that all attempts at conspiracy and high treason against the State which may come to the knowledge of the Party have to be made known to the Secret State Police. It is not the business of the Party to undertake on its own initiative searches and inquiries into these matters, what-ever their nature."

There was no question of getting rid of legality or formality. In 1931 Schweder wrote in *Politische Polizei* that the Nazi State did not derive from the Republic nor Nazi philosophy from Liberalism. Furthermore, the police, on account of its character as an instrument of the power of the State, still reflected the nature of the State and could not be the result of the transformation of a Republican organization into a Nazi body. "Something new was needed."

And new it was! The Gestapo bore no resemblance to any police force in civilized society. As soon as a possible opponent was detected, the Gestapo neutralized him. "Whosoever in future raises a hand against a representative of the National Socialist Movement or of the State," said Goering on July 24, 1933, "must know that he will lose his life without delay. It will even suffice to prove that he nursed the *intention* of committing this act, or that having been committed, this act had not caused death but only a wound." In the new Nazi State the intention sufficed. Gerland, one of the principal Nazi jurists at this period, issued instructions to German magistrates: "the term 'terror,'" he wrote, "must be respected once more in the penal code."

Thus the political police, the Gestapo, eluded all control; its members could commit any excesses without being called to account. For three years it was to work illegally without defining limits being placed on its functions or its powers. It could deprive any German citizen of his freedom by using the words "protective custody," authorized by two decrees (decrees of February 28, 1933, and of March 8, 1934), but no law had ever determined its prerogatives.

The public had to get used to this strange regime, by gradually becoming resigned to a mixture of despotism and discipline. Periodically, however, official orders proclaimed that the police were above the common law. And no one dared to say that this was a sign of the moral decomposition of the State, the end of true justice and legality.

On May 2, 1935, the Prussian Administrative Court "ruled" that the Secret Police would no longer be subject to judicial control, a ruling which a Prussian law was to codify on February 10, 1936: "The orders and affairs of the Secret Police are not subject to examination by administrative courts."

The absence of judicial foundations for Gestapo action disturbed no one. Professor Huber wrote: "The authority of the political police rests on the customary law of the Reich." And Dr. Best, a high official from the Ministry of the Interior, considered that his powers stemmed from the "new philosophy" and needed no specific legal foundation.

In May 1935 the Prussian Administrative Court issued an order that a sentence of "protective custody" could not be contested by a court. In March 1936 a Protestant pastor had dared to preach in his church against a well-known bishop who had joined the Nazis. The following day the Gestapo ordered him to leave his parish. The pastor refused, appealing to the court. The court replied that an order given by the Gestapo was exempt from judicial decision and that he was powerless to contest it (decree of March 19, 1936).

Another case was that of a Catholic priest. The local Gestapo had demanded information from him concerning the ecclesiastical organizations and also about his congregation. He, too, protested but his appeal was rejected: "When the Gestapo gives an order one does not discuss—one obeys."

The octopus extended its tentacles. Permits were necessary in order to exercise certain commercial businesses, and the police would only issue these permits after an inquiry into the applicant's "morality." The Gestapo saw in this a new field for control. It contested the validity of these commercial licenses and took the matter up with the Court of Saxony. The judgment was a masterpiece of servility. "Since tradesmen can carry out their business in a manner which might permit the development of subversive activities, the trade authority is duty-bound to consult the Gestapo before issuing permits." Thus the Gestapo was able to exercise pressures of all kinds on tradesmen who were politically suspect.

Officially the Gestapo could without prejudice apply three sanctions: a warning, protective custody, and the concentration camp. These "legal" sanctions allowed the arrest of an acquitted political defendant as he left the court and his subsequent internment. In addition to these methods there were also kidnapings, murders, killings camouflaged as accidents or suicides. Klausener, the director of Catholic Action in Berlin, was murdered on June 30, 1934, during the Roehm purge. It was officially announced that he had committed suicide; and the insurance company refused to pay the widow the sum due on the life policy since it was a suicide, pleading in addition that it would be dangerous to dispute the verdict.

Frau Klausener's lawyer approached the Ministry of the Interior. He was told that he must bring an action if he wanted the matter to be investigated. He received the same reply from the Ministry of Justice. This was a convenient method of getting rid of a nuisance; a written complaint questioning the Gestapo was tantamount to a suicide. But the Gestapo, having got wind of the proceedings, considered that they constituted an intrusion into its activities. The lawyer was arrested and kept in prison for several weeks for having dared to doubt a suicide confirmed by the Gestapo.

Dr. Best described the position in precise terms: "No judicial fetters must interfere with the defense of the State, which has to adapt itself to the strategy of the enemy. This is the task of the Gestapo, which claims the status of an army and which, like an army, cannot allow judicial regulations to thwart its initiative in the struggle."

In a few years public opinion and the law were enslaved. This was the period when Goering said to Schacht, the Minister of Finance, "And I tell you that, when the Fuehrer wishes it, two and two make five." When, despite all precautions, the most alarming rumors were current in Germany of the atrocities suffered by the unfortunates who fell into the clutches of the Gestapo, those whose consciences rebelled and who expressed their indignation were neutralized by invoking "the patriotic duty of silence." According to Nazi criteria, it was not the torturer and the murderer who caused their country irrevocable harm; on the contrary, those who denounced them must be considered as traitors and chastised as such. This theory was affirmed at the commencement of the Nazi military operations in 1938. To speak was to rise up against the sadist and the criminals; it was to supply the enemy with propaganda weapons against Germany.

These arguments were accepted with relief by the "good citizens," who asked nothing better than to be left in ignorance. As Gisevius wrote: "Millions of Germans played at hide-and-seek with themselves, or at least feigned ignorance, and it was extraordinarily difficult to touch them because the ignorance they affected was genuine. For they never took the trouble to seek further information! As loyal citizens they were content to know what they were officially intended to know."

As for those whom some fortuitous event roused in spite of themselves from this passivity, they were content to deplore the excesses committed by irresponsible subordinates. "Ah, if only Hitler knew!" was doubtless the exclamation most often heard during those years. The poor Fuehrer! Lost in his cloud, wrestling with colossal difficulties, struggling for the good of the people, and unaware of the abuses and horrors committed in his name! He would undoubtedly have dealt seriously with them had he known. But it was impossible to warn him.

The opponents of the regime went underground. Gisevius remarked very appositely that "totalitarianism and an opposition are two diametrically opposed political conceptions." The German opposition, in actual fact, from 1934 was reduced to its most simple expression. The political or trade union organizations which could have served as a structure for resistance movements—even clandestine—had been destroyed on the seizure of power. The leaders capable of re-forming them had been imprisoned or had fled. The rare cells which had re-formed could only have a reduced activity, felt themselves constantly spied upon, sometimes even betrayed by one of their own men. This triumph did not prevent the Nazis from being vigilant. They knew that this submission was only apparent, and that a hotbed of hatred was fomenting underground. The *émigrés*, particularly the Communists, secretly smuggled into Germany pamphlets and well-documented tracts of anti-Nazi propaganda. The Gestapo hounded the distributors of these pamphlets. To be in possession of one was punishable by dispatch to a concentration camp, or perhaps a silent death in a cellar of the Prinz Albrechtstrasse.

Had not Goering when explaining the reason for its creation stated: "Although at one blow I arrested thousands of Communist officials in order to counter at the outset of immediate danger, the danger itself had by no means been averted. It was necessary to act against the network of secret societies and to keep them under constant observation. For this a specialized police was necessary."

This "specialization" was "on the right path," thanks to the extraordinary powers which the Gestapo had won step by step. Soon Schweder would be able to write: "Our political police embraces everything because it is omnipotent. It strikes inflexibility by means of sanctions which it has the right to impose, but at the same time it is elastic toward the lively development of the Nation and the State it serves." And Professor Huber, the Nazi jurist, was to state that "it must put an end to trends and intentions before they take shape in overt acts." The moment was approaching when the men of the Gestapo were to give an astounding demonstration of this theory.

Chapter 8
The Gestapo versus Roehm

With Himmler, Reichsfuehrer S.S., as its Supreme Commander and Heydrich, head of the S.D. and of the head office, the Gestapo was entirely in the hands of the S.S. In the spring of 1934 Himmler stabilized his power, and the long-standing rivalry between himself and Roehm now took a more acute turn. In theory Himmler was still Roehm's subordinate, since the S.S. were only a special detachment of the S.A. In practice Roehm had practically no power over the S.S., but Himmler was burning to free himself entirely. The Gestapo, over which he had absolute control, and into which Roehm had no right to pry, was to permit this. Goering, for his part, was waiting for an opportunity to destroy his old enemy. Roehm and the S.A. staff were kept under continual surveillance. Himmler, Heydrich, and Goering had decided to compile a dossier sufficiently damning to ask Hitler for the head of the man who, despite his excesses, had remained his oldest friend and who in the past had been his most effective support.

Like Goering and Himmler, Roehm was a Bavarian of middle-class origin. He was a fat, though muscular, red-faced, husky man. Roehm was not obese, like Goering, but the banquets at which he gorged himself for hours on end could not be balanced by the riding exercise he constantly took. Above this replete but powerful body rested the most brutal head imaginable. The almost round face with its double chin and dewlaps was flushed and blood-flecked, covered with a network of fine violet veins. Beneath a broad low forehead were a pair of small, alert eyes, deep-set and drowned by the huge fat cheeks. A deep scar marred his face and accentuated his brutal expression. It ran in a broad cleft from the left cheekbone ending at the nose, which it had almost cut in two. The bridge had been crushed and flattened, and the tip of this nose, which was round and red, came to a point. His face would have been comical had it been less disturbing. A short, stiff triangular mustache hid a very long upper lip and shadowed his broad, tight mouth.

Contrary to Prussian military tradition, Roehm did not wear his head shaved, but his hair was cut short and was always well combed. His huge ears curved abruptly outward into a point.

From a sort of dissolute bravado, Roehm surrounded himself with youths whom he chose for their great physical beauty. He carefully corrupted them if they had not already been corrupted. His entourage, down to his chauffeur and his orderly, consisted of homosexuals. Roehm had acquired his homosexual tastes in the Army. When a democratic newspaper published Roehm's love letters to one of his friends, a former officer, Hitler was indignant and questioned him. Roehm replied with a leer that he was "bisexual," and Hitler finally refrained from interfering since Roehm had made the S.A. more and more formidable. He had created thirty-four Gaustuerme and ten S.A. Gruppen which, placed under his orders, embraced 400,000 men by the middle of 1931. Although imbued with the Nazi ideology, Roehm could not shed the stigmata of his officer profession. People have tried to make Hitler the "natural child of the Versailles Treaty." This definition applies admirably to Roehm, for, behind each of his gestures, at the back of his creation lay the idea of a military revenge, whereas Hitler was dominated by the counterrevolution, by the conflict against the "Reds," in other words the Democrats and the Republicans.

Roehm, however, rejected and despised the former cadres of the German Army because they had not managed to win the war. In fact, while remaining subconsciously tied to a certain traditionalism, he envisaged the restoration of Germany's military grandeur by erasing all conformity.

Goering and Himmler kept him under observation. As soon as the Nazis came to power and the S.A. had fulfilled its role by launching a reign of terror in the streets, the two allies began to undermine him with Hitler. This was the period when Hitler, who had become Reich Chancellor, was susceptible to international opinion. In the summer of 1933 he wanted to give the world the impression of a disciplined country. The noisy, ill-mannered S.A. had become a nuisance. Like Strasser, head of the P.O., they had taken the Socialist side of the Party propaganda seriously and spoke of nationalization, agrarian reform, etc. Forgetting that Gregor Strasser had been forced to resign for these reasons in December 1932, they too accused Hitler of betraying the revolution. For Roehm the seizure of power was only a first step. The rallying cry of the S.A. at this period, "Don't take off your belts," was a call to vigilance. The S.A. were not the only ones to recall the Socialist principles of the N.S.D.A.P. On May 9, 1933, at Beuthen, Brueckner, President of Upper Silesia, violently attacked the big industrialists, "whose life is a perpetual provocation." He was dismissed, thrown out of the Party, and arrested the following year. In Berlin, Koeler of the Nazi Workers' Federation stressed: "Capitalism arrogates to itself the exclusive right of giving work in conditions which it fixes itself. This domination is immoral and must be broken." In July, Kube, leader of the Nazi group in the Prussian *Landtag*, attacked the Junkers. "The National Socialist Government," he said, "must force the great landowners to parcel out their estates and cede a great portion of them to the peasants."

These naïve creatures forgot that, according to the Fuehrerprinzip, these orders should have come from the top. In actual fact orders from above bore no resemblance to these inflammatory speeches. When Hitler proceeded to reorganize German industry "according to the new ideas," he appointed as its leader Herr Krupp of Bohlen.[1]

This gossip did not disturb Hitler. It was easy to deal with. Roehm on the contrary preoccupied him far more. It was all very well Hitler being in theory Supreme Head of the S.A. Roehm, its commander in chief, had transformed it into his own private Army. And this Army was formidable, more powerful than the Reichswehr itself. It was essential therefore to nip in the bud a revolt which could not have failed to swallow up Hitler and his "trusties." On July 1 Hitler summoned the S.A. leaders to Bad Reichenhall in Bavaria, and announced to them that there would be no second revolution. This news was at the same time an undisguised warning. "I am resolved," he said, "to repress ruthlessly any attempt which might serve to disturb the existing order. I shall oppose with the greatest energy a second revolutionary wave, for it would result in a chaos. Anyone, no matter what his position, who rises against the regular authority of the State will be putting his head into a noose."

On July 6 Hitler, speaking to the Statthaelter, repeated this warning. "The revolution cannot be a permanent state. The torrent of the revolution must be directed into the peaceful bed of evolution ... Above all order must be maintained in the economic machinery ... for the economy is a living organism which cannot be transformed at a single blow. It is founded on primitive laws which are rooted in human nature." Those who wanted to drive the machine into another direction were only "carriers of the germs of harmful ideas" and must be rendered harmless "for they were a danger to the State and the Nation." The Statthaelter were also encouraged to see that no organization of the Party interfered in economic matters, this domain being the exclusive responsibility of the Minister of Economics. On July 11

[1] The "General Council for Economy," created on July 15, comprising seventeen members, included the big German industrialists—Krupp, Siemens, Bosch, Thyssen, Voegler, and the big bankers, Schroeder, Reinhardt, and von Frick. National "Socialism" was applied in a curious manner. As for Point 17 of the Nazi program, which envisaged agrarian reform by expropriation without compensation, not a word had been mentioned about it since 1928.

a decree signed by Frick, Minister of the Interior, notified the conclusion of the "victorious German revolution," which had now entered "the phase of evolution."

Thus Roehm had been warned. The replacement of Hugenburg by the candidate of the big industrialists, Schmidt, at the Ministry of Economics, underlined the new orders. Numerous articles were published in the important Nazi newspapers *Kreuzzeitung*, *Deutsche Allgemeine Zeitung*, commenting on the Fuehrer's speech and applauding this "full stop to the German revolution." Roehm, however, tossed these warnings aside and cold-bloodedly assessed the possibility of a conflict with Hitler. Doubtless he saw it merely as an internal conflict within the N.S.D.A.P., in which Hitler's predominance was by no means assured. If the Nazis as a whole had to arbitrate in the debate, it was by no means certain that Hitler would win the day.

There was, however, a force which Roehm had forgotten. This was the double Army commanded by Himmler. The S.S. was a formidable Praetorian Guard. Although numerically inferior to the S.A., it totaled 200,000 men at the beginning of 1934. Grouped into eighty-five regiments, the latter formed properly trained units infinitely superior to the S.A. storm troops.

Furthermore Roehm did not take into account Himmler's hidden army, the Gestapo. Confident of his strength, he did not bother to hide his feelings. In actual fact he wanted to obtain the post of Minister for the Reichswehr in Hitler's first cabinet. This was his dearest ambition, the sole means of forging the army of which he dreamed, a traditionalist yet popular army, an army of political soldiers who would govern the country. It was in order to obtain this post that he had returned from Bolivia at the behest of the Fuehrer. He had made the G.H.Q. of his S.A. in Munich, and when he came to Berlin rashly received all the people who more or less openly criticized Hitler's policy at the Hotel Fasanenhof in the Charlottenburg district where he always stayed. He usually lunched at Kempinski's in the Leipzigerstrasse and invited them to his table. The conversations were all more or less seditious. Roehm set the tone. "Adolf is disgraceful," he said, "he is betraying us all. He only frequents reactionaries and takes into his confidence those generals from East Prussia! Adolf was at my school. It was from me that he learned all he knows of military matters. But Adolf has remained a civilian, a scribbler, a dreamer, a *petit bourgeois*." Roehm was chafing at the bit and did not trouble to hide it. He was furious to see himself cheated of his victory.

Hitler had thought to quench his thirst for power and honors by appointing him Minister without Portfolio on the assimilation of the Party to the State by the law of December 1, 1933. But Roehm had simply remarked that this distinction had also been given the same day to Rudolf Hess, the Fuehrer's deputy, as head of the Central Political Commission of the N.S.D.A.P.

At the beginning of 1934 Roehm's attitude had become frankly hostile. The Gestapo, which kept him under close observation, recorded that many Right Wing opponents were in contact with him. Reports reminded Hitler almost daily that Roehm criticized him, and this disturbed the Fuehrer. For Himmler and Goering, Roehm was Enemy No. 1. His deeds and gestures were interpreted without indulgence. The S.A. itself was under surveillance. The S.A. men liked to drink and bawl obscene and revolutionary songs in the streets.

> Hoist the Hohenzollerns to the lamp post!
> Let the dogs sway there until they fall,
> Hang a black pig in the synagogue
> And hurl hand grenades into the churches.

These were the words of one of their favorite songs, the text of which some diligent hand laid on Hitler's desk. The Fuehrer was annoyed. He had tried to show that the Nazis were people who respected institutions and religion. Moreover, old Hindenburg obviously held the Hohenzollerns in high esteem.

Ignoring all remonstrances, Roehm flaunted himself in company with his youths in repugnant drinking bouts. The propaganda processions which he organized were often marred by scandalous incidents. His outbursts were very public. His "trusties" committed the gravest abuses. Karl Ernst, for example, the former butcher, lift boy, and café waiter (promoted head of the Berlin S.A.), spent the money from public collections in dissolute orgies. These facts were carefully reported to Hitler. Goering was enjoying himself. He was taking his revenge for the cruel jests which Roehm made with regard to his pretensions as a patron of the arts. But none of this sufficed to wring a decision from Hitler. A vague fear of openly opposing Roehm, probably a little gratitude for what he owed him, a confused feeling of inferiority, a memory of the respect of the former corporal for the captain—all this despite the Gestapo reports prevented him from sacrificing Roehm and delivering him to his enemies.

At the beginning of 1934 something more serious threatened Roehm. Hitler knew the hostility of the Army toward the new regime. Wishing to reassure the Reichswehr in the same way that he had pacified the big industrialists and the Eastern landowners, he proposed to give the soldiers control of the S.A. The Reichswehr, however, regarded this suggestion with considerable suspicion. They took the view that Roehm's scoundrels would destroy the traditionalist elements in the Army.

Hitler could not forget that a regime incapable of relying on its Army could not be sure of survival. He had attacked all the institutions of the opposition, except one: his demagogy had balked at the Army. Just as the Republic had bartered with the soldiers, so Hitler chose to come to terms. The only military victim of the *Gleichschaltung* had been General von Hammerstein, Commander in Chief of the Reichswehr, who was axed at the end of 1933 because of his ties with ex-Chancellor von Schleicher. The post had been given to von Fritsch, a traditionalist general and friend of Hindenburg. This proof of good will inspired confidence in the generals. In a speech at Ulm, Blomberg, speaking in the name of the generals, declared, "We for our part give our full confidence, our unreserved adherence, our unshakable devotion to our profession and it is our determination to live, to work, and if necessary to die in this new Reich which has been animated with new blood."

For the soldiers Hitler modified the rules of the new State. The organization of the bureaucrats which evolved automatically from the racial principles of the Third Reich were applied on April 7, 1933. Jewish officials, or those having Jewish ancestors, were expelled without the slightest consideration. The same purges were due to take place in the Army, but the application of the law was postponed until May 31, 1934. It was foreseeable that a great many would be dismissed, for most of the families of the German nobility could count Jewish ancestors in their coat of arms. The "ax" therefore was very discreet—it disposed of five officers, two cadet officers, thirty-one N.C.O.'s and men.

A reconciliation was on the way. The obstacle which prevented its conclusion now bore a single name—Roehm. The latter took fright. Since the Army was now on the side of the regime, Roehm turned to the Socialist wing of the Party and revived forbidden orders of the day. On April 18, 1934, speaking to representatives of the foreign press at the Ministry of Propaganda, he was not afraid to state, "The revolution which we made is not a national revolution but a National Socialist one. We wish to stress the last word, Socialist." And Roehm's first lieutenant, Heines, declared at the end of May in Silesia, "We have assumed the duty of remaining revolutionaries. We are only at the beginning. We shall only lay down our arms when the German revolution is complete."

But the Gestapo was on the watch. It kept the Fuehrer constantly informed. The ground was being prepared.

At the beginning of April, Hitler went for a short cruise aboard the pocket battleship *Deutschland*. Off Kiel he met Blomberg, and it was said that the latter had demanded the dismissal of Roehm and the S.A. staff, a sacrifice to which Hitler agreed in order to complete his conquest of the soldiers. This is only a hypothesis. It is however evident that the idea of eliminating Roehm at this time made great progress in the mind of Hitler. Subjected to pressure from the soldiers, from Goering, from Hess and the P.O., from Himmler and his Gestapo, he hesitated for a long while as was his custom. After a long period of wavering an irrational decision of characteristic brutality was reached. This was what Hitler called "intuition" and it bore the mark of his "genius."

Chapter 9
"The Night of the Long Knives"

It was in this atmosphere of brewing crisis that Hitler left for Italy on June 14, 1934. Invited by Mussolini, he flew to Venice with a reduced staff. Here he met the Minister von Neurath and the German ambassador von Hassell. On the Italian side, Mussolini was accompanied by his son-in-law Ciano, Undersecretary for State Suvich, and the Italian ambassador in Berlin, Cerutti. This was the first time the dictators met. Mussolini treated the man he considered his pupil somewhat airily. Hitler was rather disappointed by the meager results of his journey. To this deception was to be added an incident whose consequences were to be serious in the extreme.

On June 17 the ex-Chancellor von Papen, at that time Vice-Chancellor, made a speech to the students of the little town of Marburg. Despite Hitler's outlawing of the "second revolutionary wave," he said, despite the pledges given openly to the bourgeois economic powers, the conservative parties were disturbed by the threats of the extremist Nazis and the members of the S.A. It was in the name of the conservatives that von Papen addressed the Fuehrer, calling upon him not to forget the agreement which, by bringing him the support of the conservative parties, had enabled him to rise to power.

Von Papen's dearest wish was that there should be a halt to discrediting people who had always been good citizens and patriots, and to ridiculing intellectual and spiritual preoccupations, particularly religion, which Roehm and his friends coarsely attacked. In fact he went so far as to question one of the fundamentals of the totalitarian State: the regime of a single party. There must be a trend toward free elections and the re-establishment of certain parties.

Hitler heeded the warning. Following the Army lead, the middle classes were demanding Roehm's head. Von Papen's speech had immediately received the approval of the old Field Marshal-President, who congratulated him by telegram. It was also approved by the Reichswehr and the representatives of finance and industry. Realizing that von Papen's speech was something of an ultimatum, Hitler acted at once. The German press was sternly "invited" not to print the speech. Goering, Goebbels, and Hess spoke on the radio, threatening "the ridiculous scamps" who thought to stop the Nazis from exercising their power. Nevertheless, the position hardened and Roehm, already barred from the officers' clubs, was sent on leave to nurse a rheumatic condition of the arm.

It was impossible to strike directly at the Vice-Chancellor. The Gestapo was ordered to register a black mark for future revenge. Thanks to telephone tapping and espionage among von Papen's staff, it had no difficulty in discovering that the real author of the speech, which the Vice-Chancellor had merely read, was a young writer, the lawyer Dr. Edgar Jung, one of the founders of the theory of a "conservative revolution," a liberal intellectual who had begun to acquire a certain following. On June 21, four days after the speech,

Dr. Jung was alone in his Munich home for a few hours. On her return, his wife found that he had disappeared, and on searching the house she found the single word "Gestapo" scrawled by her husband on the bathroom wall. His body was found on June 30 in a ditch on the road to Oranienburg. It was learned later that, before being shot in a cell in the Munich prison, he had been given a lengthy interrogation and had suffered appalling tortures.

Heydrich was very proud of this demonstration by his Gestapo, whose methods were truly "swift, clean, and effective." This exercise was merely a rehearsal. Now an attack had to be launched against Roehm. Hitler had decided to get rid of him, but was still hesitant as to the means to be employed. Himmler and Goering undertook to influence him. Goering was prancing with impatience. His killer instincts were aroused.

In feverish haste the Gestapo assembled the documents they had collected for some months on Roehm and his clique. The most trivial notes were examined. The visits Roehm had received, the most banal encounter, the most harmless conversation became the subject of a veritable exegesis. The Hermann Goering Institute had dealt in the same way with the records of tapped telephone conversations. From all these documents a passage, a phrase, a word, a few names had been extracted. From these disparate elements it was necessary to make a coherent whole, a conspectus capable of frightening Hitler and making him take the brutal decision which was expected of him. Only the announcement of a conspiracy, an imminent *coup d'état* which would endanger his life, could arouse him from his indecision.

The document took shape. It was easy to give a little distortion to the truth. Roehm wanted to force Hitler to create a revolutionary people's Army of which he would be commander in chief. To achieve his ends, he was prepared to use violence, in other words to provoke a conflict which would place Hitler's new allies in a position of inferiority and force him to revert to his old friends, his faithful veterans, the S.A. combatants. But the violence of Roehm's language, his excesses, his outbursts, and his imprudences had been recorded by the Gestapo, who found in them the proof of the existence of a plot, designed not to force the Fuehrer's hand, but to overthrow him and, if necessary, to assassinate him.

Sensing the danger, Roehm took the initiative and, in a communiqué published on June 19 by the *Voelkischer Beobachter*, dismissed the S.A. for a month, beginning July 1. The men on leave were forbidden to wear their uniforms during this holiday. This was to reassure Hitler that the rumors which had been circulated of a rising were without foundation. To confirm it, Roehm left for Bad Wiessee, a small Bavarian spa south of Munich. This withdrawal merely aroused the worst suspicions of Goering and Hitler. They could not let their prey escape.

Obergruppenfuehrer Victor Lutze, formerly Pfeffer's assistant, who had never forgiven Roehm for usurping the place which he considered his right on Pfeffer's departure, visited von Reichenau, one of the leading soldiers now adhering to the Nazis, and informed him of Roehm's plans to force Hitler to make a decision. Events now gathered speed. Himmler and Goering nagged at Hitler, assuring him that the putsch was imminent. Various signs, however, denoted, that no putsch was to be feared in the immediate future. For example, Karl Ernst, commander of the Berlin-Brandenburg S.A., who would have played a leading role in any revolt, had, with Roehm's permission, packed his bags to go on a cruise to Madeira and the Canaries. Many of the other S.A. leaders had arranged trips, to profit by the unexpected month's holiday, which was to begin on July 1. To mark this separation, Roehm organized a farewell dinner. He invited all the leaders of the S.A. groups to join him around the same table at Bad Wiessee. Himmler and Heydrich immediately sent report after report to Hitler, informing him that the putsch was to be launched in Munich on the day of the banquet, which was only an excuse to bring the S.A. leaders together. From hour to hour new details arrived.

The Gestapo prepared to act. From the 28th the police forces were on duty in readiness. Nevertheless, Hitler left Berlin the same day for Essen to attend the marriage of Gauleiter Terboven. This journey was not on his normal schedule. Terboven was not an important enough member of the Party for the Fuehrer to put himself out, particularly in a period which was apparently so fraught with menace.

An even more significant fact: Goering accompanied Hitler, and Terboven blushed with pleasure and confusion at being so greatly honored. The truth is that Hitler had seized upon this excuse to leave Berlin and the pressures being exerted upon him. In his usual manner, he recoiled before the decision to be made. But Goering had sensed the danger and, to prevent the Fuehrer from evading the issue, had preferred to accompany him. Diels joined him in Essen to give him support.

On the 29th the *Voelkischer Beobachter* published an article by General von Blomberg. Under the title "The Army in the Third Reich," the Commander in Chief of the Reichswehr, on the pretext of replying to the foreign news services which spoke of "a reactionary plot supported by the Army," assured Hitler of the loyalty of the military to the new regime. At the same time the article contained a new threat for the S.A. "The Praetorian spirit is alien to the spirit of our soldier," wrote the General. "The action of the Fuehrer, summoned by the Marshal-President to the head of government, has given the soldier the august right to be the bearer of the arms of a regenerated nation. The German soldier is aware that he is involved in the political life of a unified country." This blunt reference to the existence of *Landsknechte* sounded the death knell of the S.A.

The same day, June 29, an unforeseen arrival set in motion the final mechanism of the operation. After Terboven's wedding, Hitler inspected a labor camp in Westphalia, and proceeded to Bad Godesberg on the Rhine to spend the weekend at the Hotel Dreesen, whose proprietor he knew.

That same morning Himmler flew in by the Berlin plane. He brought the latest "reports" from his agents. According to this faked compilation, the S.A. was to launch the attack on the following day by occupying the government buildings. A commando had already been detailed to kill Hitler. The armed S.A. would go into action in the streets. An agreement had been reached between Roehm and one of his old friends, the artillery general von Leeb, commanding the Munich military zone, that the weapons still stored in the old clandestine Army depots should be issued to the S.A. In actual fact an agreement had been made that these arms were to be placed in police custody during the S.A. holiday period in order to avoid any initiative on the part of individuals left to their own devices. An almost permanent liaison was established between Bad Godesberg and Gestapo headquarters in Berlin. During the course of the day, a message announced that agents of the S.D. in Munich had seen arms being loaded into a truck, a proof that the putsch was imminent!

At the Hotel Dreesen the government General Staff held a council of war. Hitler was attended by Goering, Goebbels, Himmler, Diels, Lutze, and other Nazis of minor importance. The hotel was guarded by a cordon of S.S.

In the dining room, with its magnificent view of the Westerwald Mountains and the Rhine Valley, Hitler paced up and down like a bear in a cage.

He still faltered, hesitated to condemn to a traitor's death the man who had been his stoutest supporter, his oldest comrade in arms, and the only member of the Party with whom he used the familiar du form of address. But Goering, Himmler, and Goebbels brought pressure to bear on him. He *must* strike with force and terrible energy before the S.A. had time to take the first steps.

The weather was stormy, the sky laden with heavy clouds, and the atmosphere stifling. Toward evening the storm finally burst, and a torrent of rain brought a little coolness. It was not until after dinner that Hitler suddenly took the decision which he had evaded for two weeks. In a few words he gave his instructions; Goering and Himmler were to leave for Berlin immediately to carry out repressive measures, while he himself went to Munich with Goebbels.

During the night, accompanied by Goebbels and four of his trusted henchmen, Hitler took a three-engine aircraft at Hangelaar airfield. The machine landed at Oberwiesenfeld, near Munich, at four o'clock in the morning on June 30. During the journey, the Munich Reichswehr had been given orders to occupy the Brown House. The airfield of Oberwiesenfeld was guarded by the S.S. Hitler drove straight to the Bavarian Home Office and sent for the chief of police, Major Schneidhuber (retired) and the Munich S.A. leader, Schmidt. Both men had already been detained by Gauleiter Wagner. With a typical display of histrionics, Hitler rushed up to them, tore off their badges and stripes, and insulted them. Both men were dispatched to Stadelheim prison.

Toward five o'clock in the morning, Hitler and his suite, accompanied by S.S., members of the Gestapo, and the military, left by car for Bad Wiessee. A Reichswehr armored car protected the long column of cars, a superfluous precaution since not even the smallest body of armed men was encountered along the whole forty-mile route. It was nearly seven o'clock when the convoy arrived at Bad Wiessee, and the little lakeside town was still slumbering peacefully.

They made their way to the Hotel Hanslbauer, where Roehm and his comrades were staying. The S.A. guard at the door allowed himself to be arrested without resistance. In the hotel no one was yet abroad, a curious state of affairs for conspirators on the morning of a *coup d'état*, at the very moment when the occupation of public buildings was due to begin! The dining room was prepared for the banquet. Hitler did not appear to notice these anomalies. A prey to his wild excitement, he entered the building at the head of his troops. Some of his oldest fighting comrades from the time of the Bavarian putsch had joined him. The first person they met was young Graf Anton von Spreti, Roehm's aide-de-camp, renowned for his exceptional good looks. Awakened by the noise, he had got up to discover the source. Hitler rushed at him and, with his old hippopotamus hide crop—the gift of some admirers from his early days—struck him so violently in the face that the blood spurted. Leaving him in the hands of his S.S. men, Hitler burst into Roehm's bedroom. Fast asleep and taken by surprise, he was arrested without being able to make a move, while Hitler berated him. According to Goebbels, who participated in the operation although keeping very much in the background, Obergruppenfuehrer Heines, Roehm's old friend, was found in a neighboring bedroom asleep with his chauffeur, whom Goebbels called a *Lustknabe*, a "joyboy." Heines having attempted to defend himself, both men were killed on the spot before they had time to get out of bed.

A detachment of S.A. which had come to relieve the guard allowed itself to be disarmed without protest. The main operation; which was to arrest the leaders of the plot, had been carried out without the slightest difficulty in a few minutes. Heines and his chauffeur had been killed unnecessarily, but these two victims added spice to the "bag" of what might have been called "the conspiracy of the sleepers."

At about eight o'clock, the convoy set out on the return journey to Munich, taking Roehm and his comrades, summarily dressed and in handcuffs. On the way they met several cars bringing S.A. leaders to Bad Wiessee for the farewell banquet. They were halted and the occupants arrested. By midmorning Hitler was back in Munich with his prisoners, who had been officially described as "prisoners of state." Since early dawn the S.S. and the Gestapo in the city had begun to arrest all persons figuring on the "lists," which had been prepared by the Gestapo over a period of several weeks. At midday Hitler summoned the S.S. and the members of the S.A. who did not figure on the lists to the Brown House, and announced that Roehm, deprived of his functions, had been replaced by Victor Lutze.

The prisoners were herded into the Brown House and guarded by heavily armed S.S. men, who had orders to shoot at the least sign of resistance.

At about 2 P.M. more than two hundred persons had been detained, and it was decided to send them to Stadelheim prison. Among these prisoners, and among those who continued to be brought in, were not only S.A. leaders. On the contrary, the majority of those arrested were political opponents who had no ties with Roehm and the S.A. The opportunity to eliminate them had been taken.

During the afternoon Hitler took the Gestapo list, ticked 110 names in red pencil, and gave orders that they were to be executed. Frank, the Bavarian Minister of Justice, appalled by the number of victims, interceded with Hitler and succeeded in having the list revised. Finally there were only nineteen names, including that of Roehm. Hitler wanted to spare him an ignominious death before a firing squad. Possibly he feared a final speech or the revelation of some secret. On his orders, a visit was paid to Roehm in Cell 474 in Stadelheim prison, with the suggestion that he should commit suicide, but Roehm turned a deaf ear.

Later that evening the final order arrived: if Roehm refused the chance he had been given, he would be executed. A prison warder entered his cell, laid a revolver on the table, and left without a word. Roehm was watched through the grille. He stared at the revolver without touching it and then seemed to forget it. Ten minutes passed. The warder entered the cell once more, picked up the revolver, and left, still without a word having been uttered. A moment later two men in turn entered the cell, carrying revolvers. One of them was the S.S. man Eicke, commandant of Dachau concentration camp. On seeing them, Roehm rose to his feet. He was stripped to the waist, and the sweat suddenly glistened on his skin.

"What's the meaning of this?" he asked.

"No time to waste words," said Eicke.

Calmly raising his weapon, he aimed and fired several bullets, as though at target practice. Roehm slumped to the ground. Eicke bent down and administered the *coup de grâce*. Thus ended the career of the all-powerful chief of the S.A., the first true pioneer of Hitler's career.

As early as the evening of the 30th the Gestapo men visited the prison with their first list of six men to be executed, and claimed them from Warden Koch. The latter had timidly suggested that a red pencil tick as an execution order did not seem to him "to comply with the regulations." They brushed him aside, and the six men were taken out into the courtyard of the prison and shot by an

S.S. squad commanded by Sepp Dietrich. The first to be executed was August Schneidhuber, S.A. leader and Munich prefect of police.

In Berlin, Goering and Hitler directed the purge. For the occasion Hitler had given Goering executive power for the whole of North Germany, and the latter used it without discretion. The arrests began at 10:30 A.M., proving that the Gestapo leaders had no anxiety about a putsch by the S.A. Although the action was to have been confined in principle to Munich, since that was the city from which the signal for the putsch was to be given, it was even more ferocious in Berlin. In North Germany, the S.S. and the Gestapo carried out a host of arrests. Goering wished finally to decapitate the S.A. in his region, and to settle accounts with his personal enemies. Himmler had prepared his list and Heydrich added his own.

Karl Ernst, chief of the Berlin-Brandenburg S.A., had left for his cruise in the South Atlantic. This decision could possibly have saved his life. He had been in Bremen since the previous evening, but, unfortunately for him, the boat was not due to sail until the evening of the 30th. Surprised at finding himself arrested by the S.S., he protested vociferously. It was inconceivable that anyone should dare to lay hands on such an exalted personage—a deputy of the Reichstag and a councilor of state. He forgot that he had committed the crime of speaking disparagingly in private of Himmler, whom he referred to by the name invented by Otto Strasser, "the black Jesuit." This had long since been recorded in the Gestapo files. The hour of retribution had arrived.

Ernst was also condemned for another reason: he had led the commando of S.A. incendiaries ordered to set fire to the Reichstag. Apparently he had not always held his tongue. He had betrayed dangerous confidences which the Gestapo ear had not failed to record. It is significant that of the ten surviving S.A. men who took part in the arson (Rall, the eleventh, had long since been liquidated), nine were murdered on June 30, 1934. Only one was spared, Heini Gewert, the Reichstag deputy. He enjoyed the high protection of Himmler or of Heydrich, for shortly after this he entered the Gestapo as a police officer. In this capacity he went to the East front in 1942, where he was killed.

The zealous clerk of the court Reineking, who had denounced Rall's relevation to the Gestapo, was spared, but he was arrested and sent to Dachau. He died there at the beginning of 1935. All these men who had been so useful in February 1933 had become a nuisance by June 1934. They had to disappear, and, first and foremost, their leader Ernst had to go.

Brought back to Berlin by air, he was imprisoned in the Lichterfelde barracks and shot two hours later. All those who had not been shot down on the spot or who had been unable to escape were brought here. Some of them were given a vague interrogation; most of them were reviled and beaten up, and nearly all faced a firing squad in the barracks courtyard. Throughout the whole of Saturday and Sunday, July 1, the Lichterfelde district echoed with the sound of salvos. The firing squad took up its position five yards from the condemned men. The wall against which they had leaned remained stained with blood for many months. The salvos were ordered to cries of: "Heil Hitler! It is the Fuehrer's will!"

Gestapo headquarters was a hive of activity during those turbulent days. It was from these well-organized offices that the murder orders were dispatched. It was here that the reports of the executions were received, the notifications of arrests, of escapes, the news of murders committed on the persons of those who had tried to resist or to flee, and on those against whom orders had been given to shoot on sight. For the sake of secrecy, all those whose names figured on the lists were designated by a serial number. On the telephone, in telegrams and messages, the information was limited to: "No. 8 has arrived; Nos. 17, 35, 37, 68, and 84 have been arrested; Nos. 32, 43, 47, and 59 have been shot; No. 5 is still missing." When the names that these numbers concealed gradually became known during the next few hours, the whole of Germany was struck with amazement and terror.

It has already been said that the Gestapo killers did not confine themselves to striking at the S.A. leaders. To quote the phrase used by Dr. Frick in his statement at the Nuremberg trials: "Among the people murdered during the Roehm purge, many had nothing to do with the internal revolt of the S.A., but were *not very popular.*"

"Not very popular," for example, was the journalist Walter Schotte, von Papen's collaborator and spokesman for the Barons of the Herrenklub. In 1932 he had worked out a political tactic which almost ruined the electoral hopes of the Nazis. In a book entitled *Die Regierung Papen-Schleicherr-Gayl* (The Papen-Schleicher-Gayl Government), he had defined the methods of the Nazi party so perfectly that this revelation had cost Hitler two million votes at the elections of November 6, 1932. He had not been forgiven this: the Gestapo murdered him on the morning of the 30th.

Gregor Strasser was not popular either. Hitler had not forgotten the man who had done so much toward the political organization of the Party, and who had proudly left it without a word on December 8, 1932, a victim of the intrigues of Goering and Goebbels. The Fuehrer had retained a certain respect for him. He had given orders that he should be left unharmed, but Goering, strong in the powers delegated to him, ignored this. Otto Strasser had fled to Austria, where he had founded the anti-Hitlerian Schwarze Front. His brother Gregor had retired from politics. He ran the pharmaceutical firm of Schering-Kahlbaum. This was not enough to disarm his enemies, Goering and Himmler. Himmler had entrusted Heydrich personally with the task of seeing that this old score was settled. On the morning of the 30th Strasser was taken to Colombiahaus, the Gestapo prison. There he was incarcerated with the S.A. leaders who had already been arrested. During the afternoon an S.S. man called to take him, he said, to a cell where he would be alone. The S.S. man opened the door of the cell, made way for Strasser, closed the door, and left. Less than a minute later a shot rang out. Strasser was not dead; an artery had been severed by the bullet. Stretched on his bunk, he felt his life ebbing away in the jet of blood which spurted onto the wall. The prisoner in the neighboring cell heard his groans for more than an hour. Heydrich, fulfilling his duty, verified in person that the Reichsfuehrer had been obeyed, and gave the order, "Let this swine who will not die bleed to death."

In Berlin the Gestapo agents operated in small groups. On the morning of the 30th two very correctly dressed gentlemen called at the Reich Chancellery, on behalf of Vice-Chancellor von Papen, asking to see his private secretary, Oberregierungsrat Bose. The latter was busy and had a visitor in his office. Protesting that their communication was of the utmost urgency, the two men asked him to come out and see them for a moment. Von Bose appeared in the anteroom. The two "gentlemen" each brought out a revolver and laid him low without a word, leaving him dying on the carpet.

At Neu Babelsberg, in the suburbs of Berlin, two visitors rang the bell at the villa of General von Schleicher, the former Reich Chancellor. Without a word, they pushed aside the maid, entered the house, and, still in deathly silence, shot first the General and then his wife, the daughter of Cavalry General von

Hennings, who had run up at the sound of the shots. The maid fled in terror. Their twelve-year-old daughter found them on her return from school.

The killers also visited the Ministry of Transport, entered the office of Director Klausener, and shot him at his desk before he had time to rise from his chair. The minister, von Eltz-Ruebenach, who ran in at the sound of the shot was threatened and forced to retire. Klausener was the head of Catholic Action. His execution caused a great stir, and the Gestapo coldly insisted that he had committed suicide at the moment he had been asked for some piece of information.

Nothing is more monotonous than mass murder. Everywhere that sinister Saturday, men fell to the bullets of their murderers: von Bredow, a Reichswehr general like Schleicher; old von Kahr, the former Bavarian Premier, whom Hitler had never forgiven for his attitude during the 1923 putsch; Captain Ehrhardt, former chief of the famous Freikorps, once glorified by Hitler; Gehrt, the flying ace who had won the Pour le Mérite in the field; Ramshorn, the Gleiwitz chief of police, and Schraegmuller, the Magdeburg chief of police; Karl Ernst's staff—Voss, Sander, Beulwitz, not forgetting "Fräulein Schmidt," boy friend and aide-decamp of Heines.

Glaser, a lawyer, had been rash enough to fall out with the Nazi jurist Frank, and to plead against the Party newspapers. He was shot down outside his door. Professor Stempfle, a militant Catholic who had supported Hitler at the outset and then turned from him in terror, was also shot. The leader of the Catholic students, Beck, was murdered in a wood, and the Düsseldorf Youth Leader Probst was shot "when attempting to escape."

Others were killed in error, like the music critic Schmidt, who was shot in mistake for a doctor of the same name. Or like the head of the Saxony Hitler Jugend Laemmermann, whose name suddenly appeared inexplicably on the list of people to be shot. Their widows received their ashes through the post with a letter of apology.

Goering purged Berlin with "a fist of mail," but throughout this industrial operation he made every effort to give it some semblance of legality. On his orders, the Gestapo had organized courts-martial. A significant detail: the commander of the military zone and the town commandant presided in turn as representatives of the Reichstag. The court judged the prisoners in a few minutes, but the verdict was read out to them before they were sent to the firing squad composed of Leibstandarte S.S. Some were executed on the S.S.

parade ground at Lichterfelde, and the inhabitants of the buildings on the Finkensteinallee were able to witness the scene from their windows.

Some of the firing squads consisted of Allgemeine S.S. troops, which had been brought the night before to the barracks of the Leibstandarte S.S. elite. Since the Allgemeine S.S. were not normally armed, they had been given firearms by the police or the Reichswehr, another enlightening detail concerning the role played by the generals in this affair.

On the evening of Saturday, June 30, Hitler returned to Berlin by plane. Goering, Himmler, Frick, and Daluege awaited him with their escort of police at Templehof airfield. Goering and Himmler were puffed up with pride. On the runway Goering handed Hitler the list of dead. The Fuehrer shuddered on reading the name of Strasser, but Himmler explained that he had committed suicide. A few days later Hitler gave orders that provision should be made for Strasser's widow.

The following day, Sunday, July 1, after the firing squads had been in action the whole morning, Goering "interceded" with Hitler at about two o'clock in the afternoon, asking him to stop the executions. Enough blood had flowed. Hitler agreed. Goering had not informed him that there were only two names left on the list.

Not all the men arrested on June 30 died in front of a firing squad. Hundreds of prisoners languished for months in prison; others, like Lieutenant Colonel Dusterberg, landed in concentration camps, where many died and where others remained for several years. General Milch admitted at Nuremberg that in 1935 there were still seven to eight hundred victims of the Roehm purge in Dachau.

According to certain Nazi statements, there were only seventy-one executions; according to other Nazis, there were between 250 and 300 victims. Estimates have spoken of fifteen hundred dead, but this figure appears to be exaggerated. In all probability there were several hundred victims, perhaps a thousand, including two hundred of the S.A. The Nuremberg tribunal itself refrained from establishing the exact number, but the figure has been given as 1,076.

On Monday, July 2, in the early hours of the morning, the Gestapo, S.S., and Security Police authorities received the following telegram signed by Goering and Himmler, the text of which has been preserved by Gisevius: "The Minister-President of Prussia and the chief of the State Secret Police has been invested with full police powers. On orders from above, all documents relating to the action of the past two days are to be burned. Report to be furnished immediately after execution."

A thousand dead in forty-eight hours! Even for the Nazi regime, which was prodigal enough in human life, this was rather a tall order. On Saturday evening the Party press office published a rather embarrassed communiqué. The same evening Goering made a statement to the reporters who had been summoned to the Propaganda Ministry. It was vital to give an official version of the events, because several provincial papers had already published special numbers, and the foreign press was beginning to ask awkward questions.

Goering, resplendent in his gala uniform, spoke in a solemn but far from convincing tone. It was a question, he said, of plans for a putsch staged by Roehm, the sexual depravities of his entourage, the obstinacy of certain elements in trying to make a second revolution, and treachery from the "forces of reaction." He announced that von Schleicher, who was conspiring with a foreign power, had tried to defend himself when about to be arrested, and that this gesture had cost him his life. He added that Roehm was no longer in the land of the living, but ignored the murder of Strasser, of Bose in von Papen's anteroom, and of Klausener in his office. Referring to the orders given to him by the Fuehrer, Goering said quite simply, "I enlarged my mission." It was by means of this "enlargement" of orders for suppressing a "plot" by the extreme Socialist wing of the Party that it had been possible to strike a blow at the conservatives and Catholics.

In announcing the appointment of Victor Lutze as chief of staff of the S.A., Hitler issued an order of the day to the S.A. Passages of this proclamation which, in addition to the Brown Shirts, was addressed to all the opponents in power, display a certain unconscious wit. The Fuehrer stigmatizes those "revolutionaries whose relations with the State were disturbed in 1918, and who had lost all close contact with the social order, who had devoted themselves to the revolution and who would have liked to see the latter permanently established. ... Incapable of any honest collaboration, resolved to oppose all established order, filled with hatred against all authority, their anxiety and instability finds satisfaction alone in ceaseless conspiracy and in plotting the destruction of the existing order. ... This pathological group of enemies of the State is dangerous because it constitutes a reserve of voluntary participants in all attempts at rebellion, until a new order begins to take shape after a period of chaotic decomposition."

The chief of state was striving to repel those who yesterday had placed him in the position he occupied, exactly by refusing "all honest collaboration" with the Republic, by plotting "the destruction of the existing order," and by watching for "all attempts at rebellion." Hitler thus broke with his origins and denied them, rejecting those who had had the impertinence to remind him of the dubious means which had carried him to power.

On July 3 the ministers held a cabinet meeting. The murders had to be legalized. None of the men present had the courage to protest, not even Guertner, though the Reich Minister for Justice had personal friends among the Right Wing men who had fallen to the bullets of the killers.

Von Papen did not attend this meeting, having resigned from the Vice-Chancellorship the same day. This was the sole hostile reaction to these purges by the man to whom Hitler owed so much. The suggestions of his Marburg speech had been followed, since the revolutionaries had been liquidated, but he had been shown that it was dangerous to voice the least criticism. His closest collaborators had been murdered, one of them actually in the Chancellery. He contented himself with this formal protest. His retirement, however, was of short duration. He continued to work with the Nazis and rendered them long service as ambassador in Vienna and later in Ankara.

Nor did the conservatives react. The ministers thanked Hitler for having saved Germany from revolutionary chaos and unanimously adopted a law, Article I of which included the following: "The measures taken on June 30, July 1 and 2, 1934, to thwart attempts at treason and high treason, are considered as essential measures for national defense." This was the epitaph of the victims.

Old Field Marshal Hindenburg was alarmed to hear that two generals of the Reichswehr had been deliberately assassinated, but since the Army had not reacted and his advisers assured him that everything was in order, he agreed to sign a telegram of congratulation addressed to Hitler, compiled by the Fuehrer himself: "According to reports I have just received, I confirm that by your resolution and personal courage you have crushed in the bud the intentions of traitors. With this telegram I wish to express my deep gratitude and my very best thanks. With my best regards." Secretary of State

Otto Meissner, chief of the Presidential Chancellery, guaranteed to make the old man sign the text in order to earn the gratitude of his new masters. The dotard of Neudeck had the excuse of senility and ill-health. Blomberg was neither old nor sick. In an order of the day to the Army he had given his guarantee: "The Fuehrer has attacked and crushed the mutineers with military resolution and exemplary courage. The Wehrmacht, as the sole armed force of the entire nation, while remaining apart from the conflicts of internal politics, will express its gratitude by its devotion and fidelity."

On July 13 Hitler made a great speech before the Reichstag. Where details of the putsch, of the activities of Roehm and his accomplices, of the secret bond between Schleicher and Strasser, of clandestine contacts with a "foreign power" (there had been talk of France and the Ambassador François Poncet), had been expected, there was only a long self-justification. Speaking of Karl Ernst, Hitler declared that he had remained in Berlin to direct in person the revolutionary action," whereas everyone knew that Ernst had been arrested in Bremen just as he was about to embark upon a holiday cruise. The argument, according to which Hitler's action had prevented a "national bolshevist revolution," was little appreciated. People could not understand how conservatives like von Bose and Klausener could be embroiled in such an adventure. Finally, he declared that according to an "eternal iron law," he had made himself the "supreme judicial arbiter of the German people." High-sounding phrases are far better than detailed explanations.

During the month of July 1934 the political situation was very strange. June 30 had been a new "day of dupes," and the soldiers were the dupes. They had played a considerable part in Hitler's decision. They were convinced that he was now their prisoner and that they had annexed the new regime. Not only had they given their "moral" sanction to the operation, but they had participated materially and physically. They had been among the first to be informed of the preparations for the operation. From Monday, June 25, the Reichswehr had been asked to hold itself in readiness. All leave had been canceled and all officers on leave had been recalled. Motorcycle detachments of the N.S.K.K. were armed and units of the S.S. infantry issued with rifles and 120 cartridges per man, provided by the Reichswehr armories.

Finally, in Berlin, the Reichswehr officers sat "in their own right" on the punitive courts-martial at Lichterfelde. Blomberg and the generals were convinced that the sacrifice of their competitors the S.A. was being done to reassure them. A fortnight later they had an opportunity for giving the Fuehrer a proof of their gratitude.

At the end of July, Field Marshal Hindenburg became seriously ill, and his state of health aroused the keenest interest in certain quarters. His successor was automatically expected to come from the conservative aristocracy. Such views coincided with the monarchist ideas of Hindenburg himself. The names of Prince August William of Prussia, of Prince Oscar of Prussia, and of Duke Ernst Augustus of Brunswick-Luneburg had been put forward. What would happen in the event of the old Marshal having pronounced in his will for the return of the monarchy?

In theory the constitution, still legally applicable, laid down that, in the case of the death of the President, his burden would be temporarily shouldered by the president of the Supreme Court of Justice. But Hitler, by a law dated January 30, 1934, had authorized himself to apply the constitution in a different manner.

To prevent any last-minute maneuver on the part of the "reactionaries," the S.S. invested Hindenburg's home at Neudeck at the moment the old man was on his deathbed. Oberfuehrer Behrens, a killer who had organized the murders in Silesia on June 30, was in charge of a special commando. The guardians remained at their posts until the death of the Field Marshal, and the Reichswehr officers were only allowed to approach to mount a guard of honor around the dead man's bed when he closed his eyes on August 2.

The previous day, August 1, Hitler had promulgated a law appropriating to himself the functions of Chancellor and President of the Reich. The problem of Hindenburg's succession had been settled. A significant detail: Blomberg had agreed to append his signature to this law, pledging the support of the Army and an assurance that there would be no opposition to this *coup d'état*. The following day, August 2, as soon as the death of the President had been announced, Hitler swore in members of the Reichswehr. The oath committed them personally to Adolf Hitler: "I swear before God to obey without reservation, Adolf Hitler, Fuehrer of the Reich, supreme chief of the Wehrmacht, and I pledge myself as a courageous soldier always to observe this oath, even at the risk of my life."

The same evening Blomberg issued an order of the day to the Army, which read as follows: "We will devote all our efforts and even our lives if necessary in the service of the new Germany. The Field Marshal has opened to us the gates of this new Germany, and in doing so has realized the vow born of several centuries of German victories. Inspired by the memory of this great heroic figure, we shall march toward the future full of confidence in the German Fuehrer, Adolf Hitler."

The Field Marshal's will was not published until the 12th. No one had the slightest doubt that this document had been falsified. In it were several phrases which had obviously been written at Adolf Hitler's dictation, since they agreed with his most recent ideas, particularly with regard to the Reichswehr. It ended as follows: "My Chancellor Adolf Hitler and his movement have made the German people take a decisive step of a historical nature toward internal unity, above all against differences of class and social status. I leave my German people in the firm hope that what I desired in 1919, and what has slowly matured until January 30, 1933, will continue to ripen in view of the wholehearted accomplishment of the historic mission of our people. In this firm hope in the future of the Fatherland I can close my eyes in peace."

A week later, on August 19, Hitler called upon the nation to approve his new functions by a well-orchestrated plebiscite. The support of the Army, the posthumous blessing of the "old gentleman," the disappearance of all opposition, the terror which muzzled the few nonconformist survivors, all guaranteed its success—added to the fact that the Gestapo and the S.D. had organized a secret checking of the voting papers, which would insure success and the unmasking of the last opponents. The result was a triumph: 30,362,760 "ayes" against 4,294,654 "noes," and 872,296 papers spoiled.

Thanks to the aid of the generals and the constant action of the Gestapo, Hitler had become absolute master of Germany. No obstacle now remained on the road to National Socialism, the war, and the ultimate debacle.

Chapter 10
The New Organization of the Police

At the precise moment they could have overthrown the regime the soldiers consolidated it. By sacrificing his oldest partisan, Hitler had made the Army the official defender of the regime.

The German generals were unafraid of war, they only feared to be dragged into one with an insufficiently trained and numerically weak Army. The first rearmament measures announced by the Fuehrer at the beginning of 1934 had reassured them. They soon realized that Hitler, too, wanted a striking military revenge and the domination of Europe. They had chosen to be soldiers because they considered, as von Manstein has said, "the glory of war as something very great." From this time onward Hitler was assured of their support, provided he allowed them in exchange to resume their old status. By eliminating Roehm they believed, as General Reinecke remarked, that "the two pillars of the Third Reich would be the Party and the Army," and that both would be indissolubly bound to the success or failure of the other. It is true that the Wehrmacht owed its resurrection to the Nazi party, and that the Party for its part owed a portion of its prestige to the first military successes of the early years of the war. But by thinking to insure for themselves political control, to annex Hitler, and keep the Party under control, the soldiers made a false calculation. They had considered the role played by the Gestapo to be negligible. The powerful influence of Himmler, Heydrich, and their ally, Goering, was not clear to them. They had underestimated these silent bureaucrats and believed that the police services had worked for them. Now the real victors of the purge were Himmler and Heydrich, and the second pillar of the regime would be the Gestapo and not the Army. One day it would even be the sole foundation of the system. By the time the soldiers understood this, it was too late, for the die had been cast.

The conditions dictated by Blomberg for the secret agreement prior to June 30 are known. The main points were the assurance given by Hitler to leave the effective command of the Army to the soldiers, the promise of swift and grand-scale rearmament, and the guarantee that the Army would be the only body of the State responsible for the defense of the country and the only one authorized to carry weapons. The purge of June 30, by decapitating the S.A. and transforming it progressively into a simple organization of military preparation, seemed to confirm the execution of the clauses of this agreement.

The forces of the S.A., swollen after the accession to power to four million in 1934, swiftly decreased to become stabilized at a figure of a million and a half members.

With regard to the Supreme Command of the Army, it fell by right, according to the Weimar Constitution, to the President of the Reich, but Hitler had agreed to renounce effective command by agreeing that laws applicable to the Army could only be operative when signed both by the President and by the Minister of the Reichswehr, a measure made public in the *Voelkischer Beobachter* of August 5, 1934. It was subject to this condition that Blomberg had appended his signature to the law of August 1, making Hitler President of the Reich.

After the oath of fidelity sworn by the Reichswehr, Hitler sent a letter of thanks to Blomberg. "I shall always consider it my supreme duty to protect the existence and inviolability of the Army," he wrote. "I shall abide by the testament of the late Marshal and remain faithful to my will to make the Reichswehr the sole armed force of the nation."

On July 2 in an order of the day to the S.A. leaders Hitler said: "I demand from all the S.A. leaders unconditional loyalty. Furthermore I demand that they give proof of an unreserved loyalty and fidelity to the Army of the Reich."

Strong in these assurances, repeated during the following months in various speeches, articles, proclamations, and orders of the day, the soldiers paid no attention to the discreet measures which were being prepared to end their dream of political direction and autonomy.

The Gestapo had not only drawn up the technical details of the purge of June 30 and provided the lists, but it had also carried out murders in private houses and part of the executions. As Goering said at Nuremberg, "In any case it was the Gestapo who had been entrusted with the job. It was a question of action against the enemies of the State."

June 30 was the last outward manifestation of violence, or vestige of the revolutionary period—at least within Germany. This was the last time that the world was to see embarrassing personalities liquidated so brutally. In future the Gestapo would see that they disappeared more discreetly. In the course of this blood bath, it had burnished its halo of terror. "Everyone is terrified and yet everyone is certain that they will recommence if similar orders are given and if it proves necessary," said Himmler, speaking of the S.S.

The execution orders were nearly all signed by Himmler and Heydrich, not only for Berlin but for North Germany. Von Eberstein, at that time head of the S.S. Oberabschnict of the Center, had been summoned to Berlin by

Himmler a week before the purge and told to keep his S.S. men in a state of alert. On June 30 an S.D. agent arrived in Dresden, with an order prescribing the arrest in that city of twenty-eight persons, eight of whom were to be executed immediately. This order, signed by Heydrich, merely read: "By order of the Fuehrer and Reich Chancellor—is to be executed for high treason." These orders given in the name of an authority which had no power to give them and signed by an equally unauthorized official were scrupulously carried out. Admirable discipline!

During the events of June 30 Heydrich acquired a reputation for unequaled cruelty. His extraordinary determination made even the toughest old guard of the Party tremble. Frick, Minister of the Interior, a confirmed Nazi, declared to Gisevius in May 1935, "It is possible that as a result I shall be forced to admit Himmler into the Ministry, but in no case will the murderer Heydrich be admitted."

During the latter months of 1934 and the beginning of 1935 unknown killers murdered nearly 150 S.S. leaders. On the corpses was pinned a little card bearing the initials "R.R." (this meant *Rächer Roehm*, the avengers of Roehm). They were probably carried out by an underground group of S.A. who had remained faithful to their former chief, but apparently the Gestapo was never able to identify them.

Himmler had deserved a reward. On July 20 Hitler signed the following order: "In consideration of the eminent services rendered by the S.S., notably after the events of June 30, 1934, I raise the S.S. to the rank of an independent organization within the N.S.D.A.P. The Reichsfuehrer S.S. will in future in his quality as chief of staff be under the direct orders of the Commander in Chief of the S.A." The Commander in Chief of the S.A., of course, was Hitler himself.

The July 20 decree placed Himmler on a footing with Lutze and made the S.S. independent of the S.A. organization, of which it had previously been a detached section. Himmler now had to answer to Hitler alone.

It also had another effect: having become independent, Himmler could take any steps he judged useful within the S.S., for example to arm and create S.S. troops. Thus at the moment Hitler had given his pledge to Blomberg to make the Reichswehr the sole organization permitted to bear the arms of the nation, his promise had already been broken. The only unit of which the S.S. disposed until then had been the Leibstandarte Adolf Hitler, entrusted with the personal protection of the Fuehrer. After June 30 we find the creation and considerable development of the *Verfuegungstruppen* (infantry in readiness), which soon constituted Hitler's private army, and also the creation of the *Totenkopfe* regiments, the sinister Death's-Head units which ruled with unmitigated savagery for eleven years over concentration camps.

Himmler, master of the Gestapo, profited by his independence to complete the infiltration of S.S. into the administrative machinery. This technique was followed throughout Germany in the functions of police prefects of the German towns being entrusted to the S.S. leaders of those towns. The superintendent of police and of the S.S. could issue no police order on his own initiative. He was merely Himmler's personal representative; he had to confine himself to transmitting orders and to seeing that they were carried out.

The Army was alarmed by this development of the S.S., and clashes with the S.S. resulted. To reassure the soldiers Hitler ostensibly took their part. The moment had not yet come to show them the truth. The soldiers believed in his promises.

The two heads of the Gestapo, Himmler and Heydrich, prepared their weapons. As a first step the S.D., Heydrich's old service, was subjected to the most revolutionary transformations in the second half of 1934. Originally an internal security service of the S.S., it now became by a decree of June 9, 1934, the sole intelligence service of the Party, a timely move which had allowed it to play an important role in the Roehm purge. The S.D. was not, however, a state organization and in theory had no authority except within the organizations of the Party. But the latter were so numerous and regimented such a high percentage of the population that the field was already immense.

Heydrich had three thousand agents in the S.D. They had officially recognized offices, and in the small towns in particular their activity could not remain secret for long. The intelligence tasks they performed could, however, suffer from adverse publicity. Hate piled up against Himmler and Heydrich; after June 30 the murders bearing the signature "Avengers of Roehm" showed the need for creating a "parallel" secret network. It was in this spirit that Heydrich gave an impetus to the recruitment of "well-wishers."

From its very start the S.D. had employed stool pigeons who had been modestly baptized "well-wishers"—political sympathizers who adopted police spying from political conviction and personal taste. Before the accession to power the S.D. could not boast of more than thirty to fifty permanent agents and a similar number of well-wishers.

From the middle of 1934 the number of S.D. agents increased considerably and that of the well-wishers even more, until a final figure of over thirty thousand was reached. These camouflaged agents were recruited from every class of the community. Most of the university professors were kept under surveillance. The well-wishers recruited from among the pupils took down notes of the courses which, when forwarded to the S.D., allowed their political attitude to be assessed. At the end of the war women formed the majority of these informer networks. The well-wishers had been baptized *V. Maenner,* in other words "men of trust."

From July 1934 Heydrich through the S.D. carried out a considerable work of documentation. On the pretext of making a social survey, which would allow him to establish rules for a political education designed to convert those who still clung to the ancient ideologies to National Socialism, the S.D. made scientific studies of the operation and methods of the former sections of the community—Marxists, Jews, Freemasons, Liberal Republicans, religious and cultural groups among whom the Nazis thought an opposition might be reborn. Under cover of these ideological studies, the S.D. amassed important records which allowed it to keep potential opponents under surveillance and to bring down the ax in its ranks each time political necessity demanded the sacrifice of scapegoats.

In theory, therefore, the S.D. enjoyed a kind of monopoly of political intelligence. On the other hand, it had no executive power, the latter being exclusively retained by the Gestapo which alone had the right to carry out arrests, interrogations, or house searches, and also the right to place people in protective custody, to send them to concentration camps, etc. Nevertheless the Gestapo services never ceased carrying out their own intelligence work, while at the same time using information provided by the S.D.

Intelligence abroad, observation of the political activities of the *émigrés,* the preparations for aggression against foreign countries and the role of a Fifth Column, the exploitation of ideological warfare allowing allies and agents to be planted in the enemies' camp, gave rise to the second branch of the S.D.—S.D. Ausland, which was also called the "Foreign Secret Service." This service employed scarcely more than four hundred permanent members to recruit abroad paid auxiliaries and above all numerous well-wishers, who

were often unaware of the role they were being made to play. The remarkable
organization of the S.D. was not technically the work of Heydrich. The true
creators of the administrative organization of the S.D. were Oberfuehrer
Dr. Mehlhorn, who later distinguished himself in Poland in November 1939
by decreeing severe anti-Semitic measures, and Dr. Werner Best, later
Oberregierungsrat in the Berlin Gestapo, and then Reich Commissioner for
occupied Denmark. Dr. Best was a former judge who had entered the administration in 1933. His middle-class origin and legal education made him a
valuable asset, and Heydrich often used him for delicate missions, in particular to pacify high-ranking bureaucrats whom the methods of the Gestapo,
to which they were not accustomed, were still terrifying. He became one
of the official jurists of the Nazi party, publishing later a work entitled *Die
Deutsche Polizei*, a kind of breviary of the organization and functions of the
police services.

Dr. Mehlhorn was a Saxon lawyer with a talent for organization, and
was engaged by Dr. Best, whose main duties were to supervise the technical
administration of the services, materiel, the general budget of the S.D. and
its distribution. These two men perfected the system of "honorary agents,"
particularly distinguished well-wishers chosen from people best placed and
most competent in their professions. Thanks to them, valuable information
regularly reached the central services of the S.D., which could thus keep its
ear to the general trend of public opinion. On the materiel plane these two
men made the S.D. the most modern and best equipped intelligence service
of modern times. Mehlhorn perfected the filing system. The cards of most
important individuals were housed in a huge, tall, circular filing cabinet,
containing five thousand cards. A single operator could run this formidable
machine. Driven by an electric motor, the cabinet revolved and immediately
produced the card required by mere pressure on a button. Since then the
system of perforated cards has produced better results, but at that period this
type probably existed nowhere else.

As soon as his collaborators had completed their tasks, Heydrich eliminated them in order to take the credit for the instrument they had perfected.
Accused of "indiscretion," Mehlhorn, as a disciplinary measure, was sent on
a mission to the Far East and the United States. Dr. Best was transferred to
the Ministry of the Interior, where he was entrusted with the affairs of the
Security Police.

On their departure Heydrich had an opportunity of putting into practice certain of his own ideas in the way of intelligence. One of his most significant creations was the "Kitty Salon." Heydrich's depraved taste led him to frequent the dens and red light districts of Berlin. He had a predilection for brothels and loved to gossip at length with the inmates. He soon discovered in the course of these conversations that their clients often revealed all manner of confidences. Heydrich wanted to profit by this state of affairs and, at his orders, a comfortable hotel was rented through an intermediary and luxuriously appointed as a "cat house." With the aid of S.D. and Gestapo technicians the rooms and intimate corners of the bar bristled with microphones. Tape recorders were installed in the cellars of the building. Artur Nebe, an excellent criminologist and an early recruit to National Socialism, remembered that he had once belonged to the vice squad, and was therefore ordered to recruit the girls. They were selected not only for their charm and beauty but also for their intelligence, culture, knowledge of languages, and their "patriotism." Walter Schellenberg, who has related this curious story, maintains that because of their "patriotism" there was no lack of volunteers, not only from the demimonde but from the best society.

The house known as "Kitty Salon" was soon frequented by a select clientele, among them foreign diplomats, to whom well-intentioned friends did not fail to give the address. Important information was obtained in this manner. This form of eliciting information was sometimes preferable to the normal methods of Heydrich's services. The latter, proud of his creation, made frequent personal inspections of the "Kitty Salon"—but he insisted that the microphones be disconnected while he was there.

The period from the bloody triumph of 1934 to its consecration in 1936 was used mainly for reorganization and consolidation. Heydrich then truly created the vital cog-wheels which were to transform his services into the implacable machine which was to become notorious throughout the world. He forged not only the machinery of the Gestapo but also selected the men who were to be at the controls.

In 1934 a twenty-seven-year-old Nazi, previously living in Austria and only just arrived in Germany, entered the S.D. and was posted to the card index service. He was particularly talented, methodical, and hard working. Here was a born organizer, a man to watch. He was to have a brilliant career, was later transferred to the Gestapo, and was to become chief of the

service which would insure him worldwide notoriety. His name was Adolf
Eichmann.

Another youth also started in the S.D. in 1934. He was only twenty-three
and had entered the S.S. the same year. He had taken a law degree at Bonn
University, was passionately interested in history, with a predilection for the
Renaissance and its political consequences. Heydrich noticed his specialized
knowledge and also that he spoke several languages. This cultured young
man, Walter Schellenberg, was one day to become the Supreme Head of the
German espionage services.

Heydrich also assessed the old policemen who had retained their jobs.
One of them, Artur Nebe, was a valuable professional. Under the Weimar
Republic, as head of the Berlin criminal police, he had made a name for himself as a criminologist. He wrote an authoritative treatise on police techniques
and started a laboratory for criminal expertise, in which he perfected some
new ones. Nebe soon became a disciple of National Socialism, and Heydrich
swiftly appropriated him. Nebe also posted to special Gestapo laboratories
a number of specialists from the criminal police, thus forming a highly efficient team of experts.

Heydrich's second-in-command at the Gestapo, Heinrich Mueller, was
a former member of the Munich criminal police, where he had dealt heavy
blows to the Nazis during Hitler's years of struggle. He had applied for
admission to the Party but had been refused, a fact that did not prevent his
becoming an executive of the Gestapo.

Thus progressively, thanks to the various talents which Heydrich knew
how to exploit, the specialization took shape. One section dealt with
political opponents; another followed the activities of the former members
of philosophic or religious bodies and Freemasons; a third supervised the
strict application of the first anti-Semitic measures—its activity was to
be intensified from September 1935, when the Nuremberg racial laws were
decreed; another was in charge of protective custody arrests which allowed
internment in concentration camps; another section fought "saboteurs,"
who became more and more numerous, for the least sign of laziness or
a working error was qualified as "sabotage," and finally a group was organized for "special missions to come."

From 1935 it appears that the new regime already nursed aggressive plans
with regard to most of the neighboring countries. It was realized military

victories and territorial expansion alone could consolidate the regime and make the German people accept the dictatorship of the Party, by bringing them moral and material rewards.

On March 1, 1935, the Saar, given independence by the Versailles Treaty, was reattached to the Reich, after voting its return to the Fatherland by a crushing majority in the plebiscite of January 13 (90.36 percent of the votes). The agents of the S.D. and the Party played a considerable part in the preparation of the plebiscite. They had "spotted" the opponents and played their old "terror" card, spreading the report that those who voted against the return to the Reich would be considered as traitors to the Fatherland and punished accordingly.

From March 1 the Gestapo began to work in the Saar. It was through the Saar that, during the fourteen months which had elapsed since the accession to power, the refugees living abroad had smuggled their clandestine literature into Germany: from there it circulated undercover, preserving hope in the hearts of the Nazis' enemies. It was from the Saar, too, that the most audacious sorties were carried into the Reich to re-create underground organizations and to circulate the anti-Nazi orders of the day. The Gestapo arrested the opposition leaders in the Saar and posted provocative orders of the day inciting the population to lynch the "separatists" and the "French spies."

Events progressed fast in that month of March 1935. Hitler, who had left the League of Nations in October 1933, slamming the door behind him, allowed his intentions to be revealed. The clandestine rearmament which had begun by the creation of a secret air force was now to be carried out in broad daylight. On March 10 the creation of the Luftwaffe under Goering was announced. This decision shows that Hitler not only realized the importance of aviation in a future war (the air fleet rose from 36 aircraft in 1932 to 5,000 in 1936, and to more than 9,000 in 1939), but also that he did not trust the soldiers, since he gave a veteran Nazi the job of supervising the first stages of the rearmament.

The 1935 budget allotted 262 million marks for National Socialist activities abroad. From these funds twenty-nine million marks were earmarked for the agents of Himmler's foreign services, while in the same budget the Reichswehr had been kept at an "adequate figure." Blomberg protested, but Hitler replied that the Gestapo agents were in all circumstances the best cooperators with the German Army. He promised to create a liaison service between the Regular Army General Staff and his own staff. Poor consolation with which Blomberg had to be content.

On March 16 a new decree brought balm to these wounds: the military law promulgated that day restored conscription and fixed the composition of the new Army of the Reich at twelve corps and thirty-six divisions, in other words, half a million men. The press described the event as "the most important which had happened since 1919." "The shame of defeat has now been wiped out," wrote the newspapers. "This is the first great step taken in the liquidation of Versailles." Important ceremonies took place while France and her allies were content to protest through diplomatic channels.

While waiting for this Army to be capable of setting out to conquer Europe, the S.D. and the Gestapo began to organize the occupation of their prospective victims. They prepared, in particular, for the occupation of France, and while Hitler reaffirmed his peaceful intentions they fixed the physical details for the installation of their services in Paris.

One of the main principles of the Gestapo, which was to become characteristic of most of the official German organizations, was perfected at this period—secrecy.

Intelligence and to a lesser degree the police generally knew the importance of secrecy in their work. Never, however, had this care been pushed to such lengths as under Hitler, to the point where the precautions taken and the orders given sometimes reached the heights of absurdity. In these measures we can see the personal mark of Heydrich, his equivocal character, his dissimulation, and his unhealthy taste for mystery.

This care even extended to "precautionary" assassinations. Colonel Guenther Krappe, military attaché in Budapest, who negotiated preparations for attacking the U.S.S.R. in 1940 with the Hungarian Government, reported that one of his colleagues was killed by the Gestapo to prevent his committing some indiscretion in the future!

In the offices of the Gestapo and the S.D. placards were to be seen: "You must know nothing except what concerns your service. Whatever you learn you must keep to yourself." A Gestapo official was shot for having informed a brother official, belonging to another service of the Gestapo, about the work on which he was engaged.

Affairs could be "confidential," "highly confidential," "confidential for commanders alone," and "Reich Top Secret."

Shortly before the war a directive on these measures was issued, signed by Hitler himself. Dated May 23, 1939, it read:

1. No one must have any knowledge of secret affairs which are outside his own province.
2. No one is to be given more information than is strictly necessary for carrying out his task.
3. No one must be informed of the obligations incumbent upon him earlier than is necessary.
4. No one is to pass on to subordinate services more than is necessary of the orders essential to carrying out a task and before it becomes necessary.

These rigorous measures allowed a veil to be drawn over the horrors which were secretly perpetrated in the Nazi services. The responsible officials, particularly those of the concentration camps, could commit the most abominable atrocities with absolute impunity, in the safe assurance that they would never be exposed. Subordinates who might have denounced them dared not do so for fear of the sanctions which would apply to any person who revealed what happened in the services.

The reason given out for this secrecy was the "patriotic duty of silence," which prevented the divulging of anything that might tarnish the prestige of the country. In this way for twelve years those Germans whose consciences might have revolted against the actions of the Gestapo torturers or the treatment applied in the camps were silenced. They feared "helping enemy propaganda."

These directions applied in 1939 to the organization of the whole police force. A clear and constant separation was established between the services which received the information and those which exploited it. It was an empirical rule that the service who had drawn up the plan for an operation was never charged with its execution.

During the closing months of the war secrecy still played its part. When it became obvious to the military leaders that things were hopeless; when all of them were convinced that the war was irrevocably lost, Hitler forbade the utterance of a single hint about the real situation: "Whoever disobeys this order will be shot without regard to his rank or his prestige, and his family will be imprisoned." Thus, under the pretext of fighting against defeatism, the real German plight was concealed until the very end; hundreds of thousands of men continued to perish, the German cities were destroyed under the Allied bombing, until the country totally collapsed.

This work of organization, of selecting men, of determining principles and methods, of materiel installation, took two years and brought Himmler's services and public opinion to the necessary "temperature" to cross the next fence—the seizure of the entire German police. This annexation took place in two stages.

On February 10, 1936, Goering, as Premier of Prussia, signed the text subsequently known as the "fundamental law" of the Gestapo. This law stipulated that the duty of the Gestapo was to investigate throughout the entire State all forces hostile to the State: it further declared that the orders and the affairs of the Gestapo could not be subject to revision before administrative tribunals. We quote Article 1 of this document: "The Gestapo has the task of investigating all intentions which jeopardize the State and of combatting them, of assembling and exploiting the results of their inquiries, of informing the government, of keeping the authorities informed of facts of importance to them, and initiating action as required."

This article defined the true role of the Gestapo as embracing moral questions, unlike that of the normal police service. The Gestapo agents played the role of grand inquisitors, since their mission allowed them to inquire into all "intentions," being at the same time the "conscience" of the Nazi authorities since they had "to provide them with leads."

The ratification of this law, under the joint signatures of Goering and Frick, indicates that the Gestapo had authority to order measures valid throughout the whole State. One paragraph in this decree had been inspired by Heydrich. It pointed out that the Gestapo would "administer" the concentration camps. This was the result of skilful maneuvering on the part of Heydrich to insure for himself the control of the camps, from which he hoped to make a considerable profit. According to his usual tactics, Himmler did not oppose his subordinate, whose ambitions he feared. The text was passed, but Himmler arranged that its application should not be implemented. A specialized section of the S.S. was entrusted until the end with the administration of the camps.

The decree of June 17, 1936, consecrated Himmler's triumph by naming him Supreme Commander of all the German Police Forces. This insured the entire services of uniformed and civil police coming under his authority. In practice this centralization existed *de facto* since Himmler had insured control of all the political police forces in the spring of 1934, but it had only been vested in him without any document to confirm it. The decree of June 17 finally gave a legal status to the Gestapo. It withdrew the police forces from the jurisdiction of the *Laender*, and placed them under that of the Reich. The police officials, however, continued to be paid out of the budgets of the *Laender*, and it was not until March 19, 1937, that their salaries and generous expenses were offset against the Reich's budget.

From June 17 the Gestapo was attached for appearances' sake to the Ministry of the Interior, but Himmler became the same day official Minister of Police, autonomous and responsible solely to Hitler, since he took part in the cabinet meetings of the Reich each time police matters were discussed. This was the first stage toward becoming Minister of the Interior, a post which Himmler coveted and which he finally obtained in 1943.

The preamble to this decree of unification specified the National Socialist conception of the police. "Having become National Socialist, the police has the sole mission of safeguarding an order established by a parliamentary and constitutional regime. It is there: firstly to carry out the will of a single leader, and secondly to defend the German people against all attempts of destruction by enemies within and outside the country. To achieve this goal, the police needs to be all-powerful."

Grand master of the whole police system of the Reich, Himmler regrouped his services and divided them into two branches: the ORPO (*Ordnungspolizei*), ordinary police, and the SIPO (*Sicherheitspolizei*), the Security Police, including the plain-clothes men. This strongly unified, centralized, militarized, and Nazified police force was entrusted to men whom Himmler had put to the test during the period of "running in."

His first order, signed June 25, a week after taking over his duties, confirmed these good servants of the Nazi order in their functions and extended them.

The ORPO was given to S.S. Obergruppenfuehrer (General) Daluege. It comprised the *Schutzpolizei*, or SCHUPO, the urban police corresponding to our constables; the *Verwaltungspolizei*, or administrative police, the police of the waterways; the coastal police; the fire service; the passive defense and its technical auxiliary police.

The SIPO was entrusted to Heydrich. This "security police" ensured the smooth functioning of the police machine. In actual fact it comprised the Gestapo, the State Secret Police, and the KRIPO (*Kriminalpolizei*).

A work published the following year in Munich specified that the SIPO dealt with enemies of the State, and that the following persons must be considered as aggressors:

"No. 1. Individuals who, as a result of physical or moral degeneracy, are separated from the community and who in their own particular interest violate the measures taken to preserve the general interest. Against these malefactors the criminal police will act.

"No. 2. Individuals who, as emissaries of political enemies of the National Socialist German people, want to destroy national unity and annihilate the power of the State. Against these aggressors the Gestapo will fight untiringly."

In future the political and the criminal police were to work together for the greater glory of Himmler and the prosperity of the Nazi machine. Heydrich entrusted the direction of the Gestapo to his second in command, Heinrich Mueller, who had been the virtual chief since 1935, and the leadership of the KRIPO to the veteran technician, Artur Nebe, who thus reverted to his original duties.

As for the S.D., Heydrich retained the leadership and became head both of the SIPO and the S.D., the latter service, a Party organization, still retaining its independence of the State bodies.

The soldiers did not appear to react against this new progress of the Party within the State. Doubtless the importance of this regrouping escaped their notice. They were soon to have an opportunity of realizing its efficiency.

PART THREE

**THE GESTAPO PREPARES FOR THE INVASION
1936–39**

Chapter 11
The Gestapo Tackles the Army

The reason why the Army had paid so little attention to Himmler's reinforcement of the police machine in June 1936 was because it was too busy enjoying the first fruits of revenge.

Three months earlier, on March 7, 1936, Hitler had denounced the Locarno Treaty and reoccupied the demilitarized zone of the Rhineland. At the very moment diplomatic notes were being handed to the ambassadors of France, Great Britain, Italy, and to the Belgian *chargé d'affaires*, German troops were marching down the avenues of Coblenz. About twenty thousand men crossed the Rhine that spring morning. To the cheers of the public, they occupied the old Rhenish garrisons which had not seen a German regiment since 1918. These "symbolic detachments," as von Neurath called them, amounted to thirteen battalions of infantry and thirteen batteries of artillery. The reaction in Paris and London was one of surprise. There was talk of counteraction by sending troops to reoccupy Saarbrucken, but the soldiers opposed it. General Gamelin would only agree to intervene if a general mobilization was carried out beforehand. The West was content to make diplomatic protests. The German troops entering the Rhineland had been given strict orders to retire should any French military action occur, however slight it might be. A setback of this nature, so easy to stage, would have dealt a serious blow to Hitler's prestige and must be recorded on the list of lost opportunities.

From 1936 onward Germany took the road toward war. Her economic and financial arrangements had no other object than to steer Germany toward a war economy. That year saw the start of scientific work and research into substitute products, the famous ersatz which provided material for our humorists and amused the French, who did not suspect that they would be obliged to do the same in the near future. On May 12, 1936, Goering declared, "If we have a war tomorrow we shall have to use synthetic products. This being the case, we must be ready to create the preliminary conditions in peacetime." And on May 27 he added, "All measures have to be considered from the point of view of the certainty of a war."

In the autumn the second four-year plan was announced, and Goering was entrusted with its execution. He was to procure for Germany the foreign currency she urgently needed for armaments. Industry received energetic directives to increase productivity. A new concern came into being: the Hermann Goering Works, a research institute with a capital which increased to four hundred million marks. Ordered to exploit poor-grade ores, it was to become a gigantic industrial nexus—it finally employed 700,000 workers, the Iron ore and coal trust being directed solely toward war production.

Two directorates of the Ministry of Economics came under military control: General von Loeb became responsible for raw materials and General von Hanneken for industrial production.

These measures were not unwelcome to the soldiers, who sensed the probability of a return to their old supremacy. This blinded them to the perfecting of Himmler's services and kept them from paying the slightest attention to the people who spun their webs in the gloomy offices of the Prinz Albrechtstrasse. The new head of the Gestapo, Heinrich Mueller, with the meticulous care of the bureaucrat, prepared the taming of the Army by the Party.

Despite his gestures to the contrary, Hitler had never been able to shed his distrust of the officers. This had originated in the inferiority complex of an ex-corporal, whom a long-conditioned reflex forced to stand to attention as soon as he found himself in the presence of an officer. He finally became accustomed to these colonels and generals with whom he rubbed shoulders and who now approached him as petitioners. He always looked upon them, however, as strangers.

He referred to those who wanted to assume the responsibilities of the "old Germany" and had not succeeded with contemptuous mistrust as the *Die Oberschicht* (the upper crust). Possibly he also nursed the rancor of the former foot slogger for these generals who had often never seen any fighting except from miles behind the lines, and who had treated the men whose lives were in their hands as cannon fodder. On this point he had been influenced by the theories of Roehm on the need for "popularizing" the Army.

His associates felt the same mistrust. He easily persuaded himself of the need for placing the Army under iron control to avoid the risk of seeing it rebel against him. For he was under no illusion as to the "conversion" of the Army to National Socialism: "My Army," he said, "is reactionary, my Navy Christian, and my Air Force National Socialist." The Luftwaffe had been fashioned by Goering with the aid of new cadres provided by the Party, but the Army remained deeply monarchist and did not hide the fact when it celebrated the Emperor's birthday. Since Hitler was convinced that his military genius was superior to all the techniques taught in the academies and military schools, it appeared to him essential that he should control the Army to impose his strategic concepts on a timorous general staff.

The grand masters of the Gestapo, Himmler and Heydrich, encouraged him to deliver the *coup de grâce* to their only remaining opponent. In their view their triumph would not be complete until they had succeeded in decapitating the General Staff of the Army. It was with this goal in mind that Himmler, in 1935, had sown the seeds of a well-designed scheme. It aimed at the two highest figures responsible for the German Army, Field Marshal von Blomberg and General von Fritsch. To destroy these two the Gestapo chose to dishonor them.

The man whom Heydrich appointed to carry out the plan of operation was the Gestapo leader Mueller. A bureaucrat to the fingertips, he was entirely wrapped up in red tape and statistics. He was only at home in a world of notes, memos, and regulations. His concern in life was "advancement"—his own. That his background was made up of denouncements, anonymous letters, medieval tortures, and secret executions mattered little to him. These horrors arrived in his office reduced to a state of reports or notes, transformed into administrative fodder.

Heinrich Mueller was a Bavarian with the square head of a peasant. His short stature, stocky, rather heavy appearance, his clumsy loping gait betrayed his peasant origin. Not overintelligent, but extraordinarily stubborn and self-opinionated, he had escaped from his laborer's fate by working hard at school with an ambition to become a bureaucrat, a situation which, in his milieu, appeared particularly enviable, since there was a pension attached to it. He managed to enter the Munich State Police. Here Himmler appreciated his qualities of blind discipline and professional competence. Mueller, like all the officials of the political police, had worked against the Nazis until 1933. Himmler did not hold this against him, convinced that he would display the same zeal in the service of his new masters. Mueller strove to live down his past and above all to overcome the hostility which certain influential members of the Party continued to show toward him—but his admission to the Party was obstinately refused for six years, and he did not become a member until 1939. Thus paradoxically, the regime's main instrument of domination, the Gestapo, was directed by a man whose political orthodoxy did not seem sufficient to entitle him to call himself a Nazi. In actual fact this ostracism had two completely different causes: the hostility of rivals and the deliberate policy of his superiors, who thought that Mueller would make ever greater efforts to overcome resistance.

These calculations proved correct, and Mueller made it a point of honor to get himself pardoned. It is equally true to say that he had been easily and sincerely converted to the Nazi dogmas. He was neither an intellectual nor a sentimentalist. Beneath a very protruding forehead his face was hard, dry, and expressionless, slashed by a pair of cold, thin lips. His small brown eyes bestowed on an interlocutor a piercing look, which his heavy eyelids often veiled. He still shaved his head in the old fashion, keeping only a few short hairs on top and on the forehead. His hands, like his face, were the hands of a peasant—square, broad, and massive, with slightly spatulate fingers. His enemies insisted that he had the hands of a strangler.

Mueller devoted himself to a veritable cult of force. This explains his docility to the orders of his masters, and the excessive zeal to be found in many of his initiatives. The corollary of this cult was the hatred he nursed for anything that might symbolize wit and intelligence. He once remarked to Schellenberg that the intellectuals should be sent down a coal mine and blown up.

Like all late converts, Mueller was always afraid of being surpassed or of being found weak. This state of mind forced him to keep up a constant competition with the S.D., which he hated, suspecting this service of being at the root of the difficulties which the Party put in his way. Professionally the S.D. was a rival service, which Mueller despised, because at the outset it was composed solely of amateurs whom he himself, an old professional of the political police, outclassed without difficulty.

His competence earned him Himmler's esteem. He trusted him until the very end. This high protection allowed Mueller to make a career and, thanks to the transformation of the Gestapo, to conserve a privileged and astonishingly independent position in the bosom of this ensemble.

To get into Heydrich's good graces he carried out the meanest tasks, spying on his own colleagues and helping in the liquidation of those who had offended. He was a party to all the machinations staged by Himmler. He was entrusted with most of the "delicate" missions. These tasks needed a man without scruples. His first brilliant coup and undoubtedly his masterpiece was the Blomberg-Fritsch affair.

In the spring of 1933 the command of the German armies was in the hands of three men: General von Blomberg, Minister of War; General von Fritsch, Commander in Chief of the Army, and General Beck, the General Chief of Staff. These three men were traditionalist generals, loved and respected by the whole German Army, although Blomberg was sometimes harshly criticized for having compromised with the Nazis. He had been one of the first to display sympathy for the Nazi Movement. In 1931 when the parties of the Center and the Right still resisted the Nazi assault, he had met Hitler and had not concealed the admiration this man had inspired in him. Blomberg at the time was commander of the 1st military region in East Prussia, and his G.S.O. 1 was Colonel von Reichenau. The latter's uncle, the former Ambassador von Reichenau, was a fervent admirer of Hitler, and the uncle's political convictions had found favor with the nephew. Blomberg was intelligent but unstable and very easily influenced. At the period when a collaboration had been established between the Reichswehr and the Red Army, he admitted that he himself had almost become a Bolshevik. Influenced by Reichenau, he just as easily became a Nazi. As Minister of War he created an atmosphere for the purpose of debating questions of interest to the Wehrmacht with the State and the Party: this office caused him grave difficulties with the General Staff, which reproached him for being too accommodating to the Party.

Blomberg played a very important part in the military reoccupation of the Rhineland. He drew up the plans for remilitarization in close collaboration with the Party leaders. As a reward Hitler appointed him Field Marshal when the troops entered the Rhineland. This appointment was a reward for the servility Blomberg had shown during the Roehm purge by acquiescing to the murder of his comrades, Generals von Schleicher and von Bredow, and then swearing the oath of fidelity to Hitler.

Despite everything, however, Blomberg retained a certain prestige with some of the soldiers. At Nuremberg the Luftwaffe General Milch said,

"Blomberg was capable of resisting and often did so. Hitler respected him and listened to his advice. He was the only soldier with sufficient intelligence to reconcile military and political questions." It is true that this opinion is attenuated by the verdict given von Rundstedt who said, "Blomberg has always been a stranger among us. He sailed in other spheres. He was of the Steiner School, a bit of a theosophist, etc., and to be perfectly frank no one liked him very much." The nickname which Blomberg had been given by his enemies was "the pinchbeck lion."

The elimination of Blomberg does not seem to have been caused by personal motives but by reasons of principle. The whole of Germany had been subjected to the Fuehrerprinzip. Now this principle was incompatible with certain traditions of the Staff. For example, Field Marshal von Manstein recounted that "in the old Army the chief of staff, holding a different opinion to that of his superior, could express his opinion, while being obliged, of course, to carry out any orders received." Field Marshal Kesselring indicated that the "co-responsibility of the Chiefs of the General Staff accepted in the old days fell into disuse as being incompatible with the Fuehrerprinzip."

Hitler could not bear his orders being discussed, or even that different suggestions should be put forward; he may have feared (and Himmler managed to persuade him of this) lest the soldiers, terrified by his too audacious plans, should secretly foment a *coup d'état* against the regime, if necessary with foreign aid. There was even a rumor current of secret contacts with General Gamelin.

On June 24, 1937, Blomberg had drawn up a report on the international situation which provided arguments for the opponents of the aggressive policy prepared by Hitler: "The general political situation," he wrote, "justifies the supposition that Germany has no need to envisage an attack from any side whatsoever. The reason for this, apart from the absence of aggressive desires on the part of nearly all the nations, particularly the Western powers, is the lack of preparedness for war in the numerous states, and in Russia in particular."

Hitler had not relished these conclusions which contradicted his ideas. He was psychologically ready to accept the plot which would leave Himmler and the Gestapo masters of the field. It was carried out with exceptional cynicism, and was the first illustration of the new technique of humiliation or petty persecution, less spectacular than the former violent and bloody methods, but just as effective in the liquidation of embarrassing opponents.

Things started one day in January 1938. On January 12 the German newspapers announced that Field Marshal von Blomberg, Minister of War, had married Fräulein Erna Gruhn in Berlin. The witnesses to the marriage, which took place in private, were Adolf Hitler and Hermann Goering. Oddly enough, the press published no photographs and no comment, which was surprising in view of the bridegroom's rank. The wedding had been celebrated very discreetly. There was no religious ceremony, not unusual at a period when the churches were the object of very violent attacks from the Party.

It was known that the Marshal, a widower, was the father of grown-up children. One of his daughters had married General Keitel's son. On the other hand, practically nothing was known of the new bride, of whom it was merely reported that she was of very modest origin. This was perfectly in accord with the Socialist propaganda of the new regime. The Berlin shopgirls were delighted with the idea of the shepherdess marrying Prince Charming, even if the latter was old enough to be her father.

A strange shepherdess, however, whose occupation seemed to have been far from pastoral. Less than a week after the ceremony ugly rumors about the young Frau Marshallin, spread in official circles and therefore difficult to refute (thanks to the strange circumstances which had surrounded the wedding), began to circulate. The ceremony had taken place in "indecent" haste and in excessive privacy. It was maintained that the bride has been excused from producing the innumerable official documents required, particularly the police record and the status of the great-grandparents. And finally, the married couple had left immediately on their honeymoon for an unknown destination.

A few days after the marriage the press published an agency photograph. A reporter had surprised the couple walking in the Leipzig Zoo, and had taken a snap of them outside the big monkey cage. This photo arrived on the desk of Count Helldorf, the Berlin prefect of police. Informed of the rumors on the Field Marshal's new wife, he ordered a discreet inquiry on January 20, and the dossier which he was given contained such disturbing details that he could hardly believe his eyes.

According to this dossier, Erna Gruhn was born in 1914 at Neukoelln, a working class district of Berlin, and although she was hardly twenty-four her past had been singularly eventful. Her mother ran a very suspect massage salon in the Elizabethstrasse. "Mother" Gruhn, watched by the police, had been convicted twice. Young Erna, a rather pretty girl, had followed her mother's example. She prostituted herself and had already been arrested several times by the vice squads of seven German towns. She had also been in trouble with the law in 1933 after the Nazis seized power. A traffic in pornographic photos had been discovered, and after an inquiry held by the "Central Office for the Prevention of Licentious Pictures and Writings" she had been identified and arrested as having posed for these photographs. At the time she was only nineteen, but declared in her defense that, abandoned by her lover and finding herself without resources, she had to accept this "work" because it paid sixty marks.

Helldorf compared one of these photographs, preserved in the records, with the one the press had just published. There was no possible doubt: the young woman smiling in front of the monkey cage was the same as the one who had posed for these obscene photographs. And finally the identity department of the Berlin police was in possession of her measurements and fingerprints, which had been taken during a case of robbery of which she had been accused.

The prefect of police, Helldorf, somewhat disturbed by these discoveries, notified General Keitel, Blomberg's closest collaborator and friend— thus committing a grave infraction of the rules of secrecy, a lapse which Himmler would not fail to seize upon if he learned of it. Helldorf hoped that Keitel would warn Blomberg of the danger which threatened him. But Keitel was evasive and seemed annoyed at having received such a confidence. He cleared himself by sending Helldorf and his dossier to, of all people, Goering, whose ambition, as everyone knew, was to be the future Minister of War.

Goering received these revelations rather nervously. He seemed genuinely distressed and confessed to Helldorf that Blomberg had warned both himself and the Fuehrer that his fiancée had had a "past." Naturally neither he nor Hitler had imagined that this past could be so weighty, and Hitler had not opposed the marriage. Goering promised Helldorf that he would take the necessary steps.

This interview took place on January 22. Hitler had left Berlin to visit Munich. Next day Goering, Himmler, and Heydrich met for what amounted to a council of war at Goering's. The "alliance" which had permitted the liquidation of Roehm had now been convened.

On January 24 Hitler returned, and Goering hastened to announce the news. According to his custom, Hitler wept and then decided that the marriage must immediately be annulled. On the advice of Goering, he ordered Blomberg to report to the Chancellery wearing his uniform. Always the "devoted slave," Goering took it upon himself to notify Blomberg of his Fuehrer's decisions. He feared that Hitler would consider the matter closed after the divorce and that everything would have to start again. Thus he hurried to Blomberg and, as he had done at the time of the Roehm purge, slightly "enlarged" his own mission and modified the Fuehrer's directives.

"You must go," he said to Blomberg, "you must go into hiding abroad." Dumfounded by these revelations and the threat of scandal, the Field Marshal, who had grown very attached to this young, charming woman, eagerly agreed to Goering's suggestions. He declared that he was ready to go on a long journey, a solution which was even more tempting, since Goering had handed him a substantial viaticum in foreign currency. Hitler decreed that he was forbidden to set foot on German soil for a year, and at the end of January the Field Marshal and his wife left for Rome and Capri.

In higher army circles the news gradually spread. How had such a marriage ever taken place? How had the police, which must have known the bride's past, allowed it to take place? How could Hitler have acted as a witness? Minister-Marshals, officers of the old school, had not been accustomed to haunting working-class districts or places frequented by girls of Erna's type, and even less to look for wives there. Who had introduced to the old, ingenuous soldier a young and pretty whore, undoubtedly delighted by this gift from heaven?

Himmler, Heydrich, and Mueller could have answered these questions. They could have explained why they had not revealed Erna Gruhn's past, which they had long since known. How could they have ignored it, since the "Central Office for the Prevention of Licentious Pictures and Writings," which had arrested Erna in 1933, came under the orders of their faithful collaborator and friend, Artur Nebe, and since the squad which had taken her fingerprints was also his department. And even had they forgotten—a highly unlikely eventuality—to make the traditional investigation of the bride on the announcement of the marriage, von Blomberg himself would have had to notify them. In any event the Field Marshal had had some scruples about marrying Erna after discovering a few details of her past. For some incomprehensible reason he confided in Goering. "Can I marry a young woman of low extraction?" he asked. Fat Hermann had reassured him. "It will be a very good marriage for Party propaganda," he replied. "Marry your 'working girl' without fear." Encouraged by this, the Marshal returned a few days later. A former lover had started to badger his bride. He wanted Hermann to intervene discreetly with the police to get rid of the nuisance. The police did in fact intervene, but they "forgot" to inform the Marshal that Erna's former lover was a well-known ponce and that to insure his discretion they had sent him to South America, after generously lining his pocketbook and threatening him with a particularly unpleasant end should he have the imprudence to return to Germany.

Precautions had therefore been taken so that the good Marshal could remarry with a tranquil mind. All this discretion had become pointless, since by some miracle Helldorf had discovered the fly in the ointment and revealed the scandal prematurely. But this lamentable affair would still allow of a full-scale operation, a *coup d'état* in the new style of the "gentlemen" of the Prinz Albrechtstrasse.

With Blomberg safely on his way to Italy, the way lay open to Goering, who already saw himself Minister of War, and for Himmler, who hoped to profit by the occasion to enter the great family of the generals. His S.S. regiments represented a quarter of the Wehrmacht, but there was still one more obstacle to overcome. This obstacle was the artillery general, Werner von Fritsch, Commander in Chief of the Army, second in the hierarchy after Blomberg. In addition, von Fritsch was very popular in the Army. He had been appointed Colonel General by Hitler, and had received from the Fuehrer's hands the gold badge of the Party, a very much coveted distinction. Hitler mentioned his name as Blomberg's replacement, but Goering and Himmler brought up an incident which had been quashed in 1935 and introduced him to the dossier of another sordid story.

In 1935 the Gestapo had discovered an excellent means of extending its activities. On the pretext that homosexuality was rife in the ranks of the Hitler Movement (there had been several scandals), it had arrogated to itself a monopoly of dealing with these moral delinquencies and investigated wherever it pleased. In the "search for truth" it did not hesitate to release convicted prisoners and to extract from them the names of their former "accomplices."

In this way it laid hands one day on a certain blackmailer of a particular type. Hans Schmidt, himself a notorious male prostitute, had made a specialty of spying on rich homosexuals for purposes of blackmail. He occasionally managed to surprise them in the act. Pretending to be a policeman and under the threat of prosecution, he extorted large sums of money from them.

Schmidt was taken from the central prison where he was serving a sentence (he had had several convictions) and interrogated at length. Complacently he spoke of his clients and his victims. He enumerated all those he had known—high officials, doctors, lawyers, tradesmen, industrialists, artists—and among them he quoted a certain von Fritsch from whom he had extorted money at the end of 1935. One winter evening, he confessed, he had noticed at the Wannsee railway station a well-dressed gentleman who had been "picked up" by a colleague, a male prostitute known to the police.

The person accosted looked like a former officer—fur jacket, green hat, silver-topped cane, and monocle. Schmidt had followed the two men, and after a short and sordid interview on an empty building site behind the station had accosted the old gentleman. The usual scene took place. Police … the threat of scandal and … the pay-off. As the man had little money in his notecase, Schmidt had accompanied him home to a flat in Lichtefelde-Est. For several weeks Schmidt had blackmailed him, even forcing him to draw money from his bank. The old gentleman was called von Frisch or Fritsch.

The Gestapo immediately seized upon this unhoped-for opportunity. If the old gentleman was von Fritsch, the Commander in Chief, the well-known monarchist, what a marvelous motive for liquidating him! Hitler, on being consulted, refused his consent, ordered the destruction of the Schmidt interrogation, and silence on all these *Schweinereien*.

Notwithstanding this, in January 1938 the complete dossier miraculously reappeared in the hands of Heydrich. To be accurate, the dossier shown to Hitler had only the appearance of a full dossier, and a professional policeman would have noticed certain significant "holes" in it. But Hitler was a layman in such matters. For example, the address of von Fritsch at the period of the misdemeanors did not appear to have been verified. There was no proof that he had ever lived at Lichterfelde-Est, or had a flat there. There were no details of the withdrawals from von Fritsch's bank account at the end of 1935 and the beginning of 1936. It had not even been verified whether he had had an account in a bank near the Lichterfelde-Est station, to which Schmidt pretended he had accompanied him. In short the story was singularly lacking in corroboration.

An investigation had, however, been carried out by Chief Inspector Meisinger, a former Munich detective who had come to the Gestapo with Mueller. Meisinger, one of the protagonists of the June 30, 1934, purge, was a personal friend and confidant of Mueller, who entrusted him with the most shady tasks. As a reward he had been given the special office dealing with expropriated Jewish property, which allowed him a substantial rake-off. He was later sent on a mission to Japan, in particular to check up on the activities in Tokyo of the remarkable double agent, Richard Sorge, a *Frankfurter Zeitung* reporter who had become a Gestapo and S.D. agent.

Heydrich, therefore, exhumed the dossier compiled by Meisinger three years earlier, and this time Hitler did not reject the accusing pages. He did not even ask why they had not been destroyed according to his orders, and summoned Fritsch to the Chancellery. Without suspecting for a moment the accusation which hung over his head, the General reported. When Hitler questioned him he protested his innocence with the greatest indignation. An incredible scene ensued. Hitler suddenly opened the door to allow Schmidt to enter, and there in the office of Reich Chancellor, the head of State, the all-powerful Fuehrer, confronted the Commander in Chief of the Army with an ex-convict and pederast. Schmidt looked at von Fritsch and merely said, "That's him."

The General was thunderstruck. This incredible scene left him speechless. He could only continue his denials, dumbfounded by the appalling plot of which he was the victim. Impotent rage, stupefaction, and contempt slowed down his reflexes. Hitler watched him blushing and turning pale in turn. Convinced of his guilt, he demanded his resignation. But von Fritsch pulled himself together. He refused, repeating that he was innocent and demanding a court-martial. This stormy interview took place on January 24, 1938. On the 27th von Fritsch was given leave, for "reasons of health," but this decision was not published until February 4. In the meantime Goering, who had at first been violently opposed to the inquiry, had finally given the order to the Gestapo. We see, therefore, a new paradox: the Commander in Chief of yesterday being convoked by Heydrich's men and, an even more extraordinary fact, obeying this convocation.

Despite the precautions taken to throw a veil of secrecy around this operation until its completion, the news spread in the Army. Coming after the Blomberg affair, of which no precise details were as yet known, it caused anxiety. Two scandals in such quick succession were enough to cause surprise. The soldiers sensed a plot and thought that the Army's prestige would be dealt a serious blow. There were many questions. For a long time homosexuality had had many addicts in the German Army. At the beginning of the century it had become the fashion, since the Emperor himself (who was not "queer") liked to surround himself with those whom he called "the Byzantines," because he appreciated their artistic gifts. They numbered in their ranks ambassadors, a prince, several generals, and the Emperor's own cabinet chief, Count Huelsen-Haeseler, who collapsed with a heart attack in 1906 when dancing on the table dressed as a female ballet dancer. The Army had not forgotten the scandal which in 1907 had brought about the sentencing and exile of Prince Philip Eulenberg for his uproarious "affair" with the cuirassier, Kuno von Moltke.

Von Fritsch had never laid himself open to criticism. His morals appeared pure, but one never knew. … These vague doubts and fears probably weighed on the soldiers as much as the fear of openly crossing swords with Gestapo, whom no one doubted was pulling the strings in this affair. This hesitation lasted several days.

A brutal decision put an end to it: on February 4 the veil was lifted on the Fuehrer's secret instructions. In a broadcast speech Hitler announced the departure of Blomberg from the Ministry of War. He had been retired, but the reason for his departure was not given. As regards the Commander in Chief of the Land Forces, von Fritsch, he had "asked to be relieved of his command for health reasons." Hitler announced to the German people that he had decided to abolish the Ministry of War and to place the Army, of which he was already Supreme Commander as President, directly under his control. The pledge, taken by him in 1934, to submit all plans concerning the Army to the approval of the Ministry of War now became null and void.

To replace von Fritsch, it would have been normal to appoint General Beck. But the latter had been injudicious enough in 1934 to make a speech which had offended Hitler. "Nothing would be more dangerous," he said, apropos of the desired resurrection of the Army, "than to abandon oneself to spontaneous inspirations, insufficiently matured, however opportune and however brilliant they might appear." It was common knowledge that Hitler relied on his "brilliant intuitions." The phrase had rankled, and it cost Beck his post. Nor was von Reichenau appointed, although he was the most Nazi of all the generals, because Hitler would not have an officer politician at any price. As Goering said, "The generals of the Third Reich had no right whatsoever to engage in any political activity." Von Brauchitsch, until then commander of the East Prussian military zone, replaced von Fritsch. And finally Hitler founded a new organization to crown all the services of the General Staff, the Oberkommando der Wehrmacht, the O.K.W. or High Command of the Armed Forces, and placed at its head General Keitel. The latter was well known for his docility. It had earned him the nickname in the Army "Lakai-tel" (laquaistel, the lackey).

Thirteen other generals were relieved of their commands, forty-four others transferred or retired, and a number of high-ranking officers met with the same fate. Those who had the misfortune to displease, or whom the Gestapo had designated as reactionaries, monarchists, or too religious, were the victims. Among the beneficiaries of this bloodless revolution was General Guderian, the mechanized warfare expert, appointed commander of the 16th Korps, the only armored corps existing at the time.

The soldiers were not the only ones affected. Their friends, whose reactions were feared, had not been spared. Baron von Neurath, Minister for Foreign Affairs, was axed and replaced by a confirmed Nazi, Joachim von Ribbentrop. Three ambassadors, Hassell in Rome, von Papen in Vienna, and von Dirksen in Tokyo, were replaced. Goering, who saw the coveted War Ministry eluding his grasp, received a consolation prize. He was appointed *Generalfeldmarschall.* In this way he became the highest German military dignitary. And finally Dr. Schacht, who had resigned from the Ministry of Economics in November 1937, was replaced by Funk. It was common knowledge in Germany that Funk was a homosexual.

Himmler and Heydrich took pains not to let their part in the plot be unmasked. Nevertheless the soldiers still had some support. Soon they were able to reconstruct the point of departure of the story: everything rested on a similarity of names. The real culprit was a retired cavalry captain, von Frisch, without a *t.* His apartment was discovered without difficulty in Lichterfelde-Est, where he had lived for ten years. But the Captain was bedridden and seriously ill. His housekeeper said that men from the Gestapo had arrived on January 15, nine days before the confrontation of the blackmailer Schmidt with General von Fritsch.

The following day soldiers were sent to take the invalid into safe custody, but the Gestapo had removed him the night before. He died a few days later. The investigators, helped by an official from the Ministry of Justice, learned that von Frisch's bank account, which recorded the withdrawals made at the dates given by Schmidt, had been seized together with all the correspondence on January 15 by the Gestapo. At the same time, a sergeant major, General von Fritsch's former orderly, had been kidnaped from a barracks in Furstenwald. They had tried to extort ambiguous statements from him. The General's housekeeper, arrested in the provinces where she was on holiday, was "grilled" in the same manner. Finally it was learned that on January 24, before going to the Chancellery, Schmidt had been taken to Goering's house, where Himmler and Goering himself had explained that unless he "recognized" the General with whom the Fuehrer would confront him later, he might as well prepare himself for an extremely disagreeable death.

The generals, therefore, possessed a bundle of damning proofs that the conspiracy had been contrived by the Gestapo. Would they demand from Hitler reparation for General von Fritsch and ruthless sanctions against the Gestapo leaders? How could Hitler, when threatened with an exposure of these practices, be able to refuse to render justice? But the generals' protest was merely academic. They knew that they were lost in the political desert which life in Germany had become. They were, however, given the "reparations" they requested. The court-martial demanded by von Fritsch was convened. Its composition was a masterpiece of cynicism: von Brauchitsch, von Fritsch's successor, Raeder, the new head of the Navy, the two main beneficiaries of the purge, two military judges, and, as president of this strange tribunal, Field Marshal Goering himself, the master artisan of the plot.

The court-martial sat on March 10. It was short-lived. At midday an aide-de-camp brought an order from Hitler adjourning the court and summoning Goering, Brauchitsch, and Raeder to the Chancellery.

What lay behind this *coup de théâtre*? The reply was given thirty-six hours later. On March 12 German troops crossed the Austrian frontier. That evening Hitler was in Linz, and the following day in Vienna. The Wehrmacht advanced to thunderous applause. How could they complain of the Gestapo methods? How could they demand the rehabilitation of von Fritsch?

On March 17, however, the court-martial reconvened and proceeded to interrogate the blackmailer Schmidt. Goering pressed him with questions and adjured him to tell the "truth" by promising him his life. Then, according to a script carefully composed in advance, Schmidt confessed that he had been mistaken. He had at first thought that it was the Commander in Chief von Fritsch, then on discovering his mistake he had not dared to admit it for fear of reprisals. The comedy was over. The court-martial found that von Fritsch had been the victim of a regrettable series of misunderstandings and acquitted him. Nobody had demanded the appearance of Himmler and Heydrich. No one had dreamed for a moment of subpoenaing them. As for Schmidt, although Goering had given him his word of honor before the court that he would go unscathed, the Gestapo shot him a few days later. Like van de Lubbe, he had played his part and had to disappear.

Although von Fritsch had been "rehabilitated," he had not been called back to active service. In his premature retirement he may perhaps have meditated on the conversation he had had with Ludendorff at the end of 1937. Fritsch had maintained that, like his superior, Blomberg, he now had the Fuehrer's confidence. Ludendorff replied, "Then it won't be long before he betrays you." On December 22, 1937, Blomberg and Fritsch had followed Ludendorff's bier without thinking that his predictions would be so rapidly realized.

Von Fritsch's end was rather strange. During the violation of Poland in September 1939, his own plan of operations was adopted. Paradoxically he was forced to follow the operations from his retirement. He could not submit to this and followed his old artillery regiment, of which he still remained honorary colonel, in a staff car. He was killed before Warsaw. Many people were convinced that he had been murdered by the Gestapo. His obsequies were magnificent. It is far more easy to render justice to the dead than to the living.

Chapter 12
The Gestapo Installs Itself in Europe

The humiliation inflicted on the generals in February 1938 was soon forgotten. The easy victory of the entry into Austria on March 12 was the first balm.

Full-scale rearmament showed them that war would not be long delayed, and they thought that, once war was declared, the political power would fall into the hands of the Army. How wrong they were.

Few of them had realized the importance of the decree signed by Hitler on February 4, 1938: "In future I shall assume directly and personally the supreme command of the entire armed forces." In this brief phrase Hitler arrogated to himself more powers than any other German had ever possessed, including Bismarck and William II. He now had complete and absolute power.

General Ludwig Beck was one of the few soldiers to grasp the gravity of the situation. The fact that Hitler allowed his generals no influence whatsoever on his political decisions appeared to Beck as a proof that, in future, war or peace would depend upon one of those "brilliant pieces of intuition" which formed the keystone of his regime.

The trend of Hitler's foreign policy showed that he proposed an imminent attack of Czechoslovakia. In the spring of 1938 he summoned the generals to Jüterborg, a small town south of Berlin, and in a rambling speech revealed his bellicose intentions. Beck was horrified. He was also indignant because Hitler had taken his decisions without consulting his chief of staff—in blissful ignorance of the military realities and possibilities, judging the situation as a visionary for whom political faith and conviction weighed more heavily than any army. Beck was above all disturbed to discover that Hitler had not bothered about international reactions. He was convinced that an aggression of this nature, devoid of any justification, would unleash a full-scale conflict which the German Army, in the throes of reorganization, was incapable of bearing.

On May 30 Hitler signed the new "green plan," a plan of attack against Czechoslovakia. Beck, as Chief of the General Staff, then wrote a long memo of protest against this adventure. The memo ended with his resignation. He hoped that the other generals would follow suit, but they did not. The resignation went to Brauchitsch, who, with a sinking heart, was forced to pass it on to Hitler. The Fuehrer refused to accept his resignation. Beck, however, left on August 18, to be replaced by General Halder. There was now no obstacle on the road to war.

At the period when General Beck tried in vain to let the voice of reason be heard, the other generals were aware that the true artisans of the Anschluss were not the soldiers. The long preparation which had allowed its realization was almost entirely the work of the grand masters of the Gestapo, Himmler, Heydrich, and their agents.

The idea of the union of Austria and Germany was an ancient one. In 1921 plebiscites had been organized in various regions of Austria and then banned by the Allies. They had indicated the desire of part of the population to see their country united to their neighbor. The Socialist population of the great cities, Vienna in particular, wanted to join the Republican Germany of Weimar, while the rural reactionary population awaited the return of the Habsburgs.

It was on this soil that the Nazis were to sow their seeds of hatred. They worked simultaneously on the rural masses in the frontier regions of Innsbruck and Linz and the Social Democrat working masses in Vienna, whom they dazzled with their Socialist program. The setting up of the Dollfuss Government aggravated the situation still further, and these measures could only spur the Austrian Nazis, supported by the external organization. In actual fact their directives came from Munich, and an "Austrian legion" had been created in Germany to group the Austrian Nazis living there, and to train them in underground activity. The S.D. fomented a permanent agitation in Austria.

After a street demonstration by the Socialists on February 11, 1934, which was brutally repressed, a wave of outrages was organized in Austria. It was at this time that the special sabotage and murder squad of the S.D.-Ausland perfected the technique it was to use in the years to come.

At the end of July there was a revival of terrorism. Dollfuss, whom Mussolini openly protected, was invited to spend a few days with the Duce in Italy, where his family was already staying. He was to leave on the 25th.

On July 25, about midday, 145 men of the S.S. Austrian Standarte 89, led by the S.S. man Holzweber, wearing the uniform of the Austrian civic guard, took the Chancellery by storm in a few minutes thanks to the complicity of Major Fey, the chief of police.

Dollfuss was mortally wounded and laid on a sofa in the Hall of Congress. Instead of being given first aid he was ordered to resign. He refused. A pen and paper were left at his side, and he was allowed to writhe in agony while being pressed for his signature. He died at 6 P.M. without seeing either the doctor or the priest he had begged for, but without having capitulated.

In the meantime the loyal troops and the police had encircled the parliament building. That evening it was learned that Mussolini, reacting violently to this *coup d'état*, had mobilized five divisions, which were massing on the Brenner frontier. An hour later the rebels surrendered. For the sake of appearances, Hitler recalled Dr. Rieth, the German ambassador in Vienna, with whom the rebels had remained in telephonic communication throughout the 25th. Once more the brutal method had failed. Hitler sensed that such procedure always entailed great danger unless immediately crowned with success. In future he would have to adopt well-tried underground methods and allow the S.D. and the organizations it controlled to act on their own. The Gestapo could now intervene.

Hitler had not for a moment given up his plan for annexing Austria. He summoned the Nazi leaders on September 29 and 30, 1934 (two months after the abortive putsch), at Bad Aibling in Bavaria. The instructions which were given at the end of this two-day conference are significant of the true intentions of the Nazis. The Gestapo had naturally played a leading role.

In these instructions we find the two classic elements of Nazi action: terrorism and police inquisition for the liquidation of opponents. These two aspects of the clandestine struggle were the province of the S.D. The Gestapo also collaborated in the search for adversaries of the regime. This was the period when Hitler explained to Rauschning how he interpreted the work of the Secret Service. "We shall act nowhere," he said, "until we have a solid phalanx of people who devote themselves entirely to their task and find in it their sole pleasure." The officials were loth to do this work: it was necessary to use women, particularly women of the world, blasé creatures attracted by adventure. The abnormal or fanatical could also be used.

Hitler had taken the trouble to dictate the questionnaire which the special services were required to compile. He wanted it to include "only information which counts," in other words if a man were venal, if there were any other way of buying him apart from money—for example, if he were vain. It was important to know his erotic inclinations, what type of woman he preferred or if he were homosexual—a particularly important point. His past must also be delved into. Did he hide some secret? Could he be blackmailed in some manner? Was he an alcoholic? Did he gamble? Everything had to be known about each important man—his habits, favorite sports, whether he liked traveling, or whether he had artistic tastes or pretensions. It was intended to exploit a veritable catalogue of vices and human weaknesses. "This is my Realpolitik, how I attract people to my cause, how I force them to work for me and insure my penetration and my influence in every country."

In Vienna, however, Schuschnigg, Dollfuss's successor, realized that his resistance could not last much longer. He tried to compromise, but finally concluded with Germany the treaty of July 11, 1936. According to this agreement, Austria undertook to preserve a friendly attitude toward Germany and to consider herself as a German state. In exchange Germany recognized the sovereignty of Austria and her independence, promising to exercise no influence on her foreign politics. To consolidate these dispositions, Schuschnigg appointed Austrian Nazis to various posts in the administration, agreed to admit some of their organizations into the Vaterlaendische Front, and finally he released several thousand Nazis from the prisons. This was the Nazis' hour of victory. It was an exact repetition of the maneuver which had allowed the destruction of the Weimar Republic.

The Party and the S.D. speeded up their work of undermining. As early as the autumn of 1934 a monthly budget of 200,000 marks had been secretly placed at the disposal of Engineer Reithaler, the former leader of the Nazi peasants, now the hidden leader of the Austrian Nazi party.

The frontier became more and more permeable. A constant stream of agents from the S.D., the Gestapo, and the N.S.D.A.P. left their tracks in Austria. The Socialists and Catholic opponents were disturbed because they knew that they were defeated. The Austrian police were paralyzed, and the American ambassador in Vienna, Mr. Messersmith, was able to write to the State Department: "The prospect of seeing the Nazis seize power prevents any effective police or judicial action against them, for fear of reprisals on the part of a future Nazi Government against those who, even within their rights, took measures against them."

The work of setting up cells was intensified by the creation of the *Ostmarkische Verein* (the Union of the Eastern Marches) controlled by Glaise-Horstenau, who had been appointed Minister of the Interior. From this moment the Nazi efforts converged, allowing them to place one of their trusted men at the head of the Austrian Police Praesidium. They exercised on the Austrian Government and the population what von Papen called a "slowly intensified psychological pressure."

This pressure became so acute that on February 12, 1938, Schuschnigg was forced to obey Hitler's summons to Berchtesgaden. At the end of the meeting, at which he gave the impression of a man on trial, he was forced, under threat of an immediate military invasion, to accept three measures which were tantamount to his condemnation:

1. Dr. Seyss-Inquart, a member of the Nazi party since 1931, was appointed Minister of the Interior and Police, which gave the Nazis absolute control over the Austrian police.
2. A new general political amnesty released Nazis condemned for crimes.
3. The Austrian Nazi party entered the Vaterlaendische Front.

On March 9, 1938, Schuschnigg tried a last-minute maneuver. Hoping to discourage the Nazis and to show international opinion that the Austrians desired to remain independent, he announced a plebiscite for the following Sunday, March 13. Hitler saw the danger and gave orders to set in motion the measures preparatory to invasion.

On March 11 Schuschnigg was forced to resign, but the President of the Republic, Miklas, at first refused to entrust Seyss-Inquart with the formation of a government. At 12:15 P.M. he capitulated.

At dawn on March 12, German troops entered Austria. At the same moment Himmler arrived in Vienna. According to Nazi practices, the purging of the police and the neutralization of the political opposition had always to be the first acts of government. Thus the Gestapo represented the first impression of the German administration received by the Viennese. During the night Himmler and Schellenberg, one of the leaders of S.D.-Ausland, had taken a plane with Hess and various Austrian leaders. A second plane full of S.S. men escorted them. At four o'clock in the morning Himmler was in Vienna as the leading representative of the Nazi Government. Heydrich, who had flown in his own private aircraft, joined them a little later. The Gestapo made its headquarters on the Mortzinplatz. Chancellor Schuschnigg was detained there for several weeks and treated in the most inhuman manner before being interned in a concentration camp, where he remained until 1945. At the beginning of April, Himmler and Heydrich were busy building a concentration camp in Austria. This was Mauthausen, whose sinister reputation was to spread throughout the entire world.

The Gestapo premises also sheltered another prisoner of note, Baron Ferdinand von Rothschild, one of the first to be arrested. His private residence, a palace on Auf der Wieden, was occupied by the S.D. Heydrich had declared that the Baron was to be considered his personal prisoner. His meals were brought in by a Viennese restaurateur, and there were a host of conjectures as to the reasons for this privileged treatment. The explanation may lie in the fact that the Baron was on good terms with the Duke of Windsor. The latter had stayed with him in Vienna after abdicating in December 1936. Now Hitler was trying to ingratiate himself with certain British circles. Lord Redesdale's daughter, the eccentric Unity Mitford, was at one time one of his intimates. It seems probable that news of the benevolent treatment of Baron Rothschild, friend of the ex-King Edward VIII, was intended to reach the latter secondhand. Heydrich, however, took the opportunity to do a profitable "deal" and obtained from the Baron the release of all his wealth in Germany in exchange for his freedom, that is to say permission to leave the Reich freely for Paris.

The purge began on the morning of the 12th, when Schellenberg carried out *his* mission, which consisted in seizing the statute books and records of the Austrian Secret Service chief, Colonel Ronge, before the members of military intelligence, the Abwehr, which only arrived with the first troops.

In Vienna the crowd hailed the conquerors, but the Socialists awaited the course of events anxiously, and the Jews, knowing the measures carried out in Germany against their coreligionists, fled or committed suicide. Several members of the former Austrian ruling class followed suit. The number of victims was never published, but it is certain that they amounted to several hundred. To these must be added the host of people murdered by the Gestapo during the first three days of the occupation.

Scores of others were arrested and sent to concentration camps. Among them were Grand Duke Max and Prince Ernst von Hogenberg, son of Franz Ferdinand by a morganatic marriage. The Socialists and other Left Wing opponents were arrested en masse. By mid-April there had been ninety thousand arrests in Vienna alone.

And finally the Gestapo showed its hand with two staggering murders. The day the German troops entered Austria the Gestapo agents kidnaped the Embassy councilor, Baron von Ketteler, who had been the closest adviser of von Papen, at that time German ambassador in Vienna. After three weeks the Danube washed up his corpse. Although the motives for this murder have never been clarified, it seems to have served as a kind of veiled warning to von Papen, who was suspected of playing a double game. Heydrich believed that Ketteler had deposited certain important papers for safety in Switzerland at the request of von Papen. Simultaneously von Papen was permanently relieved of his duties in Vienna. A little later he was sent to Ankara. Displaying his usual "discretion," he did not protest against the murder of Ketteler any more than he had protested against the murders of Edgar Jung and von Bose, during the June 30 killings.

The second murder was less surprising. General Zehner, whom President Miklas had wanted to appoint as Schuschnigg's successor, fell to the bullets of the black killers, who had not forgiven his opposition to the 1934 putsch. Major Fey, although he had played a considerable part in the abortive putsch of 1934, committed suicide after killing his wife and son with his own hands.

The Seyss-Inquart Government formed on the morning of the 12th included Dr. Ernst Kaltenbrunner, head of the Austrian S.S., Minister of Police, and Dr. Hueber, notary and brother-in-law of Goering, Minister of Justice. Finally Seyss-Inquart, promoted Reichstatthalter, was supported by two underlings nominated by the Party, the *chargé d'affaires* Keppler, and the Reich Commissioner Buerckel, a specialist in *Gleichschaltung*.

The fate of the Austrians was now in "good" hands.

On March 13 at 7 P.M., Hitler made a triumphal entry into Vienna accompanied by Keitel, the Commander in Chief of the Wehrmacht. The same day a law was promulgated, uniting Austria to the Reich under the name of Ostmark, "the Eastern March," a measure which Hitler announced on the 15th in the Vienna Hofburg in the following terms: "I announce to the German people the accomplishment of the most important mission of my life."

Thus six million Austrians were linked to the fate of Germany and obliged to share it until the final catastrophe. And in order that the "bringing into line" should be complete, a decree issued by Frick, Minister of the Interior, on March 18, 1938, authorized Reichsfuehrer S.S. Himmler to take "all the security measures he deemed necessary in Austria."

Although the police services of the S.D., S.S., and Gestapo had weighed heavily in the Austrian affair, their role was to be less important in the

Czechoslovakian crisis. The procedure used in Austria corresponded with the line of conduct followed so far in Germany for the maintenance of the Nazi order.

The ethnic medley in the Czechoslovak nation, which was formed by the Treaty of Versailles from part of the territories of the former Austro-Hungarian Empire, allowed the Nazis to base their action on the same pretexts as those which had given the Anschluss its sentimental justification. The fact that Czechoslovakia was the most democratic state in Central Europe acted as an aphrodisiac on the Nazis.

On February 20, 1938, Hitler had made a great speech in the Reichstag. After insisting upon the indissoluble union of the Party, the Army, and the State, he had asserted that the Germans were no longer prepared to allow ten million of their brothers living beyond the frontiers of the Reich to be oppressed. The Anschluss had allowed him to bring back six and a half million Austrians into the fold of the German Fatherland, and it was understood that those who were still expatriated were the Germans living in Czechoslovakia.

The Czech nation consisted of about seven million Czechs, three million Slovaks, 700,000 Hungarians, 400,000 Ruthenians, 100,000 Poles, and 3,600,000 Germans. The Germans constituted the largest ethnic minority of the country and lived for the most part in the region known as Sudetenland, which forms a crescent bordering on the German frontier and almost completely surrounding Bohemia and Moravia. This region was to excite the greed of the Nazis, for concentrated there were many prosperous concerns, the glass and luxury industries grouped around particularly rich iron and coal mines.

Since it could muster 2,900,000 Germans it was easy, as in the case of Austria, to invoke the democratic principle of the rights of nations to dispose of themselves. The whole maneuver consisted in skillfully provoking an inclination toward this popular "disposition."

As early as 1923 the Nazis had implanted several associations among the Sudeten Germans to propagate the National Socialist orders of the day, stressing Pan-Germanism and German patriotism. But, while basing their efforts on clandestine action, they needed an organization which could defend their theories in the open.

It was a non-Nazi who, skillfully guided, was to form this organization. On October 1, 1934, the gym instructor Conrad Henlein, born of a German father and a Czech mother, created the Deutsche Heimat Front, the patriotic

German Front. Henlein demanded autonomy for the Sudeten Germans within the framework of the Czechoslovak State and proposed the formation of a Federal State similar to the system of the Swiss cantons, which would give the ethnic minorities a feeling of independence without harming the national unity.

Nevertheless, Henlein's party was organized on the Fuehrerprinzip. This sinister characteristic should have aroused distrust. In 1935, having already collected a number of important adherents, the German patriotic front changed its name and became the *Sudetendeutsche Partei* (S.D.P.), the Sudeten German party. Then as the power of the Nazis increased the tone of the claims mounted. From 1936 the S.D.P. functioned as a Fifth Column in Czechoslovakia, receiving funds through the Volksdeutsche Mittelstelle, which S.S. Obergruppenfuehrer Lorenz controlled on Himmler's behalf. The German Embassy in Prague handed the funds to Henlein, just as it also transmitted the orders for espionage. The A.O. (Auslands Organisation) under State Secretary Bohle, also distributed money (fifteen thousand marks a month) to Henlein, and organized intelligence networks. These activities remained secret. From 1937 Henlein began to demand autonomy for the Sudeten Germans, and his political program became openly pro-Nazi and anti-Semitic. The summer of 1938 saw an increase of Nazi activity similar to that in Austria before the Anschluss. The Gestapo services were at work.

On precise instructions from S.D.-Ausland, which had taken control of the Secret Service in Czechoslovakia, the Sudeten Nazis infiltrated all regional or local organizations, sporting societies, sailing clubs, choral and musical societies, veteran and cultural associations, transforming them into so many pro-Nazi cells. Thus they detected the possible opponents to Nazi principles or to annexation by Germany and amassed a considerable documentation on the political, economic, and military situation of Czechoslovakia. They penetrated various enterprises, recruited directors of factories and banks, or, when the latter resisted, their main collaborators.

These various organizations functioned so efficiently that, according to Schellenberg, it was necessary to install at two points of the frontier special telephone lines to transmit it to Berlin. Sudetenland was literally teeming with German agents. The S.D. and the Gestapo shared the work. While utilizing Henlein and his staff, the Gestapo kept them under close and obvious surveillance, in order to counter any "faltering" on their part.

On the German side of the frontier a corps of volunteers similar to the 1937 Austrian Legion had been formed—the German Sudetenfreikorps, with its headquarters at the Schloss Donndorf, near Bayreuth.

Hitler wished to find some pretext for a military invasion of Czechoslovakia. The control posts of the Nazi network in Sudetenland, known as Sudetendeutsche Kontrollstelle, were ordered to organize a series of provocations starting in September 1938. On September 12 Hitler made a very violent speech at the Nuremberg Party Congress, accusing President Beneš of torturing Sudeten Germans and trying to exterminate them. Henlein and his second-in-command, Franck, left for Germany.

In reply to these threats the Czech Government, whose apathy had allowed the installation on its territory of the most dangerous Nazi organizations, arrested a certain number of Sudeten Nazis. The Gestapo took reprisals, and on the night of September 15–16 arrested 150 Czechs in Germany.

On September 19 the Freikorps went into action in small groups of twelve men. It carried out more than three hundred missions, taking more than fifteen hundred prisoners, with numerous dead and wounded, capturing machine guns, light arms, and equipment.

On September 22 Chamberlain had flown to Bad Godesberg, and the Munich Conference opened on the 29th. Mussolini, Hitler, Chamberlain, and Daladier decided the fate of Czechoslovakia without a single representative from that country having been heard. On the 30th it was decided that Czechoslovakia should evacuate the Sudeten Germans between October 1 and 10. The Czech Government protested, President Beneš resigned, but no one paid the slightest attention, and all over Europe this triumph of "peace saved at the last moment" was fêted.

This episode showed Hitler that the French and British Intelligence Services were not up to their task. While he assured everyone that he would make no further territorial claims, preparations for the invasions of Czechoslovakia had begun. The warning signs should have been noticed long before.

As soon as the Munich Agreement had permitted the peaceful occupation of Sudetenland, Henlein's Freikorps was placed under the orders of Himmler, "to be assigned police tasks like the rest of the police, with the agreement of the Reichsfuehrer S.S."

The democracies had just lost a decisive battle which they might have won.

Earlier a small resistance troop had been formed in certain military circles, which, like General Beck, thought that Hitler's aggressive policy could not be victoriously upheld by the German Army alone against a Europe which they believed must combine against the Nazi expansion, and that the logical conclusion of such behavior could only be the total collapse and ruin of Germany. They had also finally taken a decision from which many had recoiled since the beginnings of Nazism: they determined to use the opportunity of aggression against Czechoslovakia to seize power and arraign Hitler before a tribunal. This would have meant the end of Nazism, and the fate of Europe would have been completely changed.

In mid-August the conspirators sent an envoy to London, von Kleist, to inform the British Government of the situation and to encourage it to stand firm. But while Churchill, who was not a member of the government, encouraged the German generals in their plan and assured them of his support, Chamberlain continued to vacillate. At the beginning of September a new emissary was sent to London. A few days later a diplomat from the German Embassy in London confirmed the information to the British. Unfortunately these assurances could not make the Chamberlain-Daladier Government alter their decision to abandon Czechoslovakia.

(In the autumn of 1944, after the setback of the July 20 plot, the Gestapo discovered in Kleist's home documents referring to his journey to London in August 1938 and his contact with the British Government. He was condemned to death and executed in the spring of 1945.)

On October 21, 1938, Hitler signed an order marked "very confidential," ordering the O.K.W.:

1. To assure the German frontiers and to protect them against surprise air attack.
2. To liquidate all that remained of Czechoslovakia.
3. To occupy Memel.

So far he had always managed to conceal his aggression by lying protests about "the solidarity due to our oppressed brothers." Since this time there was no longer the smallest German minority remaining in Czechoslovakia, something else had to be invented.

With appeasement on record, the Prague Government of old President Hácha accorded Slovakia a generous internal autonomy: a parliament and an autonomous cabinet were created in Bratislava. But this first step was only to facilitate the end of the operation. The heads of the Slovak extremist party, Durcansky and Mach, on the orders of Goering, who had summoned them to Germany, demanded total independence for Slovakia with close economic, political, and military ties with Germany. In exchange they promised the "solution" of the Jewish problem and the outlawing of the Communist party.

During the winter 1938–39 the infiltration campaign began in Bohemia and Moravia. The Nazi student organizations of the Sudeten Germans, controlled by the S.S. and the Gestapo, played a considerable role. The Gestapo and the S.D. were thus able to suppress the public and private Czech institutions and when, at dawn on March 15, 1939, the German troops, without prior warning, entered what remained of Czechoslovakia, the Nazi agents were already installed in all the strategic posts, paralyzing all resistance and in control of the police. At Brno, in particular, the direction of the police immediately fell into their hands. Everywhere the commandos prevented the destruction of political and police records, to allow a rapid purge of all opponents. The chief members of these Nazi student associations were finally incorporated into the S.S. by Himmler and Heydrich, and many were subsequently employed by the Gestapo in France.

German intervention had been prepared by an act of provocation: the Slovak cabinet had virtually broken with Prague and the central government had been constrained to dissolve it by reason of its systematic opposition.

On March 12 two S.D. agents called on Monseigneur Tiso, the Slovak Premier, and flew him to Berlin in a special plane. On the 14th Tiso, in accordance with orders received, proclaimed the independence of Slovakia.

It was, therefore, to bring aid to the oppressed Slovakian patriots that the German troops violated Czechoslovakian soil. The same day Hitler, in an order of the day to the armed forces, proclaimed: "Czechoslovakia has ceased to exist." The following day a decree created the Protectorate of Bohemia-Moravia, incorporated within the German Reich, and the appointment of von Neurath as Protector of this unfortunate country.

On March 15 Hitler went to Prague with his armies. As in Vienna, he was accompanied by Himmler and Heydrich. Schellenberg, who traveled with them, reports that Himmler was delighted with the quality of the Czech police, whom he described as "exceptional human material," and decided on the spot to incorporate them into the S.S. He immediately appointed as chief of police, with the title of Secretary of State to the Protectorate, the former second-in-command of Henlein's Sudeten German party, Karl Hermann Franck.

At the same time Franck was given the rank of Gruppenfuehrer S.S. (divisional general). He was to excel himself in his new duties by his incredible ferocity.

The Czechoslovak people entered an apocalyptic period in which they were spared no suffering. The treachery of those who had become Nazi agents was responsible for this. It was with the complicity of men blinded by political passion, by the thirst for power, by ideologies in which the most bigoted racialism combined with a perversion of patriotic sentiment, that the Nazi agents had managed to complete their task. It was thanks to them that the men of the S.D. and the Gestapo had been able to pursue their termite work and to gnaw from within the whole living substance of the nation, leaving only an envelope ready to crumble to dust at the first shock. And once more the conservatives of the Right and the Center had ingenuously given their support to this undertaking of which they were to be the first victims.

Seen in retrospect, and with a knowledge of the secrets of Nazi policy revealed by the records seized in 1945, we can assert once more that Hitler's political triumph rested exclusively on his knowledge of human weaknesses. Nazi policy consisted of a speculation on and exploiting of human cowardice and ferocity, and that is why a terror organization such as the Gestapo held such a leading place in it.

Chapter 13
Himmler Shapes His Organization

Hitler's policy of aggression having proved so successful, there was no question of the Nazis changing their methods. At the end of 1938 the decision was taken to annihilate Poland. The free city of Danzig, isolated in Polish territory by the Treaty of Versailles, was to provide the excuse. The Hitlerian aims did not necessitate a *mise-en-scène* comparable to those staged in the cases of Austria and Czechoslovakia. Poland was to be transformed into a territory for expansion and repopulation. It constituted the first stage in the conquest of the *Lebensraum*, that "vital living space" which Hitler had claimed since the beginnings of Nazism.

Poland was in a poor state for dealing with the aggression now in preparation. The Minister for Foreign Affairs, Colonel József Beck, had for a long time shown keen sympathy for the Nazi dictatorship. From 1926 to 1936 Poland, previously led by a democratic government, had lived under the dictatorship of Marshal Pilsudski, who before his death had signed a non-aggression pact with Hitler Germany. Considering themselves sufficiently protected by this, the military junta of colonels, successors to Pilsudski, had opposed all agreements with the democratic countries, in particular with Czechoslovakia. Poland had shared in the dismemberment of Czechoslovakia by appropriating the district of Teschen, with its coal mines and 230,000 inhabitants.

Hitler, on May 23, 1939, declared at a conference with the generals: "There is no question of sparing Poland, it remains to decide an attack on Poland at the first favorable opportunity." The latest date was fixed for September 3.

The plan bore the code name of "Fall Weiss" (Operation White). The plan against Czechoslovakia had been called "Fall Grün" (Operation Green).

To stage an incident which would allow the Poles to be accused of provocation, Hitler naturally thought of Himmler. On June 23 the Reichsfuehrer S.S. was present at the meeting of the Council for the Defense of the Reich, summoned for only the second time since its creation in 1935. The main dispositions in view of the imminent war were laid down. Naturally there was not the slightest allusion to the role envisaged for Himmler's men. This was never fully revealed until the Nuremberg trials.

The scheme conceived by Himmler, and entrusted to Heydrich to implement, was given the code name of "Operation Himmler." To put it into practice Heydrich chose one of his trusted henchmen, Alfred Helmut Naujocks, an old friend whom he had known at Kiel. Naujocks had joined the S.S. in 1931. He was a mechanic and well-known amateur boxer, popular among the Kiel dockers, and was a useful recruit for the street fighting of those days. In 1934 Heydrich enrolled him in the S.D., where in 1939 he was head of a subsection of Section III of S.D.-Ausland (Secret Service abroad), at that time directed by S.S. Oberfuehrer Heinz Jost.

The group led by Naujocks, which was later given the name Group VI F, was allowed special duties. From his office in the Delbrückstrasse, Berlin, Naujocks ran various workshops where reliable men busied themselves with mysterious tasks. Group F formed what might be called the "technical subdivision" of the S.D. Here were fabricated false papers, passports, identity cards, safe-conducts of all nationalities, and the other necessities for S.D. agents operating abroad. Later Group F even printed forged notes. This group of forgers was led by Haupsturmfuehrer S.S. Krueger. Another workshop, located in a suburban bungalow, was the radio section. After supervising these highly confidential activities, Naujocks was axed in January 1941 and transferred to the Waffen S.S. for having dared to dispute an order from Heydrich. The latter continued to pursue him with vigilant hatred and insisted that Naujocks be sent to a front-line combat unit on the Eastern front. But Hitler's orders forbade "the repositories of State secrets" to be put in posts where they might fall into the hands of the enemy. This saved him. Finally, after carrying out his duties in Denmark, and occupying a post in the economic services of the occupying troops in Belgium, Naujocks deserted to the American troops in November 1944. He did not know that his name would figure on the list of war criminals. In 1946, when due to appear before an Allied tribunal, and in custody in Germany, he managed to escape and to disappear.

On August 10, 1939, Naujocks was still one of Heydrich's trusted men, when the latter summoned him to his office in the Prinz Albrechtstrasse. Heydrich explained to him that he was to make a feigned attack on the German radio station at Gleiwitz in Upper Silesia, near the Polish frontier. This feint was to look as though it were an act of aggression committed against the station by a Polish force. "For the foreign press and for German propaganda we need material proofs of these Polish attacks," said Heydrich.

Naujocks chose six particularly reliable men of the S.D. and set out on the 15th for Gleiwitz. Absolute secrecy had to be observed, an order easily facilitated by the frontier police who in 1937 had passed into the control of the Gestapo. Naujocks had to wait for a message in code from Heydrich to launch the operation. He knew that Germans wearing Polish uniforms were to be placed at his disposal for the attack. The plan arranged by Heydrich stipulated that the phony commando was to capture the transmitter and hold it sufficiently long for a Polish-speaking German to broadcast a violent denunciation compiled by Heydrich. "This message," said Naujocks, "declared that the hour of the German-Polish war had sounded, and that the united Poles were to crush all resistance on the part of the Germans."

The Abwehr, the military intelligence, directly responsible to the O.K.W., had provided the uniforms, weapons, and identity cards for the "Polish" soldiers who were to take part in the raid. Himmler insisted upon genuine Polish uniforms, genuine Polish military papers, although Naujocks' Workshop F was able without difficulty to fabricate perfect copies of false papers.

Canaris, the head of the Abwehr, had tried to prevent this type of operation, or at least to exclude his service from participation, but could do nothing since Keitel had given his consent. He was content to stand aside, and Oberfuehrer S.S. Mehlhorn was ordered by Heydrich to coordinate the different tasks of each service.

At the end of August, Naujocks, who was still awaiting Heydrich's orders at Gleiwitz, was summoned to Oppeln, a small Silesian town forty miles north of Gleiwitz. Mueller and Mehlhorn were there to discuss the final details of the operation. Mueller, as head of the Gestapo, had been ordered by Heydrich to provide the most important "material," to which he had given the significant code name "canned goods." These "canned goods" were in actual fact a dozen men under death sentence taken from the camps by Mueller.

To quote Naujocks' testimony at Nuremberg: "Mueller declared that he had twelve or thirteen condemned criminals who would be dressed in Polish uniforms and left for dead on the spot to show that they had been killed in the course of the attack. To this end they had to be given mortal injections by a doctor of Heydrich's service. Later they would also be given genuine wounds inflicted by firearms. After the incident members of the press and other persons were to be taken to the spot. A police report would then be made. Mueller told me that he had an order from Heydrich telling him to put one of these criminals at my disposal for the Gleiwitz action."

Everything was thus worked out down to the smallest detail: "On August 31 at midday I received a telephone call from Heydrich giving me the code word of the attack which was to take place at eight o'clock the same evening. Heydrich said, 'Before carrying out the attack ask Mueller for the "canned goods."' I did this and gave Mueller instructions to bring the man to a spot near the radio station. He was alive but barely conscious. I tried to open his eyes but I could not tell from his glance if he was still alive, only by his breathing." Mueller had promised the condemned men whom he was about to have murdered that, in exchange for their patriotic participation in this action, they would be pardoned and released.

At the appointed hour the fake attack took place. As arranged, the message composed by Heydrich was read in Polish on an emergency transmitter, which took only three or four minutes. Then Naujocks and his men retired, leaving the "canned goods" on the scene.

Next day, September 1, when the German troops had been advancing into Polish territory since dawn, Hitler, speaking before the Reichstag, enumerated some of the frontier violations committed by the Poles (since August 23 the Germans had increased their provocation) and mentioned the incident of the Gleiwitz post "attacked by regular Polish troops." Ribbentrop, for his part, informed the German embassies abroad in a communiqué mentioning that the Wehrmacht had been forced to take action in "reply" to Polish attacks, a formula which was reiterated in the High Command communiqués. The German and certain foreign newspapers published details of the attack on the station. It was six years before the truth of this affair was revealed. As for the members of the S.D. who took part in the operation, S.S. Haupsturmfuehrer Birckel insisted that they had all been "liquidated" with the exception of Naujocks.

The Nazis often used procedures of the same nature, using uniforms and materiel of the enemy, in violation of international law. The last and most extraordinary example was "Operation Greif," a commando action staged by the S.S. man Skorzeny, to support von Runstedt's desperate offensive in the Ardennes in December 1944. "Operation Greif" used more than three thousand S.S. dressed in American uniforms with Sherman tanks, American trucks, and jeeps; the plan was to spread confusion behind the Allied lines, which they managed to penetrate in depth, and to carry out the most audacious acts of sabotage.

"Operation Himmler" at Gleiwitz, however, shows the cooperation established at this period between the S.S. services and the Army. We have here in fact the S.D., the Gestapo, and the Abwehr, on orders from the German High Command, participating at the same time.

On the third day of the war, the German troops having already conquered a large slice of Polish territory—the Panzers entered Warsaw on the

8th—Hitler decided to transfer his headquarters to a place near the front. Three special trains appointed for this purpose crossed the Polish frontier in the region of Kattowitz, not far from Gleiwitz, and, crossing Poland in a northerly direction, came to a halt at Zoppot, the tiny harbor of the former free city of Danzig, which had officially been reattached to the Reich by a decree dated September 1. Hitler remained there until the end of September. The first special train was Hitler's, the second Goering's, and the third Himmler's.

Thus Himmler was one of the first to enter Poland as he had been to enter Austria and Czechoslovakia. Followed as usual by his faithful aide-de-camp Obergruppenfuehrer Wolff, he attended all the important staff conferences and supervised the posting of his services in conquered territory. Each service had sent a representative. A notable figure was Walter Schellenberg. This choice was no accident, for Schellenberg had previously been entrusted with the task of carrying out negotiations with the Army by Heydrich, and of arranging the plan of action for Himmler's men in the areas behind the front line. Special commandos from the Gestapo and the S.D. entered Poland after the first waves of assault troops to "insure the safety" of the rear, but above all to begin carrying out measures which had long since been arranged by Himmler against the Polish population.

SIPO detachments composed of men of the Gestapo and the S.D. formed an *Einsatzgruppe* (combat group), itself subdivided into Einsatzkommandos. No agreement had been established with the Army. The soldiers had learned in detail the measures prescribed by Hitler for the liquidation of Poland and had been appalled. The bombing of Warsaw was decided, although it was not a military necessity—the population had to be harassed; Hitler ordered the political "cleaning up" of Poland, and the generals knew what excesses this would entail. Finally various provocations were planned. Ribbentrop in particular had informed Admiral Canaris of the organization of a faked uprising of the Ukranian minorities against the Poles, which would allow all the farms and Polish houses in those regions to be burned.

Canaris had warned Keitel of the risks these activities entailed for the Army. Some of the generals agreed with Canaris when he exclaimed, "The world will one day hold the Wehrmacht, with whose connivance these events took place, responsible for such methods." Under pressure from these generals, Keitel and Brauchitsch informed Hitler personally of their objections to the use of Himmler's commandos behind the troops. Their security was adequately insured, they maintained.

To the generals' surprise Hitler at first agreed with them, but later reversed his decision and gave Keitel orders to accept the presence of Himmler's men. Keitel, as usual, acquiesced and informed the generals that he could do nothing to influence the progress of events since it was a question of an order from the Fuehrer. Thus was accepted the bombing of Warsaw and the mass execution of certain categories of the population: the intellectuals, the nobility, the clergy, and, naturally, the Jews. The three first categories were considered dangerous by Himmler and Heydrich because they were the only ones capable of organizing an internal resistance—a resistance which would be far more difficult for a population deprived of intellectual and moral cadres. As for the Jews, the order to exterminate them in Poland was the beginning of "the final solution."

During a meeting in Hitler's train, General Johannes von Blaskowitz, who had worked out the Polish plan of attack and commanded an army during this campaign, protested energetically and produced a detailed report on the atrocities committed in Poland by the S.S. and the Einsatzkommandos against the Jews and the Polish elite. He sent his report direct to Hitler, but only succeeded in plunging the latter into one of his spectacular rages. These difficulties led to the conclusion of a written agreement between the O.K.W. and Himmler for the use of the Einsatzgruppen in the campaign against the U.S.S.R., in the course of which these detachments were to surpass in their actions all previous bounds of horror.

There were very few generals who dared to protest during that month of September 1939. Canaris, Blaskowitz, and to a lesser degree Brauchitsch, had with difficulty succeeded in manipulating Keitel, but the attempt had petered out.

In general the Army approved and supported Hitler. The generals hoped for a *Blumenkrieg*, what we call "a walkover," and the operations in Austria and Czechoslovakia, followed by the blitzkrieg in Poland, appeared to prove them right. They feared measuring their strength against French and British armies, but Hitler insisted that the French campaign would be just as easy. In the autumn of 1939 the generals held an eminent place in the Nazi State. They had won their laurels in the East and were preparing to face the democracies of the West; at home many of them held key posts in the war economy. The remoteness of the occupied territories, the duties they had to carry out there, should have given them an unusual independence, and helped them shake off the tutelage of the Party and the control of the Gestapo and the S.D.

Faced with this situation, what was the attitude of Himmler and the Gestapo? At first a certain number of precautions were taken to limit the autonomy of the military. For example, the greater part of the Army transports were entrusted to the N.S.K.K., the Party's motorized corps. Without its transports and drivers, the Army would be incapable on its own account of insuring adequate supplies. The Party had thus retained an easy method of controlling the soldiers.

On the other hand, at the request of Hitler and contrary to custom, the soldiers were never given police powers either in Czechoslovakia or in Poland. These powers had been assumed at the outset by Himmler's services both in Czechoslovakia and Austria. In Poland they were assumed as soon as actual fighting ceased and the country was occupied.

The appearance of S.D. and Gestapo agents formed into Einsatzkommandos immediately to the rear of the fighting troops was a novelty and a "bold initiative" on the part of Himmler. This creation, which enabled the agents of his two main services to work together, reflects the important transformation which was in the process of being carried out.[1]

As soon as Himmler became Supreme Head of all Police Services in Germany on June 17, 1936, a certain number of transformations were carried out. On August 28, 1936, a circular had stipulated that from the following October 1, the political police services of the *Laender* would all bear the name of Geheime Staatspolizei (Gestapo) and the regional services the name of Staatspolizei (Stapo). This completed the unification of the past three years. On September 20 a circular, signed this time by Frick, Minister of the Interior, to whom the whole of the police services were attached in theory, decreed that the Gestapo head office in Berlin was in future to control the activities of the heads of the political police services in all the *Laender.*

To reinforce these directives, and to augment the speed of repression, Frick signed an order on January 25, 1938, giving the power of protective

---

[1] Einsatzkommandos of the same composition had been formed for the invasion of Czechoslovakia. Their role was different and limited in time, since they were dissolved as soon as the SIPO service had been installed in Prague.

custody to the Gestapo itself. Until then the Gestapo had confined themselves to applying the decrees established at its suggestion by the Ministry of the Interior. Now this weak control disappeared. "Protective custody," according to Frick, "can be decreed by the Secret Police of State as a coercive method against those who endanger the safety of the people and the State by their attitude, in other words to break any chance of a revolt by the enemies of the people and the State."

These orders for internment were unchallengeable. No administrative or judicial court was provided for and, as we have seen, the tribunals were forbidden to pry into the affairs of the Gestapo. All internment orders bore on the head of the paper the following note: "The arrested person has no right of appeal against this decree of protective custody." This was followed by an indication as to the reason for the internment. It was usually short and to the point, for example, "suspected of activities harmful to the State" or "strongly suspected of helping deserters"; or again "being the parent of a deserter [or of an *émigré*] is likely to take every opportunity of harming the Reich if allowed to remain at liberty."

Frick's order of January 25, followed by the decree of September 14, 1938, encouraged the N.S.D.A.P. organizations to collaborate with the Gestapo, to which the Fuehrer had given "the mission of watching and liquidating all the enemies of the Party and the National Socialist State, as well as all the forces of subversion directed against them."

The Gestapo, therefore, had totally and definitely established itself in power. All its officials were now officials of the Reich. Heydrich's forces distributed throughout Germany now comprised:

57 regional Gestapo services divided into:
21 Stapo Leitstellen (main posts)
36 Stapo Stellen (local posts)

The KRIPO, which since 1936, together with the Gestapo, formed the unit known as SIPO, disposed of:

66 regional services divided into:
20 Kriminal Polizeileitstellen (main posts)
40 Kriminal Polizeileitstellen (local posts)

Heydrich, who commanded the whole organization, had every reason to be satisfied. Nevertheless, although head of the SIPO, he was still in charge of his original service, the S.D., and had had a few administrative troubles. Despite all his efforts the S.D. remained a service of the Party. It was decreed on November 11, 1938, that the S.D. was to be the information service for the Party and the State. Its principal task was to assist the Security Police (SIPO = Gestapo + Kripo). In the meantime under the iron heel of Heydrich, who had taken as his model the British Intelligence Service, the S.D. had developed to the point of being much more a unit of political intelligence and of espionage in particular than an auxiliary police organization.

When the war broke out, the S.D. was therefore employed as a State Intelligence Service, though it was still a Party organization. It would remain so until the end. Nevertheless the administrative "frontier" separating it from Himmler's other organizations was such that it constantly created difficulties, despite the unity of the Himmler-Heydrich direction. The creation of Einsatzkommandos of mixed composition, for the Polish campaign, had brought these difficulties to light. Himmler therefore made a far-reaching decision during the summer: the creation of a new organization to which the decree of September 27, 1939, gave official recognition. According to this text, the Reichsfuehrer S.S. regrouped his chief services under the name of *Reichssicherheitshauptamt* (Central Security Office of the Reich), which was better known under its initials R.S.H.A.

The apparatus for investigation, house searches, criminal and political documentation was thus united into a single unit. The first result of this measure was to accentuate still further the control of the main S.S. direction over the sum total of the police services, because from its creation the R.S.H.A. was considered a government service forming part of the Ministry of the Interior and, as one of the main S.S. services, attached to the Supreme Command of the S.S. Dr. Best tried to explain it in pseudo-legal jargon, and his exposition is worth quoting: "The S.S. and the police, therefore, form a unit, both in their structure and their activities, without their private organization having lost its own character and its place among the other important branches of the Party and the State administrations, which from different points of view are of the same nature."

The same day as the creation of the R.S.H.A. another decree appointed the heads of services, confirming the former chiefs in their functions,

At the National Socialist rally in 1933. Streicher (second from the left) with Hitler and Goering. *Ullstein*.

Racial prejudice 1935 vintage. The placard exhorts Germans not to buy from Jews.

Julius Streicher blusters before the microphone, 1935.

A typical incident of early Nazidom. This girl's placard accuses her of tainting Aryan blood by "frequenting" a Jew. *Keystone.*

ehm at the Nur-
berg Party Rally,
3. *Ullstein.*

The Rivals. Goering and Streicher at Nuremberg, where both were later condemned in 1946. *Ullstein.*

Roehm and Himmler at the funeral of S.S.-Gruppenfuehrer Seidel-Dittmarschen in 1934. *Ullstein.*

Himmler and Heydrich in Vienna, 1938. *Ullstein.*

An Austrian concentration camp—Wöllersdorf-Trutzdorf. *Ullstein*.

Prisoners in the concentration camp at Oranienburg. *Ullstein*.

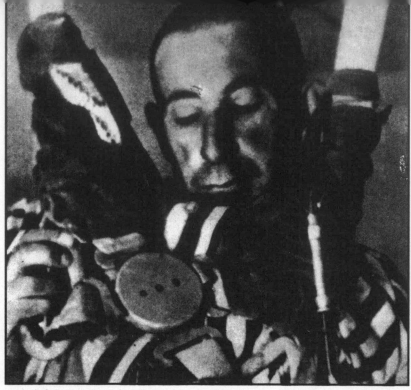

^ A human experiment for the Luftwaffe. A victim in the decompression chamber.

A round-up in Warsaw.

Heydrich himself becoming head of the R.S.H.A. From the legal point of view this amalgamation was meaningless. The term R.S.H.A. constituted a sort of camouflage, which dispensed with the use of the already notorious name Gestapo. It was for the same reason that the agents and officials of the R.S.H.A. wore on the sleeve of their uniforms the distinctive "S.D." armband, whether they belonged to the Gestapo or the KRIPO. This badge merely signified that the agent belonged to the special S.D. formation of the S.S., a formation to which the personnel of the R.S.H.A., entirely integrated into the S.S., had been attached en bloc.

The R.S.H.A.[2] was a gigantic political machine designed to centralize information, to pick up the slightest hostile rumor, and bring it, amplified and explained, to the ear of the grand master of the machine, the Reichsfuehrer S.S. Heinrich Himmler. Inversely the machine was to echo at all levels the slightest whim of the master, to transmit his orders to the farthest corners of the Nazi world, and to ensure their rapid execution.

In practice the R.S.H.A. turned out to be a very clumsy machine. The excessive partitioning imposed by the rules of secrecy took away much of its efficiency. On the other hand, the separation between intelligence and execution, and the fact that the information passed through a series of successive stages before reaching the user, falsified the view of those responsible. The groups charged with establishing syntheses from the mass of information collected at a lower level consisted of bureaucrats with no contact with reality. In their hands the content of the report was progressively stripped of all its most vivid elements. The reports arrived at the top as mere summaries, emptied of all substance: very often they bore no relation to the truth. This ultrabureaucratic conception of police work was the source of numerous errors committed by these organizations, and of the inefficiency of a great number of even the most savage measures.

The complexity of the R.S.H.A. organization called for a special formation of all the agents working within it. A circular from Heydrich issued on May 18, 1940, prescribed the progress of young agents entering the R.S.H.A. The young Nazi, fresh from the S.S. schools, or leaving a university with a law degree, had to do three consecutive stages: four months with the KRIPO,

---

[2] Cf. Appendix 1, p. 397.

where he learned the scientific elements of police work; three months with the S.D., and three months with the Gestapo. He thus acquired an overall picture of the functions of the active services, and knew what to expect from the neighboring services. He was then transferred, according to his personal aptitudes and the needs of the organization, to one of the seven *Amter*, i.e., to one of the seven offices into which the R.S.H.A. was divided.

The Gestapo formed Amt IV of the R.S.H.A.

The R.S.H.A. extended its activities to all the occupied or annexed countries. The services installed in these countries were modeled on that of the central organization, reproducing the whole machinery at all levels down to the smallest unit.

It was neither by chance nor because its name was more evocative of power that the Gestapo acquired a notoriety surpassing that of the other organizations of the R.S.H.A.[3] The Gestapo was the sole executive instrument of the whole, the pivot of the machine around which the other pieces revolved. It was here that the work of documentation, of synthesizing information, the statistics, the scientific and methodological studies carried out by the other Amter found their *raison d'être* and their final destination. It was from this administrative head that orders were transformed into a mass of human beings who had to be trapped like game, hanged, tortured, reduced to slavery, or annihilated.

At the period of its most intense activity, in the spring of 1944, the external services comprised 25 main posts, 65 local posts, and "aerials" in 300 main posts and 850 police stations of the frontier police (*Grenzpolizei*). During the Nuremberg trials Kaltenbrunner, Heydrich's successor and the last head of the R.S.H.A., stated that at the end of 1944 the personnel of the Gestapo had risen to between 35,000 and 40,000 permanent members, while the prosecution raised the figure to between 45,000 and 50,000,[4] indicating the approximate distribution of their origin. This figure seems to have been correct, for the Gestapo during the second half of 1944 absorbed a certain number of units previously responsible to other organizations.

---

[3] The seat of the Central Office of the R.S.H.A. was at No. 8 Prinz Albrechtstrasse, in the premises occupied by the Gestapo.

[4] These figures do not include "stool pigeons" (well-wishers or enforced), or the quislings recruited in occupied countries. In addition many other organizations in which the Gestapo had its agents must also be taken into account.

On the creation of the R.S.H.A., the Gestapo had already integrated certain elements of the S.D. This policy was pursued by Mueller with the support of Heydrich and Himmler. At the end of 1941 and the beginning of 1942, Mueller wanted to extend his agents' field of action to non-occupied foreign countries; on the pretext of facilitating the work of counterespionage, he claimed the powers of S.D.-Ausland. His plan was only partially successful. He obtained the right to correspond directly with the official "police attachés" or clandestine agents abroad, to ask them for information and to send them orders without passing through Amt VI (S.D.-Ausland).

To assure its predominance and control, the Gestapo at the beginning of the war had provided the necessary cadres for forming the *Geheime Feld-Polizei* (G.F.P.), the secret field police, placed under the orders of the O.K.W. With the help of the men whom he had infiltrated into it, Heydrich managed in practice to absorb the G.F.P. in the occupied countries when five thousand of its members were incorporated into the Gestapo. The agents of the "original" Gestapo amounted to some thirty-two thousand.

On October 1, 1944, an order from Himmler placed under Gestapo direction the agents of the frontier customs police (Zollgrenzschutz), previously responsible to the Ministry of Finance. The real frontier police (Grenzpolizei) had already long since been incorporated. This seizure of the customs officials[5] is an example of the arrogance of the Gestapo chiefs. The absorption of part of the Abwehr services at the end of 1944, on the contrary, was important and would have been of great advantage had the Nazi regime not collapsed a few months later. This annexation marked the end of the struggle for power waged by the Nazis against the Abwehr.

To insure control over the least of his agents, Himmler, at the beginning of 1940, signed an order by which the whole German police was subordinated for the duration of the war to the jurisdiction of the S.S.—thus robbing the tribunals of all chance of impeaching an agent of the police services. These investigations and the judicial decisions which might result were the exclusive prerogative of a special branch of the S.S. direction. In this way any control became impossible, and Himmler could reign as a despot, since investigations were ordered or not according to his pleasure. He could stop

---

[5] Half of its 54,000 agents continued to be paid by the Ministry of Finance, and a few days before the end of the war they were totally integrated.

them before their conclusion, bring weight to bear on the verdicts, break them or forbid their execution, pardon the culprits, or crush them with severity. By the beginning of 1940 Himmler had therefore perfected the formidable instrument he had begun to forge six years before. This instrument, thanks to the war, was to enjoy a field of action "worthy" of him.

PART FOUR

THE GESTAPO AT WAR
1940

Chapter 14
In Poland

During the winter of 1941–42, while the S.S. troops proceeded with their "purge" (extermination) of the civil population in the occupied regions of the U.S.S.R., Himmler made a speech to a group of S.S. officers designed to "boost their morale" (somewhat impaired by an accumulation of horrors which even they found difficult to stomach).

"The members of the Waffen S.S.," he said, "often think about the deportations of the people living here. I myself had these thoughts when I considered the difficult work carried out here by the Security Police, helped by your men who were of great service. The same thing happened in Poland at a temperature of 40 degrees below zero, when we had to transport hundreds of thousands of people, when we had to be brutal—you must understand that, but forget it immediately—and shoot thousands of Poles of repute."

Poland had been the testing bench for Nazi methods. It was in Poland, in the towns and villages of this unhappy "General Government" under the aegis of the bloodthirsty Hans Frank, that the pattern according to which the whole of Europe was soon to be decimated was perfected.

On October 7, 1939, Hitler had signed a decree, countersigned by Goering and Keitel, which appointed Himmler as Reich Commissioner and entrusted him with the "Germanization" of Poland. According to the terms of this decree, the Reichsfuehrer S.S. was ordered to bring back into the Reich true Germans living abroad, "to eliminate the sinister influence of foreign sections of the populace presenting a danger to the Reich and to the community of the German people," and to form new German colonies. In order to complete his task efficiently, he was given an absolutely free hand. Himmler immediately adapted these general instructions to his own ideas.

"It is not our duty," he said, "to Germanize the East in the old meaning of the term, that is to say to teach the people there the German language and law, but to see that only people of pure German blood live in the East." This was the natural consequence of the S.S. racial principles. "The cleansing of foreign races outside the incorporated territories is one of the essential aims to be accomplished in the German East."

In order to speed up this new type of "Germanization," Himmler ordered the appropriate measures to "prevent the increase of the Polish intellectual elite; distribute the freed lands on the liquidation of the Polish farmers to Germans and reclaim such 'good racial types' as might be discovered in such a mixture of races. I think it is our duty to adopt their children, to remove them from their surroundings, if necessary to steal or kidnap them. Where we can win good blood which we could utilize ourselves, we shall give it a place in the bosom of our people. Now gentlemen, perhaps you might find this cruel, but Nature is cruel and we shall destroy all alien and inferior blood."

Thus the Poles and the Jews found themselves expropriated, deprived of their goods, their houses, and their lands. The properties were handed to the new "colonials," who were "pure Germans" living abroad, now brought back into the German fold. The expropriated were sent to concentration camps if they were Jews or classed as possible opponents; otherwise they were sent to Germany to work in the armament factories, or as farm workers—sometimes even forced to work on their former lands as the serfs of their despoilers.

By a decree of December 12, 1940, Himmler founded the "racial register." On it had to be recorded:

(1) Pure-blooded Germans who had exercised political activity in a Nazi organization;
(2) Pure-blooded Germans who had taken no part in politics;
(3) Descendants of pure-blooded Germans or persons married to a pure-blooded German;
(4) The descendants of Germans absorbed by the Polish nation and thus considered as renegades.

The latter group had to undergo a course of re-education with a view to re-Germanizing them. Those who opposed this treatment or who failed to furnish details for this racial register were sent to a concentration camp.

The actual execution of these various measures of Germanization and colonization was entrusted to the head of the R.S.H.A., Heydrich, who carried out the expropriations, evacuations, and transport of those expelled to Germany and of the colonials in the liberated lands of annexed Poland,[1] or of the "General Government" under the iron rule of Governor Hans Frank.

"We must exterminate the Jews wherever we find them and whenever it is possible," said Frank. It was to achieve this end more easily that in 1940 the extermination camp of Auschwitz was opened near Cracow. Here, in an unhealthy marsh, millions of Jews were exterminated during the course of the next five years. Shortly after Auschwitz, two other camps were opened at Maidanek and Treblinka. Treblinka served as the prototype for the extermination camps created later.

At the end of a year the R.S.H.A. had banished from the part of Poland occupied by the Reich 1,500,000 Polish peasants or Jews and had dispatched them into the "General Government." At the end of May 1943 the expropriations had reached a total of 702,760 estates, totaling 6,367,971 hectares. This figure did not include the expropriations carried out in Danzig, East Prussia, Poznan, Zichenau, and Silesia. In these lands less than 500,000 pure-blooded Germans were installed—a third of the number of Poles expropriated. The Volksdeutsche Mittelstelle, which had opened a new branch under the control of Himmler, participated in the operation as did an "Immigration Center" with premises next to the head office of the police services and the S.S.

The Poles sent to Germany were reduced to the condition of slaves. For the first time Himmler's theory on the functioning of the future Reich was put into practice. The Poles, employed as farm workers, were subjected to a fifteen-point directive. As a start their regulation decreed: "In principle farm workers of Polish nationality have not the right to complain; in consequence no demands will be admitted by any official administration whatsoever." Thus, delivered completely to the arbitrary will of their masters, the Polish slaves had no right to leave their place of work. They had to observe a curfew from 8 P.M. to 6 A.M. in winter and from 9 P.M. to 5 A.M. in summer. They were not allowed to use bicycles except to reach their place of work, and with their employer's consent. They were forbidden to enter churches or temples, cinemas, theaters, places of cultural entertainment, or restaurants. They had

---

[1] An order of October 8, 1939, signed by Hitler, had incorporated into the Reich the four western provinces of Poland and a second order of October 12 had christened the remainder "the General Government of Poland."

no right to have sexual relations with women of any description. They had no right to hold meetings, to use any type of transport—railways, buses, etc.— and they were strictly forbidden to change employers. On the other hand, the latter had the right to inflict upon them corporal punishment "if orders and kind words failed." In this case the employer was not forced to give an account of his actions and could not be held responsible before the courts. He was also advised to keep the Polish workers away from their families. Any "crime" committed by a Polish worker was to be reported immediately by his employer under pain of serious sanctions. By the word "crime" was to be understood sabotage, "go-slow" or ill-will at work or insubordinate behavior. Severe punishments were provided for employers who "do not respect the distance which of necessity has to be kept between themselves and farm workers of Polish nationality. The same rule applies to women and young girls. The giving of supplementary rations is strictly forbidden."

The Polish women were placed as servants in German families, members of the N.S.D.A.P. having priority in obtaining one of these free servants. Between 400,000 and 500,000 of these unfortunate women, reduced to slavery "in order to bring a tangible relief to the German housewife ... to prevent her health being later impaired," were transplanted. Their situation was as wretched as that of the farm workers. "No time off is to be asked for. Female servants from the East cannot in principle leave the house except for domestic tasks. However, by way of reward they can be given the possibility of three hours' rest out of doors a week. This time off must end at nightfall, at the latest by 8 P.M." The same prohibitions which applied to men also applied to these unfortunate women: "Outside the house the Eastern servant must always carry her working permit which is to serve as her personal pass."

It will be seen that the term slavery is not exaggerated, and one is ashamed to say that the German "employers," presumably decent citizens of an ancient civilized country, accustomed themselves quite well to these regulations, which delivered into their hands other human beings, over whom they had the rights of life and death. Seven years of Nazi rule had been enough to make these iniquities acceptable. It is true that the big German industrialists sank much lower than the rest in this respect.

The Gestapo saw to it that this new code was respected. While hundreds of thousands of adults of both sexes were thus plunged into material and moral misery, thousands of children suffered an even more terrible fate—children of eight, half naked and undernourished, were used to drag carts and loads to certain labor camps.

The "work" of the Gestapo was so effective in Poland that Frank, giving an interview on February 6, 1940, to a journalist of the *Voelkischer Beobachter*, Kleist, scoffed at the terror measures taken by his opposite number, von Neurath, the Protector of Bohemia-Moravia. Neurath had placarded the walls of Czechoslovakia with red posters announcing the execution of seven Czech students. "If I ordered posters to be stuck on the wall each time we shoot seven Poles," jeered Frank, "the forests of Poland would not be large enough to provide the paper." Frank had announced on January 25, 1940, that he would deport a million Polish workers. To carry out this task the Gestapo organized police raids. They were so successful that, in August 1942 alone, 800,000 Polish workers were deported.

On May 10, 1940, the attention of the world, until then focused on Poland, was directed to another theater of operations. The German armies of the West, invading Holland, Belgium, and finally France, became the focal point for international observers. Frank wrote that he must take advantage of the fact that world interest was now concentrated on the West to liquidate thousands of Poles, commencing with the principal representatives of the Polish intelligentsia.

This extermination had been decided upon in September 1939, but to carry it out without providing too much ammunition for foreign critics, the Nazis had waited for a favorable moment. They were also careful to build up a few alibis.

In the middle of May, Frank summoned his Secretary of State, Josef Buehler, and the Reich Minister, Seyss-Inquart, to draw up the details for an operation entitled "Action A-B" (Ausserordentliche Befriedigungs-Aktion: Extraordinary action of pacification). It was carried out on the pretext of ending agitation dangerous to the security of the troops. As usual the Fuehrer, eight months earlier, had had one of his brilliant "intuitions" of events to come, since he had already decided upon the remedy.

Action A-B was entrusted exclusively to two representatives of the R.S.H.A. in Poland—Krueger, SS. Obergruppenfuehrer and General of Police, and Streckenbach, Brigadefuehrer of Amt I of the R.S.H.A., with the aid of S.S. reinforcements sent specially from Germany.

At the beginning of November 1939 the Gestapo had arrested the professors of Cracow University, and had sent them to concentration camps inside the Reich. For the number of individuals to be liquidated during Action A-B, it was considered too formidable and the transfer to Germany too complicated for this procedure to be followed. It was decided to simplify matters. "We have no need to put these elements in German concentration camps," wrote Frank after his meeting with Krueger and Streckenbach, "for that would entail difficulties and tiresome correspondence with the families. It is better to settle these questions in the country itself and in the simplest possible manner."

Mass arrests were therefore carried out, after which there was a kind of parody of a trial. (The trial was of course entirely meaningless, the cases being left entirely to the discretion of the Gestapo.) On May 30 Frank issued his final instructions:

"Any attempt made by the legal authorities to intervene in Action A-B, undertaken by the police, will be considered as high treason against the State and German interests.... The reprieve commission in my service is not to interfere in these matters. Action A-B has to be carried out exclusively by the chief of police and S.S. Krueger and his organization. It is a simple internal operation of pacification which is necessary and must be done outside the frame of regular procedure."

Thus, deprived of all legal protection, excluded from any possibility of reprieve, the Polish intellectuals were coldly "liquidated" by the Gestapo and the S.S. When this task was completed Streckenbach returned to Berlin and resumed his everyday administrative tasks. A farewell ceremony was staged for his departure. Frank made a touching little speech of thanks and congratulations for his good work. In it we read this terrible phrase: "What you, Brigadefuehrer Streckenbach, and your men have accomplished in the General Government must not be forgotten; you have no need to feel ashamed of it."

Subsequently the Gestapo extended its powers. A decree signed on October 2, 1943, by Frank gave it the possibility of legalizing the worst atrocities. By this time more than seventeen thousand Poles had already been shot as hostages. Frank commented as follows: "We must not be moved to pity when we learn that seventeen thousand persons have been shot. They, too, are the victims of the war." But "foreign propaganda" made a great stir over these executions, and a method was found to get around this. Rather than change the procedure, the word "hostage" was banished from the official vocabulary and these murders were legalized by the creation on October 2, 1943, of the *Standgerichte* (exceptional tribunals), composed exclusively of members of the Gestapo. Paragraph four of the decree stated: "The exceptional tribunals of the Security Police must be composed of a Fuehrer S.S. from the Security Police and the S.D. and two other members of the same service." Paragraph six stated: "The sentences of these exceptional tribunals of the Security Police must be carried out on the spot."

Thus the Gestapo could act at the greatest possible speed. It sought out the enemies of the people, arrested them, judged them, and executed them. On the publication of the decree, hundreds of Poles detained in the Cracow jails were "judged" and executed.

While the Gestapo and the S.D. unleashed their reign of terror on Poland, Heydrich did not neglect his other tasks.

The agitation which had been felt in certain army circles at the moment of the planned aggression in Czechoslovakia had not eluded the innumerable "feelers" of the S.D. The S.D. had got wind of von Kleist's journey to London in 1938, without being able to pinpoint the identity of this envoy of the conspirators, or the exact nature of his mission. It was believed, however, by Himmler that he had brought back a letter from Churchill, but the investigation had made no further progress. In August 1939, during the preparations for the attack on Poland, the soldiers had shown signs of becoming once more restless and frustrated. Himmler and Heydrich resolved to bring matters into the open and to discover what liaison could exist between the latent opposition and the British Intelligence Service. The inquiries carried out in Germany yielded no results, and it was then decided to start from the other direction—from the British end.

For this delicate mission Himmler and Heydrich chose two bright young S.D. men, Walter Schellenberg and Helmuth Knochen. Both were ex-university men. Heydrich had felt that, in order to make a serious contact with the British, men with civilized manners, speaking correct rather than refined English, capable of avoiding obvious conversational traps should be chosen. The results of the adventure prove that the choice was excellent.

Young Knochen had just been transferred to Amt VI (S.D.-Ausland), where he had been ordered to create new spy networks abroad. He made every effort to find exiled Germans in humble straits who might be open to "interesting" offers. Knochen had made a study of the subject and kept an eye on the *émigrés* in every country. He was thus able to recruit a certain Franz Fischer, a doctor of economics, who was living in poor circumstances in Paris. Possibly at the request of the S.D., Fischer moved to Holland where he became an agent. He was able to make contacts with British circles in Holland and soon with agents of the intelligence service, who prospected the clubs frequented by German *émigrés*. Knochen summoned Fischer to the Dutch frontier and asked him to suggest to the British that they should establish a contact with a representative of an opposition group, composed of German army officers.

By mid-October, 1939, Fischer had come to an arrangement with the British. The Polish campaign was now virtually over, and the Allies were expecting an assault in the West. Any information on a possible weakness in the German military corps would therefore be extremely valuable to them. M.I.-5 did not know that Fischer was what is known as a "double agent," and that he was "briefed" by the Düsseldorf S.D.

The preliminary setup completed, Schellenberg relieved Knochen to make the direct contact. Fischer's "trusted man" was able to organize a first meeting, which took place on October 21 in the small Dutch town of Zutphen. Schellenberg had assumed the identity of Captain Schaemmel, of the O.K.W. Transport Service. A Captain Schaemmel actually existed; the British agents were able to check him from the German army lists. As a precaution the real Schaemmel was sent on a mission to the East. Schellenberg, alias Schaemmel, managed to inspire confidence in the British agents, Major Stevens, Captain Payne-Best, and Lieutenant Coppens. Several contacts took place in Holland, where Schellenberg accompanied his interlocutors to Arnhem and to The Hague.

During one of his trips Schellenberg was accompanied by a very respectable-looking man whom he introduced as the "General," and head of a Resistance Group of the Wehrmacht. The General, who was cultured, distinguished, and a brilliant conversationalist, made an excellent impression on the British agents. Schellenberg had entrusted this difficult task to an amateur, Dr. de Crinis, a well-known Berlin psychiatrist.

A swift journey to London in a special plane was even suggested. Between visits Schellenberg returned to his headquarters at Düsseldorf to inform

Berlin as to the progress of the affair. On October 31, during a trip to The Hague, the "phony" Schaemmel was given a transmitting set, which would enable him to communicate regularly with the M.I.-5 agents in Holland, and also a special letter of credit allowing him to call a secret telephone number in The Hague. The affair seemed to have started well, and Schellenberg could hope that he would achieve his two objectives: to hoodwink the British Secret Service by giving them false information, and to be able to contact a core of hostile soldiers. A new encounter took place on November 7, once more in Holland, and a meeting was arranged for the following day.

On the afternoon of the 8th a special detachment of twelve S.S. men arrived at Düsseldorf, on orders from Himmler to insure the "protection" of Schellenberg. It was commanded by Naujocks, whose efficiency had been appreciated during the Gleiwitz incident.

The same evening, at about 9:30 P.M., Hitler spoke in the Buergerbräukeller in Munich. It was to commemorate, as he did each year, the November 9 heroes, the victims of the abortive putsch of 1923 which had started from this particular beer hall. For some reason neither Goering nor Himmler were present at this commemorative evening. Hitler made an abnormally short speech and left the beer hall immediately after the speech, whereas he usually lingered on chatting familiarly with the veterans of the Party.

A few minutes later—ten or twelve minutes according to witnesses— a tremendous explosion half destroyed the hall, leaving seven dead and sixty-three wounded. Had Hitler not left in time he would have been killed, for the bomb had been hidden in a column just behind him in the middle of the hall, at the spot where he always stood to make his speech.

An hour later Himmler telephoned to Schellenberg at Düsseldorf, informing him of the outrage and giving orders to capture the three British agents whom he was to meet the following day at Venlo, a small Dutch frontier town about forty miles from Düsseldorf. A special S.S. detachment was to help him with, his task. This was the version given by Schellenberg. It seems highly suspect. One fact alone shows the premeditation of the kidnaping and the Munich attempt itself—the arrival of the S.S. detachment in Düsseldorf a few hours *before* the bursting of the bomb in Munich. Schellenberg had no need of protection on November 8, since he had managed to win the confidence of the M.I.-5 agents. This detachment was not merely an escort but a special commando. Furthermore, Schellenberg's meetings were always arranged in Holland and often took him very far into Dutch territory. It is difficult to see how Naujocks and his twelve S.S. men could have insured his safety.

On the afternoon of November 9 Schellenberg waited for the British agents in a café near the frontier at Venlo. The moment the British opened the door of their big Buick, a car full of S.S. crashed the frontier barrier and entered Holland. Naujocks and his men opened fire at the Buick. The British replied and Lieutenant Coppens collapsed, mortally wounded. Naujocks and one of his men, Goetsch, rushed on the Buick and pulled out Best, Stevens, and the wounded men "like bundles of hay," as Schellenberg wrote later.

The S.S. leaped into the Buick and returned to the frontier, covering with their fire the retreat of the car containing the three prisoners. This kidnaping was all over in a few minutes.[2] It risked causing grave diplomatic complications, for it had necessitated a violation of the Dutch frontier and armed aggression. The crime itself had been committed in Holland; Lieutenant Coppens died a few hours later in Düsseldorf Hospital, and, thanks to his papers, was identified as being in actual fact Lieutenant Klop, of the Dutch Secret Service. These risks were not justified for such a meager capture. But Hitler and Himmler had in mind a more rewarding use for the prisoners.

On November 10 a Munich cabinetmaker, named Elser, was arrested at the frontier post of Lörrach near Basle, while trying to cross into Switzerland. He was found to be carrying a postcard showing the inside of the Buergerbräukeller. A cross had been marked in ink on the column in which the bomb had been placed. Brought back to Berlin, Elser was given a lengthy interrogation at Prinz Albrechtstrasse, where Best and Stevens had also been taken. Heydrich, Mueller, and Schellenberg conducted the interrogation. Elser showed little hesitation in admitting that he was the author of the attempt. He was even very proud of having made a bomb with a delayed-action mechanism, which allowed the explosion to be fixed ten days in advance. This technical prowess which no specialist had yet succeeded in equaling had allowed him to place the bomb in the column before the security authorities checked the hall. Best and Stevens knew nothing of the

[2] Naujocks kept the Buick which was regarded as booty and used it for months for his personal use, parading in Berlin at the wheel of this huge car, an unusual sight in that period of petrol rationing.

attempt, but Nazi propaganda devised one of those pieces of chicanery for which it became notorious and divided the responsibility between M.I.-5 and the Schwarze Front of Otto Strasser, now a refugee in Switzerland.

Elser appears to have been another van der Lubbe. The Nazis did not have the courage to stage a sensational trial, since the burning of the Reichstag case had left a nasty taste in the mouth. Elser was sent to Sachsenhausen concentration camp and then to Dachau. He remained there until 1945. Confined in the hut for prisoners of note, he was given a carpenter's bench where he could make what he pleased. He even made a lyre on which he played for hours on end. The other prisoners christened him the lyre player. By some strange chance it was in the concentration camp that Best and Stevens met for the first time their "accomplice," Elser. The latter told them that he had made his bomb at the instigation of two individuals who had introduced him by night into the Buergerbräukeller. He told them, too, that at the request of his accomplices he had equipped his bomb with a delayed-action fuse and with a second electric fuse, triggered by a simple interrupter at the end of a long thread which would allow the explosion to be caused at any given moment. Whereas Elser believed that the bomb had exploded as result of the time fuse, it is more probable that it was brought about by the second fuse after the departure of Hitler and his entourage.

Elser's accomplices took him to the Swiss frontier, where he was arrested by the Gestapo. Prior to this they had "planted" the compromising post-card upon him. The details of this affair lead one to assume that the attempt was organized by the Gestapo for propaganda purposes. The kidnaping of Best and Stevens allowed it to shift the responsibility onto M.I.-5 for the conception and realization of a plan which was too complicated for Elser, a rather limited individual, to be held as the sole author. The death of the Dutch Lieutenant Klop was exploited by the Nazis, who drew from his association with Best and Stevens the argument that collusion existed between the Dutch and the British governments against Germany, an argument that would be further produced when German troops violated the Dutch frontier in 1940.

Best and Stevens were held in custody until the arrival of the American troops. As for Elser, on a secret order from Himmler, he was murdered by the Gestapo in April 1945, and his death attributed to the Allied bombing. The Nazis had no desire for Elser to fall alive into the hands of the Allies.

The outbreak of war in September 1939 saw the centralization of German police organizations by the creation of the R.S.H.A. Another change took place at the same time within the S.S. as it was geared to the necessities of war.

Until then the S.S. troops had only had to fight unarmed civilians. Even in Czechoslovakia they had never met a military force, since that country had been delivered captive to the monster by the other European nations in a naïve attempt to satisfy its appetite.

When, in the spring of 1939, Hitler decided to attack Poland it was obvious that this time Germany would be forced to wage a real war. Himmler wanted his S.S. to play as brilliant a role as possible in the conflict. He saw an opportunity for forming a real army, not merely a home force, which would allow him to attain his ultimate objective—to become a great military leader. On the practical plane this creation of an S.S. army had the advantage of constituting a counterweight to the military power of the Wehrmacht, and its role could be capital in case of an open conflict with the generals. It could also be asked to accomplish certain tasks, which ordinary troops made up of conscripted soldiers would doubtless find it repugnant to carry out.

For a long time it had been planned that the permanent S.S. regiment at the exclusive disposal of the Fuehrer should be outside the authority of the O.K.W. An order from Hitler dated August 18, 1938, had specified that the S.S. Verfuegungstruppen were to form no part of either the Wehrmacht or the police (although they came under the orders of the Reichsfuehrer S.S. Himmler); that the period of service in these regiments was to be four years (by voluntary enlistment); and that the normal obligations of military service should be satisfied by an enlistment of equal duration in the S.S. Korps. In case of war these units were to be used "by the Commander in Chief of the Army, within the framework of the wartime Army," but would remain politically "a unit of the N.S.D.A.P." Finally, in case of moblization, Hitler reserved the right to fix the date, the strength, and conditions for "incorporating the S.S. Verfuegungstruppen in the wartime Army, taking into account the internal political situation of the moment."

On the publication of this order, Himmler reorganized the S.S. Verfuegungstruppen by motorizing them and creating new anti-tank units, and machine gun and reconnaissance battalions. In July 1939 he added an artillery regiment, thus completing the transformation of his "alert troops" into fighting units (Kampftruppen).

At the beginning of September 1939 began the conversion of the S.S. Verfuegungstruppen into Waffen S.S. troops, which Europe would soon learn to know. At the beginning of 1940, a host of volunteers had enlisted in the Waffen S.S. until they totaled about 100,000 men—60,000 volunteers and 36,000 conscripted men.

In Poland the first units of the Waffen S.S. behaved with the ferocity expected of them—with what Goering called "exemplary gallantry." Himmler then received permission to create new divisions. The Waffen S.S., after surviving the ordeal of war and growing hardened to it, was to form the home army of the police, entrusted with the maintenance of order "in critical moments." The Army saw itself deprived of any internal role within Germany. Hitler knew that maintenance of order is often an excuse for the Army to seize power. Unable to protest at this loss of police powers which the Army had always pretended to despise, the generals complained of the independence now given to the S.S. The officers repeated the formula preached by Hitler at the period of the Roehm purge: "There is only one armed force in Germany, the Wehrmacht."

Protests were in fact so strong that Hitler ordered his aide-de-camp to draw up an explanatory note. This note was never circulated; Keitel himself, in contrast to his usual docility, declared to Hitler that this gesture would be considered an affront by the Army. Finally Brauchitsch was given the job of pacifying the restless spirits by informing the officers that it was merely a question of "police troops," which would compulsorily participate in military operations.

The organizations in which every young German had to spend several years were controlled by the Party. It was easy for the S.S. to beat the propaganda drum and to recruit the best material. This "taking the cream off the top" deprived the Wehrmacht and the Luftwaffe of their future cadres. "Both the land army and the Luftwaffe have protested, quite rightly," said Goering, "because this cornering of the best volunteer elements deprives the ground troops and the Luftwaffe of men who would have made excellent officers." Hitler turned a deaf ear, and Himmler received the authorization to form his new division.

The needs of the moment, and the determination constantly to increase the size of his forces, had made Himmler abandon his famous "rules of the blood" hitherto presented as essential for the "preservation of the Nazi race and ideology." Things went still further, and now the tall, fair-haired Aryans of pure Nordic blood, the pride and *raison d'être* of the S.S., gradually assumed the most unexpected forms: the creation of the Moslem division, "Handschar," in 1943; the Albanian division, "Skanderberg"; the French division, "Charlemagne," and a Hungarian cavalry division in 1944; the Croat division, "Kama," the Flemish "Langemarck," the Walloon (Wallonia), the Dutch ("Landstorm Nederland"), and the Italian in 1945. In the meantime less important units had been formed from what Hitler called the "savage races," and we find regiments from Turkestan and the Caucasus, a battalion of Norwegian skiers, a Bulgarian and two Rumanian battalions, and three Cossack divisions. A strange medley of troops, all wearing the S.S. uniform reserved three or four years earlier for the "elite of the Germanic race," after a rigorous control of the candidate's family tree!

In this way more than a million men belonged to the Waffen S.S. The passage of these "elite troops" was marked everywhere by the worst atrocities.[3]

Chapter 15
The Gestapo in France

For the French, the war really began on May 10, 1940. For more than eight months French and British troops were bogged down in the quicksands of the "phony" war. People began to get used to this strange, static conflict, where the main preoccupation was the distraction of the conscripted men, their wireless sets and football games, rather than offensive action. The German offensive, which had been expected for some weeks by the Allied staffs, brought things into their true perspective.

No one, however, expected the hurricane of steel which was to be unleashed on the country. Events progressed at an overwhelming speed, and on June 14 the O.K.W. published the following communiqué: "As a result of the total collapse of the entire French front between the Channel and the Maginot Line near Montmédy, the French High Command has abandoned

---

[3] At the end of the war the Waffen S.S. totaled 40 divisions and 594,000 men. It had lost 320,000 men by October 1, 1944.

its original intention of defending the French capital. While this communiqué is being broadcasted the victorious German troops are entering Paris."

Paris had fallen. The troops of von Kuechler's Eighteenth Army entered Paris by the Porte de la Villette, on June 14 at 5:30 A.M., precisely thirty-six days after the offensive had begun on the Dutch frontier. Two formations advanced at dawn, one toward the Eiffel Tower and the other toward the Arc de Triomphe. They had hoisted the Swastika flag. Before midday General von Stutnitz, the first commandant of "Greater Paris," took up his quarters in the Hôtel Crillon. Everything went off according to plan, and everything seemed to have been prepared a long time ahead. During the following days a regular flow of German troops entered Paris, took up their quarters there, or crossed the city on their way south.

Among these troops a small group of men wearing the uniform of the G.F.P. (Geheime Feld-Polizei), the secret military police, passed unnoticed. It comprised only a few light vehicles, little armament, and no more than twenty men. Nevertheless this small, almost clandestine organization formed the root of the German police organization which for four years was to terrorize the French.

When the German troops entered Poland the O.K.W. formally protested at the simultaneous arrival of police-army commandos. Himmler, however, had obtained Hitler's consent; the police services entered Poland at the same time as the fighting troops, as they had done in Austria and Czechoslovakia. When the plan of attack in the West was completed, the O.K.W. objected even more energetically against the same procedure being followed in France. The behavior of the S.S. and the Gestapo in Poland had shocked some of the generals (they were eventually to become inured to it), but this time they showed such determination that Hitler yielded. No police unit, no S.D. Einsatzkommando, was authorized to accompany the Army in its advance through France. Police powers were entrusted to the military administration. The Army was thus escaping from Himmler's control.

This decision placed Himmler in a difficult position. He had realized the danger which would result for his S.S. and police organizations if the victorious Army took over the administration of the occupied territories of the West. He, therefore, had to form a "bridgehead" which would allow him progressively to undermine the powers momentarily held by the soldiers.

Himmler ordered Heydrich to form a *Sonderkommando* (an independent commando) with the mission of settling in Paris at the same time as the first troops. It was a question both of security and of prestige. Heydrich, therefore, carefully chose the detachment instructed to carry out this delicate mission. He confined himself to twenty men, a small enough force to arouse no suspicion and yet sufficient to form the first "bridgehead." To get into France he used a military stratagem. The twenty men were dressed in uniforms of the G.F.P. (military police comparable with the West's M.P.'s), and their vehicles were given military number plates. In this way the Sonderkommando could reach Paris without being challenged.

On the evening of June 14 the commando camped in the Hôtel du Louvre. Early next morning it set to work. One of its members visited the Prefecture and demanded the dossiers of the German *émigrés* and Jews and a certain number of dossiers relating to political opponents of the Nazis.

Who were these men and, more particularly, who was their leader?

To command his Sonderkommando, Heydrich had selected the young intellectual who had done so brilliantly at Venlo with the kidnaping of the two British intelligence officers—Helmuth Knochen. At the age of thirty he had shown an exceptional capacity for organization and decision. He was a first-class athlete, a university graduate, cultured, polished, with agreeable manners. Knochen chose his own team with one exception: Mueller, head of Amt IV (the Gestapo) insisted upon being represented in the group by one of his trusted men, Sturmbannfuehrer Boemelburg, an old professional policeman whose ability was well known. Boemelburg was the only representative of the Gestapo in the unit. It was obvious that initially the group would have no executive powers, and that this would possibly be the case for some time. The Gestapo, therefore, figured in it only in a consultative role. The other members of the commando were very young; several of them were university graduates, like Hagen, who at the age of twenty-seven, although a member of the S.D. since 1934, had taken his degree in Berlin in February 1940, and had since dabbled in journalism.

Amt VI (S.D.-Ausland) had provided the other members of the team apart from Boemelburg and two men detached from the Waffen S.S. who were eventually to carry out the "strong-arm stuff." All of them had specialized for a long time in the analysis of foreign circles. Since 1935 the Gestapo and the S.D. had been studying the French police administration. A vast documentation had been compiled on France and its cultural, religious, artistic, and above all its economic and political mechanization. Each sector of the Gestapo and the S.D. was ordered to study in detail a French sector corresponding to its own. Thus the agents of the Berlin region had for many years studied "Region V," in other words, Paris.

The result of this ruthless preparation enabled agents of the Gestapo and the S.D. to move about on a terrain already familiar to them. They knew all the regional customs, the behavior of the inhabitants, and even the private lives of important personalities. Knochen himself had visited Paris in 1937 to see the Exhibition.

Knochen was born on March 14, 1910, at Magdeburg of a family modest in circumstances. His father, Karl Knochen, was a schoolteacher like Himmler's father, and young Helmuth had also received a strict education. He was an industrious pupil, obtained his *Arbitur*, the equivalent of the French *baccalauréat* at Magdeburg, and then continued his studies at the universities of Leipzig, Halle, and Göttingen.

In 1935 he obtained his Ph.D. with a thesis on an English playwright. His ambition was to become a littérateur, but his fate had already been influenced by politics. Knochen's father, a patriot of the old school, a great disciplinarian, an artillery captain in the reserve, and a veteran of the 1914–18 war, had been seriously wounded at Verdun, and for a long time suffered from almost total paralysis of his right arm. When his son was sixteen, he enrolled him in the youth section of the Stahlhelm, which embarked upon a violent nationalist campaign.

To help his parents Helmuth, for several months, became a gym instructor while attending his university courses, and then began to write a few articles for the local newspapers. In the meantime the Nazis had come to power, and it became increasingly difficult for a student to obtain his degree unless he belonged to one of the Party organizations.

On May 1, 1933, he joined the S.A. and was given the modest rank of Obertruppfuehrer. He had got himself involved in a situation which was to absorb him entirely. A little later his articles appeared in the *Studentpresse*, the organ of the Ministry for Culture. He enjoyed his new journalist activities. Finding them more remunerative than a professorship, in 1936 he abandoned his studies and entered the D.N.B., the official press agency of the Party, as editor. While covering the 1936 Olympic Games, he met one of his former professors, Dr. Six, who had left the university for the S.D., where he ran the press section. Dr. Six had no difficulty in influencing his old pupil who, in 1937, also entered the main office of the S.D. in Berlin. He was given the rank of S.S. Obersturmfuehrer. Entrusted at first with the analysis of the German press, he was a little later able to study the French, Belgian, and Dutch presses. The newspapers published in these countries by refugees, and all information concerning them, were his principal task. The initiative he had shown in the Venlo operation and its success brought him into the limelight and also the award of the Iron Cross, First and Second Class. It was this success, too, which caused him to be chosen to lead the Sonder-kommando into Paris on June 14, 1940.

Knochen took up quarters in the capital, first at the Hôtel du Louvre, then at the Hôtel Scribe, later at No. 57 boulevard Lannes, and finally at No. 72 avenue Foch, where he remained until the withdrawal in August 1944. He was a slim man with an emaciated rather unpleasant face, and gray-blue eyes which rarely smiled. A straight, thin nose, a rather wide mouth, with a twist to the left giving him a rather sardonic expression, a high, somewhat domed, intellectual forehead beneath his mop of auburn hair, gave him an appearance not entirely expected in the leader of a special commando. The young man who was to make his presence felt by the German police in Paris still looked the doctor of philosophy and not the "tough" he has generally been considered. His appearance and culture were, however, no obstacle to his work.

As soon as the Army discovered Knochen's group in Paris it reminded him that he had no power and "to regularize the situation" placed him under its control. Knochen insisted that he had no intention of encroaching upon the preserves of the Army of Occupation, and explained that his sole job was to investigate the activities of anti-Nazi German and Austrian refugees, Jews, Freemasons, Communists, and all the enemies of Nazism. He agreed to call upon the aid of the G.F.P. each time "executive measures," that is to say, house searches or arrests, were necessary. Knochen maneuvered with such skill that he managed to come to an agreement with Dr. Sowa, the head of the military police. The Knochen commando immediately began to fulfill its mission: it closed the offices of the anti-Germans and anti-Nazis, seized their records, searched the houses of German refugees, Freemasons, and of certain politicians, seizing compromising documents everywhere and appealing to the military police as soon as an arrest was needed.

The soldiers believed that, although Knochen's men were rather turbulent, it would be easy to keep them in control because of their numerical weakness. Twenty men was a trifle compared with the twenty-five hundred men of the G.F.P. already in Paris, whose numbers were soon swelled to six thousand.

Knochen having solidly entrenched his bridgehead, a second Sonderkommando of a score of men under Haupsturm-fuehrer Kiefer was sent to reinforce him. At the beginning of August a third contingent arrived under S.S. Unterstrum-fuehrer Roland Nosek, with the special mission of collecting political information. Nosek was a specialist in this branch. A member of the Party since 1932, he had visited Italy, Belgium, Hungary, Turkey, Rumania, Greece, and France.

He spoke fluent French, English, and Spanish. Since 1938 he belonged to S.D.-Ausland and had selected his own group, choosing only agents who spoke perfect French. This third team was heterogeneous: it included Germans who until then had been employees or traders, including a wine merchant, a divorced countess, two Luxemburgers, and a Czech schoolteacher.

This third team was quartered in the Hôtel du Boccador, with offices on the premises of the French Sûreté, 11 rue des Saussaies, where Boemelburg, representing the Gestapo and the SIPO in France, also took up quarters with his men.

At the same time Knochen began to install his services in the provinces, and at the beginning of August ordered Hagen to open a branch at Bordeaux to keep watch along the whole Atlantic coast from the Spanish frontier to the Loire, and over the whole depth of occupied France. Hagen, having at the outset only eighteen men and a secretary, took up his quarters temporarily in the King of the Belgians' yacht, at anchor in the port, before opening offices in the rue du Médoc. Like Knochen, he soon got to work, and at the beginning of 1941 added Brittany to his sphere of action, implanting branches in the ten principal towns of his zone, each in turn being able to introduce agents to other localities.

Friction with the Army was far from being over. Von Brauchitsch, the Army Commander in Chief, issued orders to his forces to oppose the work of Himmler's men, and in any case to prevent the slightest encroachment on military powers. Knochen, therefore, confined himself to intelligence about refugees, Communists, Jews, and Freemasons. But while respecting these rules he found himself in competition with another service—the Einsatzstab Rosenberg (Rosenberg combat staff). This was a unit organized by the racial theorist of the Party to seize the records of the religious or secret societies and in particular of the Masonic lodges. A conflict soon broke out. Here, too, Knochen's men were at a disadvantage, for, although Knochen was Himmler's representative in France, the Rosenberg organization had been given special powers by the Fuehrer himself. Ultimately an agreement was reached; the Rosenberg service was to seize only archives of historical interest, leaving the political and contemporary archives to Knochen, while the latter agreed to communicate to the Einsatzstab any historical documents it might discover. The rivalry, however, continued, and in fact Knochen never passed on a single document to Rosenberg.

These quarrels had shown Knochen the need for being "covered" by a superior, capable of dealing on an equal footing with competitors. He was relieved to see arrive an S.S. Brigadefuehrer of imposing stature, General Thomas, Heydrich's personal representative, with orders to supervise all the Sonderkommandos already at work. Bearing the title of "Representative of the Head of the Security Police and the S.D. for Belgium and France," Thomas was officially entrusted with the job of insuring liaison with the German Embassy and the military command in France. The infiltration appeared to have been an unqualified success.

General Thomas was a sort of colossus, as tall as Knochen but twice as broad, powerful and blustering. While Knochen was distinguished, reserved, and hard-working, Thomas had little talent for intelligence work, and sometimes treated him with levity. Previously in charge of the security behind the Siegfried Line with headquarters at Wiesbaden, it was said of him that he was more in the casino and the night clubs of that spa than in the fortifications of the line.

He was a boisterous fellow, ideal for shock tactics, a great drinker and womanizer, indiscriminate in his choice. He was also a personal friend of Heydrich, whom he accompanied on many memorable rounds of the Berlin warehouses. General Thomas held one trump card which had earned him Heydrich's trust and his appointment to Paris. His daughter, Heydrich's mistress, had had a child by him.

In Paris, Thomas took up his quarters at 57 boulevard Lannes. He had to spend his time between Paris and Brussels, for his area included Belgium. When in France his activities consisted of haunting the cabarets of Pigalle and the Champs Elysées. He had, however, political and police pretensions and a kind of hobbyhorse, the separatist parties. He contacted representatives of Basque, Corsican, and Breton movements, convinced that the help he gave them would allow them to extend their action and play an important role in internal French policy, safe in the knowledge that their skeleton strengths barred them from any important action. At the same time Thomas received in Paris representatives of the parties which had always been prepared to collaborate with the Nazis. Among these, one movement, the C.S.A.R. (Comité-Secret d'Action Révolutionnaire), a violently anti-Republican and anti-Semitic body, was to play an important part in Thomas' ultimate undoing. Its two leaders, Deloncle and Filliol, were soon constant visitors to Thomas and to some extent became his political advisers. They then created a party known as M.S.R. (Mouvement Social Révolutionnaire).

Thomas and Knochen, the ringleader in the game, exploited those who from venality or conviction had for several years shown themselves receptive to the intense propaganda which the Nazis had poured out in France. The most insidious instrument was the Office of the German Railways, which, under cover of tourism, distributed pamphlets and brochures of all sorts, welcoming interested parties, detecting those who were susceptible to more than merely the natural and architectural beauties of Germany and offering them incredible facilities.[4] The propaganda ministry and the D.N.B. (official press agency) subsidized certain papers and, under cover of publicity contracts, obtained from them an attitude sometimes clearly favorable to or at least understanding of Nazism.

---

[4] In Switzerland the head office of the Reich railways in Zürich used the same technique. One of its directors, Streibel, was arrested and exchanged for a Swiss detained in Germany in the autumn of 1943. His "stand-in," Lemberger, was condemned on May 28, 1942, to two years' imprisonment and deportation.

A certain number of publications were fed by Nazi funds, distributed through the publicity agency, Prima. For example, *France enchainée*, the organ of the Rassemblement Antijuif de France, was founded by Louis Darquier, known as "de Pellepoix," and put itself at the disposal of the Nazis. This publication later incited persecution of the Jews in France. There was also *Le Grand Occident*, whose managing director, a certain Paul Ferdonnet, was unknown in 1937, but achieved notoriety in 1939 under the name of "The Traitor of Stuttgart."[5] An important role was also played by the Comité France-Allemagne, whose leading members were Georges Scapini and Fernand de Brinon. These newspapers and movements contributed to the shaping of part of French public opinion, bringing it progressively to look with "comprehension" and indulgence upon Nazi methods.

Frenchmen who showed themselves well disposed to the regime had long since been earmarked by two organizations: Weltdienst, with its head office at Erfurt, which published a bimonthly bulletin in six languages entitled *World Service*, and the Deutscher Fichte Bund, whose head office was in Hamburg and which distributed Pan-Germanic pamphlets and brochures. Anti-Semitism was the basis of this propaganda. It enlisted sympathizers to the German cause, from whom the S.D. and the Gestapo could recruit precious agents. Contacts with the collaborationist parties were so fruitful that Knochen detached one of his minions, Sommer, to deal with them.

Whatever the activity, the Knochen services were still under the military administration. The Military Command in France (Militärbefehlshaber), with its headquarters in the Hôtel Majestic, avenue Kléber, under General von Stuelpnagel, was divided into two branches: the staff under General Speidel, and the military administration under Dr. Schmidt.

It has been seen that, at the beginning of the occupation, the Gestapo in France was forced to confine itself strictly to intelligence and played a very significant part. This situation continued until May 1942.

---

[5] This name was given to Ferdonnet at the beginning of the war, when he was employed by Radio Stuttgart and wrote scripts for German propaganda. By some strange "premonition" his paper had published, in its April 1939 number, an editorial entitled "Pétain in Power."

In intelligence there existed only one organization empowered to deal with matters of security and military intelligence—the Abwehr. With headquarters in the Hôtel Lutétia, and run by Lieutenant Colonel Rudolf,[6] the Abwehr, in common with all spy organizations, invariably camouflaged itself under harmless social pretexts. For instance, one of its most important services in Germany was called the "Office for Recruitment of Female Staff for the Red Cross of the Twelfth Army Corps"; and in France the Nantes office was called "Direction des Travaux de Nantes."

In comparison with this vast organization the group directed by Knochen seemed very weak and defenseless. It was, however, after months of underground struggle to absorb its rival.

But in anticipation of this hard-won victory, the position of General Otto von Stuelpnagel complicated Knochen's task. Von Stuelpnagel was in fact fiercely opposed to the presence of Himmler's men in his domain, and did everything possible to prevent Knochen's units from functioning. Tension grew so strong that Stuelpnagel ordered Knochen to cease even his intelligence activities, making all contact with Heydrich impossible by suppressing Knochen's means of communication with Germany.

Knochen had found no support from any quarter. From the German Embassy he came up against silent opposition. A letter from the Minister of Foreign Affairs, dated August 3, 1940, had settled the part to be played by Abetz, the ambassador in France. He was to give a lead to both the Secret Military Police and the Secret State Police in everything regarding French internal politics, the press, radio, and propaganda. It was he, too, who was to advise what documents were to be seized for political reasons. "The Fuehrer has given express orders that Abetz alone, as ambassador, be responsible for all political questions in occupied and non-occupied France." As usual the Gestapo and the S.D. had never heeded Abetz's advice.

It was in an unexpected field that Knochen sought his revenge. He was now seen assiduously frequenting the Parisian salons—leading the life of a society man, using his culture and his wit to impress important people at whose homes he was introduced to French political figures. He was soon very popular at all the meetings and parties given by active collaborationists

---

[6] Rudolf formerly belonged to No. 1 Group of the Abwehr, commanded by Lieutenant Colonel Schmidt, alias Dr. Peterson, a land forces specialist.

in the hope of doing profitable business. Knochen was thus *au courant* not only with the lively gossip of Parisian life, but could also obtain vital information on statesmen and politicians past and present, on the true situation of economy and industry, public opinion, the trends, the leaders of the opposition, the Resistance Movement and its contacts with England and America. Some of his new friends became his agents. (It would be cruel enough to quote names now forgotten by the general public, but it is intriguing today to see some of the people formerly on Knochen's payroll giving lessons in patriotism.)

Knochen's nominal superior Dr. Thomas had chosen another way of influencing French home policy. From the start of the occupation anti-Jewish measures had been taken by the German authorities and by the Vichy Government. At the same time the anti-Semitic press, in receipt of important subsidies from the German propaganda services, opened a campaign designed to provoke anti-Semitic feelings among the French people. The sheer violence of these campaigns resulted in their failure.

Thomas, however, who preferred the Pigalle night clubs to the drawing rooms of Passy, had as his political advisers Deloncle, one of the leaders of the Cagoulards and head of the M.S.R., and Deloncle's adjutant, the killer Filliol. To "arouse public opinion" they suggested to Thomas in September 1941 that a few attempts should be organized against the Paris synagogues. This seemed a brilliant idea to Knochen's chief: it reminded him of the spontaneous pogroms organized by the Nazis in Germany in 1938. He detailed Obersturmfuehrer Hans Sommer, of Amt VI, whose special task was liaison with French collaborators, to arrange with Deloncle and Filliol the practical details of the operation with the greatest discretion and above all without the knowledge of the Army, and particularly of Stuelpnagel. Sommer caused the necessary "equipment" to be sent from Berlin.

On the night of October 2–3, the Parisians were awakened by a series of explosions. At 2:30 A.M. an explosion seriously damaged the synagogue in the rue des Tourelles; at 3:40 A.M. another charge exploded in the rue Notre Dame de Nazareth; an hour later it was the large synagogue in the rue de la Victoire; at five o'clock in the rue Sainte-Isaure, and at 5:15 in rue Copernic. Taking into account a bomb in the rue Pavée and another in a private oratory, avenue Montespan, there were therefore seven attempts on the same night, in spite of the Wehrmacht patrols. Two Wehrmacht soldiers on their rounds were in fact seriously wounded and the conflagrations caused great damage to neighboring buildings.

Deloncle was very proud of this exploit carried out by his Cagoulards.[7] Thomas was exultant. But on October 6 Stuelpnagel, on learning of the authors of these outrages, wrote to G.H.Q., complaining that Obersturm-fuehrer Sommer, on the orders of Knochen, had delivered explosives of German origin "to French criminals to carry out their attempts."

On October 21, 1941, a letter, bearing the stamp of the G.H.Q. military administration in Paris, was sent to Heydrich as head of SIPO-S.D. in Berlin. After recalling that these outrages had wounded two members of the Wehrmacht and several Frenchmen, it went on: "These crimes have been perpetrated by Frenchmen belonging to circles revolving around Deloncle. It was S.S. Obersturmfuehrer Sommer who provided the explosives. S.S. Obersturmfuehrer Sommer was fully cognizant of all details of the incidents. S.S. Obersturmfuehrer Sommer acted on the orders of the head of the Parisian service of the SIPO-S.D., S.S. Obersturmbannfuehrer Knochen. The latter has explained this affair in a joint report addressed to the military commander on October 4, 1941. His explanation that it was a purely French operation is incorrect in every respect. ... The authors and instigators of the outrages of October 2–3 must have been fully aware that their undertaking would have grave consequences for innocent people, with potentially serious political consequences."

This danger had only been avoided by the swift identification of the authors of the outrage, but the prestige of the Army of Occupation was in jeopardy, for the French police had already discovered the truth. The author of the letter—probably Dr. Best—finally came to the point:

"The responsibility for the measures taken by the Sonderkommando of the SIPO-S.D. and for the behavior of this Sonderkommando is assumed by its leader, even if it is not admitted that the latter participated directly in the affair. There must, however, be a change in the leadership of the Sonderkommando by reason of the political implications on the position of the German administration. For this reason the Commander in Chief of the German Army demands that S.S. Brigadefuehrer Thomas be relieved

---

[7] Deloncle was murdered by the Gestapo in January 1944.

of his post. The O.K.W. takes it for granted the Berlin authorities are in agreement that Dr. Knochen and S.S. Obersturmfuehrer Sommer should no longer be employed in occupied territory."

Stuelpnagel thought that he would thus be able to eliminate these irritants to his command. The sympathy shown to the French, however, seems misplaced when one thinks that the very day this letter was signed sixteen equally innocent hostages fell at Nantes to the bullets of a firing squad, and that on the following day twenty-seven more were to be shot at Châteaubriant.

On the administrative plane also Stuelpnagel was to be disappointed. Knochen was too valuable to be got rid of. General Thomas was more vulnerable, despite the high protection he enjoyed from his son-in-law on the wrong side of the blanket. Heydrich suggested a solution which satisfied everyone: Thomas asked to be relieved of his duties and a few days later was appointed head of the SIPO-S.D. for the newly occupied Eastern territories at Kiev.

Knochen found himself master of a police service without power, the butt of a punctilious surveillance by the soldiers. His intelligence and skill were, however, to enable him to extricate himself from this impasse.

Chapter 16
The Gestapo and the Army

The basic rivalry existing between the Army and the Gestapo rested on a difference of doctrine.

Article 3 of the Armistice, signed on June 22 at Rethondes, is somewhat ambiguous. It states: "In the occupied regions of France, the German Reich will exercise all the rights of an occupying power. The French Government agrees to facilitate by every possible means the regulations relative to the exercise of these rights and their execution, with the cooperation of the French administration. The French Government will immediately request all the authorities and French administrative services of the occupied territory to conform to the regulations issued by the German military authorities and to collaborate with the latter in a correct manner."

The German High Command intended to apply these conditions to the letter and assumed absolute control of the French administration of the occupied zone. The military point of view was that it must insure the administration of occupied France by the French themselves, merely seeing that the French services strictly applied the German orders. The German military administrative role, therefore, was to be limited to direction and control.

The working directions given by the military administration (Army H.Q.—Q.G. No. 800/40 of August 22, 1940) are clear.

"All activity of the military administration will be guided by the principle that only measures designed to facilitate the military occupation of the country will be taken. On the other hand, it is not the province of the military administration to concern itself with internal French policy. In all the administrative measures it will be called upon to take, the military administration will, as a matter of principle, use the channels of the French authorities."

The Army thought this procedure the most advantageous: the difficulties in execution would be solved by the French themselves, the administration would be more economical, and above all the application of German directions under a French cloak would avoid the "instinctive revulsion of the French nation to everything coming from the Germans." This attitude explains why the German authorities gave such a warm welcome to Frenchmen who agreed to collaborate with them. They did not want the annexation of France but an adjustment of her political line.

Thus, in the opinion of the soldiers, interference by the German police services risked "ruining everything." The only police branch they accepted was the anti-Jewish section directed by Dannecker, one of Boemelburg's adjutants.

Theo Dannecker was a twenty-seven-year-old Bavarian from Munich. He was under the orders of Eichmann, who had personally appointed him as his representative in Paris, where he arrived in September 1940. He was nominally placed under Knochen's administrative and disciplinary command, but actually received his orders direct from Eichmann.

Xavier Vallat, who was the first general commissioner for Jewish questions,[8] at his trial stated that Dannecker "was a fanatical Nazi who went

---

[8] Vallat was replaced by Darquier de Pellepoix on May 6, 1942.

into a trance every time the word Jew was mentioned." When the anti-Semitic measures came into force he watched the trials of the victims, giving vent to vehement notes of protest whenever the slightest compassion was shown.

Dannecker installed himself at avenue Foch and rue des Saussaies. He thought of using French anti-Semites, helping them with advice and money to create an institute for studying the Jewish question, for which he commandeered the premises of a Jewish business firm in the boulevard Haussmann. In this way, having become tools of the Gestapo, the French animators of the Institute, especially Darquier de Pellepoix's second-in-command, Captain Sézille, became the most active suppliers of the extermination camps.

German anti-Semitic propaganda had borne fruit. But Dannecker was not content. The Vichy Government had promulgated on October 3, 1940, a "statut des Juifs." This decree, after defining that any person with three grandparents of the same race, if his marriage partner was a Jew, must be regarded as Jewish, proceeded to enumerate the "public offices and mandates" forbidden to Jews, and finally barring them from certain professions.

Dannecker asked for a dozen inspectors to be transferred from the Prefecture of Police. He gave them his orders direct, thus conforming with the wishes of the military authorities "to allow the French themselves to carry out the basest tasks solicited by the Germans."

On August 24, 1941, under German pressure, a law was promulgated creating special tribunals and punishing "antinational uprisings" with death.

In October 1941 the Minister of the Interior, Pucheu, in order to "filch" from the Germans the policemen who came under their direct authority, introduced a triptych designed to pursue the "enemies" of the government, who were at the same time the enemies of the Nazis. Pucheu also created at the same time a "Police for Jewish Questions" (P.Q.J.), an "Anti-Communist Police Service" (S.P.A.C.), and a "Service for Secret Societies" (S.S.S.) for the purpose of pursuing Freemasons who were excluded from holding public office by a law of August 13, 1940, and kept under surveillance as enemies of the country.

These organizations were ruled by a disparate staff. The three directors were not police officials but men chosen from members of the extreme

Right. For example, the direction of the S.P.A.C. was entrusted to Doriot, a former leading light of the P.P.F., who received the title of executive director with a comfortable salary. His staff was composed of activists from the same movement, rounded off by a few professional police attracted by the high wages, and finally by bureaucrats who were embarrassed at finding themselves in bad company and were firmly determined not to "soil their hands" with such tasks.

Paradoxically, it was from among the members of the parties that were most vociferous in proclaiming their patriotism that the Nazis recruited their auxiliaries.

The German military authorities were disappointed in the results of their "correct" occupation policy. Since, according to Keitel's formula, the regular procedures "showed no return," the High Command embarked upon the path of repression, by deciding upon the execution of hostages each time an attempt was made against a member of the Army.

On August 22, 1941, an order signed by von Stuelpnagel decreed that all Frenchmen detained by or on behalf of the German authorities would be considered as hostages from August 24. Those who were to be shot, "according to the gravity of the acts committed," would be taken from this reserve. On September 19 a new decree added to this first category of hostages "all French males at present under arrest with the French administration, or who will be arrested in future, for Communist or Anarchist activities, must be considered as detainees on behalf of the military Commander in Chief in France." These arrangements were revised by a General Order of September 30, known as the "Hostages Code" in contempt of Article 50 of the Hague Convention, which forbids the taking of hostages.

These measures were aggravated still further when in July 1942, General Otto von Stuelpnagel having been replaced by his cousin Heinrich von Stuelpnagel, the *Pariser Zeiting* of July 16 published the following notice:

"The nearest male relatives, brothers-in-law, and cousins of troublemakers above the age of eighteen will be shot."

"All women relatives of the same degree of kinship will be condemned to forced labor."

"Children of less than eighteen years old of all the above mentioned persons will be placed in reform schools."

Throughout this whole period the various German police bodies, the Gestapo, and the S.D. had remained behind the scenes. Even if they had played no front-line role, working in the shadow of the military administration, they had nevertheless progressively increased their field of action.

From the start Knochen organized his services on the model of the R.S.H.A., dividing his men into six sections corresponding to the six Amter of the Berlin head office with the same competence. It mattered little that they were unable to work in the open; they took the opportunity of accumulating evidence and recruiting French auxiliaries chosen among criminals and members of certain parties, in the forefront of which was Doriot's P.P.F. (French People's party).

In the course of 1941 the standard of military surveillance slackened. The G.F.P., overwhelmed with work, had to allow the Gestapo to carry out house searches and arrests. The military authorities asked it to carry out investigations which the Abwehr and the G.F.P. were no longer able to carry out. It was ultimately agreed between parties that the Gestapo and the S.D. should be responsible for the security of the rear of the Army from the civil and political viewpoint, all activities of military intelligence remaining the exclusive domain of the Abwehr. But the borderline between these two activities was sometimes nebulous: Knochen's agents cheerfully crossed it and poached on their rival's reserves, hence the frequent conflicts. The relations between the Gestapo-S.D. and Abwehr were always in the nature of a dull hostility, a reflection of similar rivalry existing in Germany.

These suggestive extensions of operations increased the political importance of Knochen's services. By the end of 1941 he had a finger in every pie— with the exception of a few sections to which the soldiers reserved the exclusive rights—censorship of the press, radio, theater, cinema, the settlement of the Jewish and the economic questions of the French administration.

During the same period he had planted three branches, his "Aussenstellen" at Bordeaux, Dijon, and Rouen. One of Himmler's agents had been in Vichy from the start of the occupation. His name was Reiche and he informed Himmler direct of all the events taking place in the "provisional capital." He was not responsible to Knochen.

Since the departure of Thomas, Knochen was in sole charge of the Gestapo-S.D. in France. Thomas had been replaced by Oberfuehrer Bierkamp, but the latter simply held temporary office.

In April 1942 Himmler finally obtained Hitler's authorization to filch the police powers from the Army in France and to appoint a new personal representative. To mark the importance he attached to this post, he chose a man who had been warmly recommended by Heydrich—General Karl Oberg.

Karl Albrecht Oberg was born on January 27, 1897, in Hamburg, where his father, Dr. Karl Oberg, was a doctor. The young man studied in the Hanseatic town and obtained his *Arbitur* in 1914. He was seventeen. In August 1914 he enlisted eagerly, and in September 1916 fought on the Western front as a lieutenant. Before the end of the war he was decorated with the Iron Cross, First and Second Class.

On his return to Hamburg, his family's financial position having become strained, he took a job with a provision merchant with whom he remained until 1921. He was for a time representative to a wholesale paper merchant, and afterward employed in the Christiansen yeast factory at Flensburg near the Danish frontier. In 1923 he married Frieda Tramm, his junior by five years. Three years later the young couple returned to Hamburg, where Oberg had found a job with a wholesale tropical fruit firm, the West-India Bananenvertriebsgesellschaft. He remained there for three years before becoming the agent for a competitor house, Banjac. He was not happy there, and at the end of ten months, in the autumn of 1930, he was among the three and a half million unemployed wandering the pavements of the German cities. Thanks to a small family loan, he bought a tobacco kiosk in the middle of the town, in the Schanenburgstrasse, a commercial area near the Rathaus, the vast Hamburg town hall.

It was during this period that Oberg fell for the Nazi propaganda. Having become a cigar merchant, he found himself in a town entirely dependent upon shipping and more than any other vulnerable to the effects of the economic morass. In June 1931 he joined the N.S.D.A.P., where he received the Party Card No. 575205. Then months later he entered the S.S., using his organizing talents to advantage. The following year, on May 15, 1933, Heydrich visited Hamburg to inspect the local S.D. service, which was in full flower. For some time Oberg had felt attracted by the security branch of the Party. He approached Heydrich, who accepted his candidature. On entering the S.D., Oberg's money troubles ceased. Appointed Untersturmfuehrer on July 1, 1933, he was posted to the staff of Heydrich, and became one of his closest collaborators. He followed him to Munich in July 1933, and then to Berlin, to found the main office of the S.D. He was Heydrich's personal chief of staff in the S.D. and subsequently personnel chief of the service, a post that he held until November 1935. During his stay with Heydrich he had taken an active part in the Roehm purge.

Oberg then left the S.D. to return to active service with the S.S. and take command of the 22nd S.S. Standarte Mecklenburg, with the rank of Standartenfuehrer (colonel), subsequently becoming head of the S.S. Abschnitt IV A in Hanover until the end of December 1938. In January 1939 he was appointed president of police at Zwickau in Saxony, and in April received the stripes of an S.S. Oberfuehrer. He remained in this position until September 1941—with the exception of a short interlude. In April of that year Hitler had appointed him temporarily to the important post of president of police at Bremen, but the local Nazi pontiff, Gauleiter Kaufmann, had another candidate in view and put up such opposition that Oberg had to be brought back to Zwickau a week later.

In September 1941 Oberg was appointed S.D. und Polizeifuehrer, Chief of Police and S.S., at Radom in Poland. He took part in the extermination of the Jews and in the hunt for Polish workers. He left this post to come to Paris,[9] after being appointed Brigadefuehrer und Generalmajor der Polizei (brigadier general), which was quite a promotion for a man who had started as a second lieutenant nine years earlier.

He was forty-five when Himmler sent him to France. Then in the prime of life, a tall North German, fair-haired and pink-cheeked, stockily built with a slight pot belly. In his very elongated face a pair of blue-gray, rather globular eyes reflected neither cruelty nor particular harshness, but rather patient application. ... A pair of powerful glasses rested on his long nose which ended in an extraordinarily pointed, rather uptilted fashion. Particularly in profile, this gave his face a slightly clownish look. His pink-domed skull could be seen beneath his sparse, fair hair. In his previous post he had left behind the memory of a ponderous, patient, kindly man, quite good to his subordinates. He was a serious, orderly husband, who after thirteen years of marriage had become a father in 1936. A second child was born in 1941, and a third in 1942.

[9] Stahlecker was to be appointed, but he was killed on the Russian front, which gave Oberg his chance.

To sum up, the man whom Himmler had chosen appeared to be rather a decent fellow among the pack of wild beasts of the Gestapo and the S.S., except that he was an excessive disciplinarian.

Himmler sent Oberg to France on April 22, 1942, and he arrived on May 5. His intervention was to cause a radical change in the relationship between the German police and the Army of Occupation. To mark this transformation Oberg had been given the title of "Hoehere S.S. und Polizeifuehrer" (Supreme Head of the S.S. and the Police), and was to be regarded as Himmler's "personal representative," whereas Thomas had only been Heydrich's representative. At the same time Oberg was invested with full police powers and made responsible for insuring the liaison between the Supreme Chief of the German Police and the S.S., Himmler, and the various authorities in France, i.e., the military commander in France, von Stuelpnagel, the Commander in Chief of the West, Marshal von Rundstedt, the ambassador Abetz, and finally the French Vichy Government.

Himmler had wanted to come in person to install Oberg officially in Paris, but since his innumerable duties prevented this, he delegated Heydrich. The latter introduced Oberg to the German and French authorities with whom he was to deal during a party at the Ritz Hotel. For this ceremony Heydrich had personally summoned to Paris René Bousquet, the French chief of police, and Hilaire, the General Secretary to the Administration of the Ministry of the Interior, two men who had been appointed a fortnight earlier. In addition he received Fernand de Brinon, the French Government delegate in the occupied zone, and Darquier de Pellepoix, the new General Commissioner for Jewish Questions, who had succeeded Xavier Vallat.

Heydrich made a long speech. They were to collaborate as closely as possible with the occupying authorities in order that each one in his sphere could share in the success of a new police service which Oberg was to organize, "for the good of everyone." This speech served as a preliminary to the demands which Heydrich was to formulate in the name of the Fuehrer. These orders were addressed above all to René Bousquet, since they concerned the French chief of police. Oberg, he said, had been ordered to reorganize the German police services in occupied territories. These services were in future to possess executive powers, police powers having been wrested from the military administration. The security of the troops behind the lines was entrusted to the police services and the S.S. Himler had given Oberg a mission: "See that the troops stationed on the coasts have their backs protected."

In order that this task might be accomplished without difficulty, he ordered the French police in the occupied zone to be placed under the tutelage of the German police. This demand was claimed by Heydrich under the terms of the armistice. It was, said Heydrich, one of the rights and duties of the occupying power to see that order was maintained. Hitler and Himmler, however, did not believe that the French police, in their existing form, could offer loyal and efficient collaboration. In consequence the Reichsfuehrer S.S. demanded a revolutionary reform of the French police. It was to be directed and officered by trustworthy men chosen from the political parties which collaborated with the German services without demur, "to build a new Europe." The principal parties were Doriot's P.P.F. and Darnand's S.O.L.[10]

The Nazis could not forget that it was by "insuring order" through the S.A., and then by filling all the police organizations with men to whom obedience to the Party came before obedience to the State, that they had eliminated their enemies. In France, Thomas had tried this by protecting the men who had been Nazi agents. Pucheu had also created the three special services: P.Q.J., S.P.A.C., and S.S.S.

Heydrich had expected to find a man ready to acquiesce and he was surprised when René Bousquet refused to accept the police tutelage and to swell his squads with men from the Extremist parties. According to him, it was only by permitting the French police to carry out their task to the full that calm could be restored, providing the Germans for their part ceased to carry out blind reprisals. Heydrich appeared to agree with Bousquet. Personally, he said, he was of the opinion that these purges were unnecessary, provided Bousquet was prepared to give the French police an overall inclination toward German interests, and if a close and friendly collaboration could be established between the two services.

René Bousquet agreed on condition that the German police did not interfere in the administration and conduct of the French police, and that the two forces could operate separately. Heydrich replied that he had no power

[10] Parti Populaire Français (French People's party)—Service d'Ordre Légionnaire.

to conclude an agreement of this nature on his own account. He could only act in execution of orders received. Any further action involved referring to his superiors, Himmler and Hitler. On this tacit understanding Heydrich returned to Berlin. He was never to return to Paris.

This interview of May 5, 1942, between Heydrich and Bousquet had spared France from a very grim future. In Poland, Denmark, and Czechoslovakia the German police controlled the entire local services. In Denmark the native police had been arrested almost to a man and deported. In Czechoslovakia, Heydrich had himself been appointed Protector of Bohemia-Moravia and terror reigned. In Poland the S.S. carried out the orders of the Gestapo to annihilate the population.

One wonders whether the May 5 solution did not perhaps suit the Germans best. To police France as a whole meant immobilizing invaluable manpower, when every available fighting man was needed on the Eastern front. It was also certain to be more and more difficult to maintain order in a population groaning under the measures taken by the occupying forces rather than those prescribed by the French police themselves. For France herself it was a means of avoiding suffering ferocious measures inflicted upon her to "tame" the recalcitrant population in the style used in Eastern and Central Europe.

In Paris, Oberg began to reorganize the services now under his control.

The first transformation was the reattachment to the Secret Police and the S.D. of the section of the military administration charged with keeping an eye on the French police. On the other hand, the G.F.P. disappeared almost completely. Twenty-three out of twenty-five groups were disbanded and their staff transferred to the SIPO-S.D. or sent to the Russian front. The men taken from the G.F.P. were demustered by the Wehrmacht and re-engaged by the Gestapo and the S.D., assigned to special duties. The military administration, however, retained the surveillance of prisons and camps, the customs and the direction of the *gendarmerie* right until the end.

All this was Knochen's work, the end of a long task which he had pursued relentlessly to insure in Paris the supremacy of the Party over the Army such as existed in Germany. From this moment, and thanks to the powers invested in Oberg, this supremacy continued to assert itself and the true leadership of German policy in France lay with the police bodies, although officially the ambassador, Abetz, was still responsible.

Oberg divided the police services into two groups, corresponding to the German organization: Ordnungspolizei (ORPO), the civil police, and the Sicherheitspolizei (SIPO-S.D.), the Security Police. By applying a policy of expansion designed to take over in relays from the soldiers, a regional service was created in each district. Each of these in turn operated a number of small local posts in each of the main towns of its region, with agents in the local Kommandanturen. For example, Rouen had branches at Evreux, Caen, and Cherbourg, and three less important posts at Granville, Dieppe, and Le Havre. All these regional offices dependent upon Paris reproduced at their different levels the organization of the Paris head office, itself modeled on the R.S.H.A.

The head office of the SIPO-S.D. and its external services were therefore divided into seven sections. To their normal duties were added special tasks necessitated by the occupation of a foreign country. Section II (S.D.) in charge of the administrative management was reinforced by a second, known as II Pol, formed by the former group detached from the military administration, and in charge of relations with the French police, its surveillance, and the study of judicial problems. It insured liaison with the office of the military administration, which ran the camps and the prisons.

Section III (S.D.) kept the "Otto" list, originally established by the Propaganda Staffel, which also controlled the French press. This list scheduled banned works, either on account of the author's origin—Jew or anti-Nazi—or by reason of the subject dealt with. Section III also kept under surveillance the German purchasing offices, and finally it attended to the problems of labor and forced labor in liaison with Gauleiter Sauckel.

Section IV, as in Germany, was the actual Gestapo. It was engaged in the struggle against the enemies of the State, saboteurs, terrorists, and active counterespionage. The unfortunate people caught in its net ended in the Paris premises. It also picked up clandestine radio transmissions to London and wrote the texts of falsified transmissions.

Administratively this section was controlled by a Sonderkommando (special commando) detached from Berlin and called Sonderkommando IV J, later IV B-4, engaged in the anti-Jewish struggle. Dannecker was the guiding light of this commando, which received its orders direct from Eichmann in Berlin. It was he who initiated the "emigration" of Jews, which was then carried out by the French authorities. The Jews, arrested chiefly in raids carried out by the Commissariat for Jewish Questions, were interned at Drancy camp and then deported to Poland to be exterminated.

Present at the regular meetings arranged by Dannecker were Zeitschel, the representative of Abetz, Ernst, and Blanke, two members of the military authorities, and von Behr, a delegate from the Rosenberg service. It was in the course of these meetings that the measures were decreed which caused so much suffering for so many victims in France.

The Embassy had also appointed French "experts." These specialists were chosen from among the leaders of collaborationist and anti-Semitic groups. Among them were Bucard, Darquier de Pellepoix, Clementi, and a bogus scientist, "Professor" Georges Montandon, the racial anthropologist.

Dannecker abused his independence, and his cavalier attitude caused Knochen to take umbrage. He found a pretext to have him transferred "for disciplinary reasons." Dannecker left Paris in September 1942 and ended his career in Sofia.

In May 1943 Eichmann, considering that France was "very backward" in "liquidating the Jewish problem," compared with other European countries, sent his right-hand man, Haupsturmfuehrer Brunner, to Paris with orders to speed up the deportations. Brunner came from Salonica, where he had left behind a reputation for ruthlessness. Eichmann installed him personally in Paris: he was to return on two occasions to France to see for himself the "good" results of Brunner's activities. The French anti-Semitic newspapers, the *Pilori* in the van, having launched a campaign protesting against criminal tolerance enjoyed by the Jews in the Nice region, Eichmann went there to see if all the Jews in France had taken refuge on the Côte d'Azur as the papers maintained.

Oberg at the same time received an order from Himmler to shake up the French police, which was "too lukewarm" in chasing the Jews. But Brunner enjoyed great independence. He had brought with him a special detachment of twenty-five men and a fleet of cars. Receiving his orders from Berlin and getting them carried out by the French Commissariat for Jewish Questions, he eluded Knochen. At the end of 1943 the transit camp at Drancy came under German administration. Its external surveillance alone was undertaken by the French *gendarmerie*. Brunner could thus "speed up" the rhythm of the departures.

Section IV of the SIPO-S.D. was responsible also for deciding which of the arrested persons were to be judged by the military tribunal with its seat at 11 rue Boissy-d'Anglas, and which were to be deported without a trial. And finally it enjoyed a terrible privilege: it chose the hostages to be shot as reprisals.

It also ran two units which every Frenchman, and above all the Parisians, learned to "appreciate" without knowing their names. The Intervention-Referat, whose main office was 48 rue de Villejust, formed teams of killers recruited from the shock troops of the P.P.F. and the militia, the most notorious of which was the Carbone gang. These teams intervened when the S.D. and the Gestapo did not wish to appear in their own name. They undertook raids on certain organizations, carried out kidnapings or murders of prominent people.

A second unit, directed by the Alsatian Bickler, included Frenchmen working for the Gestapo. This section created a special school for training auxiliary agents.

These two formations were largely composed of criminals, a great number of whom were released from prison for the purpose. Their recruitment began in a curious way. A certain Henri Chamberlin, a former canteen manager of the Paris Prefecture, was interned in 1939 in Cépoy camp. There he met several German agents and escaped with them. On Knochen's arrival in Paris, Chamberlin worked for the Gestapo, first as an informer and then, at the request of his employers, as "team leader." Under the name Lafont, he formed a group which he was to lead, together with ex-inspector Bony. They took up their quarters at 93 rue Lauriston. To form his team Chamberlin-Lafont obtained the release of a score of criminals. Numerous thieves' kitchens of the same type were opened, such as that of the sinister Martin, alias Rudy de Mérode. Using the most brutal methods of interrogation, these criminals exploited the immunity conferred upon them by their permission to carry arms to commit innumerable crimes—robberies during house searches, unauthorized searches at the houses of rich people, blackmail, and traffic of all kinds. These teams worked for the Gestapo, the S.D., and the Abwehr. The Chief of Section IV until the end of 1943 was Boemelburg.

Boemelburg had been very valuable when the Knochen service began in Paris. An experienced policeman, he was very up to date in police customs and techniques, and also in international law. He had been one of the shining lights of the I.K.P.K. (the international organization of police), the forerunner of INTERPOL, whose office was at that time in Vienna, where he had got to know the chiefs of the French police—at least by reputation. In addition he spoke perfect French, even argot, having lived for a long time in Paris as a technician in a German central heating firm. At the time of King George VI's visit to France he had been delegated by the I.K.P.K. to study, with the French services, the problems of security and the measures to be taken against international terrorists, whom it was feared would go into action. The French Government still remembered acutely the Marseilles outrage, which had cost the life of King Alexander of Yugoslavia and the Foreign Minister, Louis Barthou. He had thus been able to make direct contacts, which he did not fail to renew as soon as he settled in as head of the Gestapo at the rue des Saussaies.

But in 1943 Boemelburg suddenly succumbed to the ravages of time. He seemed to age overnight, his memory, at one time formidable, became unreliable, his decisions less prompt, and his judgment less sure. This was the period when the Resistance and the political opponents intensified their activities. The Gestapo waged a pitiless war, striking with implacable cruelty. Now that Boemelburg had aged suddenly, he became ineffective. Oberg and Knochen, in agreement with the R.S.H.A., sought a solution to replace him without offending him. When Oberg's representative in Vichy, Geissler, was killed by the Resistance, the post was entrusted to Boemelburg; he was replaced in Paris by Stindt, who was to remain head of the Gestapo in France until the end of the occupation. After the evacuation of France, Boemelburg, who had accompanied the Vichy Government, was attached to the person of Pétain, at Sigmaringen. This was his last post.

Section V was the KRIPO (criminal police). Its duty in principle was to combat the black market. This duty was purely academic, for the German services were often the main organizers of the black market, to their own advantage. In collaboration with the Gestapo, its duties were the measurements of the prisoners, reporting individuals who were sought for, expertise of weapons, fingerprints, etc. Section V shared the executive powers with Section IV. It was directed by Koppenhofer, and then by Odewald.

The job of Section VI was to collect information about political groups and to watch their contacts with foreign powers. In Paris it had seven specialized commandos, whose missions were often of the strangest character. The Sonderkommando Pannwitz (from the name of its leader, Haupsturmfuehrer Pannwitz, of Amt IV of the R.S.H.A.) had been sent specially from Berlin and worked with both Sections IV and VI in the affair known as *Rote Kapelle* (the Red Chapel), to liquidate the Soviet intelligence network operating in France. The latter collected information on the activity of German troops, their strength, and the state of the divisions at rest, on their return from the Eastern front or preparatory to returning there. This information was transmitted to Moscow either by radio or through a relay station in Switzerland. Sonderkommando Pannwitz could call for its work on the aid of a second special commando, the Funkspielkommando. The Funkspielkommando (the radio for transmitting false information) was composed of specialists in picking up clandestine radio transmissions.

A third special commando insured the safety of high German officials traveling in France. It was composed of S.S. selected from the Schutzpolizei, the ordinary city police.

The fourth commando, known as Kommando Wenger, called after its leader, kept a special watch on the issue of visas. Hauptsturmfuehrer Wagner's Sonder-Referat kept a watch on French high society. Another technical commando was employed in detecting the camouflage used by the secret army vehicles. It operated in the southern zone, where the secret army had been formed. Finally the seventh and last commando recruited prostitutes for the brothels reserved for German troops, and sometimes even for those who were on duty in certain concentration camps.

In France there was no real Section VII, but specialists from Amt VII came from time to time from Berlin to study the "work" of the French anti-Jewish Institute, to catalogue the libraries confiscated by the Rosenberg-Einsatzstab, which had an office in Paris at No. 12 rue Dumont-d'Urville, and methodically pillaged *objets d'art*, antique furniture, books, silverware, jewels, furs, and all objects of value discovered in Jewish homes.

Thus at the end of May 1942 the Germans in France had set up the omniscient and ever present organization which Germany had long since endured.

Despite the partitioning of the services on the model of central offices, the separation in France was infinitely less watertight and real than in Germany.

In all these foreign sections, particularly where the total staff rarely exceeded a hundred members including the administrative staff, the agents worked indiscriminately in all branches, and as the months passed had to confine themselves more and more to the work of repression, leaving the work of intelligence to French "auxiliaries" recruited on the spot, and operating on the information and renunciations sent in by French collaborationist organizations and certain political parties.

The agents belonging to units of the SIPO-S.D. wore the same uniform, the S.S. uniform, with a distinctive band bearing the letters S.D. on the sleeve.

The power held by the Army had slipped into the hands of the Gestapo leaders. Thus the military High Command had waived the nomination of French officials in the occupied zone in favor of its rival. As soon as the Gestapo had acquired its independence, it claimed the right of intervening in each nomination capable of affecting the interests of its police duties.

After the occupation of the southern zone in November 1942, the Gestapo claimed the right in both zones to appoint prefects, and went so far as to propose its own candidates, proposals against which the military command and the Embassy fought. It is no less true to say that Section III never failed to pass the appointments through a fine sieve, to see whether the new officials might not prove an obstruction to its repressive work. Oberg finally got a man of his choice, in the person of Darnand, appointed head of the French police.

Apart from the usual sources of intelligence, the Gestapo in France shared with the Abwehr a means of information particular to the period. The shortage of raw materials, of foodstuffs, and of most manufactured goods, gave rise to ruinous black market traffic. The German economy suffered from failing productivity which grew worse as the bombing caused a new destruction in the industrial zones. At the same time the costs of the war reached figures which became more and more difficult to face. While the percentage of these expenses covered by taxes was 42 percent in 1939, it was no more than 33 percent in 1942, sinking to 19 percent in 1944. The contribution levied from the occupied countries, under the title of occupational expenses, reached 66 billion francs, and when we add sums taken or extorted on other pretexts, a total of about 100 billion marks. France alone paid 31 billion, 600 million marks for occupation expenses, which constituted the largest contribution from all the occupied countries, a weak return since the expenses of the fifth year of war alone reached 100 billion marks.[11]

Since in practice it was no longer possible to increase the tonnages imposed on France for the provision of the products demanded, the Germans decided to raise a second levy by organizing a black market for their own benefit. They created organizations known as Bureaux d'Achats, to bypass the French industrialists. These offices in fact became gigantic sources of corruption. The most incredible business took place in them, the individuals running them having realized the enormous advantages of their privileged position and Gestapo protection. The most disparate merchandise was sold, bought, and bartered. Steel, copper, tungsten, wolfram, India rubber and mercury, pharmaceutical products, wool and cotton, luxury leather goods, barbed wire, vintage wines and French brandy, champagne and hides, luxury perfumes and silk stockings, as well as wood pulp and railway lines. These offices were often entrusted to occasional agents of the Gestapo or the Abwehr in payment for their services. The profits were enormous. Certain postwar fortunes in France have no other origin. But although there were dealings in gold, shares, and foreign currency, there were also provision markets designed for the Wehrmacht. The French tradesmen and industrialists had little difficulty in overcoming their slight repugnance, dictated by a tottering patriotism, to offer their services to these purchasing offices. They became in effect intelligence agents, conscious or not, so as not to lose the benefit of these profitable orders.

All these thieves' kitchens came under a service known as Organization "Otto," with three main offices in Paris, 21 and 23 square du Bois de Boulogne, 25 rue d'Astorg, and 6 rue Adolphe-Yvon, in addition to huge sheds at Saint-Ouen and Saint-Denis.

The Otto organization was directed by two Germans: Hermann Brandl, alias "Otto"; and Robert Poeschl, or Poeschel. These two men were officially

---

[11] By the end of the war the national debt of the Reich had reached 387 billion marks: 143 billion in long and average-term loans, 235 billion in short-term bonds plus various other bonds. The cost of the war rose to a total of 670 billion marks. (In 1940 the German mark stood at 2.5 to the dollar; the franc at 43.8 to the dollar.)

in charge of all purchases of merchandise in France for the account of Germany. It is estimated that they made personal profits of several billion francs.

Brandl was the brains of the organization. He was a man of average height with a round, rather pasty face. His manners were affected, he always dressed smartly and with sophistication, his silvery-gray hair brushed back; his double chin was to be seen in all the Parisian pleasure haunts, which he preferred to visit when doing business. Everything was of interest to the "Otto" organization.

"Otto" was also interested in stocks and shares. The certificates seized or stolen by the Gestapo were often negotiated on the stock exchange by the agents of this organization. The Gestapo exercised a special control over shares. It also put pressure on certain big companies to obtain from them the cession of important blocks of shares to German companies in which the R.S.H.A. had a finger, in order to control these companies and to share in their profits. Gold, precious stones, and jewels were also bought by "Otto" and dispatched to Germany.

Brandl, a member of the Abwehr, held the rank of captain. To help him an adjutant kept in permanent contact with the Abwehr chief.

The Gestapo recruited agents among the clientele of the Bureaux d'Achats. The most terrifying were Frederic Martin, known as Rudy de Mérode, and Georges Delfane, alias Masuy, whose offices were at 101 avenue Henri Martin. He is reputed to have invented the torture of the bathtub.

After the German collapse in 1944 Poeschl tried to escape to Spain, hoping to reach South America and enjoy his enormous fortune. His flight was carefully prepared and he had salted away his capital in Lisbon. But he was arrested at the Spanish frontier by the Gestapo, transferred to Germany, condemned, and hanged.

Brandl returned to Germany with some of his wealth. On the way he had organized hiding places in France. In the outbuildings of a castle in Champagne fire extinguishers were found full of precious stones, buried by "Otto." In Germany he settled in Munich and hid more of his jewels in buckets of cement. His paintings, the Sisleys, Renoirs, Boudins, Pissaros, and Degas', tapestries, priceless furniture, collections of rare stamps, shares, antique silverware, the flower of what a methodical pillage had levied upon France during a period of four years, he placed in the safe-keeping of his friends. When Germany collapsed Brandl lived under a false identity near Dachau. He was arrested in the summer of 1946. He hanged himself in his cell in Stadelheim prison.

Thus the two accomplices shared the same fate—at the end of a rope. Only a small part of the fabulous "Otto" treasure was recovered. The paintings are probably rotting somewhere in the company of blackened silver and moldering share certificates. One wonders what accomplice is enjoying the gold, currency, and shares sent by them to Portugal and South America.

PART FIVE

**THE HELL OF THE GESTAPO
1940–44**

Chapter 17
The Gestapo at Work in France

Thanks to the apparatus organized by Knochen under the authority of Oberg; to the exploitation of the satellite organizations which gravitated into his orbit; and above all to corruption, political passion, and fear, the repression became intensified.

Oberg, a decent family man, a peaceful and meticulous bureaucrat whom his subordinates loved for his fairness and good will, obeyed his orders to the letter and, as a disciplined Nazi, became, as Taittinger was to say: "A demoniacal creature capable of doing anything for his Fuehrer. A perfect incarnation of the brute beast, he seemed to have taken on the task of making himself detested—and in this respect he succeeded perfectly." Detested is an understatement. A flood of hatred and impotent rage rose against the methods of the Gestapo.

The arrests, whose numbers increased without a halt, reached their peak between May and August 1944 in the southern zone, in particular in the Lyons area. They were of two kinds: first, individual arrests for people known for their anti-German activities, or simply suspected of practicing them, and second, collective arrests carried out by means of police raids. The most important of the latter in France were those of August and December 1941; July 1942 (roundup of the Jews); November 1943, at Strasbourg University, evacuated to Clermont-Ferrand; January 1943 at Marseilles where forty thousand people were arrested; December 24, 1943, at Grenoble; December 24, 1944, at Cluny; May 1944 at Figeac and Eysieux, and July 1944 at Saint-Paul-de-Léon and Locminé. The same procedure was used in Belgium, Holland, and Denmark. With regard to the countries of Central Europe and the East, whole populations were rounded up, transplanted or deported, and reduced to slavery.

The persons arrested individually were interrogated and usually tortured by the Gestapo. As a general rule the first interrogation did not take place until ten days after the arrest except when urgently necessary. The methods employed to make the victims talk were always the same. They were forced to kneel on a triangular bench while a torturer climbed on their shoulders; they were suspended with the arms tied behind their backs until they fainted; they were kicked, thrashed with knouts, or struck with the fist; they were revived by flinging a bucket of water over them when they fainted. Their teeth were filed, their nails torn out, and they were burned with cigarette stubs and on occasions with a soldering lamp. The electric torture was also practiced: a wire was attached to the ankles while a second wire was run over the most sensitive parts of the anatomy. The soles of the feet were slashed with a razor and the wounded man was then forced to walk on salt. Pieces of cotton wool soaked in petrol were placed between the toes and fingers and lit. The torture of the bathtub consisted in plunging the patient into a bath of icy water, his hands handcuffed behind his back, and keeping his head under water until he was on the point of drowning. He was dragged to the surface by the hair and, if he still refused to speak, was immediately plunged under water again.

Masuy, a specialist in this torture, used to cut short the sessions when the patient was on the point of losing consciousness by bringing him coffee or hot tea and sometimes brandy. When his victim had revived, the same cruelty started again.

Women were not exempt from these tortures, and it was usually upon them that the torturers used their most odious refinements. The French auxiliaries of the Gestapo rivaled their Nazi masters in inventiveness. Every Frenchman heard of these bestial tortures. Some of them denied it for political reasons, others believed that the victim's stories were exaggerated. However, there is ample medical evidence and the reports of experts, the admissions under oath of the torturers themselves, teem with details which are impossible to reproduce in this book.

Each Gestapo "office" worked for its own account, being bound by the internal partitioning and the rules of secrecy to ignore what happened in the neighboring branches; a prisoner was often claimed by several departments. Each of these services summoned him for interrogation.

The unhappy man held for questioning was brought in a police van, say to Fresnes, and placed in a temporary cell to await his turn. In the rue des Saussaies, there were cells in various parts of the building. The largest were in the basement, while various little box rooms on all the floors were summarily transformed into barred cells. Five or six prisoners were sometimes herded together for hours on end in a small airless cupboard. The handcuffs were left on their wrists the whole time, and some were chained to a ring in the wall.

Then the moment came for them to appear before their inquisitors. The first replies usually brought a hail of blows in their wake. If the unfortunate man, still chained, fell to the ground, he was kicked to his feet with such violence that fractured ribs or limbs were a commonplace.

The interrogation continued, alternating with threats with regard to the victim's family (threats often carried out), and promises or "advantageous" propositions designed to produce a little "comprehension." The accused man remained standing for several hours, badgered and beaten by teams which took it in turn to question him.

For the obstinate, the refinements were then put into practice. In this field the sadism and imagination of the torturers produced a host of variations and discoveries of which the inventors were inordinately proud, as in the Middle Ages the "questionnaires" were transmitted from father to son as family patents.

The patriotic alibi provided by Nazism and the "circumstances" caused the most appalling instincts to rise from the subconscious of these men who had once been, for the most part, decent and normal. Some of them justified themselves by following the general example for fear of being deemed traitors. But everywhere, in the meanest local office of the Gestapo, these inhuman practices flourished.

The Villa des Rosiers at Montpellier, the impasse Tivoli at Limoges, most of the French prisons, the buildings in the rue Lauriston, in the rue des Saussaies in Paris—all the buildings occupied in France by the Gestapo have echoed with the cries of tortured patriots and seen their blood flow.

In the rue des Saussaies, the cooks, whose quarters were on the second floor, were often disturbed by the screams of the victims being interrogated on the fifth floor.

This treatment was applied to unhappy creatures weakened by detention. There were forty thousand deaths in the French prisons alone, to which must be added those condemned by French tribunals, special courts, courts-martial, and internees of the French camps. Herded together in overcrowded prison cells, where the density sometimes reached fifteen prisoners in a cell of seven to eight square meters, receiving practically no rations,[1] living in almost unimaginable filth, covered with lice, receiving no mail, parcels, or visits, cut off from the outside world, it needed a fantastic morale and a superhuman will not to yield during the interrogations and to reveal the names of friends who were still at large. Some, broken morally and physically, collapsed. Who would dare to judge them?

Hundreds of others, like Jean Moulin, died under the blows or as a result of prolonged torture. Others, like Pierre Brossolette, committed suicide to escape their tormentors.[2]

When the Gestapo thought that they had extorted everything possible from a man, he was often transferred to a deportation convoy or brought before a German tribunal. This frequently meant a slow death sentence through forced labor, sickness, and ill-treatment. The transport was carried out in closed and sealed cattle trucks, and frequently lasted for three days and three nights, with a hundred to 120 persons per truck deprived of air, food, and water. The convoys arriving at Buchenwald and Dachau often numbered 25 percent dead.

Between January 1 and August 25, 1944, the date of the last dispatch, 326 convoys left France, not including the departments of the Upper Rhine, Lower Rhine, and the Moselle. Convoys consisted of anything up to two thousand persons. The rise in the number of convoys throws a light on the continuous stepping up of Nazi repression: 3 convoys in 1940, 19 in 1941, 104 in 1942 (the seizure of power by the Gestapo in Paris is immediately apparent in the graph), 257 in 1943. In France about 250,000 persons were deported, of whom only 35,000 returned,[3] indelibly marked by their experience. At Dachau the dormitories, which held 300 to 400 persons in 1942, housed 1,000 in 1943 and 3,000 or more at the beginning of 1945.

---

[1] The women detained in Fort Montluc at Lyons received, during twenty-four hours, a cup of liquid at seven o'clock in the morning, a bowl of soup and a slice of bread at five o'clock in the evening.

[2] After being tortured for several days Pierre Brossolette threw himself out of the fifth-floor window of the rue des Saussaies, for fear of talking under further torture.

[3] The Dutch hold the sad distinction in western Europe of having the smallest percentage of deportees to return: out of 126,000 deportees, 11,000 were repatriated.

The atmosphere and the life in the concentration camps have been recounted in detail in several works written by the deportees themselves.[4] This world of slaves, where men of all creeds and classes were subjected until death to the whims of a small nucleus of cruel masters, was the logical end of the oldest Nazi theories. To enter a camp was to know on arrival that one could never recover one's liberty. In these camps the S.S. said to the arrivals, "Here there is only one exit, the chimney." And in another, an enormous placard warned them as soon as they entered the camp: "Here you enter by the door and go out by the chimney." Typical Nazi jests, underlined by the nauseous smoke from the crematorium ovens.

Once inside the camp the deportee entered the domain of the S.S., governed by the Gestapo. Himmler had organized Death's-Head units to guard the camps. This was a specialized S.S. organization, the W.V.H.A. (Wirtschaft Verwaltung Haupt Amt), main office of the S.S. economic administration run by Oswald Pohl.[5] The Gestapo kept them under political surveillance. It was common talk among the Nazis that Himmler was "the sole master of the camps down to the lowest charwoman."

Himmler, Heydrich, and his successor Kaltenbrunner often visited them. They all witnessed the exhausting work to which the prisoners were subjected, checked the functioning of the gas chambers, and watched the executions. In this world of death nothing could cause surprise. When the corpses were removed from the gas chambers, the gold teeth were salvaged by the economic service. Gold-rimmed spectacles and wedding rings were also collected. Pohl was invited one day to a banquet given by the Reichsbank to various Nazi personalities. Before sitting down to table they were taken down to the bank vaults, where Pohl and his S.S. colleagues were shown the safes containing the deposits of the S.S. economic service. These included a heap of small ingots made from the gold recovered and also spectacle mounts, stylos, and teeth in their natural state, piled up in macabre heaps. After which they all went in to lunch. ...

[4] In the bibliography will be found several works on life in these camps.

[5] The first camps had been administered separately by the camp commandants. At the end of 1939 a special service was created to be directed by Death's-Head units, the main office known as K.Z. (Konzentrations-Lager) being entrusted with the administration of all the camps. At the beginning of 1942 this service was reattached to the S.S. economic administration (W.V.H.A.) under the name of Amtsgruppe D.

When the camps were liberated the final stocks which had not yet been transferred were recovered. They included 20,952 kilos of gold wedding rings and thirty-five trucks of furs.

The industrialists who used the prisoners from the camps paid wages for them to the W.V.H.A. For 1943 alone the deposits in specie made by the S.S. at the Reichsbank stood at more than a hundred million marks.

Everything had to serve a purpose. Even the bones of the dead were used to make fertilizers, and human fat to make soap. Regulations prescribed that the transit operation to the gas chamber[6] would need five minutes more for the women than for the men, the reason being that their hair had to be cut off.

When the Soviet troops liberated Auschwitz, they found there seven tons of human hair. It was not known for what purpose it was used until the day a memo dated August 6, 1942, from the camp administration was discovered. It explained that S.S. Obergruppenfuehrer Pohl had given orders that the human hair cut off in the camps "was to be used in an adequate manner"; with short-cut women's hair, slippers were made for the submarine crews and felt slippers for employees of the Reich railways. The men's hair could only be used if it reached a length of 20 millimeters, and the memo ended with this phrase: "Reports on the quantity of hair collected, under separate subheadings for men and women, are to be sent in on the 5th of each month, starting from September 5, 1942."

The Gestapo maintained the camps' population up to a constant level. Two men alone could sign the internment orders—the head of the R.S.H.A., Heydrich, and subsequently his successor Kaltenbrunner, and in his absence the head of the Gestapo, Mueller.

When there was a shortage of labor in the camp the Gestapo provided it. A circular from Mueller, dated December 17, 1942, prescribed dispatch to the camps of thirty-five thousand people capable for work before the end of January 1943.

Inside the camps the Gestapo was represented by a service known as the political section, an object of terror to the prisoners and a source of quarrels for those in command of the camp. The camp itself was directed and

---

[6] At Auschwitz, Hoess had a gas chamber built capable of containing two thousand persons.

administered by a Kommandantur, which, jealous of its privileges, was averse to the interference of the Gestapo in its day-to-day business.

On arrival every new internee had to undergo a long interrogation as to his identity, and answer a host of questions about his antecedents. His dossier, swollen by the papers giving the reason for his arrest, his civil status, etc., was then filed in the records of the political section. The latter kept a detailed card index on every prisoner.

At any moment the political section could summon a prisoner for interrogation. These summonses were the nightmare of the camps. Prisoners who had been summoned disappeared and left no trace. They were almost invariably the object of brutal ill-treatment, and it has been related that the Austrian lieutenant Heckenast died at Buchenwald from a heart attack due to the anxiety caused by the names broadcast on the loudspeaker.

The Gestapo also organized a sort of internal spy system among the prisoners. The recruitment of stool pigeons was very difficult, because the suspicion of being an informer for the political section was equivalent to a death sentence.

Prisoners who were particularly important were questioned in the camp "bunker," a kind of inner prison where the worst excesses could be perpetrated. The unfortunate people taken down to the bunker were stripped of all their clothes on arrival, and subjected to indescribable tortures before, in many cases, being murdered.

The political section also received orders from the Gestapo head office. It transmitted the death sentences which had been pronounced, sometimes several months before, on the prisoners in the camp. Orders for execution sent from Berlin thus arrived periodically without anyone knowing why a certain prisoner who had been interned for fifteen or eighteen months should be executed. Eight days before the liberation of Buchenwald, the Gestapo head office continued quite imperturbably to order executions. As a result a British officer named Perkins was executed as late as April 5, 1945.

In earlier days, when a German detainee was freed, he was obliged to report at a certain date to the Gestapo office in the town where he was to live. Before leaving the camp, the freed man had to go to the political office to sign a declaration whereby he agreed under oath to reveal nothing of what he had seen in the camp or the conditions of life of the prisoners. After 1940 there were practically no releases.

At Buchenwald the Russian prisoners, as soon as they arrived, were sent by the political section for special treatment which usually meant death, according to a specific order. The first to be executed were the political commissars, then the officers, and finally the leaders of the Young Communist League and ordinary members of the Communist party. Informers chosen from among the White Russian internees were placed in all the camps where there were Russians to find out those who held a rank or some political post.

Himmler was proud of his work. In an article published under the title "The Nature and Function of the S.S. and the Police," he wrote, on the subject of prisoners, that "they are the dregs of the criminal world and the refuse of humanity.... Among them are to be found hydrocephalics, people who squint, who are malformed, semi-Jews, and an incalculable number of products of the inferior races. Everything is to be found there. ... In a general way their education is solely disciplinary and never ideological, because for the most part these detainees are slave souls, very few of them really have any character. ... Education, therefore, is carried out by orders. Order envisages first and foremost that these people should live in clean huts. Only we Germans are capable of realizing such a thing; no other nation could show itself to be so humane."

Numerous visits from S.S. groups, delegations from the Wehrmacht and the Party were organized. A former prisoner of Dachau stated that they had the impression of being shut up in a zoo. The presentation of a cross section of the camp inmates to the visitors was calculated to amuse them and followed an almost immutable pattern. The first to be presented was a "green," an ordinary criminal from among the murderers or presented as such. Then came, say, the former Burgomaster of Vienna, Dr. Schmidt, followed by a high-ranking Czech officer, a homosexual, a gypsy, a Catholic bishop or a high dignitary of the Polish Church, and, finally, a university professor brought up the rear. The visitors roared with laughter. This method of selection which placed scholars, men of high moral integrity, civil or religious notables, beneath the authority of hardened criminals promoted to the rank of "kapos," with rights of life and death over the detainees, was the result of a long-nursed plan, the object of which was the systematic dehumanization of the man and the debasing of the enemy.

Above this scientifically induced degeneration sailed the myth of Nazism, the intangible dogma of the superiority of the German blood. A great comfort for the man who was probably to be beaten to death!

The insensate regulations were devised by the officials of the Gestapo. Their vigilance also extended to the administrative authorities of the camps, whose conduct was reported periodically to Mueller, who in his turn forwarded the reports to Heydrich and eventually to Himmler.

Reprimands were sometimes recorded against certain officials of Mauthausen camp for administrative "shortcomings." The camp doctor, for example, took two young Dutch Jews from one of the convoys arriving at the camp and had them shot—in order to make original paperweights of their skulls. These subsequently adorned his desk, because they had such fine sets of teeth. He was "rebuked."

The Nazi universe, hermetic and stifling, possessed an implacable internal logic. It escapes our comprehension because these criteria are alien to us, but murders on an industrial scale were for the S.S. normal acts, since they had been *ordered*, whereas any *administrative* error, which appears to us a trifle, was considered a grave fault because it violated the principles of the Party, outside which no truth or salvation existed.

No real Nazi regretted these murders which still dumfound us and which will haunt the conscience of men for centuries to come. Who would dream of accusing of murder the employee of a slaughterhouse who has just felled an ox or slit the throat of a few sheep? For a true Nazi it was obvious that "the members of the inferior races," or the "enemies of the Fatherland," these "dregs of humanity," were less worthy of pity than an ox or a sheep and that their annihilation was a salutary task.

The Gestapo prisoners who were not sent to a camp in Germany were rarely released, even when no genuine charge had been established against them. On the contrary, when serious "evidence" had been collected during the inquiry or confessions had been extorted under torture, the culprit was hailed before a German tribunal. In Paris this court sat at 11 rue Boissy d'Anglas.

The tribunal judged empirically, and the Gestapo could exert no pressure on it whilst it was sitting, but after pronouncement of sentence the man on trial, whether condemned or acquitted, was once more taken in custody by the Gestapo, which could dispose of him freely. The prisoners who during the preliminary inquiries had been detained in Fresnes, at the Sante or the Cherche Midi prisons were detained in Romainville fort either after their sentence or simply at the behest of the Gestapo, when the latter had judged it unnecessary to send them before a tribunal.

After June 1943,[7] the "Romainville camp," installed in the precincts of the fort, initially administered by the Wehrmacht and later by the S.S., received different categories of prisoners and formed a kind of permanent reserve of hostages.

The principle of shooting innocent individuals as reprisals for an outrage committed, although they had been detained for several months, had been adopted to inspire terror. This concept of power and human relationships impregnated the whole Nazi world so deeply that its leaders appeared incapable of envisaging any other methods of government.

At Romainville the prisoners were classified, according to the period, into four or five categories. The first of these included the privileged, who might be called "administrative detainees." Very few in number, rarely more than fifty, they were mostly personalities of a certain importance, who had either been arrested as a security measure, or reported (often by denunciation) as hostile to the Nazis and against whom no charge could be found. They included librarians, secretarial employees, and doctors. They had the right to one letter a week and a few parcels from friends outside. No hostage seems to have been included in this category. On the other hand, nearly all those who went to Romainville in this group were deported after varying lengths of imprisonment.

The second category included detainees in common law, arrested by the Germans for straightforward criminal acts. Among these were to be found German agents, Gestapo auxiliaries who had profited by their employment to cheat or steal. Some of them were recovered by the French authorities after the liberation, judged and executed. Few of these detainees were deported. Their regime more or less resembled that of the first category. Also in this class were placed children of less than fifteen, for, as in the concentration camps, many children were detained in Romainville. At one time there was even a baby of seven months there.

The third group consisted of women—mothers, daughters, and wives of political prisoners or of militants and important resistants. Their courage

---

[7] The S.S. replaced the Wehrmacht after the escape on June 1, 1943, of two prisoners, Pierre Georges (Colonel Fabien) and Albert Poirier.

and their extraordinary dynamism was a great comfort to the prisoners. It was almost invariably thanks to them that news circulated in the camp; on several occasions leading to severe reprisals. The Germans swelled their ranks with female criminals and prostitutes in order to engender a moral degradation. The failure of this idea was striking. Even the lowest women discovered a little human dignity after contact with the detainees. Most of the female political prisoners were deported.

The fourth category consisted of political prisoners kept in solitary confinement. These were allowed a material regime almost identical with that of the three former categories: a few carefully censored letters, a few Red Cross parcels, and a short daily exercise. It is from these that hostages could be taken when there were insufficient in the fifth category. A certain number of them were shot, a very few released, and the others deported.

The four above-mentioned categories were housed in the old surface buildings of the fort, formerly used as barracks, offices, and shops. The fifth category were unfortunate enough to be relegated to the old casemates and underground cellars of the fort. They were often reminded that they would be fetched one day to face a firing squad. Under the damp sweating vaults they were herded together on straw paillasses which were never changed, in almost complete darkness. The windows hermetically sealed, a small makeshift latrine, the impossibility of a change of clothing, the almost complete absence of water which made the most rudimentary hygiene impossible, combined to make the stench of these jails unbearable. Fifty-six prisoners were confined for several weeks in a casemate ten by eight meters. Herding was the general rule. The mange and lice constantly tortured the unfortunate inmates, the darkness made them almost blind at the end of a few weeks. Food was reduced to the cruelest minimum and mail and parcels were forbidden. In winter the cold and damp added to their ordeal. Some of the hostages bore these conditions for eight, ten, and sometimes twelve months. At times by way of punishment they were transferred to a nauseous underground trench, something worthy of Louis XIII's Châtelet.

In general it was from this category that the hostages were taken when a mass execution had been decided upon. Most of these prisoners had been condemned to death by the German tribunal, but among them were also people who had only received sentences of forced labor or a term of imprisonment, or even those who had never appeared before a tribunal. But the

Gestapo had classified them according to its own private standards. The bunker prisoners had nearly all been arrested for Communist or Gaullist activities.

Over this Dantesque world of suffering ruled a kind of buffoon, one of the "death officers" which Nazism spawned in profusion. Captain Reickenbach was a brutal drunkard who appreciated the stay in France which his administration afforded, spending his time in making a careful study of the wines which that country produces with such prodigality. Living in a state of chronic drunkenness, he would greet an attempt at escape with a terrible rage or a kind of frivolous interest, according to the humor of the day and the amount of alcohol he had consumed. Reickenbach, who was constantly brandishing his revolver, fired it in all directions—into the windows of the rooms, or while rolling drunkenly along the fort embankments. This mania earned him the nickname among the prisoners of "Pom-Pom." The sentries feared his rounds of inspection, which were usually punctuated by shots, and were careful to keep out of his line of fire. One of his favorite jests, when he wanted to punish a prisoner, was to have him brought out, hands tied behind his back, onto the embankment of the fort. A firing squad arrived, took up its position in front of the unfortunate man, raised their arms, and remained for several minutes in the firing position waiting for the order to fire—which never came. After this the prisoner was taken back to his cell. Pom-Pom was dismissed after the double escape of June 1943. The real head jailer was already S.S. Untersturmfuehrer Trapp, who was reputed once to have been a wine merchant in France.

It was from the bunker inmates that the greater part of the hostages shot later on Mont Valérien were taken. They had not all been arrested in the Parisian region. On the contrary, any affair of importance, whatever the region in which it had taken place, brought about the transfer of prisoners to Paris, where the Gestapo head office carried out interrogations and directed the inquiry. In this way seventy members of the Resistance, arrested by the French in the southwest in February and March 1942, were sent first to Paris, taken in custody by the "David Special Brigade" at the Prefecture of Police, handed over to the Gestapo, and conveyed to Romainville as hostages at the end of August 1942. During the inquiries seven of them were released. At Romainville one of the men managed to escape; the others were shot or deported. Among the latter only four were still alive when the camps were liberated.

The decision to execute hostages was made by the military commander, not by the Gestapo, but it was the latter who declared which prisoners were to be shot. Before June 1942 the hostages were taken to the gallows immediately after executions were ordered. Later, on an order from Himmler or from the O.K.W., executions were ordered periodically, the number of hostages to be shot varying according to the number and nature of the attempts (at sabotage, escape, etc.) committed throughout the occupied territory. This, of course, was the doctrine of collective responsibility pushed to the utmost limit of sanity. Each attempt committed in France was the object of three reports drawn up by the Feldkommandantur, the Gestapo, and the Abwehr office (one existed in each Feldkommandantur) respectively.

To these three reports were added a report from the staff of the Wehrmacht, the Luftwaffe, or the Kriegsmarine, according to whether the attempt had taken place against a member or an installation of the corresponding armed force. A second was provided by the Embassy, a third by the Propaganda Staffel—the last two reports analyzing the state of mind of the population.

The sum total of these reports presented a definite picture, according to which decisions were taken—by Keitel. The latter then gave Stuelpnagel orders to shoot a certain number of hostages. This order was transmitted to Oberg, who saw to the actual execution and its publicity. Section II Pol, of the rue des Saussaies, undertook the practical measures (transport of the prisoners, choice of place, fixation of the time and place of the executions). In Paris the firing squad was provided by the Ordnungspolizei, and in the provinces by the Wehrmacht or the police regiments. Section IV of the Gestapo chose the hostages to be shot, usually from the Romainville prisoners, sometimes from Fresnes, and in the provinces from the detainees in the German prisons. It often happened that, from a group of fifty hostages shot, only one had previously been condemned to death by a German tribunal. On the other hand, a fairly large number of those actually condemned to death were not executed but deported.

The hostages were taken from the category of bunker inmates and, if there were not enough of these, from those of the fourth category—these two categories being given the German classification of *Suehnepersonen*, "persons detained for reprisals and punishment." For example, on October 1, 1943, an order prescribed the execution of fifty hostages. Now since the preceding July 15 several convoys of deportees had taken the route for Germany and only forty hostages in Bunker 22 remained at Romainville. Ten prisoners were therefore taken from category 4 at random, to make up the required number.

In the same way in September 1942, an "outrage" having been committed in the Rex Cinema in Paris, commandeered for German soldiers, an order arrived for 125 hostages to be shot. But eighty-eight men had already been executed on August 11th (the High Command had put the number at ninety-three but actually eighty-eight had died) and the Romainville reserve had not yet been formed. Only forty-six persons could be found, and they were shot on the Mont Valérien. An order to execute seventy persons chosen from the prisoners at Fort Hâ was sent to Bordeaux. Thus Frenchmen arrested six months earlier, four hundred miles from Paris, died for an act which they did not even know had been committed.

These mass executions continued until the end. Their effect was contrary to the aim intended. Far from striking terror into the population, they revolted the masses of the people and contributed to the swelling of the ranks of the Resistance. The number of hostages shot in France reached a total of 29,660 over the whole country. An analysis of their distribution would enable a map of the Resistance to be compiled. While 11,000 hostages were executed in the region of Paris, the two regions next on this table of honor were the two capitals of the French Resistance Movement: Lyons with 3,674 hostages shot and Limoges with 2,863.

Chapter 18
The Martyrdom of the Eastern Territories

In the Eastern lands Nazi ferocity was unbridled. In Poland, in the Baltic countries, and in temporarily invaded U.S.S.R. territory, the Nazis proceeded to carry out a systematic extermination which today stupefies the imagination. While in the west of Europe they played a sort of seesaw game, alternating terror with appeals for cooperation, no attempt of this nature was made in the Eastern territories. Here it was a question of annexation for repopulation purposes and reserves of slave labor.

On July 27, 1941, an order signed by Keitel on the instructions of Hitler gave Himmler the task of keeping order in Russian-occupied territory with absolute powers to take any measures he chose and on his own responsibility, in order to carry out the Fuehrer's orders by applying, "not legal trial proceedings but the only effective measure, terror."

These terror measures were carried out by the Einsatzgruppen (combat groups) under Himmler which were composed of S.S., S.D., and Gestapo. The Einsatzgruppen had not been created specially for the Russian campaign; Schellenberg had organized them on Heydrich's orders in 1938 for the Czechoslovakian campaign, to repress any attempts at resistance on the part of the civil population and to carry out a political purge by terror methods.

It was Heydrich once more who, in 1941, planned all the measures for the extermination. We find in his orders the euphemisms he affected: he nearly always refrained from using the word "extermination," using as a substitute "filtering," "purification measures," "purges," "special measures," "special regime," and only very occasionally "liquidation" or "execution."

The Einsatzgruppen were formed in accordance with an agreement made between the R.S.H.A. and the O.K.W. In mid-May 1941 Heydrich ordered Mueller to negotiate an agreement with the military on the functioning of the Einsatzgruppen to the rear of the troops who were to fight on the Eastern front. Having secured the "cooperation" of the military first through Mueller and then through Schellenberg, Heydrich's orders were categorical. Not only must the Army tolerate the Einsatzgruppen in its rear, but the relevant corps of the Army were strictly obliged to give total support to any enterprise of the Einsatzgruppen and to the commanders of the SIPO and the S.D. It was clear that Heydrich now had a free hand in the East.

The Army was bound to help the Einsatzkommandos, to arrange for their supplies of petrol and food, and to place its liaison network at their disposal. Four Einsatzgruppen were created and the front was divided geographically among them.[8] Their leaders were hard-core Nazis, long since "cured" of any of those scruples which Hitler was pleased to stigmatize.

The strength of each Einsatzgruppe was 1,000 to 1,200 men, divided into a number of Einsatzkommandos. This composition was the result of careful

---

[8] Einsatzgruppe A: the Baltic States. B: Smolensk, Moscow. C: the Kiev region. D: Southern Ukraine.

mixing, to include every type of skill. Out of 1,000 men, there were about 350 members of the Waffen S.S., 150 drivers and mechanics, 100 members of the Gestapo, 80 members of the auxiliary police (recruited on the spot), 130 of the ordinary police, 40 to 50 from the KRIPO, and 30 to 35 from the S.D. The rest included interpreters, radio operators, teletypists, the office clerks and female staff, for there were women in these killer formations (10 to 15 per Einsatzgruppe). The headquarters staff was naturally provided by the Gestapo and, to a lesser degree, by the S.D. and the KRIPO.

The Einsatzkommandos were raised at the end of June 1941 and began to operate from the beginning of July. Their orders were that, as a first step, the Jews and political commissars had to be liquidated. These orders were issued at a conference held at Pretz by Streckenbach, who had come specially from Paris. As a result the entire Jewish population was massacred, including the children. At Riga, for example, more than 35,000 persons were executed, so that S.S. Obergruppenfuehrer von dem Bach-Zelewski could proudly write on October 31, 1941: "There is not a Jew left in Estonia."

The manner in which operations were carried out against the "partisan groups" was characteristic. Suffice to quote the balance sheet of "Operation Cottbus," carried out by the S.S. General von Gottberg against these "bands" to give some idea:

Enemy killed. 4,500
Killed, suspected of belonging to partisan bands . . . 5,000
German dead 59
Weapons recovered. 492 small arms

Less than five hundred small arms were recovered from 9,500 dead, a figure which explains why there were only fifty-nine German dead, and supporting the view that the S.S. dubbed as "partisans" any Russian peasants they met in their path. The German Commissioner for White Russia wrote in his report on "Operation Cottbus" that its "moral effect on the peace-loving population was simply horrible, on account of the numerous shootings of women and children."

These murders were accompanied by systematic pillage. Everything utilizable was collected: shoes, leather, clothes, jewels, gold, and any other objects of value. Rings were torn off women's fingers; the Jews were stripped in order to salvage their clothes before shooting them naked on the parapet of an anti-tank ditch.

Ohlendorf has related that the extermination of the Jews always began—when there was time—by a census, which forced them to attend and register. On their assembly, before being taken to their death, everything of use they possessed was confiscated and forwarded to the R.S.H.A., which in turn handed it over to the Reich Ministry of Finance.

The roundup of Jews and their executions have been described by many witnesses. The most remarkable is undoubtedly that of the German engineer, Hermann Grabe, a director of the Ukranian branch of a German construction firm at Sdolbunov. He was visiting his sites at Rovno, when the five thousand inhabitants of the Ghetto in that town were exterminated on the night of July 13, 1942. About a hundred of these unfortunate people were employed by his firm, and Grabe tried to save them by arguing labor shortage. Running from one leader to another, calling upon the authorities, he was able to follow all night the progress of this tragedy which was to be repeated a thousand times throughout the East. He told this harrowing story at Nuremberg.

At about 10 P.M. on July 13 the Ukranian militia supported by S.S. encircled the Rovno Ghetto, illuminating it with powerful projectors. The militia and the S.S. split into small groups, entered the houses, smashed the doors with rifle butts or flung grenades inside when the doors resisted. The S.S. carried dog whips and belabored the inhabitants to make them come out more quickly—just as they were, often half clothed, so quickly in fact that the children sometimes remained behind in the house. "Women called to their children to come and join them while the children cried for their parents. None of this prevented the S.S. from chasing those in front of them at the double, beating them viciously all the way to the goods train which awaited them. Every truck of the train was filled. There was a continual screaming of women and children, the cracking of rifle fire, shouts, and the hiss of whips. ... Throughout the night these people, beaten and trapped, filed along the brightly lit streets, women carrying dead children in their arms, children dragging their dead parents as far as the train by the arms and legs. ... On the way I saw hosts of corpses of both sexes and of all ages in the streets. The doors of the houses were open, the windows stoved in; clothes, shoes, stockings, jackets, hats, overcoats, etc., were scattered all over the floor. I saw a small child less than a year old with its skull smashed lying in the corner of a house. Blood and brains were spattered on the wall of the house and on the ground around the child, who was wearing only a simple shirt. The commandant, S.S. Sturmbannfuehrer Putz, strode up and down, keeping watch on the column of eighty to a hundred Jews squatting on the ground. He carried a heavy dog whip."

Tracked and hunted in this way like a terrified flock, piled into the goods truck, these unhappy creatures were taken to the spot chosen for their execution, usually some miles from the roundup, in a lonely and deserted spot. Here long trenches had been dug in advance. The condemned population was assembled out of sight of the ditches toward which they were led in groups of twenty, fifty, or one hundred. Here they were forced to undress and line up on the edge of the trench itself, or very often to descend into the trench which was already filled with a pile of corpses. Armed S.S. with whips were stationed all around. Other S.S. men, sometimes a single man, executed the people one after the other by firing a bullet into the backs of their heads. As soon as the trench was full of corpses it was filled in.

Sometimes the people were ordered to lie down on the corpses of those who had preceded them, and were killed in this position. Tens, hundreds, and thousands of Russians were murdered in this way. At Minsk, in October 1942, sixteen thousand Jews, all that remained from the Ghetto, were executed in a single day. At Kiev 195,000 persons were murdered during the war.

At Minsk an incident took place which gave rise to one of the most appalling Nazi inventions. At the end of August 1942 Himmler, on a tour of inspection, stopped in the city and expressed a wish to be present at the execution of the prisoners. The troops which carried out this task did not take any extra precautions. It often happened that people who were only seriously wounded were buried unceremoniously. This is what happened at Minsk. But when Himmler, whose orders these murderers were carrying out, saw the collapse of the victims, among them several women who continued to move and to groan feebly, he lost his proverbial impassiveness and fainted like a vulgar "intellectual."

Himmler, on his return to Berlin, impressed by this horrible sight in Minsk, gave orders that women and children were not to be subjected to the "moral torture" of the firing squad. In this way the commando troops, almost all of them married men, would no longer be forced to fire on women and children. Not for a moment was there any question of forbidding the execution of women and children. On the contrary, it was an attempt to make it more bearable for the troops. It merely had the effect of multiplying the murders. It was the "air-conditioned nightmare."

To comply with this order an S.S. engineer set to work in Berlin. From the brain of this Nazi technician, S.S. Untersturmfuehrer Dr. Becker, were born the monstrous machines known as "S" trucks. Ohlendorf has stated that "the true nature of these vans could not be seen from the outside. They were like ordinary closed wagons and were built so that when the engine was started the exhaust gas was led inside the car, bringing death to the occupants in between ten to fifteen minutes. ... The victims were loaded into the trucks, which were driven to the place of burial, the place used for mass executions. The time of the journey was enough to insure the death of all the occupants." The trucks, varying in size, could each take from fifteen to twenty-five persons. The women and children were made to climb into them, being told that they were to be transported elsewhere. Once the doors were shut, the inside, rigorously sealed, became a gas chamber on wheels.

Becker having finished designing these machines, Obersturmbannfuehrer Rauff of the R.S.H.A. group of motor transports and his adjutant, Zwabel, were ordered to build them. "S" trucks were built by the firm of Saurer, "S" being the initial of both the maker and the word *sonder*, which means special. They went into service for the first time with the Einsatzgruppen late in 1942. Engineer Becker was responsible for the trucks, the upkeep of which was entrusted to the Rauff automobile section.

Contrary to what Becker and Hitler had expected, the bringing into service of the "S" trucks by no means solved the problem of executions. The people soon began to realize what happened as soon as they climbed into these "death wagons." A stratagem was therefore necessary. Becker wrote: "I have given orders to camouflage 'S' trucks as caravans. To this end I have given the small trucks a skylight and the large ones two, similar to those one sees in the peasants' houses in the country." But later Becker was forced to admit: "In my opinion it is impossible to camouflage and to keep them secret for very long." On the other hand, the gruesome details of the results are related by Becker in the appropriate technical style: "The poisoning by carbon monoxide gas does not always take place as foreseen. In order to finish the job more quickly the drivers open the inlet valve to the full. As a result of this measure the victims are asphyxiated and not put to sleep as was foreseen. The directions I originally gave show that with the correct position of the valve death comes quicker and the condemned then fall asleep peacefully."

Can one imagine the S.S. driver of one of these trucks, at the wheel of his vehicle jolting over a Ukraine road potholed by the heavy Wehrmacht transport; behind him, bumped about at the hazard of the ruts, twenty-five women and children dying of asphyxiation in this carefully upholstered iron prison—on their last voyage at the end of which was a trench already half filled with convulsive corpses?

The drivers and the commandos soon began to complain of violent headaches. They maintained that they absorbed a large quantity of the gas when they opened the doors of the trucks on arrival. The sight which greeted their eyes inside was horrible, but they complained above all of the dirtiness of the job. They had to bring out bodies entwined together and sullied.

The "S" convoys functioned for several months and were also used in Poland and Czechoslovakia. Braunfisch, head of the Lódz Gestapo, mentioned that the Sonderkommando Kulmhof, stationed at Chelmno, had exterminated 340,000 Jews with the aid of these trucks.

The existence of this unit was top secret, and the personnel of the Einsatzkommandos was bound to absolute secrecy regarding the activities of the unit and the functioning of the trucks. At Minsk, a driver who had described his truck in a state of drunkenness, was condemned to death by a tribunal of S.S. and police. The details of this undertaking, however, were found in the German records and the activities of the "S" trucks were revealed at Nuremberg. Later, as a result of various incidents, the trucks had to be abandoned, and the executions took place by shooting or hanging as in the past.

The balance of the Einsatzgruppen activities has never been established with precision. At Nuremberg, Ohlendorf declared that, during the period he had been in command of Einsatzgruppe D, his unit had exterminated in the neighborhood of 90,000 persons. The Einsatzkommandos operating in the Baltic States executed more than 135,000 Jews in three months. It has been estimated that about 750,000 victims fell to the four Einsatzgruppen during their activity on Russian soil.

These crimes were carried out basically on orders given by Hitler in the general instructions for "Fall Barbarossa,"[9] and then renewed on December 16, 1942, by Keitel who wrote: "It is not only justified therefore but the duty of the troops to use every method without restriction, even against women and children, provided it insures success. Any act of mercy is a crime against the German people."

Keitel's attitude, incidentally, was copied by a number of soldiers. Kesselring, for example, wrote in an order of the day, issued in Italy on June 17, 1944: "I will protect any commanding officer who departs from our normal standards in the severity of the choice of measures adopted against the partisans. To this effect, the old principle still holds good: 'An error in the choice of methods of execution is preferable to a lack of time or a negligence in action.'"

In the East the Einsatzgruppen were aided in their task by thirty regiments of police composed of S.S. from the Totenkopfverbaende, whose course of action was on the same lines. At Kerch, a little boy of six was shot for humming a Soviet song in the street, and in the same town the body of another small boy of nine remained hanging for most of the summer in Sacco and Vanzetti Square: he had been picking apricots.

While the occupied regions of the U.S.S.R. bowed beneath the storm of Nazi bestiality, the other nations of East and Central Europe were not spared. Poland and Czechoslovakia suffered worse. On May 21, 1939, at the Reich Chancellery, Hitler had declared to Goering, Raeder, and Keitel, "If a conflict breaks out with the West it will be advantageous to possess vast territories in the East. We can rely on excellent harvests even if they are smaller in wartime than in peacetime. The population of the German conquered territories will do no military service and will be available for work."

On the previous March 16 a decree of Hitler had created the "Protectorate of Bohemia and Moravia," determining that this new territory would in future belong to the German Reich, while conserving an autonomous government, a puppet organization entirely under the orders of the Nazis. On the 18th a second decree appointed von Neurath Protector of Bohemia-Moravia.

---

[9] The code name for the attack on Russia.

Neurath held a special position in the Reich Government. Minister of Foreign Affairs since the accession to power, he was one of the conservative ministers chosen by Hindenburg to "stiffen" Hitler. At the beginning of 1938 he had expressed his disagreement with Hitler's foreign policy and was replaced by Ribbentrop on February 4, 1938. Becoming a Minister of the Reich without Portfolio, president of the Reich's Secret Cabinet, a phantom organization with no power, and member of the Council for the Defense of the Reich, for practical purposes he had renounced all political activity since his departure from the Foreign Office.

On the occupation of Czechoslovakia, the Gestapo installed itself throughout the country. The frontier regions constituted a special department—the Sudentenland, and two head offices were opened in Prague and Brno. Fifteen Oberlandraeter were quartered in as many Czech towns, each of them with a local service of the SIPO-S.D., the composition of which was almost identical with the organizations later introduced into France.

These fifteen Oberlandraeter were responsible to the main services in Prague and Brno, the latter being attached to the head office of the R.S.H.A. Recruitment of local staff was greatly facilitated by the presence in the Protectorate of about 400,000 German nationals, who provided almost all the agents and trusted men known as "V-Maenner."

The part of Czechoslovakia transformed by the Germans into an independent Slovak State created its own police force known as "Ustredna Stanej Bezpecnosti"—U.S.B. It was in fact entirely controlled by the Gestapo and carried out most of its missions in coordination with the German services of Bohemia-Moravia. It was not until the national Slovak insurrection of 1944 that the Gestapo and the S.D. installed their networks there.

The head of the Gestapo in Prague, Boehme, resorted to the usual methods and, between May 15 and 23, 1939, arrested in Prague and Brno 4,639 persons, most of them members of the underground Communist party. On September 1, 1939, eight thousand Czech notables, whose names figured on lists established in advance, were arrested on Boehme's orders and sent to concentration camps, where most of them died.

In 1940 Karl Frank, State Secretary to von Neurath, declared in a speech to the leaders of the "Movement for National Unity," that if the influential Czech politicians refused to sign a declaration of loyalty to the Reich, two thousand hostages would be shot.

Hitler, however, considered the measures taken by von Neurath inadequate and decided to give him the support of a more energetic Vice-Protector. Heydrich immediately saw the advantages to be gained from such a post. He entered the lists with the aid of Bormann. Himmler viewed this maneuver with displeasure. Heydrich was becoming a more and more dangerous rival, and this new function was going to increase his power. He was unable, however, to oppose it.

Wilhelm Hoettl has maintained that Heydrich obtained Hitler's promise that he would be appointed Minister of the Interior, a post which Himmler had earmarked for himself and which he later obtained. No official document confirms the existence of this promise. Whatever the truth, it is obvious that Heydrich hoped to take full advantage of his new post.

On September 23, 1941, Hitler summoned Neurath to Berlin. In very vivid terms he reproached him for his lack of firmness, then announced the appointment of Heydrich, who was to become his adjutant, with very extensive powers. Neurath protested and offered his resignation. Hitler refused it, but on the 27th Neurath was sent on leave. He remained there until August 25, 1943, the day on which he was replaced by Frick.

On September 29 Heydrich took up residence in Prague as Vice-Protector. A daily air courier and a special secret teleprinter kept him in direct contact with Berlin, not to mention the telephone lines and radio communications of the R.S.H.A. special network. Two private aircraft allowed him to be in Berlin in less than two hours in cases of urgency.

Heydrich refused to use Neurath's staff, and chose from the members of the R.S.H.A. services a reliable team, including shorthand typists. He had even wanted to take Schellenberg, but the latter, having no faith in his chief's star and possibly fearing an act of vengeance (like Ohlendorf, he had done him a disservice with Himmler by putting a brake on his rise), prudently declined the offer. As soon as he was installed in Prague, Heydrich speeded up the repression, ordering mass executions.

On October 14, 1941, the commander of the Waffen S.S. detachments in Bohemia-Moravia wrote in a report to Himmler: "All the battalions of the Waffen S.S. will be brought by motor transport into the Bohemia-Moravia Protectorate to carry out the shootings and to control the hangings. Up to the present there have been 99 shot and 21 hanged in Prague; 54 shot and 17 hanged in Brno, making a total of 191 executions, including 16 Jews."

This repression was further increased during the following month. On November 17 the students of Prague organized an anti-Nazi demonstration. Four hundred of them were arrested the same day. On the 19th nine students chosen from among the leaders of their associations were executed without trial, twelve hundred others being sent to Sachsenhausen camp.

On March 9, 1942, Heydrich obtained for the Gestapo the right to apply "protective custody" within the Protectorate. At the same time Heydrich multiplied his appeals for Germano-Czech collaboration, pursuing a policy similar to that practiced in France alternating promises and brutal sanctions, a behavior to which he had given the colorful name of "the policy of the whip and the sugar" (*Peitsche und Zucker*).

For the "sugar" Heydrich had brought with him from Berlin a "technical adviser," ordered to find out what means could be employed to make the Czech workers fall for the charms of Nazism and to persuade them to work for the German war economy. The man used an alias, but all those with a long memory recognized Torgler, the former Communist deputy who had cut such a miserable figure in the trial of the Reichstag incendiaries—Torgler, whom Heydrich had released a few years earlier from a concentration camp and whom he now used for some of his baser tasks.

The Czechs categorically refused to nibble at the sugar, and the whip began to play a more and more important part.

Seen from Berlin, Heydrich's efforts and the results he obtained, in spite of everything, made a great impression and his prestige grew. The story of the whip and the sugar was considered a masterpiece of active diplomacy, the prototype of the behavior to be adopted with regard to undisciplined people whom it was no longer a question of annihilating, for the productivity of labor potential they represented had become too valuable at a moment when the struggle in the East was assuming a more and more sinister character.

In the spring of 1942 Heydrich had reached the peak of his power, and was now a direct threat to the two other *éminences grises* of the regime— Himmler, from whom he had escaped completely, and Bormann, who had become Hitler's shadow after Hess's flight to England. Continuing to hold the posts of leader of the R.S.H.A. and Protector of Bohemia and Moravia (although not the title), he was prepared to flout the Minister of the Interior.

Himmler and Bormann joined forces to bar the progress of their dangerous competitor, when fate relieved them of the necessity.

On May 30, 1942, the D.N.B. in Berlin published the following communiqué:

"An attempt was committed by persons unknown, on May 27 in Prague, on the person of the deputy to the Protector of the Reich in Bohemia-Moravia, S.S. Obergruppenfuehrer, Reinhard Heydrich: S.S. Obergruppenfuehrer Heydrich was wounded but his life is not in danger. A reward of ten million crowns is offered for the discovery of the culprit."

The publication of this communiqué aroused a thousand suppositions in the minds of the initiated. Everyone made a mental list of Heydrich's countless enemies. Apart from Himmler and Bormann, there were other far less important figures, perfectly capable of planning an attempt, such as Naujocks, the organizer of the Gleiwitz coup, who had been axed by Heydrich and as a result nursed a hatred for him. Within the S.A. there were countless people who hardly bothered to hide their satisfaction behind a passive face. The general opinion attributed the operation to Himmler. Things were, however, infinitely more simple. Even though Heydrich's personal enemies were longing for his disappearance, the Czech Resistance Movement desired it even more. It had therefore proceeded to solve, albeit unwittingly, the Heydrich-Himmler conflict.

On the morning of May 27 Heydrich, who had just returned from Paris after a short stay in Berlin, was driving to the Hradschin, the old imperial castle of Prague, which he had made his headquarters. He had come from another castle, which he had commandeered for his country house some miles from Prague, and was enjoying the warm sun in his open Mercedes. As usual, he sat next to the chauffeur, who that morning was a new man, the veteran Nazi normally attached to Heydrich being ill.

At the approach to the suburbs of Prague, the route turned sharply and the driver had to slow down to take the bend. Two men dressed in blue workers' jeans, wheeling bicycles and carrying traditional workers' haversacks, had stopped by the roadside about twenty yards apart. Heydrich's car was easily recognizable. It sported two pennants on the mudguards, the S.S. flag and the flag of the Reich Regency. Whenever Heydrich was in Prague he took this route every morning at about the same hour.

The two workers were, in fact, members of the Free Czechs formed in England by volunteers. Their names were Jan Kubis and Josef Gabeik, and they had recently been dropped by parachute into Czechoslovakia.

As the car slowed on entering the bend, the leading worker leaped forward, brandishing a revolver, and opened fire on the occupants of the car. Losing his head, the driver did not have the presence of mind to put his foot down on the accelerator (which Heydrich's regular chauffeur would certainly have done), and the car slowed down even more. At this moment the second man took a large metal ball from his haversack and rolled it down the road in the direction of the car, beneath which it exploded.

Heydrich, who had stood up in the car to reply to the fire and had wounded the first aggressor, collapsed together with the chauffeur. The two workers fled on their bicycles, after laying a smoke screen.

Transported to the municipal hospital of Bullovka, Heydrich was immediately operated on by the leading Prague surgeon, Professor Hohlbaum.[10] He had been seriously wounded by several splinters in the region of the lungs and the stomach. A large piece of metal had entered the spleen, which had to be removed. His wounds were full of pieces of clothing and the infection was controlled by strong doses of anti-tetanus and anti-gangrene serums. In spite of the gravity of his wounds, he had seemed on the road to recovery, and had begun to take a light diet when, on June 3, he had a sudden relapse.

Gebhardt, a childhood friend and Himmler's personal doctor, and Sauerbruch, another official medical "big gun" of the Reich, dispatched with all speed to Prague, could not arrest the progress of the malady. Their treatment, which caused great discussion later, could not prevent Heydrich from dying on the morning of June 4. The post-mortem revealed that he had died of mediastinitis, an irritation of the median part of the thorax, doubtless complicated by chemical metabolism due to the removal of the spleen. Some doctors maintained that the true cause of death was the injection of serums after the removal of the spleen, which the body could not support. But this could not be verified.

---

[10] Hohlbaum, condemned immediately after the war to forced labor in Czechoslovakia for his pro-Nazi activities, was seriously wounded in 1945, while demining a suburb of Prague. No doctor was prepared to treat him but he managed to reach Leipzig, where he died.

Heydrich's death was the signal for the most bloody reprisals. More than three thousand arrests were carried out, and courts-martial at Prague and Brno pronounced 1,350 death sentences. The section leaders of the R.S.H.A., Nebe and Schellenberg, arrived in Prague on the evening of May 27 to start an inquiry. They were able to reconstitute the mechanism of the bomb, a remarkable weapon of British origin, which could be regulated according to the distance it was required to roll. It had been set for a distance of eight yards and had functioned with great precision.

The authors of the attempt had found asylum in the Church of Saint-Charles of Borromeo, where more than a hundred members of the Czech Resistance Movement were in hiding. The Gestapo discovered the existence of this hideout, and the S.S., after besieging the church, killed everyone inside, including the killers.

The inquiry petered out, probably because nobody wanted to go more deeply into the matter. The outrage was used as a pretext to track down the Resistance networks. The day of the assassination 150 Jews were executed in Berlin by way of reprisals.

Schirach, Gauleiter and Reich Governor in Vienna, seized without doubt by a feeling of solidarity with his opposite number in Prague, wrote to Bormann asking him to have a British town of cultural interest bombed by way of reprisals, since the bomb was of British manufacture.

A gigantic operation was unleashed against the Resistance and the Czech populace. An area of 15,000 square kilometers and 5,000 communes was searched and 657 persons shot on the spot. Finally it was decided to punish two villages suspected of having sheltered the authors of the crime—the communes of Lidice and Lezaki.

On the morning of June 9 a detachment of the S.S. Division "Prinz Eugen," commanded by S.S. Haupfsturmfuehrer Max Rostock, invested the hamlet of Lidice about thirty kilometers from Prague. The population was confined to the village and forbidden to leave; the men and youths of more than sixteen years old were then locked up in the barns and stables while the women and children were imprisoned in the school. The following morning the men were taken out in groups of ten into the garden behind Gorak's, the mayor of Lidice, farm and shot. By four o'clock in the afternoon 172 men of the village had been killed. Nineteen men of Lidice who worked in the neighboring mines of Kladno, or as woodcutters in the neighboring forests, were taken to Prague and shot, as were seven women from Lidice. The other 195 women of the village were deported to Ravensbruck. The newborn and babies were torn from their mothers and had their throats slit. The other infants, numbering about ninety, were sent to the Gneisenau concentration camp in Poland. Seventeen of them, placed in German families, were discovered in 1947. Finally the village itself was razed to the ground. The houses were set on fire and dynamited and the entire village demolished.

On June 11 the German newspaper *Der Neue Tag* published the following communiqué:

> In the course of the search for the murderer of Obengruppenfuehrer S.S. it was found that the population of the village of Lidice near Kladno had helped and cooperated with the perpetrators of the crime. This has been proved, although the villagers denied that they had cooperated. The attitude of the population with regard to the crime has also manifested itself by other acts hostile to the Reich. For example, underground literature, stocks of weapons and ammunition have been found as well as the existence of a transmitting set, and an illegal depot containing large quantities of rationed food. All the men of the village have been shot. The women have been deported to concentration camps and the children sent to appropriate houses for their education. All the buildings of this village have been razed to the ground and the name of the village removed from the land registers.

In this manner reprisals carried out on a peaceful peasant hamlet were brought to the knowledge of the German people, without the slightest protest being raised. This action had been ordered by State Secretary Karl Hermann Frank, subsequently known as the "Butcher of Lidice."

After the death of Heydrich the executions were just as savage. The arrests continued at an accelerated rate. People were murdered even in the prisons. In the Pankrac prison of Prague 1,700 Czechs were killed and 1,300 more in Koumic College at Brno, which had been transformed into a prison.

Until the end the Nazis harassed the Czech people without ever managing to break their resistance. It had been calculated that 200,000 people passed through the prison of Brno alone, of whom only 50,000 were liberated, the others having been killed or sent to the slow death of the concentration camps.

In all, 305,000 Czechs were deported to the camps; only 75,000 emerged alive, another 23,000 being so seriously affected that their chances of survival were very faint. The executions carried out until 1943 often received considerable publicity. After 1943 they took place almost in secret. An average of a hundred persons a month continued to be shot. By the time the Nazis had to evacuate Czecholovakia they had claimed 360,000 victims.

With the death of Heydrich, the R.S.H.A. was without a master. At the solemn obsequies in Berlin, Himmler had uttered a few ambiguous phrases into which those who might have felt tempted to court the succession most surely read a barely concealed menace. Himmler decided to take over temporarily the direction of the R.S.H.A. He could thus regain his hold on this huge apparatus, which had nearly escaped him, and choose a successor to Heydrich, being careful this time not to choose a rival.

For several months Heydrich's death mask figured prominently on Himmler's desk. No one knew whether this was a pious souvenir or a permanent reminder of final victory. Most of the R.S.H.A. leaders opted for the second supposition.

After Hess's flight to England on May 10, 1941, a silent purge had already been carried out by Mueller among his entourage. All those with access to Hess, his colleagues, aides-de-camp, secretaries, and even his chauffeur were arrested. Haushofer, his former teacher at Munich University, who had become his friend, was worried. Since Hess was interested in the teachings of Rudolf Steiner's anthroposophist groups, numerous arrests took place from among their members as among the clairvoyants and astrologers whom Hess had consulted before he left. Himmler, himself a great believer in astrology, could not oppose this measure which Heydrich had taken a cunning delight in applying.

It was thought that the death of Heydrich would provoke a purge on the same scale within Germany as had the Hess affair, but it was more limited. The section leaders of the R.S.H.A., having always sided with Himmler against Heydrich, retained their posts. Only a few newcomers introduced by Heydrich were discreetly removed. Those who had had to suffer from Heydrich's hatred, such as Hoettl, were, of course, given new posts.

It took Himmler eight months' brooding before he appointed a successor to Heydrich. When the name was ultimately revealed at the end of January 1943, it caused general surprise. The new head of the R.S.H.A. was a person in such a subordinate position that his sudden rise had been unpredictable. Himmler thought for some time of appointing Schellenberg, whose youth appeared to him sufficient guarantee against ultimate rivalry. But Hitler had refused to ratify this choice precisely because of his age, and it was Dr. Ernst Kaltenbrunner, a veteran Austrian Nazi, who was appointed by the decree of January 30, 1943.

Ernst Kaltenbrunner was born on October 4, 1903, in the valley of the Inn near Braunau, the region from which the Fuehrer also originated. This similarity of origins influenced Hitler to accept Kaltenbrunner's appointment.

The Kaltenbrunner family was one of the oldest in the district. A long line of country artisans, makers of scythes, had preceded the grandfather of the new Nazi dignitary, who had been the first to raise himself above his semi-peasant condition by becoming a lawyer. His father, Hugo Kaltenbrunner, had also been a lawyer at Raab and then at Linz. Here young Ernst completed his studies and in 1921 attained his *Arbitur*. Following his father, he studied law at Graz University, belonged to one of the first groups of National Socialist students, participated in fierce battles against the Catholic-Christian Social students, and obtained his doctorate of law in 1926, becoming a lawyer in Linz. The last two years of his studies had been difficult. His family were no longer able to give him an allowance and he had to work as a miner on night shift, in order to devote as many hours as possible to his university courses. During the following years of 1926–28 he was employed by a Salzburg lawyer, where he became familiar with court procedure.

During this period Kaltenbrunner had never ceased to engage in political activities and had been militant in the Independent Movement for a Free Austria, which led him to Nazism. In 1932 he joined the Austrian Nazi party, his membership card being No. 300,179, and at the beginning of 1933 he became a member of one of the more or less camouflaged S.S. organizations which had begun to infiltrate the Nazi combat groups in Austria. His S.S. number was 13,039. He was posted to a company one of whose former members was Adolf Eichmann.

He immediately played a leading role in the S.S. and became one of the spokesmen for the Party in Upper Austria. At the same time he organized and gave legal advice to members and sympathizers of the Party.

In 1933 he was appointed Commander of S.S. Standarte 37. His activity attracted the attention of the Austrian police. Arrested in January 1934, he was sent to Kaisersteinbruch camp with a few other Austrian Nazis. The Dollfuss Government tried to combat the Nazis by using some of their own methods, but without going to the same extremes. In the camp Kaltenbrunner swiftly gained an ascendancy over his fellow prisoners. His tall stature and physique contributed more to this than his legal knowledge. At Easter he organized a hunger strike. Secretary of State Karwinsky came in person to inspect the camp, and promised some material improvements. The strikes ceased in all the huts with the exception of one, that of Kaltenbrunner. On the eleventh day the strikers, who had been taken to a Vienna hospital, had to abandon their demonstration, because they were forbidden to take any water. A little later the prisoners were released.

In 1934 Kaltenbrunner was appointed Commander of the 8th S.S. Division, but he did not take part in the putsch of July 1934 when Dollfuss was murdered. This abstention got him chosen by the Schuschnigg Government as one of the Nazis capable of carrying out its attempts at political pacification undertaken in September 1934. Failing in this, Kaltenbrunner was arrested once more in May 1935, and accused of high treason because of his relations with the German S.S. organization. After six months in prison he appeared before a tribunal which sentenced him to six months' imprisonment for conspiracy, under benefit of the First Offenders Act. In the meantime he had been struck from the bar for his political activity. He was appointed Commander of the Austrian S.S. shortly before his arrest.

On his release Kaltenbrunner worked toward achieving the Anschluss. Using the conventional slogans of fraternity of blood, race, and language, it responded to an already deeprooted desire in the majority of the Austrian people. The bogy of Austria entering into the Great Reich and its inhabitants coming under Nazi control was brushed aside. And since the Austrians were already living under the conservative dictatorship of the Schuschnigg Government, they were inclined to overlook this kind of detail.

It was at this time that Kaltenbrunner met Seyss-Inquart. Together with him he worked on the preparation for the Anschluss, and on March 11, 1938, was appointed State Secretary for Security under Seyss-Inquart. A few hours later, at three o'clock in the morning of March 12, he met Himmler descending from his aircraft on Aspern airfield, and placed the Austrian S.S., of which he was still the leader, under the Reichsfuehrer's supreme direction. The day of the annexation Himmler appointed him S.S. Brigadefuehrer, and head of the S.S. Oberabschnitt Donau. Six months later, on September 11, he was promoted S.S. Gruppenfuehrer. He became at the same time a member of the Reichstag.

Kaltenbrunner now led the life of a regular S.S. official. Appointed successively Hoehere S.S. und Polizeifuehrer (Commander in Chief of the S.S. and the Police) for the regions of Vienna and the Upper and Lower Danube, and then, in April 1941, Lieutenant General of Police, he was not unlike an Austrian Himmler, but without any strictly personal power. He was, in fact, a simple agent for transmitting orders from Berlin, less powerful than Mueller, Nebe, or Schellenberg. This activity left him a free hand to practice the ideas he wished to try out on the organization of the intelligence services, his favorite hobby. He proceeded to create an important network, radiating from Austria in a southeasterly direction. This attracted the attention of Himmler and Hitler, and it was on account of these attributes that Himmler summoned Kaltenbrunner to Berchtesgaden in December 1942. He felt that this man, devoted solely to intelligence work, could never be a dangerous rival, and Kaltenbrunner was given the main task of creating a grand-scale intelligence service. Kaltenbrunner protested that this mission risked curtailing his executive functions, but Himmler assured him that he would continue to carry on the effective leadership of the R.S.H.A. as he had done since the death of Heydrich; this would be easy, thanks to "eminent specialists such as Mueller and Nebe," to back him up.

This arrangement was mutually satisfactory. Himmler was assured of retaining, without having to participate, effective control of all police questions, and Kaltenbrunner could at last apply his theories on a European scale. One of his favorite ideas was that the lack of liaison in the German Intelligence Service largely derived from its division into two groups—political and military. It was a strange coincidence that France also ran her intelligence service in similar fashion.

Kaltenbrunner's idea of unification was at the base of the ultimate transformation of the R.S.H.A. and also of the final victory of the Party over the Army. This limitation of Kaltenbrunner's duties was merely theoretical and designed to insure Himmler a right to inspect the workings of the services. Kaltenbrunner looked after the administration, signing joint orders, legalizing internment orders, executions, general directives, etc.

The man who arrived in Berlin at the end of January 1943 as successor to Heydrich was a veritable giant. Kaltenbrunner was nearly seven feet tall, equipped with massive broad shoulders. At the end of his huge arms were two relatively small and strangely delicate hands (nonetheless capable of immense feats of strength). On the top of this vast body sat a long, harsh, heavy, massive face. A face cut with a billhook in a piece of badly hewn wood. A great flat forehead had nothing intellectual about it; a pair of small brown hard eyes, glittering and deep-set and half covered by heavy lids; a big straight mouth like a slash, thin lips and a huge thick square chin, stressing the massive and bestial aspect of the person—such was Kaltenbrunner at this period.

The unpleasant side of this face was accentuated by deep scars, souvenirs of those German student duels in which the face was slashed, allegedly to make it look more virile. A dull voice with a strong Austrian accent, frequently husky from drink, issued from this huge body. For Kaltenbrunner, in common with many other Nazi leaders, was an incorrigible alcoholic, a defect which soon earned him the contempt of Himmler. He was a chain smoker, consuming between eighty and one hundred cigarettes a day, leaving fingers and nails brown with nicotine stains.

Kaltenbrunner drank from early in the morning—champagne and various spirits, particularly brandy which he had sent from France.

Himmler had thus given the R.S.H.A. to an essentially mediocre creature: effective control would remain in his hands. He had no fear of treachery. Kaltenbrunner was a fanatical Nazi, a convinced believer in the doctrine of the Party, which was the only thing that had put a little solidarity into him. Without the help of Schellenberg he would never have been able to see his theories put into practice. Actually the real head of the Nazi espionage was Schellenberg. He was in direct contact with Himmler, paying only lip service to his subordination to Kaltenbrunner.

Nevertheless, the Austrian took his role seriously. Like his predecessor, he was a purveyor of fodder for concentration and extermination camps. Whereas Heydrich had sometimes tried to be cunning in applying more insidious methods, as he had done in France and Czechoslovakia, in order to try and win the collaboration of at least part of the population—Kaltenbrunner had recourse to the most brutal repressions.

He did not hesitate to check in person the methods used in the camps to exterminate the prisoners. While still active in Austria in the autumn of 1942 he inspected Mauthausen, and, accompanied by the camp commandant, Zieleis, insisted upon seeing the transit to the gas chamber of a group of prisoners, watching their death agonies through a spyhole.

At the beginning of 1943 he returned to Mauthausen, and some prisoners were executed by way of experiment in his presence, using three different methods: by hanging, by a bullet in the neck, and finally by the gas chamber. The prisoners and employees of the camp have related that Kaltenbrunner arrived in excellent humor, laughing and joking all the way to the gas chamber where these experiments took place, and while waiting for the victims to be brought in.

By the time Kaltenbrunner took over the R.S.H.A. it had become a formidable machine. The German love of bureaucracy had been able to give itself free rein in this nerve center to which all wires led—bringing and transmitting information from the remotest parts of Europe. The offices, the filing systems, the listening posts, the radio center, the laboratories, and the archives had all developed to the point where they were too big for the framework of the Prinz Albrechtstrasse and sprawled over Berlin, occupying no fewer than thirty-eight huge buildings.

When the Allied bombing had seriously damaged all these buildings, Himmler found a pretext to introduce a new custom. Each day the heads of services met for lunch in the building of 116 Kurfuerstenstrasse, at Eichmann's offices. Around this table gathered all the men who made Europe tremble. Kaltenbrunner greeted Eichmann with great cordiality. Compatriots from the same region, they had many friends in common, and Kaltenbrunner never failed to inquire after the health of his family, which had remained in Linz and which he knew well. These effusions, these marks of affectionate interest exchanged by two men who that morning had with a stroke of the pen sealed the fate of a few thousand unfortunates, and from whom a word or a signature given as they left the table would doubtless signify the death of thousands more victims at the other end of Europe, were not uncommon among the Nazi hierarchy.

Himmler attended these lunches whenever he could. For him it was an opportunity of raising the morale of his colleagues, who sometimes quailed at the announcement of the military defeats which were piling up in the East, or at the balance sheet of the latest Anglo-American bombing in the very heart of Germany. Optimism and cordiality were the rule, but generally service matters were banned. It often happened, however, that Mueller or Eichmann would use this contact to ask Kaltenbrunner or Himmler for some piece of advice they needed. Thus between the dessert and the cheese, or enjoying a glass of brandy brought from France, the decision was taken to suppress or spare a certain category of prisoners, and whether a certain form of execution was to be chosen in preference to another. This monstrous type of conversation seemed to these men entirely commonplace.

It was in the course of these lunches that the details for the installation of the first gas chambers were discussed. Here, too, were debated the results of the experiments designed to exterminate the Jews. The speed, economy, and facility of the various alternative methods were compared. These sinister conversations were unlikely to cause any of the guests to lose their appetite. Nebe alone, who had gone over to the enemy and was plotting with the Abwehr to kill Hitler, must, according to Gisevius, have suffered a great deal from these exchanges of views and returned home completely exhausted.

When Himmler was absent, Kaltenbrunner was in the chair and often used these opportunities to launch splenetic attacks against subordinates he did not like, or whose direct relations with Himmler irritated him. Schellenberg, Himmler's protégé, was the most frequent object of these attacks, to the point of causing him to complain to Himmler and ask permission not to attend these meals. But the Reichsfuehrer was too fond of this institution to allow the least backsliding.

Kaltenbrunner, despite the tutelage under which Himmler had placed him, left the mark of his narrow legal mind on the R.S.H.A. Gisevius summed it up briefly: "Kaltenbrunner came and things got worse daily. We realized that the impulses of a murderer such as Heydrich were perhaps less terrible than the cold, legal logic of a lawyer who had such a dangerous instrument as the Gestapo in his hands."

In the Gestapo, Eichmann had become absolute chief of Section IV B. He was in permanent contact with Kaltenbrunner and often received direct orders from Himmler, although administratively he was still under Mueller's orders. He had been given the task of carrying out to the end the "final solution of the Jewish problem," in other words, the total extermination of the European Jews. The first ruthless and undisguised suppression of Jews in Germany on a wholesale scale was the pogrom of November 9, 1938,[11] ordered by Heydrich, and this was the culmination. According to the estimates made at Nuremberg, six million Jews were murdered in Germany and the occupied countries. Eichmann's power over the Jews became absolute after the decree of July 1, 1943, signed by Bormann; it deprived the Jews of all recourse to ordinary tribunals and placed them under the exclusive jurisdiction of the Gestapo.

A previous decree, also signed by Bormann, on October 9, 1942, had prescribed that "the permanent elimination of the Jews from the territories of Greater Germany can no longer be carried out by emigration but by the use of ruthless force in the special camps of the East."

The system of organized pogroms was applied in the East, to be followed by scientific and industrial methods of extermination. Eichmann created four camps, one of the most notorious being Mauthausen. The way in which this camp had been conceived and built shows that the policy of extermination was considered by the Nazis as a long-term task which would be carried on long after the whole of Europe had been conquered and "domesticated." After the Jews there would be many other opponents to eliminate. "Looking like an enormous stone fortress built on the top of a mountain, and flanked by huts, Mauthausen was not only a permanent building but could also house an important garrison of men and offices with all the necessary equipment. The fortress itself was the extermination factory, to which were sent prisoners already exhausted by the forced labor in neighboring camps such as Gusen and Ebensee. When blows and hunger had reduced their working capacity below a certain level, they were sent to the central camp. No one came out of the main camp alive."

Eichmann organized the system of convoys to take the European Jews to these death camps. The departures and size of convoys were fixed relative

---

[11] This pogrom, which Heydrich called "spontaneous risings," occurred after the shooting of German diplomat von Rath in Paris by a young Jew. The wanton destruction throughout Germany was such that the insurance companies protested. Goering then issued a decree on November 1938, inflicting a fine of a billion marks on the Jewish communities, confiscating their insurance polices to pay for the damage, and excluding them from the economic life of the country. According to Nazi philosophy, the victims always had to pay.

to the absorption capacity of the camps and transport of facilities of the German railways. The commandants of the death camps only killed by gas on the instructions of Eichmann. The S.S. officer in charge of each convoy received the necessary orders and could determine whether or not the train was to be directed to a camp of extermination and the treatment to be applied to its occupants. For example, the letter *A* or *M* on the escort instructions indicated Auschwitz or Maidanek, which meant that the occupants would be gassed.

At Auschwitz the following regulations applied: "Children up to the age of twelve to fourteen, persons above fifty, even the sick (or people with a police record) were transported in trucks bearing a special plaque and taken to the gas chamber on their arrival.

"The others filed in front of an S.S. doctor, who, at a first glance, indicated who was capable of working and who was not. Those found incapable went to the gas chambers while the others were distributed to the various work camps."

This second destination was obviously only temporary, the workers being rapidly exhausted by the inhuman conditions to which they were subjected, and they in turn were directed to the gas chambers.

In East Poland a diabolical procedure was used which had been conceived and perfected by Wirth, former commissioner of the KRIPO in Stuttgart.[12] Wirth spotted among the Jewish population a certain number of criminals to whom he promised great material advantages, if they would recruit collaborators ready to carry out any tasks. He obtained about five thousand men and women who, apart from the certainty of being spared, received a financial share of the pillage. They were charged with the extermination of their unfortunate coreligionists.

In the forests and marshes of East Poland, camouflaged extermination camps were built. "They were built in false perspective, like the villages of Potemkin," said an eyewitness, that is to say, the arrivals had the impression of coming to a large town or a large nexus of dwellings. The train entered a false station and, after the escort and the train staff had left, the trucks were opened and the Jews got out. They were immediately surrounded by

---

[12] In this post, Wirth had already become notorious for his special methods of investigation in criminal matters, methods which had caused him to be arraigned before the Würtemberg Landtag.

the renegade Jewish detachments and Commissioner Wirth or one of his deputies made a speech. He said to them:

"Jews, you have been brought here to be transplanted, but before organizing this new Jewish state it is obvious that you must learn a new profession. Here you will learn that everyone has to do his duty. As a first step everyone must undress, which is the regulation, so that your clothes may be disinfected, that you may be given a bath, for you must not bring any vermin into the camps."

The new arrivals were then formed up into columns. As a first step the men and women were separated and then in successive cloakrooms they had to take off their hats, jackets, shirts, and finally their shoes and socks. In exchange for each object they were given a ticket. Since all these operations were carried out by the Jews employed by Wirth, they inspired no mistrust in the newcomers, who advanced with docility, encouraged to hurry by their treacherous coreligionists, so that they might have no time to reflect. Finally they arrived at the last halt which was the bath. A group of them entered and the doors were shut. They were then gassed. Their bodies, taken out by another door, were incinerated while the following group entered in turn.

Wirth had had no difficulty in perfecting this system, for he had previously been in charge of the extermination of incurables, acording to the euthanasia decree, and it was because of the excellent results obtained by him at this period that the Reich Chancellery had appointed him for this "confidential mission."

Chapter 19
The Experiments of the Nazi Scientists

When Kaltenbrunner became head of the R.S.H.A., its functions were considerably extended. Within its new domains now figured prisoners of war and civilian workers, surveillance of whom had been entrusted to the Gestapo.

The prisoner of war camps had been placed under the control of the military, and one might have hoped that the German High Command would have respected international law and met their obligation to protect the officers and men who had fallen into its power. But the Gestapo was allowed to meddle in this field, from which it should have been excluded. Not only did the German High Command offer no resistance to these intrusions, but it cooperated actively with Himmler and his agents. This was the logical evolution after the "understanding" of the military for the pogroms and extortions committed in Germany itself, and later with regard to the action of the Einsatzgruppen. Thus the General Staff had gradually countenanced the most sinister assassinations, and had even introduced these methods into its daily routine.

The first measures were taken against the Russian prisoners of war. In July 1941 General Reinecke (chief of the army administrative branch at GHQ), Breuer (of the prisoner of war branch), Lahousen (representing Admiral Canaris and the Abwehr), and Mueller (head of the Gestapo representing the R.S.H.A.), met in conference. In the course of this meeting, certain decisions were taken, the implementation of which was entrusted to Mueller.

They were transcribed in a document published on September 8, 1941. "The Bolshevik soldier," we read, "has forfeited all right to be treated as an honorable foe, in the light of the Geneva Convention. … Orders must be given to act with ruthless energy at the slightest sign of insubordination, in particular when it is a question of fanatical Bolsheviks. Insubordination, active or passive resistance, must be immediately broken by force of arms (bayonets, rifle butts, and firearms). Anyone carrying out this order without using his arms, or with insufficient energy, is liable to punishment. Prisoners who try to escape must be shot immediately, without being challenged. Warning shots are strictly forbidden. … The use of weapons against prisoners of war is legal as a general rule."

For the application of these dispositions a special section for prisoners of war was created by the Gestapo: Group IVa under S.S. Hauptsturmfuehrer Franz Koenigshaus. At the beginning of 1943 this group was attached to subgroup IV B-2a under S.S. Sturmbannfuehrer Hans-Helmuth Wolf.

This section issued its orders to the Gestapo representatives already installed in the camps. In actual fact, Gestapo and S.D. agents had been drafted to all the stalags, where they were often disguised by some fictitious rank. An order from Mueller dated July 17, 1941, had enjoined them to detect in the prisoner of war camps "all political, criminal or undesirable elements of whatever nature," in order to liquidate them or submit them to "special treatment," as well as "all persons who could be employed in the reconstruction of the occupied territories." At the same time this order urged them to seek among the prisoners "those who seemed trustworthy," with a view to employing them as spies within the camp and, thanks to them, to discovering among the prisoners those who had to be suppressed. The methods of the Gestapo never varied.

Most of the fighting men of the last war who had experience of the German stalags remember the columns of Russian prisoners who were brought there in the autumn of 1941, gaunt and emaciated, tottering with hunger and fatigue. The convoys sometimes arrived after a march of several hundred miles. Subjected to the worst treatment, the unfortunate creatures died of physical starvation in the thousands at the roadside. The survivors of these nightmare journeys were herded into barbed-wire enclosures. An order from Himmler dated November 22, 1941, prescribed: "Every Russian prisoner of war brought back to the camp after an attempted evasion must automatically be handed over to the nearest Gestapo office." This amounted to a death sentence. In 1941, 2,000 Russian prisoners were interned in Flossenburg camp; only 102 survived. More than 20,000 Russians were killed in Auschwitz.

On July 20, 1942, Keitel signed an order requiring the branding of those who possessed the will power to survive: "The brand mark should form an angle of 45 degrees, the longer line measuring 1 centimeter pointing upward: it is to be imprinted with a red-hot iron on the left buttock." It could also be performed with the aid of a lancet and India ink, thus constituting an indelible tattoo. This example shows to what a point the Nazi ideology had been able to pervert the German Army when a Field Marshal did not hesitate to sign such an order, reducing men to cattle. But the German High Command was to give even more revolting orders—among them those for the murder of French generals who were prisoners of war.

From 1940 onward the German High Command had recognized murder as an accepted form of political action, in this respect following the example of the Party. At a conference held on December 23, 1940, consisting of Canaris, three heads of the home sections of the Abwehr, and Admiral Buerckner (head of the foreign section), Canaris revealed that Keitel had ordered him to liquidate General Weygand who, at that time, was in North Africa. Keitel feared that he might organize a center of resistance there with those elements of the French Army which had remained intact, and had given the order to have him shot by killers. But an anti-Nazi cell had just begun to form within the Abwehr, and Canaris evaded the order, later making the excuse that he had been unable to carry out the execution for technical reasons.[13]

In the same way, when General Giraud escaped from the fortress of Koenigstein in April 1942, the German High Command, after considering the idea of having him kidnaped at Vichy by a small special S.S. commando, ordered the Abwehr to have him murdered. Keitel gave the order to Canaris, who transmitted it to one of his section leaders, Lahousen. The latter, who showed no inclination to carry out his orders, was sent off once more in pursuit by Keitel in August. The operation had been given the code name of "Gustav." Lahousen "omitted" to contact Mueller and come to an arrangement with him as Keitel had ordered. Things began to take a bad turn for the Abwehr, whose reluctance was becoming too obvious. Canaris managed to shelve his responsibility by pretending that, during the conference of Section III in Prague, Heydrich had asked to be allowed to carry out the mission himself. He had consented. Reassured by this arrangement, Canaris had let the matter drop. Since Heydrich died June 4, Canaris ran no risk of being contradicted, and the business was shelved. But neither the German High Command nor the Gestapo intended to be robbed of their vengeance. When Giraud fled to North Africa in November 1942, reprisals were carried out against his family. The General's daughter, Madame Granger, was arrested, together with her four children, one of whom was only two years old, her brother-in-law, and her young maid. When Madame Granger died in Germany in September 1943 for lack of hospital attention, it was at first decided to repatriate the children. But the Gestapo opposed this at the last moment, and indeed their unfortunate grandmother joined them in captivity six months later. In all seventeen persons of the Giraud family were arrested and deported.

So far it had proved impossible to carry out these two assassinations of French generals. But the Nazis were persistent in their efforts since they made plans of the same nature at the end of 1944. Possibly to intimidate

---

[13] On the invasion of the unoccupied zone of France, Weygand was finally arrested on November 12, 1942, by S.S. near Vichy and taken to Germany.

the imprisoned generals and prevent them from escaping, it was decided to simulate an attempted escape, and to liquidate one or two of them. Orders were given that some of the seventy-five French generals detained in the fortress of Koenigstein were to be transferred to the reprisal camp of Colditz, less than sixty miles away. The faked escape was to take place during the journey. Kaltenbrunner was given orders to supervise the organization of this plot, in cooperation with von Ribbentrop. The Foreign Minister was to prepare to reply to questions which might be asked, as a result of this affair, by the International Red Cross, or by the "protecting power." Agreement was also reached with the German High Command, whose cooperation was essential.

Kaltenbrunner entrusted the technical details to Obergruppenfuehrer Panzinger, former chief of IVa, and, after the death of Nebe, his successor as head of Amt V (KRIPO). Panzinger, with the help of one of his associates Schultze, was in favor of a well-tried method, the "S" trucks. A variant was to be used, a kind of miniature "S" truck specially equipped for the operation. The officer chosen to be the first victim was General René Mortemard de Boisse. At the end of November 1944 the plans perfected during conversations between Panzinger and Wagner (Ribbentrop's representative) were revealed to Kaltenbrunner in a memo which was discovered later:

1. In the course of a transfer of five persons in three cars with military number plates, the escape incident is to occur at the moment when the rear car has a break down.
2. Carbon monoxide is to be released by the driver into the rear of the car, which will be sealed. The apparatus can be installed in the most simple manner and removed at once. An appropriate vehicle is now at our disposal.
3. Other possibilities such as poisoning by food or drink were also envisaged but rejected as being too dangerous.
4. Measures for completing the subsequent work, such as notification, autopsy, evidence, and interment, have been taken. The leader of the convoy and the driver will be provided by the R.S.H.A. and will wear military uniform. They will be issued with army pay book.

The name of General de Boisse having been mentioned several times in the course of telephonic communications, it was decided at the last moment to choose another victim for fear of a possible leakage which might sound the alarm abroad. It was on such details that the thread of a human life hung under the Nazi regime!

Everything having thus been finalized, the transfer of the six generals was arranged for January 19, 1945. They were to travel in three cars; in the first Generals Daine and de Boisse; in the second Generals Flavigny and Buisson, and in the third Generals Mesny and Vauthier. The vehicles were to leave at fifteen-minute intervals, the first leaving Koenigstein at 6 A.M. This car left on time, but the departures of the two others were changed at the last moment, and General Mesny left alone in the second car at 7 A.M., the transfer of General Vauthier having suddenly been canceled.

General Mesny never arrived at Colditz. The following morning, on arrival at the camp, the four generals were informed by Major Prawill, the commandant of Oflag IV/C, that General Mesny had been killed in Dresden while trying to escape.

"He has been buried in Dresden with full military honors by a detachment of the Wehrmacht," added Prawill. This last detail was true, since the Nazis did not shrink from this kind of staging.

General Mesny's attempt at escape appeared suspect to his comrades in captivity. They knew that Mesny had abandoned all idea of flight since his eldest son had been deported to Germany for Resistance activities, and for fear that his second son would be shot in reprisal. But it was not until after the war, in the course of an inquiry, that the truth was revealed.

Sir David Maxwell-Fyfe,[14] one of the British prosecutors, aptly summed up this affair at Nuremberg: "In the whole of this particularly sordid episode, one could observe the outstanding feature of National Socialism: hypocrisy. It was a murder committed in kid gloves, carried out on orders, bearing the stamp of the Ministry for Foreign Affairs, carrying the cold imprint of the S.D., of Kaltenbrunner's Gestapo, supported and upheld by the outwardly respectable apparatus of the Regular Army."

The repressive measures taken against prisoners of war were to some extent codified in a document issued by the German High Command; it was given one of those evocative names so dear to the Nazis—the "Kugel"

[14] Now Lord Kilmuir.

decree (the "bullet"). According to this decree, signed on July 17, 1944, and distributed stamped "Government top secret" to the commandants of prisoner of war camps and to the local branches of the Gestapo: "Every escaped prisoner of war who is recaptured, every nonworking officer or N.C.O. with the exception of British or American prisoners of war, must be handed over to the chief of the security police or to the S.D. This measure must not be revealed under any pretext. The other prisoners will not be informed, and army intelligence will report them as escaped and not recaptured. Their mail will be franked to this effect and a reply will be given to questions from the International Red Cross and also requests from the protecting power." In actual fact these measures were already in force as a result of instructions issued by Gestapo headquarters since March 4, 1944.

At the same time Mueller ordered the heads of the Gestapo branches to send the prisoners handed over to them to Mauthausen camp, advising the commandant that the transfer was carried out within the framework of operation "Kugel." This was equivalent to a death sentence. The officers and N.C.O.'s affected by the "Kugel" decree had to be executed by a bullet in the neck on their arrival at Mauthausen. A second "Kugel" decree applied the same measures to foreign civilian workers who had made several attempts to escape from the labor camps.

Prisoners arriving at Mauthausen in these conditions were called "K" prisoners; they were not even registered in the camp records, they were given no serial number but were sent immediately to the camp prison. Here they were taken to the showers, made to undress, and, on the pretext of taking their measurements, placed under an apparatus which automatically fired a bullet into their necks as soon as it reached the tops of their heads. When there was too great an influx of prisoners, they were asphyxiated in the shower, whose pipes could release either water or deadly gases.

The camp commandant was also allowed to use his own initiative. At the beginning of September 1944 a group of forty-seven British, American, and Dutch airmen, who had bailed out after their machines had been shot down during raids on Germany, arrived at Mauthausen. They had been condemned to death after more than eighteen months' detention, having tried to escape. Instead of having them shot on the spot, the camp commandant sent them to the Mauthausen where they met with an atrocious death.

There was a gigantic basin into which one descended by a staircase roughly hewn in the stone, consisting of eighty-six steps. The forty-seven prisoners, barefooted and clothed only in a shirt and shorts, were laden with stones weighing fifty to seventy-five pounds, which they had to carry on their backs or in their arms to the top of the steps under a hail of truncheon blows and kicks. As soon as they had deposited their burdens at the top, they had to descend at the double and fetch a slightly heavier stone than before. By the first evening twenty-one of them were dead. The remaining twenty-six were subjected to the same torture on the following day. Not a single one remained alive by the evening of the second day.

That same month Himmler came to inspect the camp and was offered as an attraction the execution of fifty Russian officers.

Another prisoner of war incident also aroused a great stir: that of the fugitives from Sagan. In Sagan, a little Silesian town near Breslau, nearly ten thousand British and American airmen were detained in Stalag Luft III. They were very active men with but one thought in mind—to escape. By the end of February 1944 ninety-nine escape tunnels had been discovered by the guards before completion. Especially vigorous surveillance, entrusted to the reserve troops, composed of S.A. under the orders of Juettner, could not prevent new and even successful attempts to escape, for the hundredth tunnel was ultimately completed. About eighty British officers escaped on the night of March 24–25, 1944. This infuriated Hitler and Himmler. As soon as the escape was discovered in the early hours of the 25th, the general alarm was sounded. The Gestapo in Breslau were notified, and a comprehensive search was set in motion. The first fugitives, discovered a few miles from Sagan, were brought back to the camp, but on Sunday the 26th, Mueller gave the Gestapo the order to shoot those who were recaptured.

On the 27th a conference took place at R.S.H.A. between Colonel Walde, representing the Air Ministry, Colonel von Reurmont, representing the German High Command, Mueller, and Nebe. On the agenda were the measures to be taken, but Mueller finally announced that, on Hitler's orders, directives had already been issued to his services, which had been applied on the morning of the 26th and that between twelve and fifteen fugitives had already been shot. This decision aroused great protests. It was feared that the German airmen imprisoned in Great Britain would be killed in reprisal, and that the Luftwaffe crews with missions over England would worry about the future consequences of these measures. Hitler would allow only the first prisoners brought back to the camp to be spared. The death sentence for the rest held good. The Gestapo in Breslau, commanded by S.S. Obersturmbannfuehrer Scharpwinkel, was ordered to proceed with the executions.[15] The fugitives who were recaptured—some of them at Kiel and some even at Strasbourg—were sent to Breslau and shot. Fifty young officers thus paid with their lives for their daring and courage. With the customary Gestapo prudence, Mueller had forbidden any written evidence of this affair. All orders had to be transmitted verbally.

Since the news of these executions had leaked despite the precautions, Kaltenbrunner gave orders that they were to be presented as isolated cases: some of the prisoners were to have been killed in the bombing; others shot down when putting up an active resistance at the moment of arrest; others for having showed violence to their guards, who were forced to fire in self-defense; others again had been seriously wounded trying to escape a second time while being brought back to the camp. Ultimately a statement to this effect was published. It was given no credence; on the contrary it confirmed what everyone had feared and what was officially established after the war.

The Gestapo had two other new domains to exploit. First, the immense and far from spectacular task of helping the German war effort to satisfy its enormous and continual demand for manpower. The recruitment of voluntary workers for Germany had proved a resounding failure. A levy had to be introduced which took various forms, from the "release" of prisoners (a piece of moral roguery accepted by the French Government, which agreed to an exchange of five workers for one prisoner of war, a proportion which was never made public) to the S.T.O. (the compulsory labor service), which allowed whole classes of young men to be levied and sent to Germany. The expert in recruiting labor, Gauleiter Sauckel, admitted that of the five million foreign workers, only 200,000 were volunteers. Defections were numerous and many men took to the Maquis on receiving their papers for the S.T.O. Ultimately 875,952 French workers left for Germany. If one remembers that,

---

[15] The Gestapo in Breslau was notorious for its savagery. It installed a guillotine in the town prison and, between 1938 and 1945, executed more than one thousand political detainees, including eleven Frenchmen. The former Burgomaster of Brussels, Louis Schmidt, died from a beating up in the course of an interrogation in the Gestapo office which had been installed in the prison.

at the end of 1942, 1,036,319 Frenchmen had been taken prisoner, it will be seen that, if we add the political deportees and resistants, more than two million Frenchmen were prisoners of the Nazis in various capacities and under various regimes.

The second domain of the Gestapo was the extraordinary organization set up to conduct what were termed "medical experiments." In order to understand how doctors, including men of quality, could be corrupted to this point by Nazi principles and agree to perform these "experiments," the very negation of the Hippocratic ethic, one must recall the way in which the Nazis had already infiltrated into German medical circles.

On the assumption that scientists, doctors, and professors were liberals, reactionaries, Jews, or Freemasons, a purge had been carried out in their ranks which had banished 40 percent of their effectives. Finally Himmler's passion for scientific—or rather pseudo-scientific experiment—especially in the domain of racial research—had induced him in 1933 to create the Ahnenerbe (ancestral inheritance),[16] from the year 1935 for the purpose of studying everything concerning the spirit, actions, traditions, character, and heritage of the "Nordic-Germanic race." On January 1, 1939, it received a new directive ordering "scientific researches," which led to the experiments in the camps. On January 1, 1942, the Ahnenerbe Society was attached to Himmler's personal staff and became an S.S. organization. The board consisted of Himmler as president, Dr. Wuest, rector of Munich University, with Sievers (a former bookseller who had become a colonel in the S.S.) as secretary to the Society, playing a very important role.

It was the Ahnenerbe which instigated, organized, and financed most of the experiments. This body grew rapidly and ultimately disposed of fifty specialized scientific institutes. The initiation of the experiments seems to have been a request sent to Himmler by Dr. Sigmund Rascher.

Rascher was a reservist M.O. of the Luftwaffe. He was married to Nini Diehls, his elder by fifteen years, and he met Himmler through his wife. A member of the S.S. at the beginning of 1941, he was in charge of the medical courses at Luftgaukommando VII in Munich. His lectures dealt in particular with human reactions, with psychological and physiological troubles

---

[16] The head office of the Ahnenerbe was at 16 Pücklerstrasse, Berlin-Dahlem.

in the course of high-altitude flights.[17] On May 15, 1941, Rascher wrote to Himmler: "I have noticed with regret that no experiment on human material has yet been introduced here, because the tests are very dangerous and no volunteers have offered their services. For this reason, I ask in all seriousness: 'Is there any possibility of obtaining from you two or three professional criminals to be placed at our disposal?' These tests, in the course of which the 'guinea pigs' may die, would be carried out under my supervision. They are absolutely indispensable to research into high-altitude flying, and cannot be carried out, as has been so far attempted, on monkeys, whose reactions are completely different."

This request was less surprising than it appears. There had already been the precedent of euthanasia practiced on incurables and insane people at the beginning of the war.

As regards the genuine experiments, they had been tried out first on German prisoners: in October and November 1938 Dr. Samestrang had been authorized to use the prisoners of the Sachsenhausen camp for his cold water experiments, which were subsequently resumed at Dachau.

All this led Himmler enthusiastically to accept Rascher's request, which satisfied his own "scientific" mania, and on May 22, 1941, Karl Brandt, Himmler's secretary, replied: "Naturally we shall be delighted to place some prisoners at your disposal for your research into high-altitude flying."

Low-pressure chambers were installed at Dachau, in the very center of that inexhaustible reserve of human guinea pigs. The results were diabolical. A doctor prisoner at Dachau, Dr. Antòn Pacholegg, whom Rascher used as an assistant,[18] has told the story.

"I personally saw," he declared, "through the observation window of the chamber, how a prisoner inside was subjected to a vacuum until his lungs burst. Certain experiments produced such a pressure in the men's heads that they went mad, tearing their hair out in an effort to relieve it. They lacerated their heads and faces with their nails, mutilating themselves in their frenzy. They beat on the wall and roared to release the pressure on the eardrums.

---

[17] At that time the Germans were trying to raise the flight ceiling of their aircraft, which was below that of the British machines which had just come into service.

[18] Dr. Pacholegg was due to be executed in order to insure his silence, but he managed to escape at the beginning of 1944. This enabled his testimony to be published after the war.

"These processes of producing an absolute vacuum usually ended in the death of the subject. An extreme experiment was so sure of ending in death, that in many cases the chamber was subsequently used purely as a method of execution and not for experiments."

These experiments continued until May 1942. About two hundred prisoners took part in them; eighty of them died in the low-pressure chamber, the others emerged more or less permanently injured. Rascher then began a series of new tests on the effects of cold. The purpose was to discover the best flying suit for airmen carrying out raids on England, who were often shot down into the North Sea. Many of them who reached the water unharmed died of cold after an immersion of a few hours.

Rascher installed at Dachau special tanks and a refrigerating plant. The Luftwaffe followed his work with interest, and Rascher called for assistants. Before accepting Professors Jarisch of Innsbruck, Holzloehner of Kiel, and Singer, he requested the Gestapo to carry out a careful screening of these doctors, to insure that they were "politically irreproachable." Rascher wanted the assurance that the most absolute secrecy would be observed during these experiments. The cold tests continued from August 1942 to May 1943. For the experiments on the effects of dry cold, the subjects were exposed to the icy German winter, completely naked in the open air for nights on end. Their body temperature fell to 25°C. They were brought in unconscious and then experiments for warming and restoration were carried out. Himmler insisted that warming by "animal heat" should be tried, and four women were brought in from Ravensbruck. They had to lie naked on the icy bodies of the victims, to try and bring them back to life. Naturally this was fruitless. The problem of swift restoration of frozen bodies was solved in 1880, by the Russian doctor Lepczinsky, whose work the Nazi "scientists" obviously did not know.

For their experiments on the effects of damp cold the subjects were plunged in icy water, either naked or clothed in a flying suit. A lifebelt prevented them from sinking. Dr. Pacholegg has recounted one of these experiments: "The worst of all these experiments was carried out at Dachau on two Russian officers.

"The two men were brought up from the bunker. They were forbidden to speak to each other. ... Rascher made them undress and enter the basin naked. Two hours later they were still conscious. Our appeals to Rascher to give them an injection remained unheeded. During the third hour one of the Russians said to the other, 'Comrade, tell this officer to finish us off with a bullet,' to which the other replied, 'Don't expect anything from this dog.'

"When his words were translated from the Russian by a young Pole (who toned down the expression) Rascher returned to his office. The young Pole tried to chloroform them, but Rascher returned and threatened him with a revolver. 'Don't interfere,' he said, 'and don't go near them.' The experiment continued for about five hours before ending in death. The corpses were sent to Munich for a postmortem."

Rascher believed that he had discovered a miraculous anti-hemorrhagic which he called Polygal. He made numerous experiments with this product. Both his father and his uncle were doctors. Brought up in a strictly orthodox medical atmosphere, one wonders how he could have allowed himself to be thus degraded by the Nazi doctrines. His political convictions were the cause of violent disagreements with his father, Dr. Hans August Rascher. At the instigation of his wife, Rascher junior did not hesitate to denounce his father to the Gestapo, who arrested him twice, detaining him on the first occasion for five and on the second for nine days.

His uncle, a doctor in Hamburg, reproached him one day for these experiments. The discussion lasted throughout a whole night, Rascher trying to defend the Nazi theories, such as those of Dr. Guett, who was one of the first to attack the "false love of inferior and anti-social creatures," while his uncle pointed out the importance of fidelity to Hippocratic principles. Rascher finally admitted to his uncle "that he no longer dared to think, that he knew he was on the wrong path, but could see no way of getting out of it."

Not all the German doctors behaved like Rascher. When Dr. Weltz proposed that he should work on human beings, Dr. Lutz replied, "I don't think I am tough enough for that type of experiment. It is already difficult enough to experiment on a dog which looks at you."

The Nazi doctors were never troubled by this type of scruple. Rascher was openly contemptuous of his colleagues. One day he said to the physiologist Rein, "You think you're a physiologist but your experience is limited to guinea pigs and mice. I am the only person in the world who really knows human physiology, for I experiment on men and not on mice."

Himmler favored the pursuit of these experiments and wrote several letters in which he repeated that the S.S. alone was in a position to provide the necessary human material. He himself was often present at them, and did not cease trying to overcome such objections as were (all too rarely) made.

"The researches of Dr. Rascher," he wrote to General Milch in November 1942, "relate to experiments of capital importance. I personally assume responsibility for finding anti-social individuals and criminals. These individuals who merit only death come from concentration camps.

"The difficulties, mainly based on religious objections, which run counter to the experiments (for which I take full responsibility) can be eliminated. I have personally attended these experiments and can safely say that I have participated in each phase of this scientific work, by giving my aid and my inspiration.

"It will take us at least ten years to overcome the narrow-mindedness of our people. I suggest that a non-Christian doctor of good scientific reputation, not prone to intellectual activity, should be given the job of liaison between the Luftwaffe and the S.S."

In a letter to Rascher he went much further and even resorted to threats. "I consider people who, even today, reject experiments on human beings—preferring to let brave German soldiers die rather than use the results of these experiments—as veritable traitors to their country. I shall not hesitate to communicate their names to the competent authorities, and I authorize you to inform these authorities of my views."

Himmler's protection did not prevent Rascher and his wife from coming to a tragic, if well-deserved, end. In 1943 a curious scandal occurred. Madame Rascher, already mother of two children (Rascher had married her while she was expecting her second child), gave out that she was pregnant once more and produced a baby as being her own. It was soon discovered that her pregnancy was a fake and that the child had been stolen. For a man who held suffering and human life so cheap, and in a milieu where the most revolting crimes were committed daily, this story seems trifling enough. But Nazi morality was deeply affronted. Anything touching upon race and birth assumed a sacred character, and this attempt at fraudulent introduction of a child of possibly "impure" blood into the community of the "pure," complicated by a lie to the Reichsfuehrer S.S., was considered a crime that merited the rope. The Raschers disappeared, only to be arrested at the end of 1943. The doctor and his wife were thrown in prison and placed on trial. During the final advance of the Allied troops in Germany, Himmler gave strict orders that the Raschers must not fall alive into the hands of the enemy. He knew that both of them, particularly the woman, were indiscreet and feared their eventual revelations. Frau Rascher was finally hanged at Ravensbruck. Her husband was brought back to Dachau and imprisoned in a cell in the bunker; at the end of April 1945 he was killed by a shot fired through the open door as he was being handed his food.

Many other experiments were carried out in the camps. Numerous vaccines and defense measures against bacterial warfare were tried out. A little-known incident lay at the root of these researches. In the Caucasus the S.S. troops had refused to advance because there was a rumor that they were entering a zone where a plague epidemic was raging. This is probably the only example of the S.S. refusing to obey an order.

Human beings were utilized to produce vaccines: typhus bacilli were injected into men who were used as virus "reservoirs" at Buchenwald. At Dachau malaria was the subject of intensive study, and anopheles was bred to infect more than one thousand subjects, chosen from among Polish priests. In September 1943 an epidemic of infectious jaundice raged on the Eastern front (there were 180,000 cases in one month). Experiments were carried out at Auschwitz and subsequently at Sachsenhausen on Jews of the Polish Resistance.

Among other researches carried out on the prisoners: tests of new drugs; tests of nutrition[19] and of food concentrates at Oranienburg; artificial hormones at Buchenwald; anti-gangrene serums; hematological and serological experiments; tests of an ointment designed to heal phosphorus burns; the artificial culture of phlegmons, abscesses, and septicemias at Dachau; tests with sulphonamides; surgical experiments on bones, nerves, and muscular fibers. Euthanasia was performed with injections of phenol, which killed a man in less than a second. Tests were made with ammunition poisoned with aconitin (the clinical descriptions of the effect of these poisoned bullets are revolting). Research was carried out on decontamination processes of water poisoned by gases; alkaloids and unknown poisons were studied; the tablets destined for the suicide of the leaders were tried out on the prisoners; experiments, too, on the effects of gases in warfare, both hyperite and phosegene.

Experiments were also carried out on methods of sterilization designed to exterminate, or at least to limit the birth rate of races reduced to slavery

---

[19] The experiments in hunger and thirst made at Dachau were extremely painful. Youths of sixteen and seventeen were the principal victims.

after the final victory which was to make the Nazis masters of Europe. A letter addressed to Himmler by Dr. Pokorny, informing him of the state of research into sterilization by the absorption of a drug, is edifying. "If we could produce, as rapidly as possible, as a result of these researches, a drug which, after a relatively short period, would lead to a sterilization of individuals, we should have at our disposal a new and very effective weapon. The very idea that three million Bolsheviks in captivity today in Germany could be sterilized, while remaining available for work, although incapable of procreation, opens up vast prospects. Dr. Madaus has discovered that the juice of the plant *Caladium seguinum* taken orally or intravenously produces permanent sterility after a certain time, particularly in male animals but also in females."

The effect of the juice being rather slow, and the culture of this tropical plant proving too difficult, Dr. Brack perfected a more simple process:[20] sterilization by X rays. Brack in the course of experiments carried out on prisoners was able to establish that permanent sterilization could be obtained by a local radiation of 500 to 600 R.[21] For two minutes in the case of men and of 300 to 350 R for three minutes in the case of women. The difficulty lay in the method of applying this therapy without the knowledge of the patients. Brack then had a brilliant idea which he hastened to communicate to his "most honored Reichsfuehrer."

"A practical procedure would consist in making the persons to be treated approach a counter where they would be asked to reply to certain questions or to fill out forms for two or three minutes. The person sitting behind the counter could work the apparatus by turning a switch which would bring two lamps into action simultaneously." (The radiations had to be transmitted from either side.)

"By installing two lamps, between 150 and 200 persons could be sterilized daily and, in consequence, with twenty installations of this type, 3,000 to 4,000 individuals could be sterilized every day."

Happily the fortunes of war did not allow the Nazis to carry out this particular program of scientific genocide. Everything was ready, however, and it is certain that, had the outcome of the war been different, methods of this nature would have been put into practice.

---

[20] Numerous tests were also made with surgical processes, direct injections of caustic products, inoculations, etc.

[21] R = Roentgen (after the inventor of X rays): a unit for measuring radiation.

In general the political bureaus of the camps, the Gestapo, were responsible for choosing the victims to serve as guinea pigs. A sign, a word, a little cross on a list by a member of the Gestapo, sufficed to send a healthy young man into the low-pressure chamber where, an hour later, he would cough up his lungs, or send a young woman in the prime of life to a doctor who would sterilize her with a good dose of X rays.

Sometimes orders from above, issued by Himmler to his agents in the camps, directed the using, for example, of Polish resistants for experiments on infectious jaundice in Auschwitz, or of Russian officers (chosen for their endurance to cold) for the work of Rascher in the refrigerated tanks of Dachau.

The Gestapo also carried out "selections," to satisfy the demand for anatomical specimens, requested by the Nazi institutes. The camps were utilized as a kind of reservoir of experimental material. Here the high peak of horror was reached, a kind of Grand Guignol paroxysm in the pseudoscientific style of certain horror films, where a mad scientist murders his unfortunate victims to satisfy his maniacal research. The official correspondence exchanged relative to this traffic is hardly credible.

The first example goes back to the period of the euthanasia program affecting Germans. In Berlin there existed an institute specializing in brain research called the Kaiser Wilhelm Institute, with three branches in Munich, Göttingen, and Dillenburg. The last-named establishment was run by Dr. Hallervorden. One day Dr. Hallervorden learned that certain invalids were to be killed with carbon monoxide and immediately decided to take advantage of this. He visited those responsible for carrying out the task and said to them, " 'Listen, my friends, if you're going to kill all those people, at least keep their brains so that they can be of some use.' 'How many could you examine?' they asked me. 'An unlimited number,' I replied. 'The more the merrier.' "

The way in which all this was effected has also been related by Dr. Hallervorden. "Most of the establishments were short of doctors. As a result of overwork or indifference, most of them left the choice to the nurses and hospital orderlies. Anyone who appeared ill or who in the eyes of the nurses and orderlies appeared to be a 'case,' was put on a list and dispatched to the place of destruction. The worst feature of this affair was the brutality exercised by the staff. They simply chose those whom they did not like and entered them on the lists." The Kaiser Wilhelm Institute soon had more brains than it could examine, thanks to National Socialism.

The second incident which shows the "logical" purpose behind the Nazi scientific methods of execution took place in 1941. This time they were no longer content to experiment on the corpses of people condemned to death, as Hallervorden had done, but decided to murder men solely to use their corpses as material for study.

The Germans, occupying the Strasbourg Faculty of Medicine, installed there one of their own men, S.S. Sturmbann-fuehrer Dr. Hirt. The doctor was steeped in Nazi philosophy and his *idée fixe* was naturally the racial question. He conceived the plan of forming at Strasbourg a collection of skeletons and skulls of Jews. He wrote to Himmler, to whom all these requests had to be submitted.

"We have here," said the professor, "an almost complete collection of the skulls of all races and nations. In the case of the Jewish race, however, we have so far few specimens of skulls at our disposal, so that it is almost impossible to arrive at definitive conclusions by their examination. The war in the East now gives us an opportunity to fill this gap. And the Judaeo-Bolshevik commissars, who display the repugnant, characteristic signs of degenerate humanity, can contribute their skulls, and afford us the possibility of obtaining a concrete scientific documentation."

It was therefore arranged that the Jewish Soviet commissars were to be captured alive and handed over to the military police, who would keep them until the arrival of a special envoy. The latter would photograph them, take a certain number of anthropological measurements, and collect all possible indications as to the status and origins of the prisoner, after which he would be put to death so that his head could be cut off and sent to Strasbourg.

"After the execution of these Jews," wrote Hirt, "the head must not be damaged. The envoy will sever the head from the trunk and dispatch it to its destination in hermetically sealed tin boxes. These boxes will contain a liquid to preserve the heads in perfect condition."

These instructions were carried out, and the university at Strasbourg began to receive a number of strange parcels.

But soon the heads did not satisfy Hirt, who now demanded entire skeletons, not only of "Judaeo-Bolshevik commissars." Auschwitz camp received orders to provide him with 150 skeletons. Since the camp was in no position to prepare these skeletons, and since Hirt wanted measurements of the bodies, it was decided that the most suitable solution was to send the subject alive to Natzweiler camp near Strasbourg. In June 1943, 115 persons selected by the Gestapo at Auschwitz arrived at Natzweiler camp. These were followed in August by a further eighty. S.S. Hauptsturmfuehrer Kramer, who operated in most of the camps and ended his career as commandant of the camp at Bergen-Belsen (where he earned the name of the "Beast of Belsen"), undertook the execution of these wretched victims, gassing them with cyanide, a process which did not damage the body. In this way Hirt received corpses which were still warm on his dissecting table. His anatomical collection had grown considerably by the time the American and French troops approached the city. The Nazis took fright because the refrigerating chests in the university morgue still contained eighty corpses which were liable to prove compromising. Hirt asked for instructions. Was he to preserve the collection, or destroy it. It was a question of removing the flesh from the corpses to render them unrecognizable, and to declare that they were bodies abandoned by the French. Finally, on October 26, Sievers, the General Secretary of the Ahnenerbe, who had followed this affair with the keenest attention, gave the assurance that the collection had been destroyed. The information was false. Hirt's assistant had been unable to dissect the corpses sufficiently rapidly. Some of them were still in Hirt's "reserve," when the Allied troops entered Strasbourg. They were discovered by men of the 2nd French Armored Division. Hirt disappeared and was never found. No vestige of information has ever come to light as to his fate. He was one of the very few Nazi "experimenters" who eluded the search, and who did not join his colleagues who were judged at Nuremberg at the "trial of the doctors."

Perhaps, under a false name, he is leading the peaceful life of a country doctor in some remote region, tapping the chests of his patients with the same meticulous care that he used in completing his collection.

Chapter 20

The Gestapo Operates Throughout the Whole of France

In Paris, as in the rest of occupied Europe, Hitler had his own private policy. According to Knochen, it was "not the same as that pursued by Ribbentrop and Abetz." Ambassador Abetz relied entirely upon Laval. Although Abetz appeared to accord considerable importance to Déat, it was only a maneuver on his part to play on Laval's jealousy, a maneuver which Abetz knew could only have a limited effect, Déat being particularly unpopular in France. Abetz was inspired by long-term views. His aim was to obtain, thanks to Laval, complete collaboration from the French.

Himmler's objectives were more immediate. He wanted to obtain at all possible speed an active collaboration, that is to say an essentially military one, and, in default of the Vichy Government contracting an anti-Bolshevik alliance, the formation of several Waffen S.S. divisions to fight on the Russian front. This view took into account the events in the East, where the winter campaign had just cost the Wehrmacht a million men. To recruit men was absolutely essential, since the military situation could not be entirely restored in the course of the summer campaign. On the other hand, by obtaining these indispensable troops and placing them under the flag of the Waffen S.S., Himmler would increase his power and make progress toward achieving the secret ambition of his life—to become commander in chief of an army in the field.

It was in this spirit that he had given his instructions to Oberg "to support to the maximum the pro-Nazi political movements." Himmler's policy had recorded an initial success, since on July 7, 1941, Deloncle had called a meeting of the leaders of the pro-Nazi parties,[22] a meeting which was to give birth to the "Légion antibolchevique," later christened "Légion des volontaires Français" (L.V.F.).

All this was done without the blessing of the Embassy which, consulted by Councilor Westrick, showed itself to be lukewarm, since it was not an order from the Vichy Government, to which some attention had to be paid. The L.V.H. was not publicly recognized until eighteen months later by a decree of Laval's dated February 11, 1943.

Oberg adhered to the policy outlined by Himmler. For him, according to Knochen, Darnand and Doriot were more interesting than Laval. He was

---

[22] This meeting, held at the Hôtel Majestic, Paris, commandeered by the Germans, united Deloncle, Doriot, Déat, Constantini, Clementi, Boissel, and Paul Chack. The first volunteers were enrolled at Versailles on August 27, 1941. It was at the moment of presenting the colors that Laval nearly succumbed to the attempt to kill him made by Paul Colette.

to attain his goal during the summer of 1942, which saw the start of the recruitment of Waffen S.S. in France.

Despite and perhaps because of these differences of trend, Oberg and Abetz got on very well together. Each of them worked in his own sphere, Abetz merely controlling the "high policy" at government level.

Oberg also cooperated with Stuelpnagel, under whom he had served in 1918. In Paris he was his subordinate on matters of armament and personnel, but on the police level he received his orders from Himmler direct.

On his arrival in Paris, Oberg chose his private quarters at 57 boulevard Lannes; he remained there until the end. His personal staff consisted of two orderly officers, Hagen and Beck (the latter replaced by Jungst in February 1943), six N.C.O.'s, two shorthand typists, and three telephonists.

He immediately started to reorganize the police services under his control. He had received special powers which can be summed up as follows: The office for measures of security and repression was centralized in Paris. In case of any conflict with the military authorities (Stuelpnagel) and with the Foreign Office (Abetz), Oberg could appeal to Himmler against their decisions. In the case of serious incidents he had complete power to "crush" by all means "dangerous groups, parties, or individuals."

As Supreme Head of the S.S. in French-occupied territory, he could use for his repressive missions S.S. formations and Frenchmen recruited by the S.S. Furthermore, he was able to insure the obedience of the collaborationist and militia groups. Oberg exploited this trump card to the maximum. He had not forgotten the lessons learned in the contest for power in Germany. He made every effort, therefore, to aid groups formed on the model of the S.A. or the S.S., without realizing that these movements were often well-organized "rackets," which would allow unscrupulous individuals to make enormous sums of money in exchange for which they would recruit mere skeleton formations.

In the same spirit, Heydrich had introduced Oberg to the representatives of the French administration. René Bousquet and Georges Hilaire were summoned to Paris to hear the measures which were required from the Vichy Government, and to learn that the police powers were to be handed over to the leaders of the pro-Nazi parties. At the beginning of May, René Bousquet had discussed these decisions and obtained a postponement from Heydrich. He continued to try to persuade the Germans to renounce these measures. In exchange he undertook that the French police would maintain order and repress uprisings which, according to him, were far more "anti-national" than anti-German. His goal was the abrogation of the *Code des Otages* (Hostages Code) of September 30, 1941. Negotiations were then started with Oberg with a view to clarifying a kind of common declaration, which was to be the basis of relations between the two police forces, and to limit their respective domains.

These negotiations were disrupted by the death of Heydrich. The latter was due to return to Paris, and it was hoped that he would accept the agreement. His death left everything in abeyance. The instructions which Heydrich had agreed temporarily to suspend were given to Laval. At the same time the collaborationist parties, and Doriot in particular, launched a violent press campaign and organized meetings against the policy of Vichy, which they accused of flabbiness, cowardice, and even of complicity with the "enemies of Europe," openly accusing Bousquet of protecting Jews, Freemasons, etc.

On July 29 what is known as the Oberg-Bousquet agreement, according to the term used by Knochen, was concluded. It was an agreement the final text of which was settled—according to Bousquet's own statement—after he had obtained some modifications.

The terms having been definitely decreed, this agreement was made public. "During a banquet at my house, attended by the regional prefects and the police superintendents," said Oberg, "Bousquet and I read to the company the document we had compiled."[23]

As it was read that day, the agreement seemed to be a victory for Bousquet, since it marked an express limitation of the functions of the Germans and the almost complete independence of the French police. It included, above all, an extremely important point, which might have led one to expect a modification of the repression and above all an end of the hostages. It was in fact stated that the French police would never be put into the position of choosing hostages, and that the persons apprehended by it would in no circumstances be the object of reprisals on the part of the German authorities. French nationals, guilty of political crimes, as well as those guilty of misdemeanors in common law, would in future be judged and punished according to French law

---

[23] M. Bousquet says that negotiations continued until the last moment. Even when Oberg's French and German guests had arrived, the general secretary of the police tried to extort from Oberg a few final concessions. They eventually sat down to lunch an hour late.

by French tribunals. The authors of incidents directed against the Army and the occupying authorities alone could be claimed by the German police. Again, individuals arrested by the Germans were *in no circumstance* to be the object of reprisals or to be taken as hostages.

It is understandable that the general secretary of the police could at this moment rightly feel proud. The agreement was communicated to all the authorities in the French police services and to all the leaders of SIPO-S.D. and ORPO posts. After the occupation of the southern zone it was held to be applicable over the whole of France. This was the second Oberg-Bousquet agreement of April 18, 1943.[24] This second version recapitulated the important points of the first text and repeated that French nationals, arrested by French police, should be arraigned before their own tribunals and judged according to French law.

These promises, alas, were merely on paper. The agreement solemnly published on July 29, 1942, was a long way from being effective in practice, and did not prevent the execution of hostages. What was the day-to-day truth *after* the agreement?

The Germans, according to the text signed by Oberg, could neither arrest nor claim a Frenchman except in the case of an offense against the troops or the occupying authorities. Moreover, proof of culpability was needed, and they were to be brought to court.

Tragic events allowed the tangible result of these promises to be appreciated. On August 5, a week after the publication of the Oberg-Bousquet agreement, three men hiding behind a hedge in the Jean-Bouin Stadium in Paris threw two hand grenades at a group of fifty German soldiers training on the track, causing eight deaths and thirteen wounded. This was a direct offense against members of the occupying forces mentioned in the agreement. The inquiry opened by the Gestapo revealed the identity of the three culprits; Martunek, a Hungarian, and the Rumanians Copla and Cracium, who were arrested on October 19 and shot on March 9, 1943, after being sentenced by a German military tribunal. But on August 11 the Parisian press published a notice announcing that "ninety-three terrorists convicted of having committed acts of terrorism, or of having been accomplices," had

---

[24] The whole text will be found in Appendix II (page 401). To our knowledge it has never before been published.

been shot the same morning. This notice was signed "Oberg." This execution of hostages was a violation of the agreement signed thirteen days earlier.

In fact, on August 11, between seven and eleven o'clock in the morning, eighty-eight men (not ninety-three) were shot on the Mont Valérien—seventy Frenchmen and eighteen foreigners. Three alone had been arrested by the Gestapo, the sixty-seven others had been seized by the French police, in other words, by the special brigades of the prefecture. Only nine of them had participated in actions against German troops. Three had tried to derail a train of soldiers on leave, four had sabotaged a German telephone line, one had fired on German soldiers, and another had placed a bomb in an establishment frequented by the occupying troops. Only one of the victims had been judged by a German military tribunal—Dutrieux—who was condemned to death on June 27, by the Epinal tribunal.

But even if we discard the case of the eighteen foreigners, arrested solely for their political activities by the French police and handed over to the Germans, and that of the three Frenchmen arrested by the Gestapo, the nine authors of attempts and that of the single man condemned to death, the fact remains that fifty-seven Frenchmen who had committed no offense against the Germans were shot that day as hostages in absolute violation of the agreement of July 29. *All of them* had been arrested by the French police for their "political activities" such as violation of the decree ordering the dissolution of the Communist party; fabrication, distribution, or mere possession of pamphlets; sheltering militant Communists living underground; etc. All these acts were crimes in the eyes of the French law at that time, and it was therefore French law which should have been applied by a French court in accordance with the terms of the agreement. Certain cases were even more flagrant: Ethis was arrested as a Communist sympathizer and for having fed deserters from the Compiègne camp; Fillatre, for having loaned his bicycle to a militant Communist; Scordia, because he was suspected of being in touch with a member of a special organization of the Communist party. Arrested before the attempt, none of them had been able to participate in it. Two had been taken into custody after the Oberg-Bousquet agreement: Deschanciaux, arrested on August 1, and Bretagne on August 3. They were both handed over to the Gestapo. And finally, on August 10, five of the men to be shot were still in the hands of the French police: Boatti, detained at Fresnes, Jean Compagnon, Henri Dauboeuf, and

François Wouters, who were still at police headquarters, and were handed over to the Germans on August 10 to be shot the following morning, and Raine, arrested by the French special brigade on June 18, and taken to Fort Romainville on August 10.

These men were in the hands of the French administration. It could sentence them or intern them, according to the agreement. One of them had even been sentenced and was, therefore, normally under the protection of the French penitentiary authorities: Louis Thorez, arrested in October 1940, was sentenced to ten years' imprisonment for distributing pamphlets. Sent to jail at the outset and then interned in Chateaubriant camp, he was handed over to the Germans and interned in Compiègne camp from which he managed to escape on June 22, 1942. Recaptured on July 10 by the special brigade, he was once more handed over to the Germans.

Thus fifty-seven Frenchmen arrested for their opinions fell to the German bullets at the very moment René Bousquet thought he had obtained the suppression of the system of hostages. Did this violation of the agreement bring about any reaction on the part of the Vichy Government? Did it at least understand that the signature and word of Oberg had no value, and that the Gestapo intended to act as it pleased and to continue the reign of terror?

The tragedy of August 11 does not appear to have influenced the attitude of the government, since it agreed to a renewal of the agreement in 1943. Doubtless this document must be added to the Vichy line of maintaining "French sovereignty," in other words, that caricature of authority which sufficed those in power.

Oberg continued to order the execution of hostages as before. Many Frenchmen arrested by the French special brigades were regularly handed over to the Gestapo. On September 19, less than two months after the publication of the agreement, Oberg published a notice in the Parisian press announcing that as reprisals for the outrage committed on September 17 in the Rex Cinema in Paris, 116 hostages were to be shot. This was the largest mass execution that so far had been seen in France. And the 116 hostages were in fact executed on September 21 (forty-six in Paris and seventy in Bordeaux). Out of the forty-six shot in Paris, one single man only had been condemned by a German tribunal, and none of them had participated in an act of violence.

The secretary general of police had done his best. But it is only fair to say that the Bousquet-Oberg agreement had had very limited effect.

While these futile negotiations were taking place, Oberg had continued the reorganization of his command. The police services were divided into two main branches: the ordinary police (ORPO) and the Security Police (SIPO-S.D.). Knochen, head of this second branch, divided it into two groups each with duties corresponding to the conception of police work as it existed in Berlin. The first group was intrusted with internal security in France. The second formed the political intelligence and espionage services, which kept France and the neutral countries (including the Vatican) under observation. The first group alone enjoyed the right of carrying out arrests. The executive body had its headquarters at No. 11 rue des Saussaies and its staff was provided by the Gestapo.

The main organ of the second group, for France, remained Section III of the SIPO-S.D. direction in Paris. Divided into four groups, this service collected all the general information on the internal situation of France. Its fourth group, D, was itself divided into five subgroups to study:

 I. Food and agriculture;
 II. Trade and circulation;
 III. Banking and stock exchange;
 IV. Industry;
 V. Questions of manpower and social questions.

The head of Section III, Maulaz, was a very able man. Cultured, a man of the world, he knew how to make important contacts, frequented the salons, and was able to turn a surprising number of well-known people into informers—big industrialists, bankers and stockbrokers, wives and mistresses of politicians, etc. A certain bank director kept him informed of the true financial position of certain companies, the share holdings, the true strength of the companies. This enabled him to profit by business transactions, which could only be done by people with a "fine nose." A certain head of an enormous multiple organization, which still flourishes today, revealed to him the business ramifications of his competitors, their genuine production figures, and the real potential of those who tried to escape requisitions. The informer hoped that industrial collaboration would be established after the German victory, and also that it would be profitable to himself. Another big trader informed him about competitor houses run by Jews, or denounced well-camouflaged Jews, which brought him fruitful jobs as administrator of their confiscated goods. A certain mistress of a politician sold Maulaz the confidences of her lover and his political activities.

Maulaz threaded his way easily through this maze. He adored society life. The information he obtained allowed his patrons to batten still further on the French economy. If someone maintained that his productivity figure had reached its maximum, he could reply with the evidence in his hand that the agricultural or industrial production could really rise to a far greater level; this allowed him to increase his requisitions. From personal greed, the very distinguished friends of this elegant Maulaz became accomplices in the pillage of their country. In this twilight period in France, a section of Parisian high society truly afforded an astonishingly sordid picture.

At the same time Oberg installed a series of new offices on the avenue Foch. Each of them marked the superiority acquired by the police services over the military, since they annexed domains previously considered as the preserves of the military administration. Oberg now had a new service of political intelligence, organized and run by elements of the S.D. (Section VI); a service for surveillance of the press, letters and the arts, the cinema and the theater; a service for surveillance of the Catholic and Protestant churches; a new anti-Communist service; a counterespionage service in enemy countries and for intelligence in the neutral countries—all these were attached to the second group of Knochen's services.

Knochen had enjoyed Heydrich's absolute support. The death of Heydrich altered the situation. Since Kaltenbrunner was uninterested in police matters, Mueller became in practice sole master within the Gestapo. He sent precise orders, insisting that they be carried out to the letter. Knochen tried to apply more subtle methods in France, by adapting himself as closely as possible to the circumstances. Mueller's rigid orders often embarrassed him, and he sometimes ignored them deliberately. His independent temperament, his very keen sense of his own value, his private conviction that the German police organization in France was his work, all these elements often inspired an attitude of almost overt insubordination to Mueller.

Mueller openly accused Knochen, not only of being Francophile, but "Westophile," to use his own expression—in fact that he had been won over to the mode of thought and the habits of the people of the West and full of dangerous indulgence for them. These attacks, of which the French could enjoy the bitter fruit, became so acute that Himmler had to intervene. Knochen defended himself with fierce energy, and was very effectively supported by Oberg, who had learned to appreciate his qualities.

In Paris, Knochen displayed the same arrogance with regard to the military authorities. In theory all the dossiers and all the detainees not released in the course of interrogation had to pass into the hands of the military. In actual fact the people acquitted by the military tribunals were taken back by the Gestapo. It occasionally happened that the Gestapo executed prisoners before they were ever sent before a tribunal. This custom was not peculiar to the services of Knochen, but was current in Germany, to the point where on April 12, 1943, Kaltenbrunner had to circulate an urgent note, to all his services:

"It *often* happens that tribunals open a case against an individual who has already been executed by the Gestapo, this execution not having been reported.

"For this reason the Reichsfuehrer orders that in future the Gestapo must warn local tribunals of all executions carried out. The information is to be limited to the name of the individual and the crime for which he has been executed. The methods of execution will not be revealed."

These direct methods could only increase after the arrival of Oberg. Firstly, because he had received categorical orders from Himmler himself, and also because in the spring of 1942 harshness was more than ever the rule of the Gestapo. A note of June 10, 1942, circulated by the head office of the R.S.H.A. to all SIPO-S.D. services specified the regulations to be respected for "intensified interrogations."

1. Intensified interrogations are only to be applied when it transpires during the former interrogation that the prisoner is in possession of important intelligence concerning the enemy, or concerning liaison or plans which he refuses to communicate.
2. These additional interrogations can only be applied against Communists, Marxists, *Bibelforscher* (Bible students and Jehovah's Witnesses), saboteurs, terrorists, members of the Resistance, liaison agents, anti-social persons, refractory Polish or Russian workers and vagabonds.
3. In all other cases, in principle, previous authority is required.

The summer of 1942 was a period of negotiations in France. While the Oberg-Bousquet agreement was being argued, other discussions took place in Paris during June 1942. Darlan, who had been Commander in Chief of Land, Sea, and Air Forces from April 17, and General Bridoux, Secretary of State for War, took steps to try to obtain from the Germans the authorization to increase the strength of the armistice army by fifty thousand men. It was a puerile demand, justified presumably by motives of personal pride and of "prestige" typical of the period. Far from outright rejection of a demand which they had no intention of gratifying, the Germans parleyed. At the beginning of September a conference met in Paris at the Hôtel Lutétia, the headquarters of the Abwehr services, two French officers representing Darlan and Bridoux with powers to negotiate with the Germans.

Admiral Canaris, head of the Abwehr, was in Paris at the time. The embassy councilor, Rahn, a specialist in intelligence affairs, invited Canaris and the two French officers to dinner. Two meetings took place later at the Lutétia. At the first Canaris was represented by Colonel Reile, one of his departmental chiefs, but next day he was present in person to "conclude the matter."

As an initial step the Abwehr proposed an effective collaboration between their agents and those of the French Deuzième Bureau in North Africa. Agreement was quickly reached in principle, and the French envisaged passing on to Canaris's agents their reports concerning the movements of shipping between Dakar and the British port of Bathurst. But Canaris had other plans more speedily realizable. The Germans wanted to obtain from Vichy the authorization to send an important police mission into the southern non-occupied zone—a mission which would allow them to work freely, operating under forged French papers.

The Abwehr ran a special service for discovering clandestine transmitting sets, subsection III F fu (Fahndung Funk)—a radar and listening service. A second service, the W.N.V. Fu III[25], 64 boulevard Suchet, which had installed its listening posts at Bois-le-Roi and at Chartrettes (Seine-et-Marne) disposed of a mobile section. The ORPO also had a listening service under Captain Schuster.

[25] Wehrmacht Nachrichten Verbindung Funk Referat III.

These spotting stations had detected an important network of clandestine transmitters in daily contact with England, and had located them in the southern zone, in particular in the Lyons region. It would have been an easy matter for the German authorities to force the Vichy Government to clamp down on these activities, which obviously had important military repercussions. But the ambitions of the Abwehr and the Gestapo were on a grander scale. The Gestapo in fact wanted to operate in the free zone with the maximum of discretion. For the moment the operation was presented as "Franco-German collaboration for the liquidation of the clandestine transmitting posts." This friendly collaboration might have a favorable influence on the French demand for increasing the armistice army.

The French representatives, after referring the matter to Vichy, had obtained the promise that the French arrested in the course of these operations would be handed over to French justice, which was the least that could be done for people taken in the free zone. The agreement having been signed, the Germans demanded forged French papers—identity cards, ration cards, laissez-passer, etc. Asked to produce these papers through his services, René Bousquet turned a deaf ear, but called to order by Laval had to agree.

On September 28 the special composite commando entered the southern zone. It comprised 280 men of the Abwehr, the Gestapo, and the ORPO. All of them operated under false French identities. It was an incredible intrusion by the German services into the Vichy domain and an unprecedented attack on the famous "sovereignty," on which the latter laid such emphasis. The consequences of this affair were to be of exceptional gravity.

This commando of 280 took up their abode in billets which had been prepared for them in Lyons, Marseilles, and Montpelier. The command was given to Boemelburg, assisted by Dernbach, representing the Abwehr, and Schuster representing the ORPO. The operation as a whole had been christened "Action Donar."[26] All the men spoke French.

The first phase involved the pinpointing of the transmitters, which had been gradually located from the northern zone. Friedrich Dernbach, the man delegated by the Abwehr, was a leading technician in the underground network, and also a veteran of the political police. Like many of the old agents

---

[26] Boemelburg christened the operation. Donar was the God of Thunder, and had been chosen as the patron saint of Radio in Germany.

in the German services, he had once belonged to the infamous "Freikorps Balte" from which Roehm had chosen his friends. He had later belonged to the Black Reichswehr, joining the Bremen political police in 1925 and the Abwehr in 1929. He finally became head of Abteilung III F, at Saarbrucken, after specializing in radio. He had no difficulty in rapidly locating the whole clandestine network. When the net descended it was on the fifteen or twenty posts situated in the Lyons region. Several other transmitters were found at the same time at Marseilles, Toulouse, and in the region of Pau. Nearly all the radio operators and their assistants were arrested.

Boemelburg's men now appeared on the scene. One of the first commandos which had reinforced the small Knochen group in Paris in 1940 was the Kiefer group, called after its leader. Kiefer had remained in France as a counterespionage specialist; a modest man with no personal ambition, he lived for his profession. He was a specialist in the virtuoso work which the Germans called Funkspiel. On the arrest of the operators the real work began. A Funkspiel was a delicate operation of substitution which, on the capture of a clandestine transmitter, allowed a continuation of the broadcasts in order to have direct relations with the enemy. It was an extremely difficult operation to carry out. To begin with there were the operational difficulties—codes, precise hours for transmission, the correct call signals, etc. A preliminary listening in of sufficient length gradually allowed most of these difficulties to be solved before direct intervention began. But it was also necessary to "receive" and "send" like the usual operator. In effect it established between two operators at either end of the "line" a whole gamut of indefinable customs. They could "feel" anything abnormal. Each operator had his own way of "sending," to such a point that, in the case of a post with several operators, the correspondent could immediately recognize the man at the other end. The Funkspiel duties then entailed forcing the arrested operator to continue his transmissions without giving away that he was in the hands of the enemy. A particularly skilled surveillance was necessary to prevent him signaling the danger even by a slightly unusual touch. In actual fact, if the correspondent understood what was happening, not only would the Funkspiel fail to produce the expected result but would on the contrary turn against its users, who could easily be "bluffed." The second solution—less satisfactory because it was infinitely more difficult—was to replace the operator by imitating his touch.

Boemelburg and Kiefer, with the help of the great German specialist Kopkow, managed to carry out this Funkspiel admirably. Many of the captured posts continued to transmit regularly, maintaining liaison with London, which was still unaware that the operators had been arrested. The results were catastrophic for the French Resistance Movement. The Germans received several parachute deliveries of weapons (about twenty thousand weapons were seized in this manner), ammunition, and money. They received documents, spotted agents and networks, particularly in Normandy, the Orléans region, Angers, and in the Parisian zone. Numerous arrests were carried out.

The members of the "Donar" commando did not return to the northern zone.[27] On November 11, when the German troops crossed into the unoccupied zone, they were still operating. Thanks to a patient mosaic work, completed from items of information picked up in the course of interrogations, from listening posts, etc., the Gestapo had been able to reconstitute a certain number of elements which allowed it to engage in radio communication with the French network of the Intelligence Service, known as the French Section. Having successfully made contact with London, the envoys dropped by parachute could be captured, their documents seized, and the arrests carried out. Ultimately nearly the entire British organization in France was revealed and dismantled. The exploitation of this success lasted until May 1944.

The actual Funkspiel had finished a long time before. The Gestapo wanted to close it with a witticism. A last message transmitted to London, alluding to the "parachutings" received by the Germans, read: "Thank you for your collaboration and for the weapons you have sent us." But the British operator was not to be outdone. He replied: "Think nothing of it. These weapons were a mere bagatelle for us. It was a luxury we could easily afford. We shall soon be coming to fetch them."

The Germans did not know that London had discovered several weeks before that the Brittany posts were in the hands of the enemy. The latter had continued to be fed by volunteers. Under this cover they had been able to reintroduce agents who had formed new networks elsewhere.

---

[27] Boemelburg had been replaced by Mueller, who spoke French almost as correctly as himself, and had returned to Paris.

The results of these Funkspiel operations were extremely serious both for the French Resistance and the Allied Intelligence Services. It took several months' work and heavy losses to repair the damage caused. Many members of the Resistance and Allied agents fell into the hands of the Gestapo, to be executed or deported. This period must be numbered among the most somber pages in the history of the Resistance.

On November 11, 1942, the State Secretaries for National Defense, Bridoux, Auphan, and Jannekeyn, having given orders to the troops of the armistice army to put up no resistance, and René Bousquet having transmitted this order to the police, the German troops entered the free zone without incident.

The British and Americans having landed in North Africa on the 8th, the Germans invaded Tunisia. They feared an Allied landing on the Mediterranean coast, and were under no illusions as to the welcome that the French population would give to the Americans. On the night of November 10-11, a note informed the Vichy Government of the need for German troops to occupy the Mediterranean coast. On the 11th, at 7 A.M., the units of the Wehrmacht crossed the demarcation line and pushed southward, carrying out a plan which had been worked out long in advance under the name of "Operation Anton." That morning von Rundstedt went to Vichy to give official notice to Pétain of the occupation of the zone, formerly called free. The regiments of the armistice army, which had been given orders on the 9th to leave their garrisons, were confined to their barracks by a last-minute counterorder given by Bridoux, at the risk of seeing them taken prisoner.

While the Germans sped south, six Einsatzkommandos drove toward the six French towns where they were to take up their quarters. These were the men of Oberg and Knochen, who were to open new "branches" in the southern zone.

The Gestapo and the S.D. had long since posted their observers in the southern zone. Under cover of the armistice commission, the German consulates and the German Red Cross, the agents had for some months carried out their underground work of documentation. At Vichy, Haupsturmfuehrer Geissler had officially opened in February the Deutsche Polizei Delegation, which proceeded to carry out arrests on the morning of November 11.

From November 11, 12, and 13, according to the regions, the Gestapo officially established itself. An Einsatzkommando was installed in each capital of the military regions of the southern zone. At the beginning of December they were transformed into as many SIPO-S.D. commandos, in other words into regional services identical to those of the northern zone, now quartered at Limoges, Lyons, Marseilles, Montpellier, Toulouse, and Vichy. The German police system now covered the whole of France in a close network which, on April 1, was composed as follows:

The head Paris office controlled the whole of France, apart from the North and the Pas-de-Calais, which were attached to Brussels; the Upper and Lower Rhine and the Moselle were responsible to the German regions. Upon this head office depended seventeen regional services installed in Paris, Angers, Bordeaux, Châlons-sur-Marne, Dijon, Nancy, Orléans, Poitiers, Rennes, Rouen, Saint-Quentin, Limoges, Lyons, Marseilles, Montpellier, Toulouse, and Vichy. These seventeen services possessed forty-five branch sections (there would be fifty-five in June 1944), eighteen branch posts of lesser importance (reduced to fifteen in June 1944), and three special frontier police stations (there would be six in June 1944) plus eighteen frontier posts. This made a sum total of eleven hundred services dependent upon orders from Paris; they would insure the stranglehold of the Gestapo on France at the moment of the Allied landing. By adding the three regional services of Lille, Metz, and Strasbourg, and their branches, a total of 131 services was reached.[28]

To these must be added again the innumerable auxiliary services: teams of mercenary killers, specialized services of all kinds, Sonderkommandos of every category, which would continue to increase and multiply everywhere, not to mention the constant aid, in the course of 1943 and the first six months of 1944, provided by the active collaborators, P.P.F., French Nazis, militia, etc.

When one thinks that each of these Gestapo services constantly circulated agents, installing them in organizations and administrative offices where they could work best: Kommandanturen, labor exchanges, "propaganda" services, etc.; that the agents in their turn recruited a host of informers, stool

---

[28] To this police force must be added the sixty-nine services of the Abwehr, those of the G.F.P., and the Feldgendarmerie.

pigeons, "well-wishing" or paid denouncers, one can almost feel in retrospect a shudder of fear, and imagine what would have been the fate of France and Frenchmen had the outcome of the conflict been different.

During April, Himmler came to Paris to make a personal inspection of his chief offices. He had every cause to be satisfied: his policy had begun to bear fruit. A decree of January 30 had created the militia, the leadership of which was entrusted to Darnand, a man of whom Oberg had high hopes. It needed only a little patience and he could be duplicated, and the French police, which could not be trusted, could be replaced by politically reliable volunteers who would play the role which the S.A. had once played in Germany.

A decree of February 11 gave the official seal to the L.V.F. by declaring it "a public utility," after nineteen months of existence. The volunteers recruited in France with the aid of propaganda strongly encouraged by the bait of high pay[29] passed under German control on their entry to the Versailles depot, whence they were sent to the training center of Kruzina in the forests of Poland.

At last Himmler's favorite child, the Waffen S.S., began to recruit throughout France. The recruitment was launched at a meeting of the "Friends of the Waffen S.S." in the autumn of 1942. Headed by Paul Marion, Secretary of State and head of Intelligence, Doriot, Déat, Lousteau, Darnand, Knipping, and Cance, commanding the first brigade of the Waffen S.S., it appealed to public opinion to give moral and material aid to these combatants who were to "defend France"—wearing German uniform.

In Germany itself the year 1943 was particularly auspicious for Himmler. At the end of the year he was to be Minister of the Interior, head of all the German police, arbiter in all the questions of race and Germanization so vital to the Nazi regime, which gave him a free hand over the "new Germans" recovered from the conquered territories; entrusted with the repatriation of Germans into the Reich and, as a side line, Minister of Public Health since the duties of this ministry had been transferred to the Ministry of the Interior. As grand master of the S.S., he presided over a host of ancillary organizations and pseudo-scientific institutes, letting his weight be felt in the

---

[29] This ranged from 2,500 francs a month for a second-class unmarried soldier to 10,760 francs for a bachelor major, increased by various emoluments, family, and combat allowances.

scientific university and German medical organizations. He reigned supreme over the concentration camps, earning for his S.S. an astronomical revenue which was to swell the S.S. account in the Reichsbank, shamefacedly called the "Max Heiliger" account; and finally his own private army, the S.S., was to be increased, in 1943 alone, by seven new divisions—four German S.S. divisions and three foreign Waffen S.S. divisions, making a total of fifteen fighting divisions.

Thus Himmler's career followed a graph diametrically opposed to the fortunes of his country. This year of 1943, which carried him to the peak of his power, was the year in which Germany suffered military and political defeats which she could not survive: the year of Stalingrad, of the collapse in North Africa, the invasion of Italy, and the fall of Italian fascism.

At the time of Mussolini's fall, Himmler, as Minister of the Interior, was accorded full powers to administer the Reich. When the Allied bombing destroyed Hamburg and General Jeschonnek, chief of the Luftwaffe General Staff, committed suicide in despair, when Manstein retreated to the Dnieper before the formidable thrusts of the Red Army, Himmler proudly presented to his Fuehrer his new Waffen S.S. divisions which were going to fight to save Europe. He had risen to the throne on the ruins of his country and the sufferings of his people.

In France, 1943 marked the total ascendancy of the Gestapo. Not a town, not a region, escaped the vigilant espionage of Knochen's agents. At night doors and windows were blanketed to listen to the voice of the B.B.C., which brought words of encouragement and hope to the French, who were now fighting in Africa and later in Sicily and Italy. There were more executions than ever, but people died knowing that the last days of the executioners were at hand.

Prisons were full (more than forty thousand persons were arrested during the year), but the Resistance groups and the maquis organized themselves; they were armed, thanks to parachute deliveries; and their ranks swelled, thanks to the S.T.O., which forced those who refused to leave for Germany to go underground. The Gestapo had to adapt its methods to meet this new situation.

To face up to it, Oberg tried to obtain the cooperation of the French, and above all of the police services, which he continued to find too "soft" in matters of repression. In the spring he visited Vichy, accompanied by Knochen, and his adjutant Hagen. The almost secret interview with Pétain had been carefully prepared. Dr. Ménétrel had visited Oberg to arrange the details of the ceremonial due to the head of the French State.

At the Hôtel du Parc, Oberg and his two subordinates were received by the Marshal, supported by General Secretary Bousquet and Dr. Ménétrel. The interview lasted eight minutes. Its result was the second version of the Oberg-Bousquet agreement, published April 18. Oberg and his two colleagues have recounted this interview. According to them, Pétain heard this agreement quoted by Oberg, and remarked sourly to the general secretary of police that the head of state had been notified *after* the regional prefects and superintendents of police.[30] After which, he turned to Oberg and added, "Everything which happens in France is of interest to me, too." Then he added, "Personally I consider that the greatest enemies of France are the Freemasons and the Communists."

Oberg was to say later, "I was surprised at his acumen and his good state of health."

After this brief audience Oberg was received by Laval. A dinner was later given in his honor at the Hôtel Majestic: Laval, Abel Bonnard, Ménétrel, Jardel, Gabolde, Bousquet, Rochat, and Guerard on the French side; Oberg, Knochen, Hagen, General Neubronn, and the Consul Krugg von Nidda on the German side.

These official efforts to secure collaboration did nothing to change the real situation. Each day reports, coming from one or other of the regional services, informed Oberg that the maquis was becoming omnipresent and that the underground movements being organized in the towns were attacking the collaborators. The latter, for their part, began openly to demand German protection, accusing the French police of being in league with the outlaws. For even if a few traitors and mercenaries had entered the services of the occupying power, an infinitely greater number of patriotic people sabotaged the measures taken at the request of the enemy, warned those who were threatened with arrest, and created within the administration and even in the police

[30] M. René Bousquet has informed the author that, although the negotiations and the general line of the agreement had been communicated in good time to the chief of state, the latter had not been informed of the details of the agreement itself before its definite conclusion. This would account for the rather acid remark reported by Oberg; it must not be attributed to a lapse of memory due to the Marshal's age.

(including the head office of the national police at Vichy) active groups of Resistance, at peril of their lives. No state body, during this period, paid a heavier toll to Nazi savagery than the police. A special section was formed at Gestapo headquarters to keep the French police under the closest observation. Commanded by S.S. Sturmbannfuehrer Horst Laube, it was instrumental in making numerous arrests and deportations of policemen, but never managed to eliminate the networks formed within the French services.

At the beginning of spring 1943 the Gestapo demanded that its Section II Pol be kept informed of transfers, changes of station, and promotions of all police officials up to the rank of superintendent. But it was often at a higher level in the police hierarchy that the greatest anti-Nazi activity was to be found.

The ever increasing activities of the maquis disturbed the Gestapo. In mid-November 1943 what the Germans called the "Pétain-Laval divorce" took place. Abetz considered that Laval alone was of importance and really governed the country, but several Gestapo reports had warned that the Resistance might try to kidnap Pétain, an operation which risked having grave repercussions on public opinion. According to other informers placed in the head of state's entourage, Pétain intended to leave the government and Vichy, as certain personalities had advised. This possibility was judged to be equally disastrous, and Oberg prescribed strict "protective measures" which received the code name of "Operation Fuchsbau" (the fox's lair). The environs of Vichy were combed, and all dubious individuals removed or arrested. A cordon was then placed around the town. Road blocks allowed a check on all entrances and exits. Finally ORPO posts were distributed in the surrounding countryside. All these dispositions were already in force when Skorzeny arrived unannounced from Germany with a special commando. Traveling under a false identity as Dr. Wolf, Skorzeny arrived with full powers to insure the protection of Vichy. He checked and approved the arrangements for "Operation Fuchsbau," and added a certain number of protective measures at Vichy airdrome, in case the English sent a plane to rescue Pétain! Then he returned to Berlin.

At the end of 1943 Oberg was fighting to impose the man of his choice as France's police chief. For a long time he had cast his eyes on Darnand, member of the militia and the Waffen S.S. Oberg considered that the militia, in his own words, was a movement which had a close affinity with the S.S. movement, and was capable of giving a new impulse to the French police forces. It was in this spirit that he had always protected Darnand and given aid to his organization. At the end of 1943 the S.S. General Berger invited Darnand and his secretary, Gallet, to make a tour of inspection of Germany. At the end of this tour Darnand's visits to Oberg became more and more frequent. In the autumn he was appointed honorary Obersturmfuehrer of the French Waffen S.S., and Oberg was ordered to tell him of his promotion personally.

At this period Oberg, Knochen, and the military began to doubt the genuine good will of General Secretary Bousquet. They had already suggested to Laval that he should be replaced by someone a little more "politically engaged." The final Pétain-Laval break in November allowed such a ministerial reshuffle. Oberg asked Laval to seize the opportunity to get rid of Bousquet and replace him by Darnand, whose militia was already officially recognized as supernumerary police.

Laval did not show any desire to appoint Darnand, who had on several occasions attacked him as the "friend of the Freemasons, and former supporter of the Third Republic." He wanted to appoint the former regional prefect of Marseilles, Lemoine, but finally agreed to Darnand, giving Lemoine the State Secretaryship of the Interior, and axing Georges Hilaire.

On December 29 René Bousquet left the offices of the General Direction of the National Police. Before leaving he had destroyed a large number of dossiers which he did not wish to fall into the hands of his successor. Two days later, on December 31, Darnand took over the offices, which he found almost deserted. By entrusting the maintenance of order to a man of the Party, to the head of an extremist faction, the door was open to the worst abuses and the new alignment was blatantly on the Nazi model. As Oberg saw it, the militia was to behave as a French S.S. before being integrated a few months later in the ranks of Himmler's army.

René Bousquet, who had settled in Paris, was put under close surveillance. On June 6, 1944, the day of the Allied landings, he was arrested and his father was imprisoned at Montauban. But whereas the latter was released after a fortnight, the ex-secretary general remained in custody. He was later taken to Germany by car and placed in custody in a villa on the edge of the Tegernsee. His wife and son, aged five, joined him some days later.

Hardly was Darnand installed before he was given the most extensive powers. On January 10, a decree appointed him sole commander of the entire French police forces. While his predecessor had only borne the title of General Secretary of Police, he had been appointed General Secretary for the Maintenance of Order.

From this moment the militia operated in practice as an official organization. Its offices became genuine annexes of the Gestapo, with which it collaborated openly. The same methods of interrogation were used in both houses, the prisoners were summarily handed over to the Gestapo, and the official police saw itself progressively supplanted.

The number of arrests rose week by week. During the month of March 1944 alone more than ten thousand persons were arrested by the French authorities, as many as there had been during three months of 1943. Again we must add the individuals taken by the Gestapo, whose numbers remained unknown, and all the victims whom the militia detained in its jails, sometimes for several weeks, without reporting them to the judicial authorities.

On January 20 a new law created the courts-martial. These tribunals were composed of three non-magistrate judges, whose names were not divulged, who sat in secret inside the prisons, and whose sentences (without appeal) were carried out on the spot. There was neither prosecutor nor defense counsel. For a long time the Germans had demanded the creation of special jurisdiction to repress the activities of the Resistance. Oberg confessed later that he had not dared to hope for such expeditious measures.

The courts-martial began to function at Marseilles at the end of January and subsequently in Paris, where one of them sitting at the Santé condemned to death sixteen Resistants, who were immediately shot. The judges who thus murdered French compatriots, under the convenient veil of anonymity, were usually militiamen.

The author hopes that the reader will excuse him for recounting some personal memories on the manner in which the detainees in the French prisons followed in their cells the sessions of the courts-martial. The simple sequence of noises which came to their ears was enough to give them some idea of the strange concept of justice which directed these tribunals.

The courts usually sat at the beginning of the afternoon—at least it was always at this time of the day that I heard the echoes of their work. I imagine that the three mysterious dispensers of justice returned to the prison after lunch.

Inside the prison their arrival was preceded by an unchangeable ceremony. All the prisoners employed on prison routine—sweepers, cooks, collectors of mess tins, office employees, were taken back to their cells. The warders then closed the double doors, as for the night regime. A little later we heard the great double door of the prison open. A truck entered, stopped in the courtyard, and we could hear the dull thud of coffins laid on the ground. The truck left and was parked a little further away in the courtyard. It would leave later, again full of coffins.

The great gate squeaked once more, and the sound of a squad of marching men rang out between the walls and the rounds. A word of command, the sound of rifle butts echoing on the flagstones, and the firing squad was ready for action.

Silence then fell once more, and ears were cocked inside the cells. The crowd being in position, the leading actors in the tragedy were expected. A light rap on the small door which opened immediately, a noise of footsteps on the gravel of the inner courtyards, the successive squeaking of the grilles. ... The "court" was now in session in the lawyer's parlor.

The drama now developed very quickly. A vague murmur rose from the ground floor of the prison, the noise of a cell door being opened and shut and steps making their way to the parlor. ... The whole prison held its breath. There was no distinction left between political prisoners and ordinary lawbreakers, each prisoner leaned toward his neighbor, his brother, in this appalling nightmare from which he would never emerge alive.

A few minutes elapsed ... five or ten perhaps. When there were several accused, which was often the case, the session would sometimes last as long as fifteen minutes. Finally, the noise of doors and footsteps announced the end of the sitting. Sometimes a voice was raised, a cry of rage or despair quickly stifled. ... The successive grilles opened once more, the gravel crackled beneath footsteps, the little door onto the street closed on the three men who were now safely in the broad sunlight outside, while the condemned man hastily wrote his last letter.

The step of an escort approaching, a cry, a song of rage, interspersed with tears ringing out in the Chemin de ronde, usually the *Marseillaise*, or sometimes the *Internationale*. ... And then another cry in the far distance: "*Adieu, les copains! Vive la France!*" A salvo which echoed horribly rolled between the high walls, clung to it, bounced off the corners of the prison, and echoed in our heads. A sharp report, pathetic after this thunder—the *coup de grâce*.

While the platoon marched off, leaving by the big door, we could hear the blows of the hammer on the white wooden coffins. At last the truck left. It was over. . . . Darnand's justice had passed us by.

Later that evening the almoner would visit each cell, his face distraught, his poor shortsighted eyes behind his big glasses displaying all the distress in the world. "My friends, you know that your comrades . . ." His voice trembled on the words. "They died courageously. If you are believers, pray for them. And you, too, be courageous, and hope, and have trust." Then he left, going from cell to cell, distributing the same words of piety and hope to the twelve or fifteen prisoners who waited behind each door for the next sitting of the court.

I deeply regret having to write that most of the judges of these courts-martial could never be identified after the liberation.

PART SIX

COLLAPSE OF THE GESTAPO
1944

Chapter 21
Resistance in the Army

June 6, 1944. During the night vague gleams began to pierce the darkness, as the most formidable armada of all time sailed toward the French coast. Within an hour the first troops of the Anglo-American invasion armies would set foot on the beaches of Normandy and the Battle of France, the long-awaited, feared, and hoped-for ordeal, would begin.

In the shock which was to confront assailants and besieged, the Gestapo could only play a secondary role. The German Army fought fiercely, defending foot by foot positions which had been fortified for months, since the Fuehrer had forbidden any retreat. The S.S. "Das Reich" Division stationed in the southwest carried out its "mopping up" operations against the maquis with its customary ferocity. On its journey across France from Montauban to St. Lô, to engage the Allied troops, it left in its wake hundreds of corpses. The ninety-nine hanged in Tulle and the inhabitants of Oradour-sur-Glane, shot or burned alive, who fell to the S.S. at the beginning of June 1944, joined the dead of the Eastern countries in the immense martyrology of the victims of Nazism.

But the reign of cruelty was drawing to a close. The "Das Reich" Division lost 60 percent of its effectives in the battle of Saint-Lô; then the breakthrough at Avranches and the advance into Britanny forced the German troops to retreat.

In Paris, Oberg and Knochen began to be seriously alarmed. It was obvious that the Allied armies would soon reach the capital. The population and the Resistance groups, now operating almost openly, would certainly try to hamper the retreat of the last troops. Oberg, therefore, ordered the preventive arrest of all persons capable of leading this rally.

Already in April and May a first measure had been taken with this end in view. Thirteen active prefects of police had been apprehended, as well as a certain number of leading personalities.

On August 10 forty-three more people were arrested and deported. Prefects, inspectors of finance, high treasury officials, generals, colonels and commanding officers, bankers, lawyers, and professors.

These measures passed unobserved by the Parisians. They were living in a sort of hypnotic state, fascinated by the fortunes of the liberating forces taking place about two hundred kilometers from the capital. On July 14 parades behind the tricolor were staged in various districts in Paris. The Parisians did not suspect the internal "tragedy" which, on July 20, shook the German authorities in Paris—the Gestapo in particular.

For a long time certain anti-Nazi personalities had tried for reform in Germany. The vigilance of the S.D. and the Gestapo had upset their aim. Among the military, certain opposition groups had existed. They alone might have had some chances of success, but everything showed that they preferred ultimately to justify themselves and to accept without too much difficulty the numerous advantages which the regime was able to give them—easy promotion,[1] big pay, not to mention periodical donations given by Hitler to the generals.

Thus the first acts of courage are not to be found among the military. During the war it was in university circles that the first opposition to the regime was organized. The planting of Nazi spy networks within the German universities had not been able to destroy the long tradition of independence, liberty, and justice so dear to students of all countries.

In Munich the *Weisse Rose* (White Rose) group lived within the precincts of the university. For several years its activities, confined to university circles, remained secret. It printed and distributed texts of the courageous sermons of the Bishop of Münster, Mgr. von Galen, and then in the summer of 1942 extracts from the Laws of Lycurgus and Solon.

At the beginning of 1943 the members of the *Weisse Rose* came out into open opposition. On the walls the young folk dared to write in large letters "Down with Hitler," which at that time demanded high courage. After Stalingrad on February 18, 1943, pamphlets containing appeals to rebels were printed and thrown in bundles into the university amphitheaters. They also contained an urgent appeal to the Wehrmacht, to the conscience and

---

[1] On July 19, 1940, for example, twelve new marshals were appointed at the same time.

honor of the officers. Canaris and one of his staff officers, Lahousen, were summoned to Munich by Kaltenbrunner, who dealt with this affair himself. They were notified of these texts. It was February 22, the day when the authors of these pamphlets were executed, that this agonized appeal from young people, who still believed in military honor, might have found an echo in their hearts: perhaps it contributed to the final action in the passive circles of the Abwehr conspirators.

For the young members of the *Weisse Rose* were not content with distributing their pamphlets. The next day they staged a demonstration of students in the streets of Munich, an astonishing sight in the Nazi world. A Blockleiter recognized two of the of the young people, a brother and sister, as they were throwing pamphlets through a university window, and denounced them to the Gestapo.

The result was not long delayed. The Gestapo arrested three students: Christoph Probst, aged twenty-four, Hans Scholl, twenty-five, both medical students, and Sophie Scholl, twenty-two, philosophy student. On the 22nd, after three days of interrogation and tortures—Sophie Scholl had a leg broken—all three were condemned to death and executed the same evening. The investigations continued. On July 13 it was the turn of philosophy professor Kurt Huber and a medical student Alexander Schmorell. Finally, on October 12, medical student Willi Graf fell in turn. Condemned to death by a "People's Court," they were decapitated with an ax. The names of these martyrs for freedom are unknown to most French people. They paid a high enough price for us to render them this modest homage here.

The disaster of Stalingrad played the role of catalyst to the growing military resistance to Hitler. The most logical of them realized that the war was lost and that an irreversible process had just been started in the icy wastes of Russia, a process which could only end in total collapse. The Army would go down to defeat on the grand scale. It was more to try and save what could still be saved of the Army than out of revolt against Nazi crimes that the soldiers began to envisage direct action. They had witnessed appalling crimes for years, without ever trying to call a halt. The fear of defeat and a reflex move to preserve their own privileges finally managed to get them started.

Since the beginning of the Nazi regime Hitler had kept the Army under close surveillance. The security services, however, guessed that the soldiers conspired in the privacy of their staffs, sometimes with the aid of diplomats, and the R.S.H.A. put its best agents on the job. But the conspirators had a solid and practically impenetrable bastion in the Abwehr. And this was what Himmler coveted most, because he dreamed of taking over the entire intelligence services. After February 1943 Kaltenbrunner joined him in this aim. A "speed contest" then began between the Abwehr and the Gestapo, the conspirators having finally taken the decision from which they had recoiled for so long—to get rid of Hitler. The officers could have eliminated the Fuehrer much earlier by legal methods, but they had not had the courage. The decision having been taken, there were several abortive attempts. The one with the most chance of success was carried out on March 13, 1943. General von Tresckow, chief of staff of the Center Army Group on the Russian front, and General Olbricht, head of the General Administration of the Army, had planned "Operation Flash," which consisted in blowing up Hitler's personal aircraft.

On March 13, 1943, Hitler left his headquarters at Smolensk to return to Berlin; one of Tresckow's staff officers, Fabian von Schlabrendorff, handed one of the passengers in the aircraft two bottles of brandy, asking him to give them to a friend of his in Berlin. The package contained a bomb which Colonel Lahousen[2] of the Abwehr had brought from Berlin. But the contraption did not work, and Hitler arrived safe and sound. The conspirators having managed to recover the package in Berlin, the attempt was not discovered.

Other plans were elaborated and put into effect, but all of them failed. Mueller's and Schellenberg's men continued their vigilance unceasingly. On April 5, 1943, they breached the defenses of the Abwehr by arresting the chief collaborators of Major General Hans Oster, head of the Central Section of Ausland-Abwehr and one of the leading conspirators. One of the arrested men, Dr. Dohnanyi, also a member of the Abwehr, kept in his safe documents which revealed the broad outlines of the conspiracy. This

---

[2] Colonel Erwin Lahousen, a former member of the Austrian Secret Service, posted to the Abwehr after the Anschluss, was adjutant to Colonel Pieckenbrock, head of the 1(a) Branch (operational) of the Abwehr.

information, however, was too fragmentary to allow a full-scale action. Another factor also put a brake on the Gestapo's operations. Himmler, who suffered from a real complex vis-à-vis Canaris, could not make up his mind to attack him directly, a fact which allowed the head of the Abwehr to hold out for several more months.

The information collected in April was cross-checked in September during an operation of true Gestapo character, known as "Frau Solf's tea party." Frau Solf was a charming old "society" lady at whose home some of the conspirators periodically met on the pretext of taking afternoon tea. They kept in contact with anti-Nazi refugees in Switzerland and also through the latter with British and American agents. On September 10, 1943, a new guest was admitted into the circle, a Swiss doctor, Dr. Reckse, who expressed violent anti-Nazi sentiments. The conspirators were rash enough to entrust him with their mail to Switzerland. Dr. Reckse was a Gestapo agent. Once more Himmler waited before taking action. This information was still insufficient to strike a blow at Canaris.

In December, the inquiry had, however, collected enough evidence to force Oster to resign and to have him arrested. In January the seventy-five persons involved in the affair of Frau Solf's tea parties were apprehended. The most heavily compromised were judged in a few days and executed.[3]

At the beginning of 1944 new incidents revealed activities within the Abwehr which too often served as cover for the conspirators. Himmler then obtained from Hitler a measure he had demanded for some time, encouraged by Schellenberg, who suffered no paralyzing complex with regard to Canaris.

On February 14, 1944, a decree ordered the dissolution of the Abwehr. The Central Office of the Abwehr bore the exact title of *Amt Ausland Nachrichten und Abwehr*, i.e., "Foreign and Defense Intelligence Service." It formed one of the five branches of the O.K.W. and was divided into two subbranches known as *Amtsgruppe Ausland* and *Abwehr Amt*.

The decree of February 14 resulted in "bursting" the ensemble of the services. *Amtsgruppe Ausland*, working in liaison with the Foreign Office,

---

[3] All of them were judged by a People's Court, under the bloodthirsty Freisler. Frau Solf and her daughter escaped death and were sent to Ravensbruck.

which dealt with what one might call general intelligence, was reattached to the *Wehrmachtsfuehrungstab* (the Staff for the Conduct of Operations)—of the O.K.W. With regard to the *Abwehr Amt*, which was essentially the Secret Service, its four sections were absorbed by the R.S.H.A., which grouped them into a supplementary Amt called *Militarische Amt*—"Military Office" or more simply *Mil Amt*.

At the same time an order from Hitler gave complete liberty of action abroad to Amt VI, in effect to the services of Schellenberg, who thus became absolute master of the Nazi Intelligence Services. Canaris took the only step open to him. He resigned.

The Mil Amt of the R.S.H.A. was entrusted to Colonel Hansen, former leader of Abteilung I of the Abwehr, the most important branch which comprised in the main the three information services, Army, Navy, and Air. Hansen succeeded Pieckenbrock, Canaris' old friend, who had been heavily compromised. Hansen himself, together with Freytag-Loringhoven, was one of the oldest members of the underground movement within the Abwehr. He had enjoyed extraordinary good luck and the Gestapo had never suspected his activities. On becoming head of Mil Amt, he continued in the conspiracy and, like his friends, was executed after the July 20 plot.[4]

Thus the Abwehr, a rival service to the R.S.H.A. abroad, finally disappeared. Himmler triumphed over his rival Canaris, and finally installed himself in power. The conspirators were now deprived of an alibi and a refuge. The source which had provided them with false papers, briefings, explosives, etc., had definitely dried up. There was no longer a possibility of passing those who were too compromised across the frontier to Switzerland, as had often been done previously. Contacts with American and British Secret Services also became very difficult.

The coup would have been fatal for the plot had not a new recruit entered the fray shortly after the dissolution of the Abwehr: Lieutenant Colonel Graf von Stauffenberg. A staff officer who had been seriously wounded in Tunisia,[5] then chief of staff to the Reserve Army, descendant of a long line of military aristocrats, a great-grandson of Gneisenau on his mother's side,

---

[4] Freytag-Loringhoven took his own life.
[5] Stauffenberg had lost an eye and his right hand in Tunisia.

he too had believed in the excellence of the Nazi regime, and had hoped to see the rebirth of Germany's grandeur. But Stauffenberg also realized that the war was lost and that Hitler was to drag Germany and the Army into an abyss, unless he was prevented from causing further harm. He, therefore, joined the conspiracy of which Dr. Goerdeler, mayor of Leipzig and General Beck, ex-chief of General Staff, were the leading lights.

His motives have been clearly defined by Gisevius: "Stauffenberg did not want Hitler to drag the Army down into the tomb he had dug. A soldier to the fingertips, he thought that to save the Fatherland and to save the Army were one and the same thing. ... He was not the only one of his species but a representative type of the military group which led the July 20 plot. At the end of 1942 this group was reinforced at each defeat, and was animated by a firm will to react in the face of events."

Stauffenberg was essentially a man of action. For the first time, one of the leaders of the conspiracy risked his life. On December 26, 1943, summoned to the Fuehrer's headquarters at Rastenberg to present a report, he had carried in his brief case a delayed-action bomb. But Hitler[6] canceled the meeting at the last moment, and Stauffenberg had to take his bomb back to Berlin.

Stauffenberg's dynamism brought a new breath of life into the circle of conspirators. The Abwehr destroyed, he knew how to find a new asylum in the O.K.W. itself and to rally to the conspiracy a certain number of generals—or at least to insure their benevolent neutrality.

No complicity had been discovered within the Gestapo or the S.D., but two important police officials, Nazis from the very beginning, had changed sides and gave their aid to the conspirators—Nebe, head of the KRIPO, who had commanded an Einsatzgruppe in Russia, and Count Heldorff, the Berlin prefect of police, together with his adjutant, Count von der Schulenburg, another repentant Nazi. Their role in the event of a putsch could have been of the greatest importance in liaison with General von Hase, commandant in Berlin and also a member of the conspiracy.

Several military leaders of the occupying troops in the West had also given their support: von Stuelpnagel, Military Governor of France; von

---

[6] To avoid attempts on his life Hitler side-stepped any regular schedule and constantly changed his timetable at the last moment.

Falkenhausen, Military Governor of Belgium, and above all Rommel, Commander in Chief of "B" Army Group, the only marshal not to have rejected a discreet sounding out by the conspirators' envoys, as well as his chief of staff, General Hans Speidel. The crushing superiority of the invading armies had persuaded them that the German forces available could not hold the Normandy front for long and would have to fight a full-scale rearguard action. Hitler, as usual, refused to accept his marshals' arguments.

The dissolution of the Abwehr created considerable difficulties for the conspirators. While six attempts had been made in 1943 to kill Hitler, no plan could be perfected for the first six months of 1944. Stauffenberg realized that the overthrow of the regime would be possible only if Hitler himself disappeared. His presence paralyzed the generals who, in addition, considered themselves bound by their oath of fidelity to the Fuehrer, which they had sworn on the death of Hindenburg.

The Normandy landings and the first successes in the French campaign, the advance of the Allies in Italy, where Rome had just been captured, the debacle of the German troops in the East, where the Soviet armies had just entered Poland, proved to Stauffenberg that no tergiversation was possible if there was to be anything left to save.

The conspirators were convinced that the death of Hitler would allow them to treat amicably with the Western powers. They desired an immediate armistice, but rejected unconditional surrender. The peace plans drawn up by Carl Goerdeler show an astonishing lack of realism. This separate peace with the West would be accompanied by no letup in operations in the East. On the contrary, after the temporary settlement of a shortened front, and during the period of organizing a new executive power, the conspirators believed that the British and Americans would join with them to fight the Russians. This showed a complete misunderstanding of the Yalta Agreement, which goes to prove that, had the conspiracy succeeded, the course of events would not have changed very much. Even with Hitler dead and the conspirators forming a new government for Germany, their proposals as framed by Goerdeler would have been rejected by the Western powers. Apart from commitments undertaken at Yalta, which were clearly laid down, it is hard to imagine men of the caliber of Roosevelt and Churchill renouncing unconditional surrender at the moment when the military situation was safely assured. Faced with rejection of their proposals, it is possible that the new German Government would have decided to continue the war.

Contrary to the theories of Goerdeler and Beck, Stauffenberg and his closest friends apparently had a more healthy view of the situation. The collapse on all fronts proved to them that the resistance advocated by Hitler was suicide for the German nation. The prolongation of the war which was now being waged on their home soil would bring the total destruction of Germany's economy, cause hundreds of thousands of deaths, and would risk making a renaissance of Germany impossible.

It was on these precepts, while maintaining contact with the group led by Goerdeler and Beck, that Stauffenberg devised the "Valkyrie" plan to assassinate Hitler, and to set up immediately a military government in Berlin which would neutralize the most dangerous Nazi organizations—the S.S., the Gestapo, and the S.D. Stauffenberg, promoted to colonel at the end of June, was appointed at the same time chief of staff of the Home Army, a post which would give him frequent access to the meetings at the Fuehrer's headquarters. Preparations continued toward the attempt of July 20.

An important conference had been fixed for that day to launch a Russian offensive in Galicia. Keitel summoned Stauffenberg to headquarters at Rastenburg to learn details of the first units from the Home Forces, destined to fight in each German village, and finally to be known as the Volkssturm. Mussolini was also expected that day. He was now a refugee in Germany, and was due to arrive at 2:30 P.M.

Stauffenberg, therefore, arrived at the Wolfsschanz,[7] bringing in his brief case for the second time the exogen bomb—an explosive of British make from the former secret stocks of the Abwehr—firmly resolved to use it.

At 12:30 A.M. Keitel and Stauffenberg entered the hut which served as conference hall. Stauffenberg had released the delayed-action fuse a few moments earlier. The explosion was to occur about 12:40 A.M. The meeting had already begun. At 12:36 A.M., Stauffenberg placed his brief case on the floor against one of the heavy legs of the table—less than six feet away from Hitler. He then slipped discreetly out of the room, on the pretext of

---

[7] The Wolf's Lair—the name given by Hitler to his Rastenburg headquarters situated in the middle of a forest.

an urgent call he had to make to Berlin. In the meantime Colonel Brandt continued his exposition on the situation in Galicia. As he bent over the map he was disturbed by Stauffenberg's brief case. He picked it up and moved it to the other side of the table leg, which was now between the bomb and Hitler.

At 12:45 A.M. a tremendous explosion rocked the hut, although it was built with solid stone walls. Stauffenberg, who was two hundred yards away, saw the roof blown off, flames and smoke and debris of all kinds flying through the ripped-out windows. He was in no doubt that Hitler was dead together with all those who were in the hall. But, although Colonel Brandt had been killed, two generals mortally and most of the others more or less seriously wounded, Hitler had come out of it almost unharmed, thanks to the table leg, which had played the part of a protective screen.

Stauffenberg had no time to learn this. Sure of his success, he hurried to the nearest airfield and left for Berlin. There an unpleasant surprise was in store for him. Contrary to the preconceived plan, the Berlin conspirators had not gone into action. They wanted to be certain that Hitler was dead. They had not, therefore, broadcast, as had been arranged, the proclamation announcing the disappearance of the Fuehrer and the constitution of a new government, with Field Marshal von Witzleben as head of the Wehrmacht, and Beck as Chief of Staff. Stauffenberg assured them that Hitler was dead and persuaded the conspirators to act. But precious time had been lost and this delay, more than the failure of the attempt, was to prevent the success of the *coup d'État*.

While the first orders went out to the garrisons, several of the conspirators learned that Hitler had only been slightly wounded. Communication with Rastenburg, which one of Stauffenberg's accomplices had managed to cut, had been restored at about 3:30 P.M. From this moment panic took hold of the less stouthearted, who, in the hope of saving their necks, abandoned their friends and refused to play the part upon which they had agreed a few days earlier.[8]

Those who, like General Fromm, would willingly have aided the conspirators in the event of a success tried to escape or even to arrest them. Apart

---

[8] For example, General Herfurth, after starting to carry out his part, took fright and helped to repress the plot. This did not prevent him from being hanged several months later.

from a few rare exceptions, the generals became once more what they had never ceased to be and what Stauffenberg's dynamism had made them forget for a moment—that they were cowardly opportunists. At last at 7:30 P.M. Field Marshal Witzleben broadcast a telegram exorting the soldiers to assume power everywhere. Had the same order been broadcast at 1 P.M., it might have saved the situation, for it was not until after 4 P.M. that Goebbels, by this time informed of the attempt, received clearance to broadcast that the Fuehrer was safe and sound.

Himmler, appointed Commander in Chief of the Home Army (his old dream finally realized), flew to Berlin to direct the repression. Schellenberg, with the aid of Skorzeny, had already managed to rally part of the troops who were to have marched with the conspirators. At one o'clock in the morning Hitler spoke on the radio. The putsch had failed, and a bloody revenge was about to begin.

In Paris, Prague, and Vienna the soldiers among the occupying troops who shared in the plot, learned, at about 4 P.M., that the attempt had taken place as planned. At 7:30 P.M. Beck telephoned Stuelpnagel, confirming the order to carry out the prescribed measures. Stuelpnagel agreed, although a catastrophic defection from the very outset had compromised the success of the operation. Marshal von Kluge, recently appointed by Hitler to replace von Rundstedt as commander of the West forces, had promised his aid "in the event of the attempt being a success." At 7 P.M. he learned over the official radio that Hitler was only wounded and changed his mind. At 7:30 P.M. he received Witzleben's message, assuring him that Hitler was dead, and he seemed to try to rally to the conspirators. Three quarters of an hour later a direct communication with O.K.W. confirmed the failure of the plot, and once more he turned about. His refusal was of great consequence, but the Parisian conspirators had already given orders and decided to carry their rebellion to the end. Even in the case of a setback to the plot in Berlin, nothing would have prevented them from carrying out their orders in France, and openly declaring their dissidence. It is certain that such an action could have had vast repercussions in Germany had von Kluge remained firm. As it was, the plotters very nearly succeeded.

At about 9 P.M., on the orders of General von Boineberg, commandant of "Greater Paris," detachments of the second battalion of the 1st Guards Regiment, billeted in the École Militaire, invested the buildings in the avenue Foch, Oberg's private residence, the offices of the rue des Saussaies and the boulevard Lannes. Nowhere did the S.S. put up the least resistance, and at 11 P.M. nearly all the twelve hundred S.S. stationed in Paris, the Gestapo, and the S.D. were under lock and key. Oberg himself, who had been arrested by General Bremer just as he was telephoning to Abetz, allowed himself to be disarmed without a murmur. A single man was missing: Knochen. He had gone to dine with his friend, Zeitschell, at the Embassy. One of his subordinates telephoned him to come immediately to the avenue Foch. Knochen, who was suspicious, preferred to visit General Oberg on the way. There he learned of the latter's arrest and was arrested himself. Taken to the avenue Foch, he found General Bremer in his office. Shortly after midnight all the S.S. leaders, Oberg, Knochen, and the local chiefs of the Gestapo and the S.D. were prisoners, held in the Hôtel Continental, rue de Castiglione, where General Boineberg, whose offices were adjacent in the rue Maurice, had brought them while waiting to decide their fate.

In the meantime, while at the École Militaire it was being planned to shoot the heads of the Gestapo and the S.D. the next morning, von Kluge made his final *volte-face*[9] and notified Berlin, reporting the behavior of Stuelpnagel.

At the same time Stauffenberg called Stuelpnagel from Berlin and told the Parisian conspirators of the fall of the putsch. "The killers who have come to shoot me are already at my door," he said, before hanging up.

The conspirators in France might still have held on but for an unforeseen obstacle. Admiral Krancke, Commander in Chief Group West of the Navy, was notified by Berlin shortly after von Kluge had denounced Stuelpnagel. The conspirators, men used to making plans which solely concerned the Army, had not taken into account the naval forces. When Krancke received the order from Berlin to intervene, he alerted the naval troops quartered in Paris and, from his headquarters in La Muette, sent an ultimatum to Army H.Q. threatening to use force if Oberg and the

---

[9] His cowardice did not save him. Relieved of his command for not having discovered the plot in time, he committed suicide on August 19, 1944, by taking cyanide, near Clermonten-Argonne, rather than return to Germany, where he feared he would be judged and hanged.

S.S. were not immediately released. It was the *coup de grâce*. To pursue operations that had no chance of success was folly. At about one o'clock in the morning, when repression had already begun in Berlin, the soldiers in Paris had to release their prisoners and return their weapons. The following morning, order was restored and the Parisians did not suspect for a moment what extraordinary events had taken place that night in the bosom of the German hierarchy in Paris.

In Berlin, the principal heads of the conspiracy had been murdered on the night of the 20th–21st. General Fromm, Stauffenberg's immediate superior, who had been heavily compromised with the conspirators, thought to save his life by turning upon his colleagues. As soon as he was convinced that the putsch could not succeed, he rallied a few subordinate officers who, like himself, had played the turncoat, and at about 11 P.M. suddenly arrested Stauffenberg, Beck, Generals Olbricht, Hoepner, Colonels Mertz and Haeften, all leaders of the putsch, in the offices of the War Ministry in the Bendlerstrasse.

To rid himself of dangerous witnesses, Fromm declared that a court-martial had condemned four of them to death: Stauffenberg, Olbricht, Mertz, and Haeften. Beck had already been handed a revolver and enjoined to commit suicide; this he had tried to do, but so clumsily that he had only wounded himself. While Stauffenberg and his three companions were being shot in the courtyard by the light of a car's headlights, Beck missed for the second time. On Fromm's orders a sergeant took him out into the corridor and finished him with a bullet in the neck.

A few minutes later Skorzeny invaded the ministry with a platoon of S.S. At one o'clock in the morning, when Hitler could finally speak on the radio, the surviving conspirators were already in the cells of the Gestapo at Prinz Albrechtstrasse.

In a few hours the Army had been crushed by Himmler and his S.S. For the first time the soldiers had dared to challenge their rivals, but cowardice among themselves had caused the effort to collapse. Himmler was triumphant; the Gestapo achieved the absolute control of which it had dreamed for years, and instituted an inquiry which was to allow it, by prying into the most secret recesses of the staffs, to settle all its old accounts.

In Paris, Knochen entrusted the inquiry to Stindt, Boemelburg's successor at the head of the Gestapo. Lieutenant Colonel Hofacker, who had insured the liaison between Stuelpnagel and the Berlin group, was arrested, as were Colonel von Linston, Lieutenant Colonels Fink and Falkenhausen.[10]

As for Stuelpnagel, he had been summoned to Berlin the day after the putsch. Von Kluge's report had taken effect, and Stuelpnagel realized at once that he was lost. Late in the morning, on the 21st, he set out by car for Berlin. A breakdown caused him to stop at Meaux, and the second car ordered to complete the journey did not arrive until 3 P.M. Outside Verdun, Stuelpnagel ordered his chauffeur to change route and the journey continued in the direction of Sedan, across the battlefield where as a young captain he had fought in 1916. On leaving Vacheraucheville, he was forced to turn off to reach the Meuse and, getting out of the car, ordered the chauffeur to drive on to the next village where he would rejoin him on foot, to take the "stiffness out of his legs." Hardly had the car driven off than Stuelpnagel fired a bullet into his temple and slumped into the ditch.

Fished out by his chauffeur and taken to the Verdun Military Hospital, Stuelpnagel's life was saved. But the bullet which had pierced the skull made him blind.

He was sufficiently recovered to appear on August 29 with the other prisoners before the bloodthirsty Freisler and his "People's Court." Everyone was condemned to death and hanged in the courtyard of the Ploetzensee prison in Berlin. With exquisite cruelty they were slowly strangled after being suspended on butcher's hooks. Hitler had said, "I want them to be hanged like butcher's meat." Stuelpnagel had to be led by the hand to the gallows. The repression lasted for several months and was extended to the friends and families of the conspirators. Under its pseudo-judicial cover it was even more savage than the Roehm purge of 1934.

Himmler and Kaltenbrunner gave themselves over to a veritable orgy of cruelty. There were more than seven thousand arrests and probably

---

[10] Falkenhausen and Hofacker were arrested by the elegant Maulaz, the haunter of the Paris salons.

over five thousand executions.[11] Canaris had been dragged from his retirement, although he had played no part in the final plot. In prison for several months, he too was hanged on April 9, 1945. The cowardly Fromm, who had caused Beck, Stauffenberg, and their companions to be shot, was shot in March 1945. Falkenhausen was saved by the American troops in May 1945, just as he was about to be executed. He was later sentenced as a war criminal. Many of the compromised officers had preferred to commit suicide than be arrested and judged. Rommel was forced to kill himself on October 14.

In Paris, where Oberg and Knochen had resumed their activities, the rapid development of the military situation put a brake on the inquiry. General Boineberg, who had only carried out Stuelpnagel's orders and whose personal feelings were not known, was transferred to the Reserve, and the command of Greater Paris given to General von Choltitz.

Toward the end of July the Allies, by now fully consolidated on French soil, launched their offensive for the liberation of France. On the 24th the breakthrough at Avranches began. On the 28th Coutances and Granville fell, Avranches on the 30th, Rennes on August 3, Nantes and Angers on the 10th. All this time Oberg, Knochen, and the Gestapo services imperturbably carried out their tasks and busied themselves with dispatching to Germany the last convoys of deportees, emptying the Compiègne camp, Romainville fort, and the other prisons which still contained several thousand inmates. The final deportations were carried out in the middle of the battle under aerial bombing in appalling conditions. In the convoy which left from Compiègne on July 2, men went mad and fighting broke out among the prisoners. The stifling heat, the thirst, the despair of leaving just as liberation seemed imminent made these last deportees veritable martyrs.

By the time Compiègne was in sight, every truck already contained several corpses. More than six hundred prisoners perished before arrival at Dachau. In Bremen station the German Red Cross nurses remained deaf to all supplication and refused to give any water, even to the dying.

[11] The plausible figure of 4,980 executions has been put forward, but it is difficult to guarantee this as completely accurate.

On August 15, when von Kluge gave the general order to retire, and the Canadians were preparing to take Falaise, another convoy of 2,453 deportees left for Germany.

Since mid-July the representatives of the Resistance Movement had tried to negotiate with the Germans to put a stop to these deportations. M. Raoul Nordling, the Swedish Consul-General who had accepted this delicate mission, contacted von Choltitz, the newly appointed commander of Greater Paris and the German Embassy. Herr Nordling transmitted the notes and suggestions prepared by M. Parodi, the Paris representative of General Koenig, now chief of the French Home Forces, and by Count Alexandre de Saint-Phalle. But although von Choltitz and a few others were in favor of an agreement, no German dared to accept the responsibility. On August 17 Oberg completed his last preparations for leaving. His records and the Gestapo files had left Paris at the beginning of the month. During the night of August 16–17, the staff of the German police services reached Châlons-sur-Marne. On the 17th all the services left Paris for Nancy and Province. The only people to remain in the capital were Oberg himself, Knochen, and their immediate staffs. They, too, prepared their luggage.

This imminent departure gave courage to the soldiers and the diplomats. On the morning of August 17 von Choltitz suddenly decided to act, on condition that the agreement was accepted and signed by the services of the Militaerbefehlshaber at the Hôtel Majestic. But at the Majestic the offices were already deserted, the military administrative services had finished loading their records that morning, and were on their way eastward. They finally found a certain Major Huehm, who agreed to give his signature as representative of the Militaerbefehlshaber in France. The negotiators hurried to see Alexandre de Saint-Phalle, and a protocol agreement was quickly drawn up.

The three paragraphs of the protocol signed by Raoul Nordling and Major Huehm[12] prescribed that, on signature of the agreement, Herr Nordling would "assume direction, surveillance, and responsibility for all political prisoners interned in the five prisons, three hospitals, and three

---

[12] Major Fritz Huehm was killed at Würzburg in 1945.

camps used as places of detention, and also all other places of detention and all evacuation trains, without exception, at the present moment on their way to various destinations." The responsible German authorities were to hand over all their powers to Herr Nordling.

"For his part Herr Nordling agreed to obtain the exchange of five German prisoners of war against one of the above-mentioned political prisoners." This final clause was never put into practice. The Allied advance and the retreat of the Germans precluded its implementation.

The important thing was to obtain the immediate liberation of the French detainees whom, it was feared, might be massacred in their prisons as those in the prison of Caen had been. But although the gates of the Paris prisons were actually opened on August 17, things were quite different at Romainville fort and in the Compiègne camp, where the S.S. or members of the Gestapo or the S.D. refused to carry out von Choltitz' orders, maintaining that they would obey only Oberg's instructions.

At Compiègne, Haupsturmfuehrer Dr. Peter Illers refused to release his prisoners, despite the intervention of MM. de Grammont and de Laguiche, the Red Cross delegates, and even demanded the arrest of all the negotiators, who had to take to their heels. The following morning, August 18, on Oberg's instructions, a convoy of sixteen hundred prisoners was dispatched, nearly all of whom died in Germany.

This was the last order given by Oberg in the capital. On the morning of the same day Oberg, Knochen, Scheer, the head of ORPO, and the last members of the Gestapo, left Paris for Vittel, where they set up temporary headquarters, the O.K.W. having announced that the Front would be stabilized in eastern France.

On August 20 Knochen decided to send a Sonderkommando to Paris with the task of staying there as long as possible, to send radio messages announcing the progress of events. Nosek, who had been in one of the very first groups to reinforce Kochen's Sonderkommando in June 1940, was in command of this expedition. On the 21st he set out for Paris with four cars, a radio car, and eleven men, five of whom were French agents. On the 23rd, when Leclerc's division was at Rambouillet, the Sonderkommando entered the suburbs of the capital. But the atmosphere was so explosive and the Parisians so frantically excited by the imminence of their liberation, that there was a strong risk of them being taken prisoner. Nosek decided to limit his reconnaissance to the suburbs of the city. After reconnaissance as far as the Port de Vincennes and the Port de Montreuil, the commando turned about and took up its quarters at Meaux. Nosek stayed there until August 28 before beating a hasty retreat, which was very nearly cut off by American tanks.

The last units of the Gestapo left Paris under conditions similar to those of their arrival in June 1940. Knochen, the driving force, had stayed at the helm of his sinister ship from the first to the last day—from June 14, 1940, to August 18, 1944. But the French campaign was not yet over for him.

Chapter 22
The Wolves Devour Each Other

In Germany the liquidation of the July 20th conspirators and the execution of Canaris caused a final modification in the services of the R.S.H.A. Amt Mil, which had been formed in the R.S.H.A. to embrace the Abwehr services, was suppressed. Its chief, Colonel Hansen, had been hanged, the staff of the Abwehr was purged and the duties shared between different sections of Amter IV (Gestapo) and VI (S.D.-Ausland). The Gestapo took over the sections dealing with espionage and counterespionage, parachute drops, and sabotage. The S.D. took over military intelligence. Each group of the Gestapo and the S.D. was in future flanked by a subgroup, bearing the same nomenclature followed by the word "Mil."

The plot of July 20 finally persuaded Hitler that he could no longer trust the Army, that "reactionary clique" which he had resolved to tame.

At the suggestion of Martin Bormann, young members of the Party, chosen for their fanaticism, were promoted officers and posted into every unit to spy on the political attitude of their colleagues. They reported directly to Bormann, a fierce guardian of Nazi orthodoxy, anything which did not seem to them sufficiently National Socialist. Thus they denounced the defeatist attitude of the officer corps in the Silesian Army Group, because the latter, tried by a terrible and interminable campaign, had broken before the Russian assault.

Himmler had achieved his crowning ambition and had at last obtained command of an army group. The year 1944, which was just ending, had presented seven new divisions to his S.S. Two additional brigades were still to be formed at the end of the year, consisting of Dutch and French volunteers. Strange volunteers, these militiamen fleeing from their country in enemy trucks to escape punishment, and who, enrolled on the spot, were to form the S.S. Freiwilligen-Sturm-Brigade Charlemagne.

In eastern France the German troops hung on doggedly, in obedience to Hitler's demands. The Allied troops did not reach the Rhine and the German frontier as a whole until the beginning of 1945.

Oberg and Knochen made their general headquarters at Vittel on August 30. Two pieces of bad news had reached them almost as soon as they arrived. The first was an insulting letter from Himmler. The Reichsfuehrer reproached them in very abusive terms for having let themselves be arrested on July 20, without putting up any resistance, and cast a slur on their courage and their loyalty. A few days later, at the end of August, Kaltenbrunner peremptorily recalled Knochen to Berlin. Knochen was under no illusions as to what this meant. During the time he had been in Paris, no one had been able to touch him, for fear of harming the progress of the Gestapo services. The end of the French occupation also put an end to this protection, and now his enemies would have his blood. In fact, as soon as he arrived in Berlin, Kaltenbrunner told him that he was stripped of his rank and had been posted as a private soldier to the Waffen S.S.

Knochen was immediately sent to the Leibstandarte Adolf Hitler and the training camp of Benechau in Czechoslovakia to take a course in anti-tank combat. When about to be posted to a fighting unit he was called to Berlin. This was to tell him that he had been restored to Himmler's graces and that he was to be given a post in the R.S.H.A. On January 15, Knochen was posted to a service whose job it was to perfect the work of the new S.D. groups, which had now assumed the functions of the former Abwehr, where he remained until the final collapse.

At Vittel, Knochen had been replaced by Obersturmbannfuehrer Suhr, former head of the Toulouse section. Himmler had given orders to re-form an organization on the small fragment of French territory still occupied, and to use it as a base for introducing agents into liberated France. These agents were to be recruited mainly from former French collaborators who had taken refuge in Germany.

In September, Himmler visited General Blaskowitz, who after commanding Army Group "G" had just taken over command of Army Group "H" at Gérardmer. He took advantage of this to inspect his agents. This was to be Himmler's last journey to France. A little later Oberg settled at Plainfaing, near Saint-Dié. There he received a visit from Darnand and his adjutant Knipping, who had come to ask his help in obtaining an improvement in their material conditions, which were less than perfect; the militiamen were stationed in Schirmek camp, while waiting for their regroupment in Germany.

It was at Plainfaing on November 7[13] that Oberg issued his last order to the population of a French town. On November 8 the inhabitants of Saint-Dié received orders to evacuate the town. From the 9th to the 14th the town was given over to pillage. The factories were emptied of their stocks, the tools and machinery being sent to Germany. Next all the installations which could not be dismantled were blown up. After this the houses were set on fire. The conflagration lasted three days. Ten men who tried to save their furniture were shot on the spot. Finally, all men between sixteen and forty-five were commandeered to carry out defense work. In actual fact the 943 inhabitants thus collected were deported.

On November 18 Oberg left Plainfaing with his staff, and fell back on Rougemont, near Belfort. He remained there only a few days. The retreat continued via Guebwiller and Ensisheim. On December 1 Oberg, Suhr, and their staffs at last crossed the Rhine, reaching Friburg the same evening. On the 3rd the group reached Zwichau near the Czech frontier, where the services had already been reinstalled on Himmler's orders.

A little later Oberg was appointed Commander in Chief of the Weichsel Army Group, under direct orders from Himmler, who himself had assumed the title of Commander in Chief of the Army Groups of the Upper Rhine. Oberg, having ended the police phase of his career, rejoined the ranks as a fighting S.S.

---

[13] The placard posted up on the town hall of Saint-Dié explained the reason for this evacuation in halting French: "It is the intention of the Wehrmacht to remove the population as far as possible from the combat zone, in order to spare them unnecessary losses and suffering."

The Gestapo continued to busy themselves with France for another few months. Schools of sabotage and espionage were organized by Dr. Kaiser at Friburg and at Stetten, near Sigmaringen, with several specialist branches.

At Friedenthal, Skorzeny organized a training center for intelligence agents and saboteurs. These spy centers recruited their agents from among former members of the P.P.F., the R.N.P., and above all from the militia and the M.S.R. (ex-Cagoulards) who had crossed into Germany. Darnand had been the first to offer his men to Hauptsturmfuehrer Detering, given the job of recruitment at Sigmaringen with his adjutant, Oberscharfuehrer Dr. Hinrichs. Detering was head of the "Fuchs" commando ordered to introduce agents into France.

Finally Darnand received permission to create a special school for the militia, administered and directed by French militiamen and functioning with the aid of instructors from the S.D. and the Gestapo. This autonomous service was under the direction of militiaman Degans, with Filliol for adjutant. The latter was a former Cagoulard killer, who had been one of the torturers of the Militia's Deuzième Bureau.[14] Darnand finished by drawing up a plan for creating a "white maquis" in France.

These spy nets had great difficulty in introducing even a few dozen agents and saboteurs into France. Some of them were introduced clandestinely into Switzerland via the frontier post of Lörrach, near Basle. Several were arrested by the Swiss police; some managed to penetrate into France and even to return to Germany after carrying out their missions. Most of them were very swiftly picked up. Others were dropped by parachute into France in upholstered containers, for the drops had to take place at night and night jumps are dangerous for a badly trained paratrooper. Parachute drops of this type took place in particular in the department of Correze. These agents were arrested a few hours after their landing before carrying out their mission. Some of them committed suicide at the moment of their arrest with a capsule of cyanide which had been issued to them at their briefing. These attempted actions behind the Allied lines were an almost total failure. The military situation had become desperate by the beginning of 1945.

---

[14] Filliol left behind a sinister record in the region of Limoges, where he operated under the name of "Denis."

Born in violence, nourished upon crimes and horror for twelve years, Nazism slowly collapsed in ruins and blood, dragging a whole nation down in its death throes. In the Wagnerian chaos which ensued the "faithfuls" of yesterday, the pure savage Nazis, the "great leaders," the masters of the country, desperately sought their salvation, trying to play their last personal trumps.

Each of these all-powerful men was spied upon by his neighbors and each neighbor knew himself to be spied upon in turn. The slightest faulty step could cost him his life. Underground in his bunker, in the Chancellery, Hitler felt the whole ramshackle edifice of his power collapsing.[15] He knew that all those who yesterday had still acclaimed him, and had committed the most despicable deeds to gain a word of praise had no other thought today but to abandon him. Like the ancient Pharaohs he refused to disappear alone. Those whom he had carried with him to the top must follow him in death, and his maniacal glance scrutinized faces, in which fear hid behind the mask of rigidity and resolution, seeking for signs of treachery. He insisted that no one should escape his fate.

The Fuehrer, who in the old days had galvanized the masses, the great war lord, the leader of men, was now a sick man weighed down by defeat, and the burning eyes of the hunted beast glittered in a gray face already marked for death.

No one could enter the Chancellery without being checked by the S.S. guards. Responsible for his life, they were the only human beings who had retained his confidence. Alone with them, his familiars, these members of the small court who shared his close confinement were spared the contemptuous distrust with which he regarded the whole of the human race. Bormann lived in his shadow. He had triumphed over his rivals by undermining their reputation. Himmler was discredited after having come close to total triumph, to the absolute power so savored by Hitler himself.

Himmler had been the most powerful man in the Reich from August 1944 to March 1945. His last rivals liquidated after July 20, he had become commander of a group of armies—his eternal dream. At this moment he possessed more titles and functions than any other man. He was Minister

---

[15] Hitler left Rastenburg and made his general headquarters in Berlin at the end of November 1944.

of the Interior and of Health, Supreme Head of all the Police Forces, Intelligence, Secret and Espionage Services, both civil and military. Supreme Head of the S.S., he disposed of a veritable army—in the spring of 1945 with a strength of 38 divisions, 4 brigades, 10 battalions or legions (Waffen-Verbaende), 10 staff commandos, and 35 corps of troops and independent groups (Korpstruppen u. Selbstaendige Verbaende). His troops were formidable and fanatical. And finally Himmler controlled a host of Party and State organizations, the ramifications of which extended everywhere. Having become commander of these army groups, he undertook maneuvers which were to allow him to seize the remaining military powers that he lacked. His old political rival, Goering, had been practically eliminated. Despised and ignored, he lived a life of sordid looting in the most decadent luxury. Ribbentrop had also been discredited. His high diplomacy had suffered nothing but setbacks. Goering had treated him in public as a "dirty little champagne peddler," and the Fuehrer had laughed, forgetting the time when he had called him "a new Bismarck."

Goebbels remained powerful, but Bormann was far more powerful. With implacable determination this fanatic had been able to dispossess his rivals. Reichsleiter, chief of the Hess cabinet (the Fuehrer's deputy from 1933–41), then after Hess's flight to England, himself deputy and head of the Party Chancellery, he had held the reins of the whole Party since that date. On April 12, 1943, he had added to these titles that of Secretary to the Fuehrer.

Bormann was fully aware that Himmler was his most dangerous rival, and he was quick to see his aims. He knew that Himmler was no military leader and he staked all his cards on this.

Himmler had a permanent representative at the Fuehrer's headquarters, Obergruppenfuehrer Hermann Fegelein, aide-de-camp to Hitler. This former groom who had become a general insured liaison between Himmler's General Staff at Baden (and later at Prenzlau) and the Fuehrer. Now Fegelein had married Gretel Braun, Eva's sister. Unofficially the Fuehrer's brother-in-law, he lived on intimate terms with him, both as his aide-de-camp and as Eva Braun's relative. Bormann, who rubbed shoulders with him all day, regarded him as an ally.

The shortcomings of Himmler's army command were thrown up in relief, his setbacks amplified, and his inefficiency revealed. In March, after the loss of Pomerania, Himmler was relieved of his command for inefficiency.

In Hungary, where the military situation had become disastrous, the counterattacks were carried out by elite S.S. divisions under the command of veteran Nazi Sepp Dietrich. Bormann saw the opportunity of striking a decisive blow at Himmler.

The S.S. divisions in Hungary were forbidden to wear the special armband of the elite S.S. troops. Sepp Dietrich himself was affected by this sanction as well as all the officers and soldiers of the division, who were the darlings of the regime and the pride of Himmler. Also affected were Leibstandarten Adolf Hitler and Das Reich, the two oldest S.S. divisions and the Hitler Jugend, which had covered itself with glory.

This collective degradation marked the fall of Himmler. He now ceased to be a rival. His military command had kept him for several months away from his high police duties, a dangerous absence in such a tense period. Bormann and ultimately Hitler himself had got into the habit of giving orders direct to Kaltenbrunner, so that Himmler found himself ousted from the true direction, and most of the Fuehrer's instructions did not reach him.

The "Thousand-Year Reich" announced by the prophet of Nazism was in its last hours. The empire of the Herrenvolk was limited to a narrow strip of territory which shrank every hour during the last days of April 1945. The victory of the Party over its enemies, the victory of the Gestapo over its rivals, had been in vain. In the midst of the ruins of what had once been a capital, a few yards away from the smart Unter den Linden Avenue upon which the Russian shells were soon to fall, Hitler from the depths of his bunker continued to issue orders which no longer reached the troops for which they were intended. Usually these troops no longer existed.

On April 10, feigning to yield to the insistence of his entourage, Hitler decided to transport his headquarters to his Berghof eyrie, and his staff left for Berchtesgaden where he was to join them later. On the 12th a bombing attack destroyed the rest of the Chancellery, which was set on fire. On the 16th the Russians broke through on the Oder front and advanced on Berlin. But Hitler had not left. His departure, arranged for the 20th—his fifty-sixth birthday—was canceled at the last moment. The Red Army had now reached Lübben, seventy kilometers south of Berlin, and was advancing toward the city through the Spreewald. To the north, Oranienburg was captured and the Russians were thirty kilometers away.

During the night of April 20–21 three men left the ruins of the Chancellery without Hitler's consent: Ribbentrop, Goering, and Himmler. Hitler had given up the idea of going to Berchtesgaden. He knew now that his idea of defending the Bavarian "redoubt" was unrealizable. In his last birthday speech, broadcast on the evening of the 20th, he had announced his decision to remain, whatever happened, in Berlin.

Goering heard this broadcast with a shudder. He had spent this birthday with his Fuehrer and the old Nazi combatants who were still alive and in Berlin: Himmler, Goebbels, Ribbentrop, and Bormann. But Hermann had no intention of dying. To end his life at the bottom of a bunker under a hail of bombs and Russian shells did not seem to him a worthy death. He had already made his plans to leave the city. Time was pressing. Goering slipped out of the bunker and as night fell reached his residence, where a convoy of trucks awaited him.

At the beginning of April Goering had placed in safety his collections, which consisted of works of art stolen from all over Europe. Two special trains were needed to transport this vast booty to Berchtesgaden, where his second wife, the actress Emmy Sonnemann, and his daughter had taken shelter. A few trucks, loaded with the last crates, and a car to transport his staff accompanied Goering's private car in his flight to the south. Following the narrow corridor which still separated the American from the Russian troops, the caravan of the Fuehrer's most "faithful paladin" was able to reach Berchtesgaden without a hitch on the evening of April 21. He was unaware that at the same time Himmler had also fled, his example being followed by Ribbentrop a little later. Both of them, like himself, decided to play his last card, and each one was thinking of himself as the only possible successor to Hitler.

Goering could have considered himself the legitimate successor. After creating the Gestapo he had behaved as a perfect Nazi and a faithful supporter of his leader. The law of June 29, 1941, appointed Goering as Fuehrer, not only in the case of Hitler's demise but also in the case of the Fuehrer being prevented from carrying out his duties even temporarily.

On the strength of this, Goering considered on April 23 that the conditions for his succession had been fulfilled, since Hitler was in no position to govern, and since he had declared to Keitel and Jodl that when the moment came for starting peace parleys the most qualified man would be Goering.

(The Luftwaffe General Koller reported this conversation to Goering on his arrival at Berchtesgaden on April 23.) Goering considered that the least that could be said was that the moment had come. The Americans and the Russians had made contact on the Elbe, and the Red Army had completed its encirclement of Berlin. The hour for the access to supreme power had come at last. Goering, despite the circumstances, was inordinately proud of this.

He convened the Nazi personalities who were in Berchtesgaden: Dr. Lammers, head of the Chancellery; Philip Bouhler, Reichsleiter and head of Hitler's private office; General Koller and the Luftwaffe Colonel Bernd von Brauchitsch, son of the Marshal and Goering's first aide. All of them considered that the Fuehrer's decision to lock himself up in Berlin prevented him from exercising command. With their agreement Goering sent a radio message to Hitler asking for his consent to carry on the government of the Reich "with all freedom of action in foreign and home affairs." In the event of no reply being received by 8 P.M., Goering announced that he would act for the general good.

Goering sent this message out of a feeling of last-moment fear of the man who had for so long been the absolute leader. Events left little hope of the message arriving and still less of a reply being received. At 10 P.M., therefore, on April 23, 1945, Goering could consider himself as the only man qualified to start peace parleys, the tactics of which he had already worked out. But surprisingly enough the message over the air arrived at its destination. Bormann had received it and presented it to Hitler as an act of typical disloyalty and an attempt at the usurpation of power. The time limit given for the reply was, according to Bormann, in the nature of an ultimatum. Hitler flew into one of his hysterical rages, abusing Goering as "a drug addict and corrupt peddler."

Just before 10 P.M. Goering received a short message forbidding him to take any initiative. At the same time an S.S. detachment under Obersturmbannfuehrer Frank arrived and put him under arrest. This was the last maneuver on Bormann's part to settle accounts with his old enemy. He had on his own initiative sent a radio message ordering an S.S. detachment at Berchtesgaden to take the Reichsmarshall into immediate custody,[16] accused

---

[16] To elevate him above the numerous marshals he had appointed, Hitler had created a special title for Goering of "Marshal of the Great German Reich."

of high treason. At the very moment he had thought to reach the summit of his career, Goering saw himself reduced to the condition of a condemned man.

The following morning, April 24, he thought his last hour had come when Kaltenbrunner came to inspect the prisoners (Goering's aide-de-camps had been arrested) and left without saying a word. The same day the Reichsstatthalter of the Upper Danube, Eigruber, decreed that all those in his *Gau* who opposed the will of the Fuehrer would be shot on the spot whatever their rank.

General Koller, who had remained at liberty, moved heaven and earth to get Goering released. On the 29th Goering was transferred under escort to a neighboring *Schloss*.

On May 1 Bormann, taking advantage of the fact that Hitler had committed suicide the night before, sent a message to the commander of the S.S. guard telling him to see that the traitors of April 23 did not escape, but the situation deteriorated from hour to hour. The Americans could arrive at any moment, and the commander of the S.S. guard did not dare to assume responsibility for executing a marshal of the Reich. On May 5 the S.S. were only too pleased to hand over their embarrassing prisoner to a small detachment of the Luftwaffe, before disappearing into the blue. Goering was free. He took advantage of this to propose to Doenitz, Hitler's official successor, his good offices for negotiations with Eisenhower. According to his letter, he did not doubt that "a conversation between marshals" would produce propitious results. The armistice, signed on May 6, failed to make him abandon all hope of still playing a part. When taken prisoner on May 8 by the American troops who had occupied Berchtesgaden, he demanded an interview with General Eisenhower, for whom he had prepared his letter. He was extremely surprised to learn that he would be brought before an international tribunal, together with the principal Nazi leaders, to be judged as a war criminal.

Goering's successor at the head of the Gestapo, Himmler, "*der Treue Heinrich*," had also left Berlin on the night of April 23. But whereas Goering traveled south with his trucks full of pictures, Himmler made his way to the Danish frontier. He intended to play his own game and, without demanding any authorization from his Fuehrer, intended to negotiate with the Allies in an attempt to pull his own irons out of the fire.

This was not merely an improvisation. The clear-thinking Schellenberg had long since realized[17] that the outcome of the war was irremediably determined, and that the fate of Germany (and above all that of the leading Nazis) could not be mitigated except by swift negotiation with the conquerors. Since August 1944 Schellenberg reigned supreme over all the German Intelligence Services and received a mass of information from every country in Europe. His agents in the neutral countries kept him *au courant* with the decisions taken by the Allies and with their intentions. It was obvious that the future boded ill for people such as he. But these same agents could facilitate certain contacts, establish liaisons, and allow conversations and ultimately secret parleys to begin. Schellenberg planned to save his skin, and in order to do this he decided to inveigle Himmler into the game and to leave the stupid Kaltenbrunner outside these maneuvers.

During the summer of 1944 Schellenberg had contrived to meet, in a Stockholm hotel, an American diplomat to whom he had mentioned the possibility of negotiation. This first attempt came to nothing, but Schellenberg informed Himmler, who, after flying into a violent rage, let himself be persuaded that such contacts, carried out in the utmost secrecy, could only be of advantage to them both. Schellenberg then started a sly wheedling campaign. He finally obtained Himmler's permission to draw up certain agreements which he considered as veritable life insurance policies.

At the beginning of 1945 another of Schellenberg's agents, Dr. Hoettl, representing Section VI in Vienna, made contacts in Berne with the American, General Donovan. The object of these maneuvers was to obtain from the Americans a separate peace and the establishment of an alliance against the Russians. This alliance was to materialize in a common pursuit of the war in the East, and to this end Schellenberg's representative tried to obtain a safeguard for Rendulic's army group and for its eventual use by the Americans against the Russians. No setback or snub could ever persuade the Nazis what their position really was. They kept plunging further up the same cul-de-sac. These proposals received no reply, despite several trips by Hoettl to Berne. It is not known whether Schellenberg notified Himmler of these steps, or whether he had decided to launch these "kites" on his own account.

---

[17] From August 1942 onward, according to Schellenberg himself, but he constantly boasts of his perspicacity.

At the end of 1944, at the great Nazi headquarters, a preventive occupation of Switzerland was discussed. Schellenberg and, on his advice, Himmler were against it and the plan was abandoned. Schellenberg had started important negotiations in Switzerland. One of his agents, Dr. Langbehn, had made contact with the Allied representative, but Mueller and Kaltenbrunner, getting wind of these negotiations, started investigations and he had to retreat.

On the other hand, the parleys started with M. Jean-Marie Musy, former President of the Swiss Federation, achieved a positive result. Faithful to Swiss tradition, M. Musy tried to obtain the release to his country of the greatest possible number of Jews detained in concentration camps whose fate seemed to have been sealed in advance: they were to be massacred as soon as the Allied armies penetrated Germany. Himmler agreed to meet M. Musy for the first time at the end of 1944, and then a second occasion on January 12, 1945, at Wiesbaden. He agreed to hand over a certain number of Jews to Switzerland, to be considered as a transit place for Jews "authorized to emigrate." But in exchange the international Jewish organizations, and in particular the American, had to pay an enormous ransom. Finally it was agreed that twelve hundred Jews were to be delivered every fortnight to Switzerland. It was a puny number compared to the tens of thousands of victims who awaited death in the camps, but a few hundred of them had already been wrested from the gas chamber. The first train arrived in Switzerland at the beginning of February 1945, and the Jewish organizations paid five million Swiss francs as ransom, deposited with M. Musy. The press reported the fact, and certain foreign newspapers suggested that as a *quid pro quo* the Swiss had agreed to give asylum after the war to the chief Nazi leaders. Hitler flew into one of his mad rages and forbade any further delivery of prisoners.

M. Musy, however, continued his efforts and did not hesitate to travel several times to Germany, despite his age,[18] the bombing and the risk such expeditions entailed. At the beginning of April he obtained Himmler's agreement that the concentration camps would not be evacuated but left intact to await the arrival of the Allied troops. Until then the prisoners had been flung onto the roads in lamentable convoys, or herded into sealed trucks which traveled in search of a new camp. In certain centers orders had been given to

---

[18] M. Musy at the time was more than seventy.

massacre the captives rather than to let them fall into the hands of the Allies, with the result that the unfortunate Jews were torn between hope and fear when they heard the sound of the approaching battle.

Other efforts were made in the same direction by Hillel Storch, representing the Jewish World Congress; by Dr. Burckhardt, president of the International Red Cross, and by the Swedish Count Folke Bernadotte. These more or less secret negotiations convinced Himmler that he could play a leading part in saving Germany (and his life) by concluding an international agreement.

He had met Count Bernadotte twice: in February and then at the beginning of April 1945. He made him the same promise as he had made to M. Musy: the concentration camps would not be evacuated. Nevertheless he hesitated a long time before committing himself further. The habit of total obedience to the Fuehrer, the fear of the terrible chastisement which awaited him if his double game was discovered, prevented him from crossing the Rubicon. But in this decisive month of April, Himmler was already in disgrace and his S.S. had been degraded; Hitler received him now very rarely, thus releasing him from the power his master had hitherto exercised over him.

On April 19 Himmler had a long conversation with the Finance Minister, Schwerin von Krosigk, while Schellenberg buttonholed Minister of Labor Seldte. Agreement was reached: Hitler was to "abdicate" or disappear, and Himmler was to succeed him and swiftly conclude an honorable peace. These last-minute plotters were as un-realistic as their predecessors. Himmler thought that he would succeed because Count Bernadotte, in the course of their last interview, had suggested that he should succeed Hitler by announcing publicly that the latter could no longer fulfill his duties because of a serious illness. After which he was to dissolve the National Socialist party. Himmler was prepared for this tardy coup, but he wanted to insure that the Allies would agree to negotiate with him.

On April 21, on leaving the Chancellery, Himmler joined Schellenberg, who was waiting to accompany him to Hohenlychen Hospital in the suburbs of Berlin, where a meeting had been arranged with Count Bernadotte. Himmler promised to prevent the evacuation of Neuengamme camp near Hamburg, then asked Count Bernadotte to transmit his proposals to General Eisenhower with whom he desired an interview. Bernadotte was obliged to dispel his illusions on the possibility of playing a political role in the future of Germany, and the meeting came to nothing.

But Himmler had decided to pursue this last straw, which seemed to elude him each time he tried to seize it. Bernadotte having left for Sweden via Lübeck, immediately after the encounter at Hohenlychen, Himmler decided to rejoin him and to make proposals for the cessation of hostilities, together with the elimination of Hitler, which he had finally accepted. Schellenberg took the Lübeck road in advance of Himmler, but on his arrival learned that Bernadotte had already crossed the Danish frontier and was at Apenrode north of Flensburg. He managed to reach him by telephone and obtained a rendezvous at Flensburg on the German-Danish frontier. Here Schellenberg used all his diplomatic skill to persuade the Count to return with him to Lübeck to meet Himmler. Although convinced of the futility of this journey, Bernadotte accepted. On April 23 at eleven o'clock in the evening, the last meeting took place in the cellar of the Swedish Consulate, by the light of candles, for Lübeck, subjected to almost continuous bombing, had been deprived of electricity. After a five-hour talk Count Bernadotte agreed to submit Himmler's proposals to his government, which alone was qualified to judge whether they should in turn be transmitted to the Allies.

Himmler immediately wrote a letter to the Minister of Foreign Affairs in Sweden, M. Christian Guenther, asking him to intercede with the Americans. The following day a declaration by President Truman, formally dismissing any idea of partial capitulation by Germany, sounded the death knell to Himmler's hopes.

On April 22 he learned that Hitler had given orders to execute his former private doctor, Dr. Brandt, because the latter had sent his wife over to the Americans. Brandt had already been arrested in Thuringia, and here was the proof that, from the depths of his bunker, the Fuehrer could still make himself obeyed.

And yet the demented Pharaoh, already half buried in his hypogeum, knew that there was no hope left. On the 22nd he had said to his collaborators, "The war is lost. I shall kill myself." Next day the news of Goering's treachery restored a little of his energy. Incited by Bormann, he thundered against the traitors and cowards and gave orders that they should be chastised. On the 24th the encirclement of Berlin was complete, but Hitler began to hope that the "Wenck" army would come and deliver the besieged city. The Wenck army was a phantom, and on April 27 it was obvious that it would never reach Berlin.

The night before an incident had already aggravated the Fuehrer's spleen. Fegelein, Eva Braun's brother, had also left the bunker. On hearing of his disappearance on the 27th, Hitler had sent a few S.S. to look for him. They had soon found him and brought him back to the bunker, this time as a prisoner. The following day the radio was tuned in to the B.B.C. when the British speaker read a communiqué from the Reuter agency via Stockholm, revealing the interview between Himmler and Count Bernadotte and his proposals for capitulation. This ultimate piece of treachery brought on one of the usual fits of rage and gave rise to a series of final decisions. The Russians, who had already entered Berlin, were approaching the Potsdamer Platz and the last assault could only be a matter of hours. To assuage his anger, Hitler had the unhappy Fegelein shot in the courtyard of the Chancellery and then hastily called a registrar. During the night he married Eva Braun, who had been his mistress for many years, then dictated his will to one of his secretaries.

Goering and Himmler were denied, degraded, and their memory expunged: "Goering and Himmler, apart from their lack of loyalty toward myself, have done considerable wrong to the people and the whole nation by negotiating secretly with the enemy without my knowledge and without my authorization, and by trying illegally to seize the power of the State." Both were expelled from the Party, deprived of all their ranks, functions, and dignities. Admiral Doenitz was appointed Hitler's successor with the title of President of the Reich and Supreme Commander of the Armed Forces.

In a second personal will Hitler designated Bormann as his executor to see that the instructions in his first will of May 2, 1938, were carried out, according to which he left his personal belongings to the Party, with various legacies to his family, servants, and a few friends.

The second phase of this will expressly indicates his decision to commit suicide. "I and my wife have chosen death to escape the shame of deposition or capitulation. It is our wish that our bodies be cremated immediately in the spot where I have carried out the greater part of my daily tasks during these twelve years, which have been devoted to the service of my people." On April 30 at 3:30 P.M. Hitler and Eva committed suicide, the former by firing a bullet through his mouth and the latter by drinking a dose of cyanide.

According to their wishes, their two bodies were carried out immediately into the Chancellery courtyard, sprinkled with petrol, and incinerated.

Hitler dead, Goebbels and his wife resolved to follow his example. At the request of the couple, a doctor who was still among the inhabitants of the bunker killed Goebbels' six children with an injection; then Goebbels and his wife asked an S.S. man to fire a bullet into their necks. The S.S. were only too ready to grant them this favor, after which the eight corpses were taken out into the garden, sprinkled with petrol, and burned. It was about 9 P.M.

While they were still burning the last survivors of the bunker slipped outside to try and cross the Russian lines under cover of darkness. Bormann was among them. He had sent a final telegram to Admiral Doenitz announcing his departure, and still clung to the hope of finding a place in the new government.

According to eyewitnesses, Bormann was killed trying to cross the Russian lines. But their testimonies differ. According to Erick Kempka, Hitler's chauffeur, Bormann was killed by a Russian shell which had burst among the group of fugitives. According to Obergebietsfuehrer Arthur Axmann, head of the Hitler Jugend, Bormann committed suicide by swallowing cyanide after having failed to cross the line.

On the strength of these two testimonies Bormann's death cannot be considered to be a certainty. The International Tribunal at Nuremberg refused to accept it, subpoenaed Bormann to appear, and then judged and sentenced him in contempt.[19] Since then the presence of Bormann has been reported periodically in various parts of the globe. In 1946 his presence was announced in northern Italy, where he had found asylum in a monastery. An S.S. man, who had also lived in hiding in Lombardy for more than two years, insisted that Bormann had died in this monastery and indicated the approximate place of his burial. The inquiry set up at the period came to nought, but it seems possible that Bormann did actually reach Italy, where he found asylum. Later he may have reached South America. Today he is believed to be in Chile, after having lived in the Argentine for several years.

While these events took place, Himmler had started on his last odyssey. On leaving Count Bernadotte at Lübeck, he had wandered around in circles

---

[19] Bormann was the only accused man who was absent. He was condemned to death.

like a wild beast which had fallen into a trap. And in actual fact this piece of land, growing narrower every moment, seemed like a trap about to close. He first made for Berlin, for he did not suspect that his treachery could be known, but found it impossible to enter the city. Then, traveling north, he arrived at his Fürstenberg headquarters.

On the 26th he learned of Goering's treachery, his setback, and the order of arrest issued against the Marshal. Himmler hastily took the road to the Danish frontier to join Schellenberg. He had told the latter to accompany Count Bernadotte to Flensburg and to pursue the negotiations, giving him plenipotentiary powers. Schellenberg made a swift trip to Denmark and arrived at Flensburg on the 30th, to learn that he had been relieved of his duties. Hitler had guessed that he was a party to the initiative taken by Himmler, and had struck at him too. He was replaced by Obersturmfuehrer Wanck, head of the political section of the S.D., and Obersturmbannfuehrer Skorzeny, head of the military section.

Schellenberg then joined his chief at Travemunde, north of Lübeck. Here on May 1 they heard the news of Hitler's suicide and the appointment of Doenitz. Himmler had seen the latter a few days before, on a visit to the combined staff at Plön, a few miles from Lübeck. He decided to confer with him on the measures to be taken.

Schellenberg, who had accompanied Himmler to Plön, contacted Schwerin von Krosigk, a member of the government, and left the following night for Denmark to continue negotiations. After a swift return to Plön he reached Stockholm, where he heard of the capitulation.

As for Himmler, he had followed the new government[20] which had left Plön on May 4 to take up its headquarters at the naval school in Mürwick near Flensburg. A bewildered stream of people milled around in the wake of the new President. Keitel, Jodl, and a number of other soldiers spoke of continuing the fight in Norway. Doenitz had sent for the Reich Commissioner Terboven and Generals Boehme and Lindermann to discuss the possibility of resistance in the Scandinavian countries. A host of Party dignitaries tried to join the new government—incorrigible backroom

---

[20] The Doenitz "government" existed in semblance until May 23, the date on which all its members were arrested. Doenitz appeared before the Nuremberg Tribunal and was condemned to ten years' imprisonment.

strategists incapable of realizing their ruin, little heeding the sufferings of a nation crushed by a total war, while the bombing continued to claim victims at every moment.

It was in this seething mass, a prey to false rumor, that Himmler hid himself when unconditional surrender was finally accepted on May 6. That day the Reichsfuehrer S.S., who had become a liability, was excluded from the new government. Himmler realized at last that he was in danger and disappeared. At midnight on May 8 hostilities ceased on all the European fronts. The guns fell silent for the first time since September 1, 1939.

The whereabouts of Himmler were unknown. It was probable that he went to ground near Flensburg, in company with a few faithful S.S. who, like himself, were eager to escape punishment. For fifteen days he eluded all the searches undertaken by the special Allied detachments, who believed that he was hiding in the neighborhood. His photograph had been distributed to the occupying troops in the region. It is probable that many Germans would have denounced him had they known his hideout.

This situation could not continue, and about May 20 Himmler decided to try and reach Bavaria, with about a dozen S.S. officers. On May 21 a small group of men coming from Hamburg took the Bremervorde road to Bremen. They were soon merged with a crowd of refugees who, chased from their country by the war, were trying to return on foot to what had once been their homes.

It is a low marshy region, a barren plain, cut by waterlogged saline lands and dotted with clusters of stunted pines. Near Teufels Moor—the Devil's Marsh—the crowd slowed down to pass the British control post. One of them approached the barrier and handed the guard a pass made out in the name of Heinrich Hitzinger. He wore a black patch over the left eye, and like most of the refugees wore a composite garb: civil trousers and the jacket of a private soldier of the Wehrmacht. His embarrassed air, his brand-new pass in a crowd of people who were without papers, made him a suspect. The official beckoned to two British soldiers, who took the man into the post and then reported to the security service of the Second Army, which had its headquarters at Luneburg, and the suspect was sent to the nearest camp and placed in a cell. No one had the slightest idea that the man with the black patch was the sinister Himmler, who had shaved off his mustache and put his spectacles in his pocket.

Himmler knew that he would soon be recognized; he decided to play his trump card and asked to speak to the camp commandant. As soon as he entered the room he took off his black patch and introduced himself. "I'm Heinrich Himmler," he said. "It is very important that I speak to Field Marshal Montgomery on a matter of urgency."

Did he still hope to play his part in a tutor government, or did he hope to escape on the subsequent journey? Whatever the case, this revelation caused him to be immediately transferred to the Luneburg headquarters.

At Luneburg all the customary precautions taken for a prisoner of his importance were carried out. A doctor examined him and his clothes were searched. In his pocket a large phial of cyanide was discovered. He was made to put on an old British uniform and locked up to await the arrival of Colonel Murphy, sent specially by Field Marshal Montgomery to attend to the prisoner. On his arrival he inquired as to what security measures had been taken.

"Have you examined his mouth?" he asked. "It is usually beneath the tongue or in a hollow tooth that the Nazis hide their cyanide capsules. The one you found on him was perhaps only a blind."

The doctor prepared to examine Himmler again. But when he ordered him to open his mouth, the latter brought down his jaws with a snap and fell to the ground, killed by the cyanide he had just absorbed.[21]

All attempts to revive him were in vain. In a few minutes the Reichsfuehrer S.S. ended his life lying on the floor among the British soldiers—who kept trying to make him vomit. Later his corpse, photographed by the Allied war correspondents, was buried in a secret place.

Heinrich Mueller, the prize bureaucrat, Himmler's favorite subordinate at the head of the Gestapo, seems to have been the only one to have escaped the death that awaited him. He disappeared at the beginning of May 1945. Several German officers, prisoners of war in Russia, after their repatriation insisted that he was in Moscow. According to Schellenberg, Mueller took advantage of the *Rote Kapelle* affair to establish contact with Soviet agents

---

[21] The Nazi leaders carried a completely watertight capsule of cyanide hidden in their mouths. It had to be crushed for the poison to work. If it were swallowed accidentally the capsule was resistant to digestive juices and had no effect.

and entered their service at the moment of Germany's collapse. Numerous members of the German services tried to save their lives by working for the American, British, and even French services. Some succeeded. Mueller may have chosen to play the same game with the Russians. Although the ruthlessness he showed in pursuing the investigation of the *Rote Kapelle* makes this rather difficult to swallow, it cannot be entirely ruled out. According to the same sources, Mueller died in Moscow in 1948. Later reports suggest that Mueller is today living in Chile with Bormann.

Kaltenbrunner was arrested like Goering, and appeared before the International Military Tribunal at Nuremberg. Both men were condemned to be hanged on October 1, 1946, after a trial which, starting on November 20, 1945, continued for 403 public sessions.

Kaltenbrunner was hanged on October 16 at the same time as Ribbentrop, Keitel, Rosenberg, Jodl, Frank, Frick, Seyss-Inquart, Sauckel, and Streicher. Goering managed to procure a capsule of cyanide. Two hours before the execution Goering crushed his capsule as Himmler had done eighteen months before.

Oberg and Knochen tried to avoid the explanations that would be demanded of them. Oberg had gone to ground on May 8, 1945, in a Tyrolean village, Kirtschberg, near Kitzbühel, under the name of Albrecht Heintze. His respite was to be short-lived. At the end of July, the American military police arrested him and on August 7 handed him over to the French authorities at Wildbad.

Knochen was more skillful. In hiding at Göttingen, in the south of Hanover, he escaped his pursuers for more than seven months. On January 14, 1946, he left his hiding place for the American zone. This was imprudent, for only his immobility had protected him so far. On his arrival on the 16th at Kronach, fifty kilometers north of Bayreuth, he was arrested by the American military police. After a stay in various camps, including Dachau, he was handed over to the French authorities, after having testified at Nuremberg in the trials of Kaltenbrunner and Ribbentrop. He arrived in Paris on November 9, 1946.

Oberg and Knochen appeared before the Parisian Military Tribunal sitting in the Cherche-Midi prison on February 22, 1954, after a difficult preparation, in the course of which Oberg was interrogated 386 times. More than ninety kilos of documents had been assembled and the prosecution's dossier amounted to no fewer than 250 pages. But the trial had to be adjourned once more, and it was not until October 9, 1954, that both Oberg and Knochen were condemned to death. The ex-ambassador Abetz had been condemned to twenty years' forced labor in 1949, but had benefitted by a pardon and been released in 1954. ...[22]

This pardon, foreseen from the very outset, had to wait ratification until April 10, 1958, the date on which a presidential decree commuted the death sentence to that of forced labor for life. The sentence was once more reduced by a decree of December 31, 1959, to twenty years' forced labor from the date of sentence.

Adolf Eichmann, directly responsible for the death of millions of innocent people, held out much longer. Having managed to reach South America in 1952, he wandered about for three years in the Argentine, Brazil, Paraguay, and Bolivia, finally settling in Buenos Aires in 1955. Rejoined by his wife and two sons, he worked in the Mercedes-Benz factory in the suburbs of Buenos Aires. He had managed to fabricate a civil status under the name of Ricardo Klement. His facade as a small, peaceful employee did not manage to save him. On May 13, 1960, a group of Israeli agents kidnaped him in the streets on his return from work. Transported in secret to Israel, Eichmann was tried at Jerusalem in a public trial which opened on April 11, 1961, and ended on December 15 with his death sentence.

Eichmann was hanged on June 1, 1962, in Ramleh prison. His body was cremated and his ashes dispersed at sea the same night. With him disappeared one of the last surviving heads of the Gestapo.

Thus the majority of the leading figures in the story of the Gestapo, suffered an end which was in keeping with their lives. This is the only just thing about their sinister existence, each one a reflection in miniature of that period of "blood, sweat, and tears."

With them the complicated edifice of the Gestapo, the pivot of Nazism, disappeared. Its masterpieces of technique, its giant filing systems which covered all Europe, its records which housed the most intimate secrets of millions of people, went up in flames under the carpet bombing rained down

---

[22] Otto Abetz and his wife were killed on May 5, 1958, in a car crash on the Cologne-Ruhr Autobahn. Abetz at the time was a reporter on the weekly **Fortschritt**.

on the German cities, or were blown away by the wind on the muddy roads, slipping from gutted trucks, under the wheels of the convoys of soldiers or refugees, driving around in circles in a country besieged from all sides. Everything that remained intact was to fall into the hands of the conquerors and formed the basis for the overwhelming charges against those who had devoted all their efforts to creating them.

The nightmare was over, and yet an immense lassitude remained; a taste of ashes and tears were mingled with the liberty restored. This prodigious edifice left in the memory a picture of an instrument of terror which had been responsible for the most incredible accumulation of suffering, tears, and mourning in history. It left also a legacy of shame. For the Gestapo has shown us man in a distorting mirror, and forced us to realize that this terrifying creature can exist among us.

The crimes of Nazism are not the crimes of one nation. Cruelty, a taste for violence, the religion of force, ferocious racialism, are not the prerogative of a period or of a people. They are of all ages and of all countries. They have biological and psychological bases which it is by no means certain that we shall escape again. The human being is a dangerous wild animal. In normal periods his evil instincts remain in the background, held in check by the conventions, habits, laws, and criteria of civilization, but let a regime come which not only liberates these terrible impulses but makes a virtue of them, then from the depths of time the snout of the beast reappears, tears aside the slender disguise imposed by civilization, and howls the death cries of forgotten ages.

What Nazism, epitomized by the Gestapo, tried to realize (and almost succeeded in realizing) was the destruction of man as we know him and as thousands of years have fashioned him. The Nazi world was an empire of total force, with no restraints. It was a world composed of masters and slaves, in which gentleness, kindness, pity, the respect for law, and a taste for freedom were no longer virtues, but inexpiable crimes. It was a world in which one could only obey by crawling, killing on orders, and dying oneself in silence if one could not howl with the wolves. It was a world where people exterminated for pleasure and where the murderers were treated as heroes. It already seems far away, like a nightmare one would prefer to forget. And yet the poisoned yeast is still ready to rise. Men have not the right to forget so quickly. They have not the right. Never. . . .

The adventure which ravaged Germany, which left that unfortunate country dislocated, broken, and tainted with opprobrium, might have happened to any nation. If a people is subjected to a regime composed of obsessional propaganda, terror, total militarization, denunciation, and surveillance, and if one inculcates in its youth the delirious principles of Nazism; if the criminals are glorified; if a nation is deprived of all morality and persuaded that it is an elect people; a Herrenvolk, the final result will always be the same. What nation could have resisted the pressure? What people could resist a similar regime tomorrow?

For the problem remains and will always remain in its entirety.

The German example is already fading. Already in the four corners of the world the survivors, those who regret the passing of Nazism, are sniffing at the changing wind. If men have short memories, if the circumstances prove favorable, when times of trouble or the absence of solid safeguards permit it, the bloody tide could once more be unleashed.

And who will be tomorrow's victims?

APPENDICES

I. THE INTERNAL STRUCTURE OF THE R.S.H.A.

From its creation, the R.S.H.A. was divided into seven Amter.[1]

Amt I[2]: *Personnel service for the entire R.S.H.A.* Successive leaders: Dr. Best from its creation to July 1940;[3] Streckenbach from July 1940 to the beginning of 1943; Schulz from the beginning of 1943 to November 1943; Ehrlinger from November 1943 to the capitulation.

Amt II: *Administrative and economic questions.* Divided into four groups:

II A: Premises, upkeep, pay, accountancy questions.

II B: Economic questions, relations with the Ministry of Justice, prisoners (with the exception of the prisons and the camps), transport of prisoners.

II C: Material administration of the active services, SIPO-S.D.

II D: Technical group (in particular car service). Successive leaders, Dr. Best from creation to July 1940, Nockemann, Siegert, Spacil.

Amt III: *Internal S.D.,[4] Party organization.* Active intelligence service divided into five groups. Its main strength comprised three to four hundred agents.

III A: Questions concerning law and the structure of the Reich. (Subgroup III A-4 compiled regular reports on public opinion and the attitude of the population.)

III B: Problems relating to the "ethnic community of the Reich." Ethnic minorities, race, and public health.

---

[1] Amt (plural **Amter**), meaning office or service.

[2] Amter I and II were the administrative services of the whole R.S.H.A.

[3] Dr. Best after this date held important posts in Paris at the Direction of Military Administration.

[4] Less the branch known as S.D.I. (Search for enemies). Absorbed by the Gestapo on the creation of R.S.H.A It was Amt III which directed the immense network of spies operating in Germany.

III C: Cultural matters, science, education, the arts, and the press. Intelligence in religious circles.[5]

III D: Economic questions, surveillance of industry and the industrialists, supplies, labor, commerce, etc. Group G: brief "honorary agents"—"high society" espionage.

Leaders: S.S. Gruppenfuehrer Otto Ohlendorf from the beginning to the end.[6]

Amt IV: *Gestapo, State organization*. Active service invested with executive powers (right of arrest) in political matters. Its head office employed fifteen hundred agents. Operational duties: The search for opponents of the regime and repression. Comprised six groups:

IV A: Opponents of National Socialism: Marxists, Communists, "reactionaries," and liberals. Countersabotage and general security measures. Group IV A comprised as many as six subgroups.

IV B: Political activity of the Catholic and Protestant churches, religious sects, Jews, Freemasons. Was divided into five subgroups. (Subgroup IV B-4, entrusted with the "final solution" of the Jewish problem, was directed by Adolf Eichmann.)

IV C: Preventive detention, protective custody. Press. The affairs of the Party, compilating of dossiers, card index.

IV D: Territories occupied by Germany. Foreign workers in Germany.

The subgroup IV D-4 was in charge of the "Western territories"— Holland, Belgium, and France. Its leader, Karl Heinz Hoffmann,[7] compiled the order "Nacht und Nebel" (Night and Fog), which resulted in the disappearance of thousands of deportees.

IV E: Counterespionage (C-E) Six groups: IV E-1: General problems of counterespionage. Counterespionage in the factories of the Reich. IV E-2: General economic problems. IV E-3; Countries of the West. IV E-4:

---

[5] Part of the personnel of III C was transferred to the Gestapo on May 12, 1941, at the most bitter moment of the struggle against the churches.

[6] Ohlendorf also commanded an Einsatzgruppe in the East. Cf. Part Five, Chap. 18.

[7] Former political adviser to the Gestapo at Düsseldorf. Later head of the SIPO in Holland, then deputy leader of the Gestapo in Denmark.

Scandinavian countries. IV E-5: Countries of the East. IV E-6: Countries of the South.

IV F: Frontier Police. Passports, identity cards. Foreign police forces.

From 1941 the head of Amt IV disposed of an additional independent group, Referat N, which supervised the centralization of intelligence.[8]

Leader: Heinrich Mueller from the beginning to the end.

Amt V: *KRIPO, State organization*. Active service with executive power in criminal matters. Its head office employed 1,200 agents. Divided into four groups:

V A: Criminal police and preventive measures.

V B: Repressive criminal police. Crimes and misdemeanors.

V C: Identification and searches.

V D: Technical criminal institute of the SIPO (Gestapo & KRIPO).

Successive leaders: Artur Nebe, until July 20, 1944.[9] Panzinger from this date until the end.

Amt VI: *External S.D. (S.D.-Ausland)*.[10] Party organization. Intelligence abroad. Its head office employed between 300 and 500 agents according to the periods. Divided into six groups and subsequently into eight in the following years.

VI A: General organization of the intelligence services. Control of the activities of the S.D. Sections.[11]

VI B: Direction of espionage activities in western Europe. Three subgroups: VI B-1: France; VI B-2: Spain and Portugal; VI B-3: North Africa.

VI C: Espionage in the zone of Russian influence. Comprised a subgroup VI C-13: Arab section, and the "Sonderreferat," VI C-Z (special section) for committing sabotage in the U.S.S.R.

VI D: Espionage in the American zone of influence.

---

[8] During its 5½ years of life Amt IV underwent various internal transformations, but its organization and attributes remained the same.

[9] Artur Nebe was hanged after the July 20 plot. He had also commanded an Einsatzgruppe in the East.

[10] A competitor of the Abwehr, the military intelligence.

[11] This attribute was withdrawn in 1941.

VI E: Espionage in eastern Europe.

VI F:[12] The necessary technical means as a whole of Amt VI.

Amt VI exploited a great number of societies abroad and briefed several thousand agents. One of the most famous was Eliazar Bazna, known as "Cicero," briefed in Ankara by S.S. Sturmbannfuehrer Moyzisch, placed in Ankara by Schellenberg.

Successive leaders: Heinz Jost until the beginning of 1941.[13] Walter Schellenberg from this date until the end.[14] In 1942 Schellenberg created Group VI G to exploit all scientific intelligence and Group S for the preparation and execution of "material, moral, and political sabotage," which was entrusted to Otto Skorzeny.

Amt VII:[15] *Written documentation.* Ideological research into the opponents of the regime: Freemasonry, Jewry, the churches, liberals, Marxists. Party organization composed of members of the S.D.

Three groups:

VII A: Research and centralization of documentation.

VII B: Exploitation of the documentation. Establishment of syntheses. Biographical notes. Written commentaries, etc.

VII C: Centralization of the records. The perfecting of methods of classification, exploitation, and filing systems. Upkeep of museum, library, photo records, for the whole of the R.S.H.A.

[12] The leader of VI F was Naujocks, the author of the faked attack at Gleiwitz, who also minted false notes in the special workshops of subgroup VI W-1.

[13] Recalled and sent to the Eastern front as a private.

[14] Formerly head of Group A. Was only thirty-two when he became head of Amt VI. Himmler called him his "Benjamin."

[15] Amter I, II, and VII were merely a home service and had no sections abroad.

II. THE SECOND OBERG-BOUSQUET AGREEMENT

OBJECT: The communal work of the German and French police forces in newly occupied territory.

At a joint meeting (April 16, 1943) of the chief of the Security Police (SIPO-S.D.), the command, and the regional prefects of the newly occupied territories, I revealed the following rules after an agreement with the general secretary of the French police, Bousquet, for the communal work of the German and French police forces in the newly occupied territories.

1. The German and French police forces are warned that their common task is to maintain law and order efficiently in the field of operations of the German Army in the newly occupied territories; to combat preventively and to preserve with all the means at their disposal the security of the German Army and the interests of the German Reich; also the pacific collaboration of the French people against the attacks of Communists, terrorists, enemy agents, and saboteurs, as well as those who incite them—Jews, Bolsheviks, and Anglo-Americans. To this end they will collaborate very closely and continuously. The French police in this domain will combat these adversaries on its own responsibility and will at the same time assist the services of the Hoehere S.S. and Polizeifuehrer by transmitting to them immediately all useful information, and by helping them in every other respect. The German police authorities will, for their part, keep the French police informed, passing on the information given the informers, which might be important in taking police measures.

2. The Hoehere S.S. and Polizeifuehrer will notify as far as possible in advance the general secretary of the French police of all the principal measures taken by the German police affecting the common task.

3. All joint police measures which may prove necessary in the interests of the security of the German troops will in principle be ordered and carried out by the local French authorities on their own responsibility. The Hoehere S.S. and Polizeifuehrer will transmit to the general secretary of the French police the corresponding German wishes.

4. The services of the Security Police and the S.D. and the services of the ordinary police will collaborate with the regional prefects and the services of the French police, in the execution of all police measures. The Hoehere S.S. and Polizeifuehrer and the general secretary of the French police—each for their part—will issue the necessary instructions.

5. The German police will conduct its own executive operations only in the case when this is found to be necessary in the course of its duty—the security of the German Army and its arrangements. Apart from this, executive measures will be left in principle to the French police.

French malefactors arrested by the French police for crimes in common or political law will be brought before French tribunals and judged according to French law.

An exception to this rule will exist for any person, irrespective of nationality, found guilty of an attempt against nationals of the German Army or of an act of sabotage against German military installations, or of preparations or attempts to this end. In these cases the persons arrested will be handed over by the French police.

In these special cases an arrangement will be made between the Hoehere S.S. and Polizeifuehrer and the general secretary of the French police. The persons arrested will remain in the hands of the French police, but will be interrogated by the German police, who are to be given access to the files.

The interrogations will take place in French police stations in the presence of a representative of the French police.

In these circumstances the request will be addressed either by the Hoehere S.S. and Polizeifuehrer to the general secretary of the French police or by the commander answerable to the regional police superintendent.

6. It is firmly understood that the services of the Hoehere S.S. and Polizeifuehrer will not force the services of the French police to choose hostages, and in no case will persons arrested by the French police be taken by the German authorities as hostages by way of reprisals.

7. The Hoehere S.S. and Polizeifuehrer, convinced that only a well-equipped police and *gendarmerie* are in a position to insure the common mission, will take steps to speed up the reorganization, re-equipment, and rearmament of the French police and *gendarmerie*.

He will cast a benevolent eye on the plans submitted to him by the general secretary of the French police.

These rules are based on the broad lines fixed on July 29, 1942, for collaboration between the German and French police forces in the formerly occupied territories. They insure the German police, by the recognition of the principle of the sovereignty of the French Government in the newly occupied territories, the prerogatives for execution incumbent upon it in its own domain. To this effect the settling of particular cases will intervene as far as they are necessary by particular agreements with the general secretary of the French police.

Signed: OBERG
Gruppenfuehrer and Generalleutnant der Polizei
At the German Embassy in Paris.

SUGGESTED BIBLIOGRAPHY FOR FURTHER READING

Publications by Allied or Neutral governments

Documents and Materials relating to the Eve of the Second World War, 1937–39. 2 vols. Moscow: Foreign Language Publishing House, 1948.

Documents Concerning German-Polish Relations and the Outbreak of Hostilities between Great Britain and Germany. London: His Majesty's Stationery Office, 1939. (The British Blue Book.)

Documents on German Foreign Policy, 1918–45. Series D, 1937–45. 10 vols. Washington: U. S. Department of State.

Le Livre Jaune Français. Documents diplomatiques, 1938–39. Paris: Ministère des Affaires Etrangères. (The French Yellow Book.)

Nazi Conspiracy and Aggression. 10 vols. Washington: U. S. Government Printing Office, 1946.

Trial of the Major War Criminals before the International Military Tribunal. 42 vols. Published at Nuremberg.

Trials of War Criminals before the Nuremberg Military Tribunals. 15 vols. Washington: U. S. Government Printing Office, 1951–52.

Publications of the N.S.D.A.P. and official German publications

In principle the publications of the N.S.D.A.P. were issued by the "Zentralverlag der N.S.D.A.P." in Munich.

Alquen, Gunther d', official historian of the S.S.: *Die S.S., N.S.D.A.P. publication*. Munich, 1939.

Baynes, Norman H., ed: *The Speeches of Adolph Hitler, April 1922-August 1939*. 2 vols. New York, 1942.

Das Nationalsozialistische Jahrbuch (Annual report of the N.S.D.A.P.). Several editions exist.

Das Schwarze Korps, the official organ of the S.S. Published under the direction of Gunther d'Alquen.

Das Organisationsbuch der N.S.D.A.P. (Organization Register). Several editions exist.

Goebbels, Joseph: *Der Nazi-Sozi*. Munich, 1932.

Goering, Hermann: *Reden und Aufsätze* (Speeches and articles). Munich, 1938.

Himmler, Heinrich: *Die S.S. als Anti-Bolchewismus Kampforganisation*, 1939.

Hitler, Adolf: *Mein Kampf.* Boston, 1943. The unexpurgated edition in English translation was published by Houghton Mifflin. (German original, Munich, 1925, 1927.)

———: *Adolf Hitler's Reden* (Hitler's Speeches). Munich, 1934.

Ley, Robert: *Der Weg zu Ordensburg* (N.S.D.A.P. publication).

Lutze, Victor: *Organisation und Ziele der S.A.*

Voelkischer Beobachter, the daily paper of the N.S.D.A.P.

General Works

Abetz, Otto, *Histoire d'une politique franco-allemande.* Paris: Stock.

Assmann, Kurt: *Deutsche Schicksaljahre.* Wiesbaden, 1950.

Bayle, François: *Croix gammée ou caducée.* Freiburg, 1950 (a documented account of the Nazi medical experiments).

———: *Psychologie et Ethique du national-socialisme.* Paris: P.U.F., 1992.

Bernadotte, Count Folke: *The Curtain Falls.* New York, 1945.

Best, Captain S. Payne: *The Venlo Incident.* London, 1950.

Billig, Joseph: *Le Commissariat aux questions juives.* Paris: Editions du Centre, 1955–57.

Boldt, Gerhard: *In the Shelter with Hitler.* London, 1948.

Bryant, Sir Arthur: *The Turn of the Tide—A History of the War Years Based on the Diaries of Field Marshal Lord Alanbrooke, Chief of the General Imperial Staff.* London, 1953.

Bullock, Alan: *Hitler—A Study in Tyranny.* New York, 1964.

Craig, Gordon A.: *The Politics of the Prussian Army, 1940–1945.* New York, 1964.

Daluces, Jean (appears to be a pseudonym): *Le Troisième Reich.* Paris: André Martel, 1950.

Desoille, H.: *L'Assassinat systématique des prisonniers malades par les médecins nazis* (La Presse médicale, mai-octobre 1945).

———: *En marge de la psychologie du bagne: Le bagne nazi* (*Archives de médecine sociale,* octobre 1946).

Desoille et Laffite: *Psychologie criminelle des hitlériens* (*Annales de médecine légale,* juin-juillet 1947).

Diels, Rudolph: *Lucifer ante Portas.* Zurich, 1950.

Documents concerning the story of the July 1934 putsch, according to official sources, Vienna, 1934.

DuBois, Josiah E., Jr.: *The Devil's Chemists.* Boston, 1952.

DuBost, Charles: *Le Procès de Nuremberg.* Paris, 1947.

Fitzgibbon, Constantine: *20th July.* New York, 1956.

François, Jean: *L'Affaire Roehm-Hitler.* Paris: Gallimard, 1946.

François-Poncet, Andre: *The Fateful Years.* New York, 1949.

Friedman, Filip: *This Was Oswiecim* (*Auschwitz*). London, 1946.

Gisevius, Hans Bernd: *To the Bitter End.* New York, 1998.

Goebbels, Joseph: *The Goebbels Diaries, 1942–1943,* edited by, Fred Taylor. New York, 1984.

Goerlitz, Walter: *History of the German General Staff, 1657–1945.* Whitefish, 2007.

———: *Der Zweite Weltkrieg, 1939–45.* 2 vols. Stuttgart, 1951.

Greiner, Joseph: *Das Ende des Hitler-Mythos.* Vienna, 1947.

Gritzbach, Erich: *Hermann Goering, the man and his work.* Newport Beach, 1986.

Guerber, André: *Himmler et ses crimes.* Paris, 1946.

Gumbel, E. I.: *Vier Jahre politische Mörde.* Berlin, 1922.

———: *Verschwörer.* Berlin, 1984.

Harris, Whitney R.: *Tyranny on Trial—the Evidence at Nuremberg.* Dallas, 1999.

Hassell, Ulrich von: *The Von Hassell Diaries, 1938–1944.* Whitefish, 2007.

Heiden, Konrad: *A History of National Socialism.* London, 1971.

———: *Hitler—A Biography.* New York, 1936.

———: *Der Führer.* New York, 1999.

Henderson, Neville: *The Failure of a Mission.* Whitefish, 2005.

Hoettl, Wilhelm (Walter Hagen): *The Secret Front: The Story of Nazi Political Espionage*. New York, 2003.

Hofer, Walther: *War Premeditated, 1939*. London, 1955.

Hossbach, General Friedrich: *Zwischen Wehrmacht und Hitler*. Hanover, 1949.

Jouvenel, Betrand de: *La Décomposition de l'Europe libérale*. Paris: Plon, 1941.

Junger, Ernst: *Diaries*. 2 vols. Paris, 1951, 1953.

Kogon, Eugen: *The Theory and Practice of Hell*. New York, 2006. (The German original: *Der SS Staat und das System der deutschen Konzentrationslager*. Munich, 1946.)

Krosigk, Count Lutz Schwerin Von: *Es geschah in Deutschland*. Tuebingen, 1951.

Le Livre Noir, La Situation des Juifs en Allemagne. Comité des Délégations juives. Paris, 1934.

Livre Brun sur l'incendie du Reichstag et la terreur hitlérienne. Paris: 1993.

Lubetzki, J.: *La Condition des Juifs en France sous l'occupation allemande. La Législation raciale*. Paris: Editions du Centre, 1945.

Lutz, E. H. G.: *Die Goldenen Hände*. French translation: *Les Mains d'Or*. Paris: Plon, 1954.

Meinecke, Friedrich: *The German Catastrophe* Cambridge, 1950.

Michelet, Edmond: *Rue de la Liberté (Dachau)*. Paris: Editions du Seuil, 1998.

Munzenberg, Willi: *Propaganda als Waffe*. Paris, 1937.

Nazifuehrer sehen Dich an 33. Paris: Editions du Carrefour, 1935. Published by the anti-Nazi refugees.

Neumann, Franz: *Behemoth, the Structure and Practice of National Socialism*. New York, 1966.

Papen, Franz Von: *Memoirs*. New York, 1953.

Pertinax: *The Grave Diggers of France*. New York, 1944.

Rauschning, Hermann: *Time of Delirium*. New York, 1946.

———: *The Revolution of Nihilism*. Whitefish, 2005.

———: *The Conservative Resolution*. New York, 1941.

———: *The Voice of Destruction*, Whitefish, 2004.

Reed, Douglas: *The Burning of the Reichstag*. New York, 1934.

Reitlinger, Gerald: *The Final Solution—The Attempt to Exterminate the Jews of Europe, 1939–1945*. Washington D.C., 1987.

———: *The SS—Alibi of a Nation*. New York, 1989.

Ropke, Wilhelm: *The German Question*.

Russell, Lord Russell of Liverpool: *The Scourge of the Swastika*. London, 2006.

Schellenberg, Walter: *Der Labyrinth* English translation: *Memoirs of Walter Schellenberg*. New York, 2000.

Schirer, William: *The Rise and Fall of the Third Reich*. London: Folio, 2004.

Schlabrendorff, Fabian von: *They Almost Killed Hitler*. Whitefish, 2007.

Scholl Inge: *Die weisse Rose*. English translation: *The White Rose*. Middle town, 1983.

Schramm, Wilhelm Von: *Der 20. Juli in Paris*. Bad Woerishorn, 1953.

Schuschnigg, Kurt Von: *Austrian Requiem*. New York, 1946.

Strasser, Otto: *Die deutsche Bartholomäusnacht*. Zurich, 1935.

Taylor, A. J. P.: *The Course of German History*. Oxford, 2001.

Trevor-Roper, H. R.: *The Last Days of Hitler*. New York, 2002.

INDEX